A HISTORY OF

MODERN CRITICISM

1750 - 1950

IN FIVE VOLUMES

OTHER BOOKS BY RENÉ WELLEK

Kant in England

The Rise of English Literary History

Theory of Literature (with Austin Warren)

Concepts of Criticism

Essays on Czech Literature

Confrontations

A HISTORY OF MODERN

Criticism: 1750-1950

BY RENÉ WELLEK

The Later Eighteenth Century

New Haven and London:

YALE UNIVERSITY PRESS

Copyright © 1965 by Yale University.
Fourth Printing, 1977.
Set in Baskerville type,
and printed in the United States of America by
The Murray Printing Company, Westford, Mass.
All rights reserved. This book may not be
reproduced, in whole or in part, in any form
(except by reviewers for the public press),
without written permission from the publishers.
Library of Congress catalog card number: 55-5989
ISBN: 0-300-01036-2
Published in Great Britain (except Canada), Europe,
Africa, and Asia (except Japan) by Yale University Press,
Ltd., London. Distributed in Latin America by
Kaiman & Polon, Inc., New York City; in Australia and
New Zealand by Book & Film Services, Artarmon, N.S.W.,
Australia; and in Japan by Harper & Row, Publishers,
Tokyo Office.

THIS IS the first volume of a four-volume history of modern literary criticism, written from a consistent point of view. The history of criticism should not be a purely antiquarian subject but should, I believe, illuminate and interpret our present situation. It will, in turn, become comprehensible only in the light of a modern literary theory. The middle of the 18th century is a meaningful point to start, as then the neoclassical system of doctrines, established since the Renaissance, began to disintegrate. To describe the changes within that system between 1500 and 1750 seems to me largely an antiquarian task, unrelated to the problems of our day; but in the later 18th century there emerge, and struggle with one another, doctrines and points of view which are relevant even today: naturalism, the view that art is expression and communication of emotion, the symbolic and mystical view of poetry, and others. The 1830's, when the European romantic movement was well on the wane, when Goethe and Hegel, Coleridge, Hazlitt, and Leopardi died, and when the new creed of realism began to emerge, seem the natural break in our story. Volume 2 ends here, and the remaining two volumes, now in active preparation, should bring the account down to our day.

The term "criticism" I shall interpret broadly to mean not only judgments of individual books and authors, "judicial" criticism, practical criticism, evidences of literary taste, but mainly what has been thought about the principles and theory of literature, its nature, its creation, its function, its effects, its relations to the other activities of man, its kinds, devices, and techniques, its origins and history. I shall try to steer a middle course between pure aesthetics on the one hand—"aesthetics from above," speculations about the nature of the beautiful and about art in general—and mere pronouncements of impressionistic taste, unsubstantiated, unargued opinions, on the other. It will be impossible to avoid some excursions into the history of abstract aesthetics and of concrete taste, since obviously the history of literary criticism cannot be totally divorced from them. But we shall discuss purely philosophical aestheticians, such as Kant, only very briefly and shall merely glance at even prominent writers if they have not given some kind of theoretical framework to their literary predilections and tastes.

The first two volumes consider only four countries: England (with Scotland), France, Germany, and Italy, though the Conclusion touches briefly on developments in other countries. In volumes 3 and 4 Spain, Russia, and the United States will be added; meanwhile, in the period under discussion, Spanish criticism seems derivative, Russian barely emerging, and the new United States still echoing England.

The only existing book which covers our topic *in extenso*, George Saintsbury's *History of Criticism and Literary Taste in Europe* (3 vols. 1900–04), while admirable in its sweep and still readable because of the liveliness of the author's exposition and style, is not only outdated by having been written fifty years ago, during the heyday of impressionism and art for art's sake, but seems to me seriously vitiated by its professed lack of interest in questions of theory and aesthetics.

To preserve the uniformity and readability of the text, all quotations are in English, but in the notes all foreign texts are given in the original in order to make a check of vocabulary and context possible. Most translations are my own, but in some cases I have used older translations freely. The spelling is modernized throughout, for it seems unnecessary, in a book devoted to ideas, to preserve the printing habits of the time. In many cases, especially the German classics available in modernized reprints, going back to the original spelling would have been an almost impossible task, irrelevant to the purpose of the book. The many superior numbers need not disturb the reader; only the infrequent notes which contain something more than a mere reference to the sources are placed at the bottom of the page. The bibliographies are selective and descriptive and allow allusions to controversial points of interpretation avoided in the text.

In three chapters (1, 5, and 6) I was able to draw on my discussion in an earlier book, *The Rise of English Literary History*

(1941). I want to thank the University of North Carolina Press for permitting me to use some passages verbatim.

I owe a heavy debt of gratitude to the Guggenheim Foundation for granting a fellowship which allowed me to devote a whole year to writing and to undertake a short trip to Europe; to Edgar S. Furniss, Provost of Yale University, who gave generously from the Fluid Research Fund to facilitate the preparation of this book; and to several friends and colleagues, Cleanth Brooks, Douglas Knight, Austin Warren, and Robert Penn Warren, for their critical reading of several chapters. Two friends between them, Lowry Nelson Jr. and William K. Wimsatt Jr., have read the whole manuscript and have made many valuable suggestions for its improvement. David Horne has helped with the proofs and Mr. and Mrs. Addison W. Ward with the indexes.

R. W.

Yale University
New Haven
Christmas 1954

CONTENTS

INTRODUCTION

1

THE HISTORY of literary criticism between the middle of the 18th century and the 1830's is the period which raises most clearly all the fundamental issues of criticism that are still with us today. It is the period in which the great system of neoclassical criticism, as it was inherited from antiquity and built up and codified in Italy and France during the 16th and 17th centuries, disintegrated, and when divers new trends emerge which early in the 19th century crystallized into romantic movements.

Today, it seems, we have escaped the dominance of romantic ideas and have come to understand the neoclassical point of view far better and far more sympathetically. There is now a large academic literature which interprets the principles, applications, and fortunes of neoclassical criticism not only with the historian's sense of detached justice but with enthusiastic endorsement of the main neoclassical doctrines and polemical fervor directed against the romantic creed. Also, in contemporary nonacademic English and American criticism we find many tendencies and ideas which could be interpreted as a revival of neoclassical principles. T. S. Eliot has described his general point of view as classicist in the famous preface to *For Lancelot Andrewes* (1928), and he is the critic who has influenced contemporary criticism most profoundly, if not on all theoretical issues then at least with his individual judgments and the general bent of his taste. Eliot's emphasis on the impersonality and objectivity of the poet, his view of the poet as "the shred of platinum" (to quote the famous simile from "Tradition and the Individual Talent"), could be interpreted as a revival of neoclassical principles, and it is surely a reaction against romantic subjectivism, lyricism, and exaltation of the ego. Eliot's constant stress on the share of the intellect in the creative process, his plea for reasonableness and toughness, and his view that poetry

1

must be at least as well written as prose could also be interpreted as neoclassical. His advocacy of the colloquial, the conversational style in poetry, could be compared with its use in Dryden and Pope. The great feeling which Eliot has for the continuity of the Western tradition, conceived of not only as a literary but as a moral and religious force, could also be interpreted as a conscious return to a similar view held less consciously and less vocally during the age of neoclassical dominance. In defining his ideal of what criticism should be, Eliot voices his preference for analysis against the impressionism and "appreciation" which we have come to associate with romantic attitudes.

If we look at other prominent contemporary critics we can find the same elements, or at least some of them. F. R. Leavis displays the banner of tradition and criticizes all poetry from the point of view of "living speech." Yvor Winters talks about prose sense, the moral idea governing a poem, of poetry as a more intense kind of prose. The recent almost universal increase of interest in economy of expression, in craftsmanship, and in rhetoric and its devices might be thought of as neoclassical. The revulsion against the lyrical cry, the purely subjective, and the merely biographical is common today. Most of the so-called New Critics in the United States criticize the English romantic poets, especially Shelley, very severely. Many favor wit, paradox, and irony as central devices of poetry.

But it would be an absurd simplification of the present critical situation if we described it merely in terms of a revival of neoclassicism. It is certainly not a total revival, and one could argue that the neoclassical doctrines are used today in a different context and with an altered meaning. One could even argue the opposite: many modern critics actually use romantic ideas more prominently in some of their most central theories. An examination of the historical antecedents of some of the key terms of recent criticism will show this. "Organic" has its origin in a passage of Aristotle's *Poetics* (chapter viii). The neoclassical "unity in variety" and the neo-Platonic "inner form" are other anticipations. But only Herder, Goethe, Schelling, and the Schlegels have drawn the ultimate consequences from the organic metaphor and used it consistently in their criticism. It reaches England with Coleridge. A further development of the organic view is the idea that a work of art represents a system of tensions and balances. T. S. Eliot and after him I. A. Richards [1] constantly quote the key passage in Coleridge's *Biographia Literaria,* describing imagination as the balance or reconciliation of opposite or discordant qualities.[2] This formula is neither neoclassical nor original with Coleridge. It is merely a reproduction of what some of the most romantic of the German aestheticians had said: the closest parallel can be found in Schelling, whom Coleridge had studied and for whom, at the time of writing the *Biographia* (1817), he professed such admiration that he thought of himself, momentarily at least, as merely an expounder of his philosophy.*

Opposites and tensions are easily associated with ironies and paradoxes. The aesthetic (not merely rhetorical) use of irony comes

* One could argue that "reconciliation of opposites" is foreshadowed in all rhetorical theories about the recognition of "similitude in dissimilitude." It dates back to Aristotle's view that in a riddle it is possible to join together absurdities by metaphor (*Poetics,* xxii), or to Longinus' analysis of a poem by Sappho, which speaks of "uniting contradictions in the feelings" (x, 24), as Allen Tate has pointed out in *Lectures in Criticism,* ed. H. Cairns (New York, 1949), p. 61. Anticipations could be seen in concettist theories, in Gracián's theories of *agudeza* (1642). Gracián arrives at a definition of agudeza as a "splendid concordance, a harmonious correlation between two or three extremes, expressed in a single act of the understanding." Quoted by Croce, "I trattatisti italiani del Concettismo e Baltasar Gracián," in *Problemi di estetica* (Bari, 1949), p. 317. Dr. Johnson's famous description of metaphysical wit in his "Life of Cowley" (*Lives of the English Poets,* ed. Hill, *1,* 11) as "a kind of *discordia concors;* a combination of dissimilar images, or discovery of occult resemblances in things apparently unlike" seems derived from such widespread theories. But they are all purely rhetorical, little more than recognitions of the distance between tenor and vehicle in a metaphor, of the opposite in antithesis, paradox, and oxymoron. They are not the reconciliation of such opposites as nature and art with its implied metaphysics, as in Coleridge.

Croce, *Storia dell' età barocca in Italia* (Bari, 1946), p. 222, refers to Tomaso Ceva (1648–1737) as speaking of the union of contraries which is poetry, of the probable and the marvelous, of unity and multiplicity, of naturalness and art, of delight and reason. But I cannot discover more than faint hints of such ideas in the actual text of Ceva's *Memorie d'alcune virtù del Signor Conte Francesco de Lemene con alcune riflessioni su le sue poesie,* Milan, 1706.

from Friedrich Schlegel. In another German critic few people read today, Karl Wilhelm Ferdinand Solger, we find at the very center of his system the view that all art is irony and paradox—and, again, Coleridge had read and annotated Solger's *Erwin* (1815). The distinction between the denotative and the connotative meaning of linguistic signs was worked out earlier, but a theory of metaphor and symbol as the prime requisite of poetry was first enunciated by Vico, Blackwell, Diderot, and Hamann; it finds its fullest elaboration in the Schlegels, who propounded a system of correspondences, of an all-pervasive symbolism in the universe which poetry reflects and expresses. To Goethe we apparently owe the distinction between allegory and symbol, which was then elaborated by Schelling and August Wilhelm Schlegel and from there taken over by Coleridge. Myth, of course, has always been a device of poetry: classical and Christian mythology were the requisites of neoclassical epic and tragedy. But the view that all poetry is myth, that there is a necessity and possibility of creating new myth, is again propounded for the first time by Herder, Schelling, and Friedrich Schlegel. The only possible anticipations, unknown or barely known in their time, were the visions and mythological fantasies of William Blake.

Most modern critics want poetry to be concrete, visual, precise, and not abstract or universal. Again some preromantic critics can be shown to be the first to have decidedly rejected the older view of poetry as abstract, universal, and wary of the "streaks of the tulip, the shades of the verdure." The shift happened late in the 18th century, and we have not returned to the neoclassical ideal. Thus if we trace the pedigree of the key concepts of many modern critics we inevitably arrive at the romantic period, though the modern critics themselves may not always be aware of the exact derivation of their particular terms. Clearly, much is not drawn directly from the original sources but rather comes through many intermediaries, through Coleridge, Poe, the French symbolists, and Croce. Paradoxically, modern professedly antiromantic criticism, while it has rejected much romantic poetry and some of the metaphysical claims advanced for poetry by romantic criticism, has nevertheless revived its basic tenets. Probably it is better to say it has achieved a curious blend of classical and romantic concepts. Of course modern criticism cannot be described as merely such a blend. It has its distinctive characteristics. The contributions to criticism of semantics, sociology, psychoanalysis, and anthropology are largely new. Yet, whatever the achievement and the originality of modern criticism may be, we should not forget that the problems it raises were raised before and that its roots are deep in the period under discussion. The view recently expressed that, with the exception of Aristotle and Coleridge, there was hardly any criticism before our age and that " 'modern' criticism does not seem to exist to any degree at this time anywhere but in England and America" seems merely ignorant.[3] Our sense of the continuity of critical tradition can be increased if we realize that the problems we discuss today have a long history and that we need not start thinking about them from scratch. The fact that modern criticism does not realize this, that every American (and not only American) critic invents his own "homebrew" vocabulary, his own shifting set of terms differing sometimes from essay to essay, is the most serious obstacle to the establishment, propagation, and final victory of an excellent cause.

Understanding these eighty years will allow us to understand the contemporary situation. But what follows should not be thought of as primarily the presentation of a thesis about the origins of modern criticism: rather I want to trace history in all its complexity and multiplicity, in its own right. At the same time such a history cannot be written without a frame of reference, a standard of selection and evaluation which will be influenced by our own time and determined by our own theory of literature.

2

The history of criticism from the beginning of the Renaissance to the middle of the 18th century consists in the establishment, elaboration, and spread of a view of literature which is substantially the same in 1750 as it was in 1550. Of course there are shifts in emphasis and changes in terminology; there are differences between individual critics, the main countries of Europe, and the different stages of development. There were three clearly recognizable stages which could be distinguished as governed by authority, reason, and finally by taste. In spite of these differences, however, one can speak of a single movement, seeing that its principles are substantially the same and that its sources are obviously the same body of texts: Aristotle's *Poetics*, Horace's *Ad Pisones*, the rhetorical tradition best codified in the *Institutiones* of Quintilian, and, at a later stage, the treatise *On the Sublime* ascribed to Longinus. Neoclassicism is a fusion of Aristotle and Horace, a restatement of their principles and views which underwent only comparatively minor changes during almost three centuries. This fact alone establishes something that many literary historians are reluctant to recognize: the deep gulf between theory and practice throughout the history of literature. For three centuries people repeated the views held by Aristotle and Horace, debated these views, put them into textbooks, learned them by heart—and actual literary creation went on its way quite independently. Substantially the same critical theory was embraced by such diverse men as the poets of the Italian Renaissance, Sidney and Ben Jonson in Elizabethan England, the French dramatists of the court of Louis XIV, and the middle-class Dr. Johnson. Literary styles had undergone profound revolutions during these three centuries, but no new or different theory of literature was ever formulated. The metaphysicals, who wrote poetry totally different in structure and local detail from that of Spenser, had scarcely any theoretical justification for what they were doing: they spoke sometimes of "wit," they spoke of "strong lines"; but if we except these few critical tags we must conclude that neither Donne nor any of his fellow poets developed a theory of literature which would really account for their astonishingly different practice. One must never forget how strong the authority of classical antiquity was in those times; how strong the craving was to conform to it and to ignore the gulf that existed between one's own age and the centuries in which Aristotle or Horace wrote. The situation can be illustrated by two drastic examples derived from the history of the fine arts. Bernini, the highly baroque sculptor who created the famous group of St. Teresa floating on a cloud of marble and the angel in the Church of Santa Maria della Vittoria in Rome, gave a lecture at the Paris Academy in which he argued that he was the true successor and imitator of the Greek sculptors. Daniel Adam Pöppelmann, the architect of that very rococo building in Dresden, the Zwinger, published a little pamphlet which tried to demonstrate in detail how closely his work conformed to all the purest principles of Vitruvius, the main theoretician of Roman architecture.[4] One must recognize that theory and practice may diverge very widely in the history of literature and that convergence or divergence differs widely from author to author. There may be authors, such as Zola or Gogol, where one can put one's finger on a real cleavage. There are others, more highly self-conscious writers, who can work out a theory closely related and even helpful to their practice. But during these centuries the weight of authority was such, the acceptance of certain presuppositions and terms so general, that one cannot find any sharply divergent formulas and original theories which would really break with the views handed down from classical antiquity.

It should be frankly recognized that the history of criticism is a topic which has its own inherent interest, even without relation to the history of the practice of writing: it is simply a branch of the history of ideas which is in only loose relationship with the actual literature produced at the time. No doubt one can show the influence of the theory on the practice and, to a minor degree, of the practice on the theory, but this is a new and difficult question which should not be confused with the internal history of criticism. We shall proceed mostly on the assumption that the relation between theory and practice is very indirect and that we can ignore it for our purposes, which are, after all, directed mainly toward an understanding of ideas. It is, of course, undeniable that these ideas should apply to actual literature, and it is obvious that we shall confront them with the general norms for literary works of art and hence with the theory of literature that we possess. Still, this is a different procedure from handling such historical questions as how much the doctrine of *ut pictura poesis* has actually stimulated the writing of descriptive poetry, how far the theory of the neoclassical epic accounts for the failure of the epics written at that time, how far the doctrines of the German "Storm and Stress" describe the nature of the poetry written by young Goethe. It is a new question which has to use quite different evidence if we inquire whether Wordsworth actually wrote poetry in the common language of men. The historian of criticism need only ask what Wordsworth meant by his doctrine, whether what he said makes sense, and what were the context, the background, and the influence on other critics of his theory. The concrete poetry written by critics will be left out of account, since an actual study of the influence of criticism on poetry and vice versa would abolish the unity of our subject matter, its continuity and independent development, and would make the history of criticism dissolve into the history of literature itself.

3

Another extremely complex problem has to be excluded if we want to keep a sharp focus on critical theory and opinions: the causal explanation of the changes we shall describe. Causal explanation, in an ultimate sense, is impossible in matters of mind: cause and effect are incommensurable, the effect of specific causes unpredictable. All causal explanation leads to an infinite regress, back to the origins of the world. Still, we might at least glance at the kind of questions raised and answers suggested. We must first recognize that there is an inner logic in the evolution of ideas: a dialectic of concepts. An idea is easily pushed to its extreme or converted into its opposite. Reaction against the preceding or prevailing critical system is the most common driving force of the history of ideas, though we cannot predict what direction a reaction will take or tell why it should come at a certain time. One has to leave something to the initiative of the individual, the luck of the gifted man devoting his thought to a particular matter at a given time.

The individual critic himself will be motivated by his personal history: his education, the demands of his calling, the requirements of his audience. To investigate such psychological causes would lead us into biography and the whole variety of personal histories. Only now and then will we be able to refer to such possible motives of critical positions.

Criticism is part of the history of culture in general and is thus set in a historical and social context. Clearly it is influenced by the general changes of intellectual climate, the history of ideas, and even by definite philosophies, though they may not have produced systematic aesthetics themselves. We shall constantly bear in mind these affiliations. The effects of Cartesian rationalism, Lockean empiricism, and Leibnizian idealism are imprinted on the criticism of the three leading nations, and seem to a large extent to account for the differences between French, English, and German criticism. It has been argued that the emergence of romantic criticism, with its emphasis on the organicity of the work of art, is due to shifts of interest from physics to biology, from Newton to Linné or Bonnet.[5] A similar shift can be observed in political theory: natural law was discarded by Burke and his German followers in favor of the organic national state. But to pursue these questions in detail would lead us too far into the history of thought and science.

The specific influence of social and general historical causes on criticism is much harder to grasp and describe. One can certainly observe the influence of the widening reading public on even the forms of criticism. In the 17th century the formal treatise, the poetics, often written in Latin, was standard, while in the 18th century the essay in the vernacular took its place. The freer form, even in formal treatises, and the less purely learned vocabulary show that the critic came to appeal to an audience wider than that of students in the library or lecture room. Critical periodicals, which even early in the 18th century were almost all abstracting media, mainly describing learned books, changed slowly into critical reviews of recent belles lettres.

Yet it seems harder to associate particular doctrines with particular social or historical changes. The idea that the breakdown of neoclassicism has something to do with the rise of the middle classes will not withstand close scrutiny. Many expounders of neoclassicism were churchmen, teachers, men of the comparatively unattached middle classes, and Dr. Johnson, Gottsched, and La Harpe must strike us as peculiarly middle class. The growing sentimentalism seems a particularly bourgeois trait when we think of the contrast between men such as the Earl of Chesterfield and Richardson; yet Chateaubriand and Byron were aristocrats who played a decisive role in the spread of romantic emotionalism. Exact social affiliations and allegiances would need much closer study and can only be alluded to when the occasion seems to demand it. More obvious is the influence of specific historical events such as the French Revolution or the defeat of Napoleon: the French emigrants in England and Germany brought back new ideas to France. The fall of the French Empire coincides with a decline of the prestige of French taste.

The differences between the national traditions of criticism are obviously connected with different political and historical institu-

tions and events. It is no mere fancy to see a connection between
the French monarchy and the neoclassical dogmatism. Surely there
is something to the view that English resistance to the French
system was based on patriotic motives, at least in part, and that,
without pressing the parallel too hard, the English political tradition, which maintained considerable local autonomy even under
the Stuarts, favored also an unsystematic, undogmatic approach in
criticism. English literature was hardly ever a court literature and
was also far less urban and centralized than French. What is called
preromanticism seems often to be the taste of men living in the
country or coming from it: the large number of clergymen or sons
of clergymen who almost lived in a churchyard has been suggested
as a "cause" of the "graveyard" school.[6]

In Germany the situation was somewhat similar to that in England: there was the same patriotic feeling directed against France,
which increased sharply during the Seven Years' War. This feeling was also aimed at the German powers who upheld French
taste, especially Frederick the Great, whose ambition was to become a French poet, who founded the Berlin Academy with a
French president and many French members, and who wrote the
famous contemptuous pamphlet against the German literature of
his time.[7] It seems no accident that the anti-French movement began in Switzerland, which had upheld its local democratic tradition most strongly and had kept up English and Italian relations,
and that men like Hamann, Herder, and Gerstenberg came from
the other outlying regions of the German-speaking world, namely
from East Prussia and Schleswig. The reaction against the Enlightenment, the attempt to revive the old Germanic traditions in literature, is connected with the defense of the Holy Roman Empire
and its institutions and local traditions against the leveling tendencies of enlightened despotism. Moreover, the local religious
tradition of Pietism resisted the spread of the secular enlightenment. The French Revolution and the Napoleonic conquests increased the reaction of German patriotism, and they are also reflected in the violent nationalism of the criticism.[8] But all these
questions lead deeper and deeper into general history. It seems
impossible to isolate one specific cause for these changes or always
to distinguish clearly between cause and effect, to decide the
priority of the chicken or the egg. We must concentrate on the de-

scription, analysis, and criticism of ideas and opinions, and even there will constantly be confronted with unsolved questions of priority and interrelationships, overwhelmed by the sheer mass of printed matter, and challenged by the necessity of rejection and selection. We can hope to master the subject only by a conscious purity of method, by a refusal to enter into related problems around us, by intense probing of the great authors and central ideas.

I have used in part the method nowadays called "history of ideas," the tracing of key concepts or what A. O. Lovejoy calls "unit-ideas," through diverse texts, but I have chosen to combine this with more traditional methods of describing and evaluating the ideas of individual great writers. Pure "history of ideas" no doubt offers some advantages which I have foregone. In experimenting with various approaches to my topic, I came to the conclusion that the history of critical terms and ideas is in many instances not yet far enough advanced to give full scope to the "history of ideas," and that the great virtue of that method, the ease in tracing dialectic sequences and shifts of meaning which it allows, is more than offset by its drawbacks. Pure "history of ideas" does not encourage any synoptic understanding of sometimes loosely put together and even self-contradictory systems of individual theorists, any development of the individuality and personality, the peculiar attitude and sensibility of the great critic. (I am not speaking of his biographical idiosyncrasy.) I have used the method of "history of ideas" here and there, where it seems to work best, with certain masses of rather unindividualized materials, but even in these areas I have shifted freely to the exposition of individual texts, to the characterization of total critical outputs. Through this history I have wished to convey an impression not only of the development of modern critical ideas and the evolution of our own critical outlook, but of the richness, diversity, and attractiveness of some of the greatest minds in literary history, working, from however diverse positions, toward a common aim: the understanding and judgment of literature.

NEOCLASSICAL criticism can be defended even today if we reinterpret its terms, though it would be folly not to recognize the
excesses of pedantry to which it could lead or the narrowness of
literary experience on which it was inevitably based. It cannot be
revived in toto because it could not cope intelligently with the
variety of modern literature, its many values and problems for
which the neoclassical creed had no vocabulary and no framework
of questions. But basically the aim of neoclassicism was sound and
right. It attempted to discover the principles or the "laws" or
"rules" of literature, of literary creation, of the structure of a literary work of art, and of the reader's response. To deny the necessity of such an attempt would lead to mere skepticism, to anarchy,
and finally to total theoretical impotence. In some extreme pronouncements of critical impressionists who think of criticism as
"the soul's adventuring among masterpieces," [1] or in theories of
total critical relativism which assume not one but many mutually
exclusive ideals of literature, we come perilously near to complete
critical shipwreck. Neoclassical criticism scarcely recognized these
dangers: it assumed a stable psychology of human nature, a fundamental set of norms in the works themselves, a uniform working
of human sensibility and intelligence allowing us to reach conclusions which would be valid for all art and all literature.

These laws were not, as the older caricature of neoclassicism
assumed, simply taken over from Aristotle or the other ancients
because of veneration for their authority as authority. We cannot
interpret the history of criticism merely as a revolt against such
authority and call any disavowal of it "romantic." There were
no doubt very literal-minded Aristotelians among the critics of
the Italian Renaissance and the French 17th century. But even
the most fanatical Aristotelians managed to reconcile their venera-

tion of Aristotle with the cult of reason. Thomas Rymer has the well-earned reputation of being the most rigid of all the English neoclassical critics. For his unimaginative mauling of Shakespeare's *Othello*, he has been pronounced by Macaulay "the worst critic that ever lived." But even Rymer would say that the laws of literature, the rules as he calls them, are based on reason and experience. "What Aristotle writes on this subject are not the dictates of his own magisterial will or dry deductions of his metaphysics: but the poets were his masters, and what was their practice he reduced to principles. Nor would the modern poets blindly resign to this practice of the ancients, were not the reasons convincing and clear as any demonstration in mathematics." [2] Dryden quoted Rapin in Rymer's translation with approval: The rules "are founded upon good sense, and sound reason, rather than on authority: for though Aristotle and Horace are produced,. yet no man must argue, that what they write is true, because they writ it." [3] Dennis said it again quite succinctly: "The rules of Aristotle are nothing but nature and good sense reduced to a method"; and his enemy, Pope, rephrased it memorably:

> Those rules of old discovered, not devised,
> Are Nature still, but Nature methodized.[4]

Almost all neoclassical critics tried to formulate a theory of literature explaining its function, the nature of the creative process, and the ways in which a work of literature is constructed. They were not authoritarians but rather rationalists.

But the term "rationalist" is misleading if it is interpreted to mean that neoclassical criticism conceives of art as a construct of the conscious intelligence to the exclusion of feeling, imagination, and even the unconscious. The theory of literature is a matter of the conscious mind, but no reputable critic has ever held that artistic creation itself is nothing but conscious rational process. The terms "genius," "inspiration," *poeta vates, furor poeticus* are the stock in trade of Renaissance poetics, and even the most rigid critics of the most formalistic kind never forgot to say that poets need "inspiration," "imagination," "invention," this last a term which covers much that later criticism would have called creative imagination. They believed in a rational theory of poetry but not that poetry was entirely rational. But, of course, neither did they believe that poetry was a merely subconscious process, something like the twittering of a bird in a tree, or automatic writing. They constantly stressed the share of judgment, discrimination, and design in the composition of poetry. Imagination needs the guide and bridle of reason. As Pope tells us of Pegasus,

> The winged courser, like a generous horse,
> Shows most true mettle when you check his course.[5]

Also, in the reader's response—his "taste," as it came to be called during the 17th century—a rational element, the share of judgment, was emphasized. Trained taste, the taste of those who had experience and knowledge, the taste of the ideal, informed, cultivated reader, was taken as the standard.

The central concept of the neoclassical theory of literature was "imitation of nature." Both its terms are today open to gross misunderstanding. "Imitation," the Aristotelian *mimesis,* does not of course mean copying, photographic naturalism, but rather representation: it merely says that the poet makes something which is not nature itself but is meant to represent it. Nor does "nature" mean "dead nature"—still-life or outdoor landscape—as it is frequently used today, but reality in general and especially human nature. This central assumption puts all emphasis on the referential side of the work of art. The poet is not primarily looking into his heart, expressing his soul or mood, or writing his autobiography, his grand confession. Nor is the poet a mystic visionary who "sees into the life of things," rises beyond reality to some transcendent absolute for which poetry is only a symbol or sign. Rather, the poet reproduces reality by his art.

But what exactly is meant by "nature" in neoclassical theory? The term meant very different things to different people. Imitation of nature was frequently understood to mean realism. The classical theory of painting in particular, with its stories about birds trying to pick painted cherries, fostered a concept of art as literal duplication of reality and even deception. Since Castelvetro's commentary on Aristotle's *Poetics* (1570) naturalistic arguments were the main support for the three unities. D'Aubignac, in his *Pratique du théâtre* (1657), was the most consistent of the critics when he argued that the time of action should be limited to three hours, the actual time of representation. Others com-

promised for twelve hours, twenty-four hours, or even (like Corneille and Dryden) allowed an extension to thirty hours. Similarly
D'Aubignac is completely consistent with regard to the unity of
space: the place cannot change for "one and the same image [the
stage] remaining in the same state, cannot represent two different
things." [6] The spectators are in Athens, and if the action shifts
from Athens to Sparta what becomes of the poor spectator? Must
he fly like a witch through the air? Or imagine himself to be in
two places at the same time?

The concept of probability was also used to enforce naturalistic
standards. The literary use of the term is based mainly on Aristotle,
who justified the "probable" against the merely true, the historical
event. Aristotle distinguished three orders of action: the real, the
possible, and the probable, and argued that in poetry the impossible probable is preferable to the possible improbable. To give
a modern instance: Ariel would be an impossible probable, while
a chance happening in a novel, an accidental death, would be a
possible improbable. Aristotle's term was a justification of fiction
against reality, but in neoclassical criticism (at least in a large part
of it) it was used rather to restrict art to commonplace reality. It
served to exclude the marvelous and supernatural. Ancient mythology was often admitted only because it was believed by the
ancients to be true. Thus standards of literal probability, of fidelity
to life, were very widespread. For instance Rymer, in his attack
on *Othello*, laughs that a "woman never loses her tongue, even
though after she is stifled." [7]

But this interpretation of "imitation of nature" as naturalism
or copying was only one strand of neoclassical criticism. Often
"nature" was rather understood to mean "general nature," the
principles and order of nature. This could mean also the typical,
that which characterizes the species man as he is everywhere and
at all times, and nonhuman nature conceived as free from purely
local and accidental conditions. Negatively this view of "general
nature" meant the exclusion of the purely local, concrete, and individual. The demand for the typical and universal was at the base
of the doctrine of decorum, *bienséance*, propriety. Propriety forbade the depiction of the horrible and ugly, the low and mean. As
La Mesnardière, an early French theoretician, formulated it, the
poet must not describe the "meanness of avarice, the infamy of

cowardice, the blackness of perfidy, the horror of cruelty, the smell of poverty." [8] Propriety on the precept of Horace forbade the display of violent events on the stage. Medea must kill her children offstage, Agamemnon must be murdered behind the scene. General characters, or types, must preserve their typical behavior and decorum. A king must behave and speak like a king, a miser like a miser. Rymer merely applies the views of his time when he condemns Shakespeare for introducing an ungrateful, scheming soldier in Iago, for soldiers are typically honest and straightforward. Mesnardière expressly prohibited "subtle Germans, modest Spaniards, and impolite Frenchmen" on the stage, though he admits that such individuals may exist in real life.[9] Clearly the principle of universality or typicality had two sides: it could and did mean in the best writings of the period a universal appeal which made its greatest works comprehensible anywhere and everywhere. This appeal to the verdict of the ages was implied in the whole concept of "classicity." A "classical" author was obviously an author who could stand beside the ancient classics because of his assumed appeal to a distant posterity, beyond the immediate public of his time. But this conception of art as imitating universal nature also meant something extremely limited and limiting. All too easily it was assumed that men are everywhere the same and that the type of man of one's own time was the only right and proper type of humanity. "Universal nature," in practice, meant very specific demands on the ethical and psychological traits of the characters represented, and implicitly the rejection of everything that did not conform to the social ideals of the time. "Universal nature" in art was part of the whole system of nature which assumed a "natural" law, "natural" rights, a "natural" theology, a system of cosmic order, and a psychology of man which was basically Stoic in its practical precepts. The age hardly ever realized how closely its universal man was tied up with a unique social and historical situation. For instance Racine, in his preface to *Iphigénie* (1675), deluded himself by the complacent assumption that the success of his plays which derived from Homer and Euripides proved that "good sense and reason are the same in all ages" and that the "taste of Paris was found to agree with that of Athens." [10]

The demands for universality and typicality easily passed into demands for idealization. Nature might mean ideal nature, nature

as it ought to be, judged by moral and aesthetic standards. Art was
to exhibit beautiful nature, *la belle nature*. This meant not only
a selection from, but a heightening, an improving of nature. This
concept was derived from a theory of the fine arts: in sculpture the
human body was to be represented not as it usually is but as it
ideally should be. The story of the painter Zeuxis who assembled
the most beautiful virgins of Crotona in order to paint the most
beautiful leg of one, the hand of another, the breast or thigh of
a third was the standard example for the view that idealization is
simply selection from nature.[11] But others saw that the standard
of selection is not given in nature, that man in "idealizing" im-
poses his idea of beauty and that he does not actually "imitate."
The consequences of this view, which would be destructive of any
simple theory of imitation, were, however, rarely acknowledged, or
rather they were avoided by the assumption that there is a complete identity of the artist's ideal with the universal, eternal essence of things. But idealization could mean an appeal to the
inner vision of the artist. A strand of neoclassical aesthetics emphasized this "internal model" in the artist's mind. It found its
philosophical affinities in the tradition of neo-Platonism. The
standard text was a passage in Plotinus which told of Phidias that
he had not "created his Zeus after something visible, but made him
such as Zeus would appear if he wanted to reveal himself to our
eyes." [12] This inner conception of the artist, which was eventually
assumed to be confirmed by reality, pervaded the art theories of
the later Renaissance. In England it inspired Sidney's *Defence of
Poesie;* through the Italian theorists of ideal beauty it re-entered
French and English speculation in the 18th century and remained a significant undercurrent which again became dominant
in Winckelmann's new proclamation of ideal beauty.

The ideal, even when conceived less exaltedly, was an important
factor in much neoclassical theory. Certainly the epic hero had
a definite function of representing ideal human nature, and the
pastoral was constantly justified as representing the golden age,
nature before the fall. Idealization in art could be defended from
two almost opposite philosophical positions: by a theology which
assumed the decay of nature and considered, as Dennis did, that
the function of art was "to restore the decays that happened to
human nature by the fall, by restoring order." [13] Or it could fol-

low from a naturalistic trust in man's power and creativeness in making another and better world, on the analogy of and almost in rivalry with Divine creation. It is no chance that a man such as Giordano Bruno exalted genius and rejected the genres and rules, since all his hope was placed on the artist's power of seeing ideas.[14]

The doctrine of poetic justice was also a version of the ethical ideal. The term apparently comes from Rymer, but the doctrine itself is much older: it was known to Scaliger, Scudéry, Corneille, and others. It was argued at length by Dennis.[15] Every character, it was assumed, should be rewarded and punished at the end of a play according to his deserts. The poet was required to present an order of the universe, free from chance and injustice, and thus became a defender of the ways of God to man. In practice, however, it often meant that the end of a play was a distribution of prizes, an untruthful rosy dream image.

Thus "imitation of nature" was a term which allowed almost all kinds of art: from literal naturalism to the most abstract idealization, and all stages in between. What specifically was recommended depended not only on the particular predilection of the critic but also on the assumption that the different genres required different kinds of imitation. In critical practice, little attention was given to the relation of image and model, art and reality, and there was hardly any "social" criticism in our sense.

If we shift attention to the neoclassical teaching of the structure of the work of art, we shall have to admit some disappointment that most neoclassical theory had a clumsy view of the relation of content and form. In Aristotle the way had been pointed toward an organic conception of a work of art: he spoke clearly of a "structural union of the parts being such that, if any one of them is displaced or removed, the whole will be disjointed and disturbed." [16] But this insight into the unity of a work of art was never regained during the Renaissance, and neoclassicism usually was content with the dichotomy of content and form. On the one hand its theory embraces formalism of an external and empty kind, and on the other it could not disengage itself from a ranking of subject matter outside of the work of art according to criteria of dignity and moral value. These two doctrines are not incompatible: rather are they the two sides of the same dilemma. In actual practice in the best authors there is an almost instinctive sense of form, a knowledge of intellectual disposition, lucidity, harmony, and symmetry of almost architectural order which is the fruit of formalism rightly understood. But among critics it amounted mostly to a breakup of the work of art into categories viewed almost in isolation: the plot, the characters, the diction, the thought, and the meter, which in Aristotle's analysis of tragedy had formed a unity, became fragments discussed separately. Attention to the details of stylistic devices (to what was called "rhetorical colors"), the classification of figures, and the tabulation of meters was imported from rhetorical theory, and increasingly the view of form as mere ornament triumphed over older, more instinctively organic conceptions. The decorative rococo was only a symptom of a tendency existing, in one form or another, in many late times of history. The rules of the genres, which were originally conceived as inherent laws, became at times the rules of a game and in practice often a set of pedantries which allowed the unimaginative reader and critic to judge by a ready-made yardstick. One can put up a convincing general defense of the rules as imposing limits which create difficulties and thus stimulate the artist to overcome them. One can explain how the introduction of the three unities led to a tightening of dramatic form salutary as a reaction against the looser formal structures of the early popular drama. But one cannot deny that the rules, especially in the most studied and most analyzed genres, the drama and the epic, had also a cramping influence even on the greatest writers. It is enough to cite the example of Corneille, who almost all his life, despite his high respect for authority in church and state and for the ancients, had to struggle for his artistic independence.

The rules were rarely defined in general terms but rather specified according to genres. The distinction between genres was basic to the neoclassical creed, so basic that its assumptions were never, to my knowledge, properly examined during this time. Aristotle and Horace were the classical authorities for the main divisions of the drama and the epic. Antiquity, however, never clearly envisaged the lyric as a single genre and rather discussed independently its different forms—the ode, the elegy, satire, and the like.[17] The ancient table of genres was enormously increased during the Middle Ages, and new genres established themselves in practice without too much theoretical resistance or even attention. The social preferences of the age for the elevated style, and the fact that Aristotle treats of tragedy and the epic and Horace mainly of the drama, focused most theories on these two genres and helped to establish an elaborate hierarchy of genres, but its exact rationale was not clear. Was it dignity of subject matter? mere size and effort involved? intensity of effect? The actual grounds of classification were extremely various and often quite obscure or purely practical. Formalistic criteria of a simple external kind, such as recognizable verse form, stood next to criteria which were based on a ranking of subject matter or moral effect. At times the detailed rules were conceived as a merely empirical characteristic of the original model of the genre. Thus Dryden said of the epic that "no man ought to dispute the authority of Homer, who gave the first being to that masterpiece of art." He recognized similar authority in Pindar for odes and even in its founders for opera.[18]

It was rarely clear whether the table of genres was closed or whether new genres could be admitted. In practice hybrids of existing genres or ruleless new genres outside of the table of categories arose and were at least tolerated. The neoclassical scheme was being undermined, however, by the success of genres for which its theory made little or no provision: the novel, the periodical essay, the serious play with a happy ending, and so on. At times, even very early, the whole theory of genres was challenged; but the challenge was usually an argument in favor of a new genre, such as the much debated romantic epic of Ariosto, or an assertion of the freedom and independence of the artist from all rules. Especially in England the rules and unities were combated during the whole of the 17th century, and in France, where the rules held sway on the stage most persistently, they were constantly questioned and debated, and frequent allowances were made even by Boileau for genius to transgress them.[19] More and more a distinction between essential principles and arbitrary rules became established. It was recognized that there were some general laws of art, such as the necessity of pleasing and the desire for conformity between style and subject matter, and that there were local rules, empirical precepts which may be modified or even totally ignored by the great artist. In practice there was wide disagreement about the line of demarcation between these two kinds of rules. On the issue of the unities, for instance, the view prevailed that those of time and place were less essential than that of action. Besides, from the beginning of French neoclassicism some realm was reserved for the unknown, the mysterious, which was called the hidden beauties, the *je ne sais quoi*, the "grace beyond the reach of art," [20] a region which eluded the systematizing of the critic and the rationalism of the theorist. Though critics could hardly have realized it, it meant an abdication before the main task of criticism, an admission that the theory held was insufficient to account for much more than a fragment of reality.

But neoclassical theory was not merely interested in the relations of art to reality and in the concept of structure and genre. Much of it was concerned with the effect of literature on its audience. The classical texts for this concern were two bits from Horace: *utile dulci* and *aut prodesse aut delectare*. Both crudely stated the union of pleasure and instruction that art was supposed to convey. There were a few writers who thought that poetry should only delight, but the majority of critics accepted moral utility as the primary aim of literature. Pleasure and delight were, however, generally considered the necessary means toward this end. In the many defenses of poetry against Puritan objections (by no means limited to Protestant countries, but common also in Catholic countries during the Counter Reformation) a constant appeal was made to the history of literature as proving its social utility and the high social status of the poet. Vossius, for instance, says bluntly that "the poets are teachers of manners." Comedy writers believed, as Molière did, that the "duty of comedy is to correct men by diverting them." [21] Tragedians praised the theater as a school of virtue. Le Bossu defined the aim of the epic as "moral instruction disguised under the allegory of action." He actually thought of the process of composition as first the selection of a moral and then the invention of an appropriate fable.[22] On the whole, the problem of art and morals proved unsolvable because the aesthetic effect was still concealed under the far too inclusive term "pleasure," and the moral effect of art was not distinguished clearly from that of the mere stating of moral precepts. It took the whole 18th century to disentangle the distinctions between the good, the useful, the true, and the beautiful. Only then could the relations between art and morality be freshly formulated.

Still, besides the pleasure-instruction formula the age had access to a subtler theory of the effect of literature: Aristotle's concept of purgation. Though this was occasionally claimed for the epic it was generally considered to be limited to tragedy. The interpretation of the difficult passage in the *Poetics* has a complex history which is not yet concluded. It can safely be said that in the neoclassical age purging was interpreted to mean hardening, becoming inured to the passions of pity and fear, just as a physician becomes indifferent to the sight of terrible wounds and a veteran soldier to the most dangerous fighting. In Corneille *catharsis* was interpreted as the purging of the spectator from the emotions in which the characters of the play indulged to their cost. Tragedy became a warning example. The misfortune of the hero should arouse our pity, and this pity should in turn arouse our fear that we might meet similar misfortunes ourselves. Corneille minimized pity and exalted "fear," the pathetic, the admiration we carry away for the suffering hero.[23]

In this theory of catharsis the emotional effect of art was central, even though it was interpreted to mean a release from emotion as the final attainment of a contemplation, "calm of mind, all passion spent." [24] But simultaneously the view that poetry is persuasion, communication, and even incitement to feeling has its ancient history. Part of the success of this second theory must be due to extraliterary circumstances, and in particular to the general rise of sentimentalism. But its theoretical justification was largely drawn from the arsenal of rhetorical theory. Poetry is to move the affections as rhetoric does. The observance of the rules and even the observance of the right relation to reality can be interpreted as a means toward achieving this emotional effect. The poet himself must be moved in order to move, as Horace knew when he said "if you would have me weep, you must first of all feel grief yourself." [25] In England John Dennis was an early exponent of this view. To him "poetry is an art, by which a poet excites passion . . . in order to satisfy and improve, to delight and to reform the mind." "The more passion there is, the better the poetry." [26] The theory of tragedy reflects the same change. Dryden argued that tragedy achieves not only an "abatement" of our pride but "insensibly works us to be helpful to, and tender, over the distressed." [27] Dubos, in his *Réflexions critiques sur la poésie et la peinture* (1719), built a whole theory of poetry purely on the ground of the communication of emotion. Art (both poetry and painting) is a means of exciting artificial passions without the dire consequences of real ones.[28] But neither Dennis nor Dubos drew the consequences from their positions. They did not see that if poetry merges with persuasion, it ceases to be art, and becomes life, excitement of experience, passion. If the aim of art is this, any kind of form and any relation to reality is justified. The question of morality disappears or rather has to be reintroduced by devious ways. But on the whole neoclassicism suffered mostly from the excesses of literal-minded moralists who thought of art as a mere intellectual statement of moral precepts. At their best and worst critics understood that literature is a part of politics in the wide sense of the word, that the poet is, willy nilly, a molder and shaper of human souls.

Thus the idea of the poet and the requirements for becoming one always included moral qualities and intellectual achievements. Although there would always be reference to the need of genius and inspiration, most insistently critics stressed art (in the sense of artistry), science, and knowledge. Even information was considered an important requisite: the epic poet especially was required to have an almost encyclopaedic knowledge. Later, however, there was an increasing suspicion of mere learning and pedantry, and the ideal of the gentleman collaborated with the demand for universality to exclude from the bulk of literature the display of information and the use of technical terms. The learned humanist, such as Milton, gave way to the cultivated gentleman as the ideal poet.

He was also the ideal audience of literature. When the critics appealed to general human nature, to man in the abstract, they often had in mind only the man of their own time, the man of taste, the civilized man educated on the classics and trained since childhood to distinguish the good from the bad. In practice the ideal reader became the self-consciously modern man, very proud of his exalted position at the pinnacle of civilization. He looked down at the barbarians, even those of antiquity like Homer, who was scorned by many for depicting Nausicaa at the family washing or Patroclus cooking meat. Fénelon put it quite bluntly: "The heroes of Homer do not resemble gentlemen, and the gods of that poet are even much below his heroes, who are unworthy of the idea we have of a gentleman." [29] Thus the universal audience supposedly appealed to actually became more and more narrowed down: it excluded the dark ages as well as the barbarous societies of one's own time, and within the "polite" nations it also excluded the bulk of the population, the poor and the lowly. But these critics did not, to my knowledge, face the paradox of a universal audience, of a true taste confined to a very few select groups.

All these difficulties were inherent in the term "taste," which was the crystallizing point of the new concepts that turned attention to the individual state of mind of the reader or listener. The term "aesthetics" comes from Baumgarten, but "taste" is much older and shows the same basic shift: the concept of general beauty is being discarded in favor of an individual standard. Taste can be found throughout the Italian and French 17th centuries as a term, but it becomes the subject of elaborate theorizing only in the early 18th century.* Père Bouhours and Dubos are the main authors who discuss it at length. Bouhours tried to reconcile it with rationalism. "Taste is the first motion, or to put it another way a kind of instinct of right reason, which works with more rapidity and more certainty than any trains of reasoning." [30] Taste was a quicker reason, a short cut to the results of reason. In Dubos it becomes a "sixth sense," a purely irrational instinct, a special faculty of the mind. On the whole, however, the 18th-century critics refused to embrace such radical anti-intellectualism. They usually managed to reconcile taste and judgment and even to identify it in some form. They defended the view that taste was both acquired and spontaneous, innate and cultivated, "sentimental" and intellectual. But these reconciliations of opposites raised a problem which proved dangerous to the basic assumptions of neoclassicism, which demanded, after all, an objective standard of value and beauty.

Neoclassical theory, expounded here in very general terms with-

* Croce cites a passage from Ludovico Zuccolo (1623) in his *Storia dell' età barocca in Italia* (Bari, 1946), p. 166, and Borgerhoff quotes a letter by Guez de Balzac (1645), in *Freedom of French Classicism*, p. 14. The widely held view that "taste" comes from Spain and particularly from Baltazar Gracián is thus untenable. See Karl Borinski, *Baltasar Gracián und die Hofliteratur in Deutschland* (Halle, 1894), pp. 39 ff.

out distinctions as to nations, authors, and diverse stages of its development, had many contradictions concealed in its system. What
happened in the 18th century was not anything like a unified romantic or preromantic revolt; rather, individual issues concealed
in the current theory were brought out into the open, critics
pushed this or that position to its logical or illogical extreme, and
theories became established which kept up connections with the
past only uneasily and formally. Thus if we take the imitation
theory as an example, many attempts were made to restate it and
to make it even more coherently applicable. Charles Batteux's *Les
Beaux Arts réduits à un même principe* (1746) is the best known
formulation of the imitation of "beautiful nature" as the general
principle of all the arts. Even music as the "imitation of passions"
was included in the scheme. The lyric, Batteux argued, is also
an imitation of emotions and passions, and not a cry of the heart.[31]
But the imitation theory broke down partly under the impact of
the shift toward the emotional effect of art and partly through the
growing emphasis on the self-expression of the artist. This creative
power of the artist could be thought of as something purely personal, a necessity for self-expression, but in these earlier stages
the creative imagination of the artist was on the Renaissance
model, increasingly conceived of as the power of creating an independent world which is a parallel or an analogue of actual
creation. This view, common in the Renaissance, was echoed by
Shaftesbury and became most widespread and effective in Germany. It allowed the development of purely imaginative poetry
cut off from ordinary reality which was to be the great feature of
German literature from Klopstock to Novalis and E. T. A. Hoffmann. On the other hand, a new turn toward naturalism becomes
obvious in the 18th century. Its rise is closely connected with the
victory of empiricism in philosophy, the growth of the scientific
spirit, the increased self-consciousness of the bourgeoisie, which
wanted its life depicted in art. Naturalism enters into many combinations with emotionalism and makes many compromises with
classicism. But one can say that a few of the greatest figures of the
18th century in all three main countries—Diderot, Dr. Johnson, and Lessing—have strong naturalistic leanings and are often
in danger of losing grip on the nature of art. This tendency
which unites such apparently diverse figures in different countries

emerges again with renewed vigor in the 30's of the 19th century, after the sudden breakdown of the romantic movement.

If we turn to theories of structure, the most important and promising event was the rebirth of the organic view of the relation of form and content. It came slowly and was by no means universally accepted; it may have had something to do with the turn of interest from physics to biology.[32] It is prominent in Herder, Goethe, and all the German romantics, and it comes back to England with Coleridge. The organic view led to a slighting of the purely rhetorical analysis of poetry and to the breakdown of the genre theory. But it took a long time before the uniqueness of the work of art was asserted with any decision, as the organic view allowed a new theory of genres on the analogy of biological species. The organic view was associated with the concept of creative imagination, as creating was thought of as an irrational process like procreating or growing.

But by far the strongest and most obvious change in the middle of the 18th century was the shift of critical concern to the reaction of the audience, which led to a dissolution of neoclassicism into emotionalism and sentimentalism. Today this tendency is wrongly identified with the romantic movement; it was a minor factor in the English and German romantic writers and is predominant only among the French. It shifted attention to the emotional effect of art, and, if pushed to its extreme as it was by writers such as the early Diderot or Madame de Staël and some theorists in England, it became destructive of the essential feature of art: its appeal to contemplation. Art became identified with persuasion, rhetoric, and even raw emotion. This flying asunder of the neoclassical positions and theories toward naturalism, emotionalism, and highly imaginative art was closely involved with a process of very great importance in history and the history of criticism: the awakening of the modern historical sense. The historical sense should not be identified simply with historical relativism. Relativism itself leads only to barren skepticism, to the old and vicious maxim of *De gustibus non est disputandum*. Rather the historical sense should be defined as a combination of the recognition of individuality with a sense of change and development in history. These two ideas are complementary, since there is no proper understanding of historical individuality without a knowledge of its development, while on the other hand there is no true historical development beyond a series of individualities. We must not, of course, think of individuality as restricted to the person of the poet. Rather, with the increased sense for the peculiarities of different human beings in different ages, the sense of individuality and its value began to be extended also to types of art: the national peculiarities of one literary tradition in opposition to another, one type of drama clearly contrasted with another. The individuality of different epochs became recognized; the "spirit of the age" was a new term used for the analysis of the peculiar characteristics of each successive period in history.

Literature was increasingly studied in the context of its environment. Individuality cannot be comprehended and described except in the context of or in contrast to some environment. In the 17th century more and more attention was paid to the climatic and geographical conditions of literature, and increasingly. literature was seen in terms of social conditions and intellectual atmosphere. People began to discuss the influence of social stability, peace and war, liberty, and despotism on literature. The concept of a national character as a determining factor in literary creation was slowly taking shape.

Development, or at least movement and change in time, was the central concept which for the first time made the writing of literary history possible. Before the 17th century Greece and Rome were considered as being on almost the same plane as France or England. Virgil and Ovid, Horace, and even Homer were discussed almost as contemporaries. There was little consciousness of the gulf of time between the ages, though everybody knew the actual facts of the chronology. The germ of the concept of historical development is in the idea of progress, which can be traced back to the Renaissance.[33] But the idea of progress itself is not sufficient to make proper literary history possible, since it merely implied a uniform advance toward one ideal of perfection. It rather tended to increase the contempt for the past and obliterated any distinctions except those of uniform improvement in the regularity of meter, for instance, or the purity of diction. Also the ancient idea of cyclical progress implied an inevitable advance and decline, which cannot be reconciled with the actual diversity of the historical process.[34] The modern concept of development could arise

only when the idea of independent, individual, national literatures had become established and accepted. The recognition of the
diversity of different national traditions and their courses of evolution was only possible when past literature had been rediscovered
and radically re-evaluated. The slow opening up of the treasures
of medieval literature and folklore was broadening the literary
horizon beyond the confines of the tradition that had descended
from classical antiquity to the Renaissance. This formerly despised
and therefore unexplored past began to be appreciated, at first
with many reservations, and then so enthusiastically as to be
exalted at the expense of the classics.

The whole process was closely bound up with the spread of
a point of view which we are now accustomed to call primitivism.[35]
It is a somewhat misleading term, since there were very few critics
who could be described as recommending an actual return to
primitive poetry. It should be stressed that the "historicity" of a
given work of literature was felt for a long time merely as a limitation and drawback and was usually used only as apology for the
"faults" of older poetry and for its violations of the rules. To give an
example from the French debate about Homer's supposed lack of
modern polite manners: La Motte defends him, saying that it is
"ridiculous to reproach Homer for faults of decorum as he could
not depict something which had not yet come into being." [36]
Homer did not describe gentlemen because there were no gentlemen at that time. But this reluctant apology soon changed into a
recognition of the existence of two kinds of poetry, the natural
poetry of rude, barbarous manners, and the universal poetry based
on the eternal principles of taste derived from Greece and Rome.
Many antiquaries and literary historians, even late in the 18th
century, upheld such a double standard of poetry. They did not
abandon their belief in neoclassical principles, but at the same
time they professed a liking for and delight in the primitive, the
popular, and the naive. Antiquarianism, literary history, was a
hobby which did not induce them to give up their basic convic-
tions. It was, however, a dangerous hobby, as more and more
admirers of primitive poetry accepted its implied standards and
began to disparage modern and classical literature. The so-called
Scottish primitivists were the first (if we ignore the forgotten Vico)
to assert definitely that the "times which we call barbarous are the

most favorable to the poetic spirit." [37] Only Herder, encouraged
by their initiative, jettisoned the neoclassical view completely.

All these elements went into the actual writing of literary history; the historical sense, the sense of individuality and development, had to combine with the antiquarian spirit, use the materials it had accumulated in the past centuries, and penetrate them
with a sense of urgency and application to its own time. At first
most literary histories were mere accumulations of biographical
and bibliographical information, huge storehouses of raw materials. Certainly the great works of antiquaries such as Muratori
and Tiraboschi in Italy and the Benedictine group which produced the *Histoire littéraire de la France* are little more than that.
But simultaneously actual narrative history of literature arose
which had a critical scheme in mind and a critical ambition to re-
evaluate the past. Though still greatly hampered by a mass of
purely inert antiquarian learning, two books with literary pretensions and presuppositions stand out: Gian Mario Crescimbeni's
Istoria della volgar poesia (1698) and, seventy-six years later, the
first *History of English Poetry*, by Thomas Warton (1774–81). But
even these books were uneasy compromises. One can speak of successful literary history only in the early 19th century, with Bouterwek, the Schlegels, Villemain, Sismondi, and Emiliani Guidici.
But this was a victory which should not make us ignore its definite
preparation during the 17th and 18th centuries. Then the materials for literary history were accumulated and then the intellectual
groundwork was laid, in the idea of development and in the new
concepts of criticism.

Originally literary history was mainly confined to national literature, since one of its main motivations was patriotism. But there
was an increasing awareness of the literatures and literary activities of other nations. There existed, of course, some remnants of
the humanist community of learning in such reviews, in France,
as *La Bibliothèque anglaise* (founded in 1716), but that was confined to reports on books in theology, archaeology, etc. Still, even
the French, though they have been the most self-sufficient of all
nations, began to discover the existence of English literature. A
very great importance has usually been ascribed to the beginnings
of this discovery. But one must not forget that the French discovered England when it was itself officially ruled by neoclassical

taste, and that they could not help seeing it through the spectacles of their own taste and the taste of their contemporaries in England. Thus a "Dissertation sur la poésie anglaise" in the *Journal littéraire* (1717), concludes with an argument of the general inferiority of English literature. Prior must bow to La Fontaine, Rochester and Dryden to Boileau, the English comedy writers to Molière, and even Milton to Fénelon.[38] Voltaire's attitude toward English literature is hardly different.

Thus about the middle of the 18th century we see the tensions of the neoclassical creed breaking out with far greater violence and sharpness. It would be an error to think, however, that these diverse reinterpretations and innovations followed a logical or chronological order. Rather all these positions were taken up almost simultaneously and became sorted out only very slowly. The baffling complexity of reality is such that we can meet it squarely only by analyzing the great critics and the important documents in some detail. We shall begin with Voltaire, who represents a late stage of French neoclassicism, and then proceed to the great critics —Diderot, Dr. Johnson, and Lessing—who restated neoclassicism in new terms. Chapters on the minor critics in France, England and Scotland, and Italy will permit us to observe the general trends of the century before we turn to the radical break with neoclassicism in Herder and its very different restatement in Goethe and Schiller.

2 : VOLTAIRE

VOLTAIRE (1694–1778) is the best representative of late French classicism. There are, it is true, other writers who summarize the position of neoclassical orthodoxy more systematically than the volatile Voltaire. But he is such a key figure in French literature, thought, and life of the 18th century, he is a lively writer of such wide range and scope, and, of course, he is so much more widely known and discussed than any of the critics who were his contemporaries that it seems best to start with him. He is, besides, of particular interest to the English-speaking world because of the considerable attention he paid to English literature and his many pronouncements on Shakespeare which are worth knowing, discussing, and understanding.

Voltaire cannot be described as a rigid neoclassicist who merely echoed the views of the 17th century. He is strongly opposed to the growing geometrical spirit, the excessive rationalism of the end of the 17th and the beginnings of the 18th century. He shares, however, some views of the party of the Moderns against the Ancients, and he found it surprising that Boileau and Sir William Temple were obstinate enough not to recognize the superiority of their own age over classical antiquity.[1] He endorsed the attacks of La Motte on Homer and generally preferred Virgil, yet he was skeptical of rigid prescriptive poetics as expounded by D'Aubignac and Le Bossu.[2] Voltaire is also never weary of defending poetry and verse against the rationalists, such as La Motte,[3] who actually wrote odes and tragedies in prose and saw the end of the age of poetry as inevitable and even desirable. Voltaire, whom we think of as the foremost representative of the Enlightenment, who certainly was proud of the achievements of his time in promoting tolerance and science and thought highly of his share in such progress, nevertheless did not believe in continuous uniform progress in civilization or, of course, in literature. He rather

shared the view which can be described as cyclical progress. He
believed that humanity had passed through four great ages of
flowering: the Athens of Pericles, the Rome of Augustus, the Rome
of Leo X, and the Paris of Louis XIV.[4] But in between there were
troughs of utter decay or ages of utter darkness, and in literature
ages of bad taste and barbarism. Voltaire was well aware how precarious the hold of civilization is on mankind. The violence of
some of his late opinions must be interpreted as the aroused feelings of an old man who sees a new flood of barbarism advancing.

Voltaire's taste was, no doubt, already substantially formed when
he arrived in England in 1726. Still, the English years (1726–28)
proved of very great importance for the widening of his literary
horizon and the actual writing of criticism. Voltaire certainly
learned to read English very well, though it may be doubted that
he ever spoke or wrote well. He met many of the literary figures
then famous in England—Pope, Swift, Edward Young, Congreve,
etc.—and he frequented the theater in London, partly to learn
English and partly to learn something about the English drama.
He saw Shakespeare's *Julius Caesar* and *Hamlet,* not to speak of
Addison's *Cato* and any number of comedies. In England he wrote
Essai sur la poésie épique, which was published as an English original as *Essay upon the Epic Poetry of the European Nations from
Homer down to Milton* in 1727. It was not, of course, a history of
the epic, but mainly served an immediate purpose: it was a defense
of Voltaire's own epic, the *Henriade,* which he was then preparing
and for which he was anxious to get English subscriptions. The
Henriade needed defense against the strict neoclassical prescriptions such as those laid down by Le Bossu, since it chose a historical
and not a mythical hero (Henri IV) and since it did not use pagan
machinery. Voltaire argues against the classicists that a modern
epic must be different from an ancient. He also wanted to anticipate any unfavorable comparison of the *Henriade* and *Paradise
Lost* by pleading that a French epic must be different from an
English epic. His defense is based on a distinction which he could
have found in Perrault and St. Évremond: there are essential beauties and conventional beauties, rules which are based on common
sense and universal reason and rules which are merely customary
and local. Machinery is local, based on national taste. Voltaire then
gives a short sketch of the history of epic poetry which is quite su-

perficial as history but argues both for the independence of modern
literatures from the classical, by pointing to a deep gulf of social
and technological changes between the two civilizations, and for
the differences between the main modern national traditions. No
attention is paid to Dante or Ariosto (Voltaire admired the latter
but excluded him from the epic), and only Trissino, Tasso,
Camões, Ercilla, and Milton are taken up in some detail. Though
the information on Camões and Ercilla is secondhand,[5] the range
of observation is remarkable for the time, and the discussion of
Milton (cautious as it is in order not to offend his hosts) is certainly novel for France for its recognition of different taste. "If the
difference of genius between nation and nation ever appeared in
its full light, it is in Milton's *Paradise Lost*," begins the discussion,
and Voltaire concedes that "he is very far from thinking that one
nation ought to judge its productions by the standard of another." [6]
In the later French version, published in 1733, Voltaire again
pleads for the importance of knowing other literatures than one's
own and for the divergencies of national taste which must be accepted as a matter of fact. "It is impossible that a whole nation
could err in matters of feeling and be wrong in being pleased." [7]
Some scholars [8] have hailed the *Essay on Epic Poetry* as the beginning of comparative literature and of true critical relativism and
toleration. But in the light of Voltaire's later writings it seems
rather doubtful that it can claim such a position, for he never gave
up the idea of one universal taste. It also seems questionable
whether total relativism is such a great advance on the neoclassical
point of view, and there is, of course, hardly anything like true
comparative literature in Voltaire's remarks on different epics,
often discussed before, or on the differences of national taste, a
topic broached by St. Évremond and many others before him.

Still, Voltaire in England did become more open minded and
interested in English literature. The *Letters concerning the English Nation* were also published first in English in 1733, while the
French original, rechristened *Lettres philosophiques*, came out a
year later. There is no need to discuss the importance of the book
in the history of French thought, but the discussions of English
literature belong to our province. The key is established in the
characterization of Shakespeare. "Shakespeare boasted of a strong,
fruitful genius: he was natural and sublime, but had not so much

as a single spark of good Taste, or knew one Rule of the Drama."
Shakespeare's influence was the ruin of the English stage, though
there are "beautiful, noble and dreadful scenes in this writer's
monstrous farces, to which the name of tragedy is given." [9] Voltaire
then gives a list of Shakespeare's most obvious "absurdities": Desdemona speaking after being strangled, the gravediggers in *Hamlet,* the jokes of the Roman cobblers in the same scene with Brutus
and Cassius. But Voltaire wants also to present some of the beauties of Shakespeare and produces a translation of "To be or not
to be":

> Demeure, il faut choisir et passer à l'instant
> De la vie à la mort, ou de l'être au néant . . .[10]

He then quotes, in his translation, a speech of Dryden's, and comments: "It is in these detached passages that the English have
hitherto excelled. Their dramatic pieces, most of which are barbarous and without decorum, order or verisimilitude, dart such
resplendent flashes through this gloom as amaze and astonish." [11]
Addison was the first writer to write a regular tragedy, *Cato,* but
Voltaire objects to the love intrigue and its general frigidity. "One
would think," he concludes, "that the English had been hitherto
formed to produce irregular beauties only. The shining monsters
of Shakespeare give infinitely more delight than the judicious
images of the moderns. Hitherto the poetical genius of the English
resembles a tufted tree planted by the hand of nature, that throws
out a thousand branches at random, and spreads unequally, but
with great vigor. It dies if you attempt to force its nature, and to
lop and dress it in the same manner as the trees of the garden of
Marly." [12] The same comparison was soon to be used in favor
of the untamed forest.

The discussion of English comedy is of far less interest. Voltaire
seems to admire Wycherley, though his summary of the *Plain
Dealer* stresses the absurdity of the intrigue, and his account of
the *Country Wife* the grossness of the situation. Rochester is then
praised as "the man of genius," "the great poet," and as an illustration of his "shining imagination" Voltaire translates a part of the
Satyr against Mankind. The same chapter gives a lukewarm account of Waller, and the next some enthusiastic praise of Butler,
Swift, and Pope. Voltaire deplores only Butler's local wit, but

Swift is preferred to Rabelais and is called, rather oddly, a "Rabelais in his senses, and frequenting the politest company." "The poetical numbers of Dean Swift are of a singular and almost inimitable taste"—a judgment which will surprise those who remember only the "Lady's Dressing-Room" or the "Progress of Love." The highest praise goes to Pope. "He is in my opinion the most elegant, the most correct poet, and at the same time the most harmonious that England ever gave birth to. He has mellowed the harsh sounds of the English trumpet to the soft accents of the flute." [13] Voltaire then translates a passage from the *Rape of the Lock* and concludes with some envious reflections on the regard shown to men of letters in England.*

But with the years Voltaire's opinion of Shakespeare grew more unfavorable. One could not say that he actually changed it. The basic assumptions stayed the same, but the tone becomes much more sharp and even bitter and the acknowledgment of beauties much less frequent and generous. One must have in mind the circumstances: in the *Lettres philosophiques* Voltaire felt himself to be a discoverer; in 1776, when his attacks were most violent, he felt that bad taste had triumphed in France and that his own countrymen were now preferring Shakespeare to Corneille and Racine, not to speak of the tragedies of Voltaire himself. A letter explains it quite honestly thus: "What is frightful is that the monster has a party in France: and to fill up the measure of calamity and horror, it is I who long ago was the first to speak of this Shakespeare. It is I who was the first to show the French some pearls which I had found in his enormous dunghill. I did not then expect that one day I should help to trample under foot the crowns of Corneille and Racine in order to adorn the brow of a barbarous stage player." [14]

The most extravagant condemnation of Shakespeare is the fa-

* One other early piece of Voltaire's throws much light on his critical opinions of French literature: the poem *Le Temple de goût* (1731–33), which has a Hell filled with commentators and philosophers and a Purgatory with La Motte, J. B. Rousseau, and Fontenelle. Then nearer the Temple of Taste we see Pascal, Rabelais, Marot, and Bayle, who still have to be purged of their sins. Finally, Paradise contains only eight authors: Fénelon, Bossuet, Corneille, Racine, La Fontaine, Boileau, Molière, and Quinault.[15]

mous letter to the French Academy which was read by D'Alembert at the Festival of St. Louis on August 25, 1776.[16] Voltaire's wrath was then overflowing because of the new translation of Shakespeare by Le Tourneur and the very high praise of Shakespeare in a prefatory epistle addressed to Louis XVI, who, together with Catherine the Great and the King of England, figured among the list of subscribers. Voltaire's method of attack is twofold. Partly it consists in more or less literal translations of what he considered crude and obscene passages in Shakespeare: the first scene of *Othello*, with Iago waking the father of Desdemona and telling him, in coarse terms, that she had run away with a blackamoor; the porter in *Macbeth;* the wooing of Catherine by Henry V; the punning of the servants at the beginning of *Romeo and Juliet;* the first scene in *King Lear,* when the Duke of Gloucester introduces Edmund as his illegitimate son and jokes about the manner of his procreation. Even details are recounted when to the taste of Voltaire they seemed undeniably "low," such as the talk of the soldiers at the beginning of *Hamlet.* To Bernardo's question: "Have you had a quiet guard?" Francisco answers, "Not a mouse stirring." The shocked Voltaire translates it "Je n'ai pas entendu une souris trotter." He is particularly angry since Lord Kames [17] had preferred these words to those of an officer of Agamemnon in Racine's *Iphigénie:* "Mais tout dort, et l'armée, et les vents, et Neptune." "Yes, sir," Voltaire comments, "a soldier may answer thus in a guard-house; but not on the stage before the first persons of a nation who express themselves with nobleness and before whom he must express himself in the same manner." [18]

The other method is one in which Voltaire excelled: the burlesque recounting of the contents of Shakespeare's plays, especially of *Hamlet,* which appears in his summary as an absurd murder story without rhyme or reason.[19] This conclusion thus seems obvious: Shakespeare is nothing but a "village clown" (*gille de village*), a "monster," a "drunken savage," a "water-carrier." But it would be a mistake to think that Voltaire has completely forgotten his praise. He constantly held to the view that Shakespeare was a "beautiful, though very savage nature," who knew no regularity, no decorum, no art, who mixed baseness and grandeur, buffoonery and the terrible: "It is a chaotic tragedy with hundreds of rays of light." [20] Shakespeare always represented to him the crude genius of nature in the beginnings of art. When Voltaire wrote his final comparison between Corneille and Racine he had in mind Scaliger's comparison of Homer and Virgil. But he also alludes to Shakespeare: "Corneille was unequal like Shakespeare, and full of genius like him: but Corneille's genius was greater than Shakespeare's as that of a nobleman is greater than that of a man of the people who was born with the same mind as he." [21] The final argument, which must have seemed to Voltaire quite unanswerable, is the view that Shakespeare is admired only locally. "He was a savage who had some imagination. He has written many happy lines: but his pieces can only please at London and in Canada. It is not a good sign for the taste of a nation when that which it admires meets with favor only at home. On no foreign stage has any piece of Shakespeare ever been performed. The French tragedies are acted in every capital of Europe from Lisbon to St. Petersburg. They are played from the borders of the Arctic sea to the sea that separates Europe from Africa. Let the same honor be done to a single piece of Shakespeare, and then we shall be able to enter into an argument." [22]

It requires a considerable effort of sympathy not to dismiss much of this criticism as totally absurd. The last argument certainly would refute Voltaire completely today; we refuse to be worried about lowness and even obscenity; we easily make allowance for improbabilities of plot and situation. Least of all can we think why Voltaire should be so annoyed by the "stirring mouse." After all, the soldiers are speaking among themselves and not to the king who may be in the audience.

We must try to describe Voltaire's taste, his different opinions and judgments, in order to arrive at something like an understanding of his view of Shakespeare. Voltaire was not a systematic thinker or even a systematic critic. He prided himself on his mobility, his distaste for mere metaphysical speculations, his refusal to become pedantic and stuffy. He has no theory of beauty, and the little he said on questions of general aesthetics would point to a radical individualism. There is the famous beginning of the article "Beau" in the *Dictionnaire philosophique:* "Ask a toad what is beauty . . . and he will answer his she-toad." [23] But actually he was far from being a mere relativist. He stressed taste and disliked judging by mere rules. To Pascal's well-known view that "a man who judges by rules is like a man who tells time by a watch compared to a man who has none," Voltaire answered dryly: "In matters of taste, in music and poetry and painting, taste takes the place of a watch: and those who judge only by rules, judge badly." [24] Taste, again, seems at first sight something purely individual. There are passages in Voltaire which suggest such conclusions. "Every man according to his taste," he would say, "I cannot convince a man that he is wrong if I bore him." [25] But actually Voltaire believes only in one universal taste, that which found its models in Roman antiquity and in the French 17th century. "Fine taste consists in a prompt feeling for beauty among faults and faults among beauties." [26] The man of taste must not judge "in the lump"; he is a born anthologist, a culler of passages. That is why Voltaire detested complete works (and would have detested the fifty-two volumes of Moland). "The mania of editors to collect everything," he says, "resembles that of sacristans who collect rags they want to have worshiped; but still just as one judges true saints by their good actions, so one should judge talents by their good works." [27]

Most of Voltaire's principles can thus be studied only in his concrete pronouncements, but these are fortunately so numerous and cover so many authors that a general view emerges with astonishing consistency. Voltaire adheres to the classical tradition of *decorum, bienséance, convenance.* "Perfection consists in knowing how to adjust one's style to the matter one treats." [28] Style, form, way of expression are always decisive for critical judgment. "As far as making the passions speak, all men have almost the same ideas; but the way of expressing them distinguishes the man of wit from the man who has none." [29] Voltaire restates the ancient doctrine of the three levels of style: each subject has its level, "natural," "tempered," or "elevated." The natural style is not, of course, the style of the barbarian, the savage, or even the natural man. Simplicity is precisely the result of civilization. Clarity, purity, ease are associated with it. Barbarous people emerge from rudeness by flying into preciosity, bombast, comparable to the drunkenness of the newcomer to Paris or the squandering of the newly rich. Voltaire is thus an enemy of anything "baroque," or what he calls "oriental." He attacks Ossian and the grandiloquence of the Old Testament,[30] and obviously the style of Shakespeare's

speeches seemed to him mere bombast. Voltaire frequently translates verse into prose to "test" it and to achieve comic effects. Simplicity of style means also homogeneity of style, unity of tone: a
view which is implicit in the whole insistence on purity of genre
and the disapproval of mixtures of style. He is extremely pedantic
and also subtle in his linguistic criticisms: only contemporary good
usage is his standard. Even Molière, La Fontaine, and Corneille
must be read with caution. The standard of clarity applies also to
poetry: "Poetry must have the clarity, the purity of the most
correct prose." [31] He praises some lines of verse by saying: "All the
ideas are closely linked, the words are the right words, and it would
be beautiful in prose." [32]

But it would be a misunderstanding of Voltaire to think of him
as a disparager of poetry. Poetry is not superfluous or obsolete.
"Verse which does not say more, better and more quickly than
prose would say it, is simply bad verse." [33] In his elaborate commentary on Corneille's plays Voltaire subjects them to a minute
linguistic criticism which points out all instances of preciosity as
a vice.[34] Clarity is thus a prime requirement of both prose and
verse. "Any verse or any sentence which requires explanation does
not deserve to be explained" [35] is his surprising statement which
makes short work of one-half of the world's literature, the half
which we seem to love most today and which our poets are aug-
menting in every issue of the little magazines. Also poetry should
impress itself on the memory and thus must be easily understood.

Still, Voltaire recognizes higher styles: above the natural style
rises the elegant, which is always based on selection, a result of
justness and agreement. Virgil and Racine are the masters of elegance and the greatest poets. Poetry is not mere rhymed prose. Voltaire thus disapproves of the prose poem advocated by La Motte,
and resents Fénelon's calling his prose epic *Télémaque* a poem.[36]
Rhyme is not a shackle: it rather forces the poet to think more
justly and to express himself more correctly.[37] Poetry, he says frequently, is the "music of the soul," [38] and in practice he stressed
the qualities of euphony in verse. Translation of poetry is thus,
he knew, all but impossible. "Don't believe," he wrote, "you know
the poets from translations; that's like wanting to see the colors of
a picture in an engraving." [39] It would be a mistake to think that
Voltaire ranked the mere reasoners in rhyme highest. He did not

admire Boileau or Pope excessively and he realized that he was living in an age of decay in French poetry. His admiration was for Virgil and Racine, their harmonious poetry, their "language of the soul." In French literature he recognized at the most, besides Racine, some passages in Corneille, in La Fontaine, and in Quinault, and possibly some stanzas in Malherbe and Racan, as perfect poetry.[40]

Beyond the poetic style there was the elevated, the dramatic, tragic style. Voltaire loved and admired the French theater above any other institution or tradition. Corneille, he said, "established a school of the greatness of soul: Molière founded one of social life." The drama is to him the supreme result of civilization, especially, of course, of French civilization. "There was no good comedy until Molière, just as there was no art of expressing true and delicate sentiments before Racine, because society had not yet arrived at the perfection it reached in their times." [41] Drama, to him, must first of all have an emotional effect; it must move us, interest us. This interest is damaged by improbability, by unnecessary complications of plot or intricate reasonings. The three unities which Voltaire defends in the early preface to *Oedipe* (1729) are merely guards against improbability. The unity of action is there "because the human mind cannot embrace several objects at the same time"; the unity of place "because a single action cannot occur in several places at the same time"; [42] and the unity of time because only the moment of decision can be interesting. The stage must never be empty, and no character must appear on it without sufficient part in the action. Tragedy, according to Voltaire, should and must be lofty, even pathetic, theatrical. He thus had no patience with the new bourgeois tragedy, which seemed to him a debasement of the true kind, though he was rather tolerant of the *comédie larmoyante* and wrote several himself. Still, to a certain extent he was discontented with some of the traditions of French 17th-century tragedy. He objected especially to love intrigues if they were not the center of the play and were only dragged in as obligatory diversion, and also to the rigid exclusion of scenes of violence and death, at least in his early period. He wanted to bring the death of Mariamne on the stage, and he was obviously at first favorably impressed with the amount of action in a play like Shakespeare's *Julius Caesar* or Otway's *Venice Pre-*

served. His own plays, *La Mort de César,* which violates the unity
of time, and *Semiramis,* which introduced a ghost in broad day-
light, are certainly examples of Voltaire's own desire and willing-
ness to experiment. But later he became more and more hostile to
stage business, to elaborate actions and costumes, and thought that
the theater was sinking back into barbarism.[43]

This short description alone should show how well defined Voltaire's taste was, how firmly rooted in the French 17th century to
which he looked back with nostalgia, with a clear feeling of the inferiority of his own time in poetic genius but with pride in the advance of freedom of thought and civil liberties. There is nothing
merely capricious about Voltaire's taste: he feels it definitely to be
an expression of a society and a standard which has the moral and
social sanction of that society. He is neither an impressionist nor a
mere dogmatist: he is a man of taste, the voice of a civilization
which may have irrevocably passed away but has left its deep impress on French literature and criticism. Clarity, measure, design,
taste are still words to conjure with in France, and French neoclassical taste represents in its purity a permanent contribution to
civilization.

Voltaire cannot be placed with the pioneers of historical criticism. No doubt he knew a great deal of history; he has been described, not unjustly, as the founder of the history of civilization,
of economic and world history. But even as a historian he was
primarily interested in the present and the future. As a critic he
was not concerned with literary antiquarianism, though he wrote
some sweeping surveys which could be called literary history: the
sketch of the epic in *Essai sur la poésie épique,* the survey of literature in *Siècle de Louis XIV,* or the slight sketch of the history of
dramatic art in the *Dictionnaire.* Occasionally Voltaire would use
historical arguments: in order either to apologize for faults or to
stress historical merit, the introduction or origination of something. Thus the bombast in Corneille's *Le Cid* would be excused
as Spanish taste which then was "the spirit of the time." [44] The
Church Fathers would be called great in spite of their bad taste for
allegories and metaphors. Voltaire would recommend indulgence
in order to understand Nausicaa or the Song of Songs, which he
translated, toning down the erotic passages. Voltaire was struck by
the similarities of all primitive literature, and by primitive he

meant any writing which was not derived from the tradition of Roman antiquity. Thus he compared the *Iliad* with the Book of Job, the ancient Greek theater with the operas of Metastasio. The *Prometheus Bound* of Aeschylus strikes him as similar to a Spanish *auto sacramental*.[45] Homer, the Bible, and Ossian he sometimes classed together as representing a kind of literature which is considered to be inferior to true taste. Still, he shows some awareness of the existence of different standards of taste in different ages and nations. On the whole, however, Voltaire recognizes only one kind of literature: classical Latin and French, or anything which, in nations other than France, seems to approach it. He is sometimes described as a pioneer of cosmopolitanism in literature; but surely his hopes for a future republic of letters, for a grand society of spirits, could be rather described as French cultural imperialism, since the "French language would be its essential idiom" and certainly French taste would be its central point of reference.[46]

In his early years Voltaire thought of the role of the English as one of contributing to a liberalizing of French taste. He recognized the existence of local beauties and the different geniuses of the main European nations. Occasionally he would give social explanations for differences of taste. In speaking of Oriental poetry, he refers to the different status of women: "Poetry will be different with a people that locks up its women in harems and with a people that gives them unlimited freedom." [47] But basically he always appeals to universal taste, and that universal taste is the classical taste which is founded on the principles of general human nature. One of his attacks on Shakespeare is called *Appel à toutes les nations de l'Europe* (1761), and he recurs again and again to the argument that an author who pleases only locally (such as Shakespeare or Lope de Vega) cannot be really great and correct. French taste he thinks of as the nucleus of European taste to which all other nations can only contribute, a view which will seem less absurd if we consider the tremendous spread of French language, taste, and customs during the 18th century. Six years after Voltaire's death Rivarol could win a prize of the Prussian Academy with his *Discours sur l'universalité de la langue française* (1784). Voltaire himself was feted at the court of Frederick the Great, whose great ambition was to be considered a French poet. In Russia French had become the language of the court and of the nobility, a state

of affairs which lasted far into the 19th century, as any reader of
Tolstoy must know. French was certainly the second language of
Italy.[48] The dominance of neoclassicism in Spain, Italy, Germany,
and even England began to be challenged only in the years immediately preceding Voltaire's death. No wonder that he saw other
literatures through the spectacles of French taste. In England, of
course, he would have to be classed among the most conservative.
His attitude toward Shakespeare is proof enough; there is no
doubt that he read and knew Rymer and even learned from his
method.[49] He certainly was, after some general professions of admiration and puzzlement, hostile also to Milton. One suspects that
the views of Pococurante, the Venetian nobleman in *Candide,* are
not too far removed from Voltaire's own.

> "Milton?" said Pococurante; "that barbarian who made a
> tedious commentary on the first chapter of Genesis in ten
> books of rugged verse? That clumsy imitator of the Greeks,
> who disfigures the creation and, instead of representing the
> Eternal Being, as Moses does, creating the universe at a word,
> makes the Messiah take a large pair of compasses from one of
> the cupboards of Heaven to draw a plan of his intended work?
> Do you expect me to appreciate the man who has spoiled
> Tasso's conception of Hell and the Devil, who disguises
> Lucifer first as a toad and then as a pigmy, who makes him
> repeat the same speeches a hundred times, and even argue
> about theology? Why, the man has so little humor as to imi-
> tate in all seriousness Ariosto's comic invention of firearms
> and make the devils fire cannon in Heaven! Neither I nor
> anyone else in Italy can take pleasure in these sorry extrava-
> gances. The marriage of Sin and Death and the snakes to
> which Sin gives birth sicken every man with any delicacy of
> taste, and his long description of a hospital will only please a
> gravedigger. This obscure, bizarre, and disagreeable poem was
> despised on publication. I judge it today as it was first judged
> by the author's fellow-countrymen. I say what I think, and
> care little whether others agree with me." [50]

Though Pococurante's memory of Milton is curiously inaccurate
(he even changes hellhounds into snakes), and though he does not
know of the biblical authority for the compasses,[51] the view ex-

pressed fits so well with Voltaire's taste that his ridicule of Pococurante does not soften the criticism of Milton.

Again, as with Shakespeare, Voltaire admired individual beauties and flights of imagination. He translated the monologue of
Satan after his fall, but the episode of Death and Sin is called
"disgusting and abominable." [52] On the whole, he concludes that
Paradise Lost is a "work rather singular than natural, more full
of imagination than of graces, of boldness than of selection, whose
subject is all ideal and seems not to have been made for man." [53]

The same attitude is behind the rather scarce pronouncements
on Dante, who is praised for being frequently naive and sometimes
sublime. But usually he is charged with "bizarre taste," and Voltaire even wrote two burlesque imitations in the *Essai sur les
mœurs* and the *Dictionnaire*.[54] Among foreign poets the one who
receives the highest praise is Ariosto, who to Voltaire combines the
invention of Homer with the elegance and taste of Virgil. He adds
the imagination of the *Arabian Nights* to the sensibility of Ti-
bullus and the pleasantry of Plautus. He is superior to La Fontaine
as a story teller and is at times equal to Racine in pathos.[55] Tasso
is also admired by Voltaire, though less fervently. Ariosto and
Tasso surpass Homer: *Orlando Furioso* is better than the *Odyssey*,
Gerusalemme Liberata than the *Iliad*. He censures them only for
too many marvels in an epic poem and admits occasional *clinquant*
with which Boileau had charged Tasso.[56]

Among the French writers Voltaire singles out Racine for the
highest praise. Voltaire's tone becomes positively lyrical when he
speaks of Racine, and in tones of deep emotion he describes *Iphigénie* and *Athalie* as masterpieces of the human mind.[57] Molière is
to him undoubtedly the greatest of all writers of comedy, while he
showers generous praise on Pascal and Bossuet, though he dis-
agreed with their views profoundly and argued against Pascal
much of his life. Among the contemporaries Voltaire naturally
disapproved of Rousseau, for personal and later ideological reasons. His satirical method shines at its wittiest when he sum-
marizes the plot *La Nouvelle Héloïse* [58] or picks holes in the gram-
mar, the images, and the morals of Rousseau's novel. But privately
Voltaire was not totally unappreciative of his eloquence and
genius. "He is a Diogenes, who sometimes speaks like Plato." [59]

One could go on giving examples of Voltaire's innumerable literary judgments. But the more one reads him, the more one is
impressed with the coherence and consistency of his taste: the uniformity of his outlook, in spite of occasional contradictions or
shifts of emphasis. His literary opinions are an almost instinctive
assertion of this taste. The main criteria are always standards of
style, composition, harmony, and eloquence, and the central concept is that of decorum, understood in terms of the French gentleman. Socially Voltaire was certainly the French aristocrat, in spite
of his religious skepticism and his hatred of despotism and intolerance. His literary judgments are never or very rarely colored by his
religious and political opinions. *Athalie,* a pernicious example of
fanaticism, is still the "chef-d'œuvre de l'esprit humain."

I thus cannot agree with Saintsbury's discussion of Voltaire as a
critic.[60] The view that Voltaire's "treasure" and heart were nowhere in literature, "that for literature he had very little genuine
love," seems to me completely mistaken. He was a man of letters,
first of all, and it seems surprising that anyone could doubt his
fervent love and interest in literature and his lifelong ambition to
be a poet. One must have narrowly romantic taste not to appreciate
the very real artistic success of some of Voltaire's tales such as
l'Ingénu and *Candide.* And within limits even his tragedies, his
burlesque poems such as *La Pucelle,* and many fugitive pieces show
genuine power. He himself knew that he was merely a follower of
the great men of the 17th century and that he could not measure
up to them. That is why he held to their standards so strongly: he
thought of himself as a defender of the poetic faith in an age of
prose, as a representative of aristocratic civilization in the age of
the rising bourgeoisie with its low "foreign" taste for the violent
and the commonplace. There may be a paradox in the fact that
Voltaire can be considered a forerunner of the French Revolution
as well as the last outpost of the age of Louis le Grand. But it can
be resolved in the unity of personality of a man who hated injustice, intolerance, obscurantism, irrationality, just as he despised
what he considered the gross, the low and the violent, the absurd
in taste and poetry. Religious skepticism and even political radicalism are not incompatible with literary conservatism and have
never been so in history.

3: DIDEROT

DENIS DIDEROT (1713–84) as a critic is a most baffling subject to deal with. The reasons for the difficulty of presenting a coherent account of Diderot's thought on literature and poetry are obvious enough. The range of his interests and the variety of literary genres in which he is apt to discuss aesthetic and literary topics are as great as in Herder. There is, besides, an obvious evolution in his views from the early pieces in the late 40's to the *Paradoxe sur le comédien* (1778). These difficulties are those one would expect: more surprising are the contradictions and shifts of emphasis in Diderot's views, which he held simultaneously and which cannot be reconciled by simply deciding that only one view was his genuine one. Finally and basically there is the volatility of his temperament, the dynamism of his personality, which is reflected in his style and composition and which makes systematization of his views all but impossible.[1]

There are several ways of handling the situation: one would be to observe the contradictory variety of Diderot's views and to decide that he was simply incoherent and possibly therefore of little account. Another would be boldly to single out what one considers his basic view and to dismiss all other theories as deviations or concessions to the times. Neither of these ways commends itself. We shall have to find some kind of common denominator among his theories in order to explain how he could hold them simultaneously. If one studies his works in strict chronological order one can trace a not unreasonable shift, and, if one pays close attention to the polemical context of pronouncements and the genres to which they are applied, one can discover a further coherence and consistency.

Diderot's early theories could be best labeled as emotionalist. Art and literature are to move us, of course, to virtue. The artist himself must be moved, and the devices, the structures he uses

must be as moving as possible. Diderot wants literature to be above
all pathetic. This is possibly a somewhat rash generalization, but
it may allow us to accommodate the seemingly contradictory theories of his early years. Later Diderot became more skeptical about
the effect of art and hence about the need of spontaneity in the
artist and of emotion in the work itself. He moves back to neoclassical idealism and speaks more insistently of an "interior
model" in the artist's mind.

His theories of the drama were the most influential of his critical writings in his time. There is a well-known discussion of
French tragedy in the indecent early novel *Les Bijoux indiscrets*
(1748) which Lessing was to quote,[2] and there are the various
dialogues and discourses which Diderot wrote to follow or introduce his plays, *Le Fils naturel* (1757) and *Le Père de famille*
(1758). It seems unfortunate that Diderot as a critic is known
mostly by these early writings on the drama. They have their great
historical importance and interest but do not seem impressively
new to those who know the English critics. They can be judged
mainly as a plea for a realistic drama as opposed to the conventions of the French stage: they are the manifestoes of a new genre,
the domestic tragedy, which was new in France but had its models,
known and admired by Diderot, in Lillo's *London Merchant* and
Edward Moore's *Gamester*. The passage in *Les Bijoux indiscrets*
implies wholly naturalistic standards: French plays are criticized
for their improbable accumulation of events within a short time,
for their set speeches, and for their unnatural gestures. He
imagines the response of a foreigner who had never seen a French
play and was promised the sight of an actual intrigue in the
palace.[3] As soon as the foreigner was admitted into the box from
which he could see the theater, which he supposed to be the
palace of the sultan, he would burst into laughter and recognize
that it was all a play, on account of the stilted walk of the actors,
the bizarreness of their costumes, the extravagance of their gestures, the emphasis of their strangely rhymed and cadenced language. Diderot seems literally to accept the view that the theater
should deceive: "The perfection of a spectacle consists in such an
exact imitation of an action that the spectator, deceived without
interruption, imagines that he witnesses the action itself." [4] In re-
porting a successful performance in Marseilles of his own *Père de*

famille, Diderot is pleased to relate that "hardly had the first scene been played before one believed oneself in a family circle and one forgot that one was in a theater. These were no longer the boards, this was a particular house." [5] But all these requirements of naturalness are not those of modern realism. They are meant to be strictly subordinate to emotional effects, as we see when we examine the two treatises Diderot annexed to his domestic plays, or his famous eulogy of Richardson (1761). Still, many concrete opinions imply naturalistic standards. In criticizing French tragedy he objects to too much speechifying, to the forced unities of place and time, to the intricate fable, to the whole social milieu of remote antiquity and remoter Orient. But what he recommends is not simply realism. It should rather be called sensationalism, in which realistic devices are valued only as contributing to an intense emotional effect.

The moderns (that is, the French of the 17th and 18th centuries) are criticized particularly for shirking this emotional intensity of real art.

> In general [he says] the more a people is civilized and polished, the less are its customs poetic; everything weakens and softens. On what occasions does nature present us with the models for our art? When children tear out their hair beside the bed of the dying father; when a mother uncovers her bosom and appeals to her son by the breasts which have nursed him; when a man cuts off his own hair, throws it at the corpse of a friend, raises the corpse and carries it to a pyre, where he collects the ashes and shuts them up in an urn to which he comes, on appointed days, to wet it with his tears; when disheveled widows tear their faces with their nails . . . when bacchantes, armed with thyrsi, wander in the forest and inspire fear and curse those whom they meet; or when other women undress without shame, open their arms to the first comer and prostitute themselves. . . . I do not say that these are good manners, only that they are poetic manners.[6]

Thus Diderot's ideal is that of emotional intensity, of spontaneity. There is, he finds, nothing in common between the modern hooped and powdered ladies with handkerchiefs in their hands

and the heroines of antiquity. Brutus, Catiline, Caesar, Cato would
not recognize themselves on the French stage. The modern audience shuns the great emotional effects of Greek tragedy and shuns
them wrongly. Philoctetes crying and moaning on his island, the
Eumenides hot on the trail of blood, Oedipus with the blood
streaming from his face—these are scenes after Diderot's heart.[7]
The dramatic poet thus "should aim not at the clapping of hands
after a striking line, but at the deep sigh which leaves the soul
after the constraint of a long silence, and which relieves it. He
should aim at the even more violent impression which puts people
as if to the rack. Then the spirits will be troubled, uncertain,
floating, lost: and the spectators will be like those who in an earthquake see the walls of their houses shake, and feel the earth open
under their feet."[8] Diderot feels as violently the effect of Richardson's novels. "When I read of the last hours of this innocent
creature [Clarissa], I am always astonished that the very stones and
walls and cold and senseless flags on which I walk are not stirred to
cry out and join their sorrow in mine."[9] He favors melodramatic
plots and situations: he sketches a harrowing scene of a *Death of
Socrates;*[10] he writes highly strained, high-pitched plays full of
impossible situations and complications. "Touch me, surprise me,
tear me; make me tremble, cry, shudder, be angry!"[11]

Diderot is dissatisfied with the ordinary means of achieving the
emotional effect on the stage. He thinks words insufficient. Passion,
he argues, does not speak in flowery, ornate set speeches. It speaks
haltingly, it resorts to pantomime, to gestures. This is why Diderot
admires the scene with Lady Macbeth sleepwalking, rubbing her
hands.[12] The situation is seen, is visualized, brought home in more
than mere words. Thus he welcomes a novelty on the Parisian
stage, the Italian dramatic pantomime, and he even sketches a
scenario for such an experiment.[13]

This naturalistic emotionalism in Diderot was perfectly compatible with traits which have been hailed as anticipations of symbolism or modern impressionism. It connects with his polemics
against the intellectualization of language and poetry, with his
particular brand of primitivism. Like Fontenelle or Vico, Diderot
voices the view that because barbarous people were more spontaneous and more violent they had more poetry.

There is more fire in barbarous people than in civilized;
more fire in the Hebrews than in the Greeks; more fire in the
Greeks than the Romans; more fire in the Romans than the
Italians or French; more fire in the English than in the last.
There is always a decline of fire and poetry in proportion to
the progress of the philosophical spirit. . . . Its cautious advance is an enemy of movement and figures. The realm of
images passes as the realm of things extends . . . as civil and
religious prejudices disappear; it is incredible what damage
this monotonous politeness does to poetry. . . . The philosophical spirit leads to a sentimentous and dry style. Abstract
expressions, which extend to a great number of appearances,
multiply and take the place of figured expressions. . . .
Which kind of poetry, do you think, requires most fire? The
ode, without doubt. It has been a long time since odes have
been written. . . . When does one see critics and grammar-
ians arise? Always after an age of genius and divine production. . . . There is only one propitious moment; when there
is enough fire and liberty to be warm, and enough judgment
and taste to be wise.[14]

Thus Diderot condemns Helvétius for his unmetaphorical, dry
style, and prefers the loose and informal Montaigne.[15] Like Voltaire he understands that the process of rationalization has been
detrimental to poetry and that it means depriving words of what
we would call their connotative rather than their denotative meaning.

Diderot has a theory of language as a system of signs. Language
has the tendency to become more and more arbitrary and fixed.
Original language was natural, i.e. a language of nonconventional
signs. The poet is a man "who passes from abstract and general
sounds to less abstract and less general sounds, until he arrives at
a sensible representation, the last resort and repose of reason." [16]
The natural sign is better, it is more concrete, and it is truer; for,
according to Locke and Condillac, only an "idea," i.e. a sense
datum, is immediately evident. It is more poetic because it appeals
directly to the senses, to the visual imagination. "We are presented
not merely with a chain of strong terms which express the idea
with force and nobility, but with a tissue of hieroglyphics heaped

one above the other which picture it. I may say that in this sense all
poetry is emblematic." [17] As Diderot's elaborate comments on
passages of poetry show, "hieroglyphics" and "emblems" do not
mean symbols which conceal an intellectual content, but stress
what we would call sound symbolism and the physiological effect
of meter. "The poet is under the necessity of finding an expression
of genius, a unique, original, and natural physiognomy, the force-
ful and strong image of an individual quality." [18]

But sometimes, instead of stressing the concreteness and visual
force of the word in art, he recommends connotation as a means for
achieving vagueness and even downright obscurity, which seems to
him sublime and moving. "Clarity is all right for convincing: it is
of no use for moving. Clarity of whatever kind damages enthusiasm. Poets, speak incessantly of eternity, infinitude, immensity,
time, space, divinity. . . . Be dark!" [19] "The vaguer is expression
in the arts, the more is imagination at ease." [20] "At ease" must here
mean free to roam, to indulge in its own play of association. This
seems the opposite of the precision of the visual, the physiognomic,
the characteristic and individual, which the preceding passages
recommended. Here is one of the contradictions of Diderot's
theory, reconcilable only if we understand that both doctrines are
directed against the ideal of purely rational language, and that
both distinct visual beauty and indistinct vague sublimity are
prized for achieving emotional impact. Diderot works toward a
rhetoric of sensation: an idea, in poetry and in the arts in general,
must not remain a mere sense datum, and of course it must become not a concept but an emotion.[21] Sensationalism and emotionalism fuse.

But Diderot pushes further. He also tries to explain the effect
of poetic images by a psychological theory which demands more
than vividness of impressions. In *Le Rêve de D'Alembert* (1769,
published 1830) there are hints for a theory of imagination as the
perception of analogies beyond the merely associational. He compares metaphoric imagination to the sympathetic vibration of
strings at unexpected intervals. The creation of original metaphors, the yoking together of remote spheres, the apprehension of
unsuspected relationships comes about through the accumulation
of delicate and varied experiences during the long life of an organism. The memory serves, so to speak, as a vault of images, stored in

the darkness of nerve centers, from where they spring in an unpredictable and often inexplicable manner, coupling themselves
to present ideas to form the metaphors of the poet and the hy-
potheses of the scientist.[22] Apparently Diderot does not distinguish
between the intuition of the philosopher and the imagination of
the poet. He defends the poet's original associations, as we could
expect, by the sensationalist theory of knowledge: they are real
because they occur in the organism of the poet and may be felt
by him with an intensity which is often lacking in direct sense impression. But Diderot breaks off these speculations by suggesting
that they may furnish the subject of a book. He leaves the poet
dangling in a world of subjective, irrelevant, interior associations
and linkages. No theory of poetry may be derived from these
passages. It seems impossible to reconcile them with the conven-
tionally neoclassical idea of the "interior model." [23]

Diderot, in accord with his age and his own gifts, paid little attention to lyrical poetry. But he thought enough about verse to
see the connection between language as metaphoric emblem and
the physical effect of sound: onomatopoeia, rhythm, and meter. He
thinks of verse rhythm as following closely the "movement of the
soul," the interior rhythm of the mind.[24] It is clear that with such
a conception of poetry Diderot understood that translating is well-
nigh impossible. Even the best translation will lack the suggestive
sounds which depend on the distribution of long and short syllables, and of vowels between consonants.[25]

Poetry, which moves our sense by physical signs, can be produced only by the moved mind, by the emotional man who is
genius and poet, the man of feeling. Diderot constantly assumes
intense emotional personal engagement as the criterion of poetic
greatness. He criticizes Saint-Lambert's version of Thomson's
Seasons as academic poetry, full of art, design, intellect. "The soul
alone, not art, must produce [the effect]. If you think of the effect,
you have failed." [26] Nothing is seen or felt in Saint-Lambert's descriptions. "His body is in the country but his soul in the town
. . . he never waited for the inspiration of nature and he has
prophesied, to use an expression of Naigeon, before the Spirit descended on him. He does not intoxicate, because he himself is not
intoxicated. At the sight of a beautiful landscape, he says: 'O, what
a beautiful view for a description'—instead of falling silent and

letting himself penetrate it deeply and only then seize the lyre." [27] "What then does Saint-Lambert lack? A soul that torments itself, a violent spirit, a strong and burning imagination, a lyre that has many chords." [28] For Diderot the poet or the artist is a tragic, melancholy figure. "Before taking up the pencil one must have trembled twenty times in the presence of the subject, lost sleep, got up in the middle of the night and have run in one's nightshirt and with bare feet in order to throw one's sketches on paper under the light of a night-lamp." [29] These are the tones of the young Goethe jumping out of bed in the middle of the night, the *Sturm und Drang,* the emotional overflow. Diderot contrasts genius, the "pure gift of nature," with taste.[30] Genius is above the rules: it can break any rule and all of them, even though rules may be useful in an age of decadence.

If this were all Diderot had written we should have a fairly consistent theory of the emotional genius, the moved spectator, and the moving work of art. But this aim is considerably modified by basic neoclassical assumptions which, with the years, became stronger and finally pushed him into a position contradictory, at least in part, to his earlier sentimentalism. Even his very influential advocacy of a new genre, the *drame bourgeois,* is made almost entirely in terms acceptable to neoclassical theory. He elaborates a hierarchy of dramatic genres, in which the domestic tragedy appears to fill the gap between tragedy and comedy, while the burlesque comedy and the marvelous play are relegated to the role of inferior subgenres.[31] Tragicomedy is expressly condemned as a bad genre which confounds two genres distinctly separated by a natural barrier. "One does not pass from one to the other by imperceptible nuances, but one falls at each stem into contrasts and thus the unity disappears." [32] Diderot censures Shakespeare and Otway for this mixture as bad taste, though less violently than Voltaire censured Shakespeare. The new genre, the *drame bourgeois,* differs from tragedy in its subject matter and also in its tone and its lack of heroic passion. Diderot thinks of it also as intermediary between the other genres in the sort of characters it exhibits. Comedy is about types, tragedy about individuals. Domestic drama is about *conditions,* a term which refers to Diderot's practice of introducing types such as the financier, the man of letters, the philosopher, the judge, the lawyer, the politician, and people in their basic family relations as father, husband, sister, brother.[33] It is difficult to see what novelty lies in these characters: Diderot could hardly have thought that *condition* can replace either individuality or the general type; it is simply good neo-classical typology. He himself says that one could write a new *Misanthrope* every fifty years,[34] an admission that a comic type can be localized in time and place. He could hardly have thought that tragic heroes are totally individual and not representative.

Art therefore, or at least the art of the drama, obviously does not mean mere emotionalism but rather the imitation of nature; and, of course, by "nature" Diderot means the typical, the universal, the assumed harmony of nature. "The harmony of the most beautiful picture is nothing but a feeble imitation of the harmony of nature." [35] There are many passages, especially in the later writings such as the *Salon* of 1767, in which Diderot takes up the concept of an internal model which the artist is to follow. Thus he accepts the neo-Platonic strain in neoclassicism and sometimes sounds exactly like Shaftesbury (whom he studied and a translation of whose essay on *Virtue and Merit* was his first publication in 1745) or Winckelmann. Diderot can even say that works of art "preach more forcefully the grandeur, the power, and the majesty of nature than nature herself." [36] Art then is idealization and implicitly a justification of nature. In the question of sculpture Diderot becomes involved in arguments about the imitation of ancients, the undesirability of imitating modern nudes who are deformed by stays and garters,[37] the difficulty of merely recommending the imitation of classical statues, and the possible ways by which antiquity may have arrived at ideal beauty (to which, in this context at least, Diderot gives a purely naturalistic interpretation). "The most beautiful model, the most perfect model of a man or woman is one which is supremely fit for all the functions of life, has arrived at the age of fullest development without, however, having fulfilled any." [38] This apparently means a biological ideal of beauty, a woman who has not yet borne children but is best capable of bearing them, an ideal which does not take one very far in aesthetics and certainly in literature suggests little beyond normality and regular beauty.

By far the most interesting application of this "idealism" is Diderot's dialogue *Le Paradoxe sur le comédien,* written between

1770 and 1778 but published only in 1830. It differs so strikingly from his earlier more naturalistic theories that attempts have been made to deny its authenticity. But it is well attested on external and internal grounds and actually fits in very well with many scattered pronouncements and the general drift of Diderot's development.[39] The argument of the *Paradoxe* refers mainly to the art of acting, but its implications for poetry, though recognized only slightly by Diderot himself, are far reaching. Diderot now argues that an actor cannot and should not identify himself with his role and should not be carried away by emotion, but rather he should imitate an interior model of the character which he has formed in his mind. There will thus be three such models: the actual man in reality, the model imagined by the poet, and the model imagined by the actor. Strangely enough Diderot now says that "the model of nature is less grand than that conceived by the poet, and that in turn is less grand than that achieved by the great actor, which is the most exaggerated" (and apparently therefore the best of the three). Naturalistic expressions of feeling are now rejected. If the actor is endowed with extreme sensibility, either he does not act or he acts ridiculously. "If I have to tell a pathetic story, some unknown trouble arises in my heart, in my head; my tongue falters; my voice is changed; my ideas disintegrate; my speech halts; I stammer; my tears flow down my cheeks and I fall silent." The other speaker objects: "But that is what succeeds." "In society, but in the theater I'll be hissed." "Why?" "Because the audience does not come to see tears but to hear moving speeches, because the truth of nature clashes with the truth of convention. Neither the dramatic system, nor the action, nor the speech of the poet are patterned from my stifled, interrupted, sighing declamation. It is not sufficient to imitate nature. One must imitate beautiful nature." [40] The argument seems to have come full circle: Diderot now considers the hissing of a French 18th-century audience as the test of dramatic art. Many arguments and anecdotes about actors are produced to strengthen this view. Some are convincing, though in bad taste: stories about actors who interrupt the passion of their role to address their fellow actors or the audience; a dying actress whispers to the actor stretched out next to her: "You smell"; another, admonished by the audience to speak louder, answers, "You be quiet." The actor, after a performance that leaves the audience in tears, is not sad but merely tired by the effort, wants to change his shirt and go to bed. The good actor is then the man who best knows how to render the external signs of emotion, not the actor who is himself most profoundly moved. Such real emotion cannot be repeated and can extend only to one or two roles, to one or two situations. Diderot recognizes that what he says about the actor must apply also to the poet, the orator, the painter, the musician. "The great poets, the great actors, and probably in general all the great imitators of nature, whatever they are, endowed with a beautiful imagination, with a good judgment, a fine tact, a sure taste, are the least sensitive of all beings. . . . They are too much occupied with looking, knowing, and imitating to be vividly affected and carried beyond themselves." [41] Diderot says of art in words strikingly similar to Wordsworth's "recollection in tranquillity":

> Do you compose a poem about death the moment after you have lost your friend or your mistress? No. . . . When the great pain has passed, when the extreme sensitivity has dulled, when one is remote from the catastrophe, when the soul is calm, when one recalls the past happiness . . . when the memory unites with the imagination, then one can speak well. One says that one weeps, but one no longer weeps when one chases a striking epithet . . . when one is occupied in making the verse harmonious; when the tears flow, the pen drops from one's hands, one surrenders to feeling and one stops composing.[42]

Diderot now recognizes that the actor does not cease to be a private person and is not transformed into the character he is portraying. What happens is something like a division of personality: "In this moment, she is double: the little Clairon and the great Agrippina." [43] Diderot now also recognizes that the figures of the stage, the Cleopatras, Meropes, Agrippinas, and Cinnas, are not historical personages, not personages at all, but "the imaginary specters of poetry: I say too much:—they are the specters of the particular character of this or that poet." [44] The theater is based on an old convention, a formula given by Aeschylus, "a protocol aged three thousand years." [45]

Also Diderot's view of the effect of art has changed. He no

longer speaks of violent emotional effects, of putting men on the
rack, of breaking up their world like an earthquake. Rather
naively he even dreamt of some fortunate island—Lampedusa,
between Tunisia and Sicily, is singled out—where on feast days
tragedies and comedies would be performed and where actors
would become the great preachers of morality.[46] He had high expectations of the immediate moral effect of the stage. "The pit of
a theater is the only place where the tears of a virtuous and a
wicked man mingle. Here the evildoer becomes indignant at the
injustices which he himself would have committed, feels pity for
the evil he himself would have occasioned, and gets angry at a
man of his own character. . . . The evildoer leaves his box less
disposed to work evil." [47] But later Diderot became more skeptical
as to the immediate moral effect of the theater. "There in the
theater I am magnanimous, just, compassionate, because I can be
so without consequence." [48] These later pronouncements certainly
show a deeper comprehension of the nature of art, the nature of
the creative process, and the effects of art than his earlier, more
influential writings, full of the emotionalism and sentimentalism
of the time.

Something must be said of his practical criticism, his rating of
the main authors, his predilections and tastes. He cannot be described as a fertile or careful critic of individual authors, nor can
his views of the history of literature be considered particularly
novel or striking. Toward antiquity he takes a sensible in-between
position. He disapproves of the wholesale adulation of antiquity
and thus seems to side with the moderns in the *Querelle*. But he
does so only very provisionally on general grounds. Actually he
admired many ancients very fervently. "When I prefer Homer to
Virgil, Virgil to Tasso, Tasso to Milton, Milton to Voltaire or
Camões, it is not a matter of date at all. I can give my reasons." [49]
He rejects the accusation of *antico-manie* but is actually quite in-
sistent on the necessity of knowing antiquity. There is no excellence of taste without a knowledge of the Greeks and Latins. One
easily recognizes a modern author who does not know the ancients.
Diderot himself read Greek and Latin very well. He emphasizes
the value of knowledge and erudition for the poet and, in criticism of the rococo poetry of his time, protests that modern poets,
"because of their lack of knowledge, sing nothing but melodious

insipidities." [50] Though nature is the source of all beauty, still the ancients furnished the greatest models of art.

Homer comes in for the highest praise. He differs from all other poets for he speaks the language of poetry as if it were his own; all other poets compared to him smack of the academy. Diderot defends Homer unreservedly against his many detractors in the wake of Bayle. He accepts Homer's heroes, his manners, his language, his technique of description. Like Lessing he singles out for praise the passage in the *Iliad* where the beauty of Helen is not described, but suggested by the effect it had on the old men of Troy.[51]

Virgil is also very great but not as great as Homer. Diderot especially admires the *Georgics*.[52] He admires Horace and thinks the *Ars poetica* a work of genius greatly preferable to Boileau's *L'Art poétique,* which seems to him merely a work of good taste.[53] He praises Tacitus as the Rembrandt of literature, admires Lucretius for his imagination but criticizes him for his "dry and chaotic style." [54]

Diderot was most deeply impressed by Greek tragedy. He admires Aeschylus as "gigantic and epic," "sublime," especially in the *Eumenides,* to which he always refers when he wants an example of moving tragic art. Sophocles' *Philoctetes* is to him the perfect masterpiece: "One cannot add a word or subtract one." [55] But he is surprisingly cool toward Euripides. He constantly appeals to Greek tragedy as a model for modern tragedy, especially extolling its simplicity of action as compared with the complex intrigues of a French tragedy. Diderot also has an inkling of the social implications of Greek tragedy: he contrasts the great public space of the Athenian stage with the little dark corners of modern theaters where only a few hundred people can gather. He tells the story of a man who thought a Parisian theater a prison.[56] Great effects like those on the Greek stage are needed, but Diderot recognizes that "we need for such a genre authors, actors, a theater, and possibly a people." [57] He belongs with the many critics of the 18th century who expected something like a reunion of the arts—of dance, pantomime, stage painting, music, and poetry—and he saw a partial fulfillment of his ideal in the Italian opera.

Diderot, quite comprehensibly, was enthusiastic about Terence. Terence depicts family life; he is pathetic and even bourgeois. He has nothing of the violence and extravagance of Aristophanes or even Molière. He is praised as having "the more tranquil and sweet Muse," [58] and the first scene of *Andria* seems to Diderot unsurpassed by anything even in Molière. He praises Colman's translation of Terence into English, hoping it may give the English a lesson in truth, unity of design, precision. It may teach them to avoid the extravagances of Vanbrugh, Wycherley, and Congreve.[59] Compared to Terence, Aristophanes is only a "jester," useful to the Athenian government.[60] And Plautus did not interest Diderot at all.

Diderot's attitude toward classical French literature is somewhat ambiguous. He opposes many features of French tragedy and comedy but cannot withhold his admiration from their great authors or suppress the feeling that the 17th century will be revered as the classical age of French literature.[61] He praises Corneille as sublime but uneven, considering only eight or nine plays really excellent. But he disapproves of the baroque features in Corneille. "Corneille is almost always at Madrid and not at Rome." Racine is "probably the greatest poet who ever existed," [62] possibly the most perfect, the purest of all writers of the world.[63] And, like Voltaire, Diderot gives the highest praise to the melody of Racine's language and verse. The actor becomes a musical instrument in his hands.[64] His poetry is charged with the subtlest "hieroglyphics." Molière is a favorite, of course, but for surprising reasons. Diderot thinks him most original in his burlesques and farces and defends these farcical features against the strictures of Boileau and Fénelon. *Tartuffe* is singled out for the skill with which the action is managed and still made perfectly probable and natural.

Diderot shows considerable interest in English literature, especially Shakespeare and Richardson and, of course, the domestic drama of the English, which anticipated his own reforms of the French stage. There are remarks on English writers, Milton, Swift, Pope, and Young, but they are undistinguished.[65] Shakespeare is seen with more sympathetic eyes than those of Voltaire, though fundamentally Diderot still considers him a natural, rude, and tasteless genius. In a curious passage he protests against the idea that one can find Shakespeare's originality only in his sublime passages. It is rather in the "extraordinary, incomprehensible, inimitable mixture of the best and the worst taste" that Shakespeare's greatness lies.[66] He condemns tragicomedy, but is lenient toward the comic scenes in Shakespeare, which he believes show little taste.[67] On the whole one should not be shocked by the violence of Shakespeare any more than by the pathos of Homer, by the sight of Oedipus with his eyes pulled out, or by the crying and moaning of Philoctetes. He ironically asks French poets if they write for a delicate, vaporous nation which enjoys only the harmonious, tender, and touching elegies of Racine and which is hurt by the butcheries of Shakespeare, for souls too feeble to support violent shocks.[68] "In Shakespeare sublimity and genius shine like lightning in a long night, but Racine is always beautiful." Homer is full of genius and Virgil of elegance,[69] but Shakespeare is a representative of almost medieval crudeness. "He will not compare him to the Apollo of Belvedere, to the Gladiator, to Antinous, or to the Hercules of Glycon, but rather to Saint Christopher of Notre Dame, a shapeless colossus, rudely carved, but between whose legs we all can pass without our forehead touching his shameful parts." [70]

Diderot expresses the greatest enthusiasm for Richardson in the famous eulogy (1761) and also in private letters to his mistress, Sophie Volland. Richardson is true to life, is moral, incites to virtuous actions, is perfect. "How good I felt, how just, how self-satisfied, after reading your books: I felt as a man does after a well-spent day." [71] "The nobler the mind, the more refined and the purer the taste, the more one knows human nature, and the greater one's love of truth, so much the more one will appreciate the works of Richardson." [72] Diderot compares Richardson's novels with the Bible. "Since I have known them I use them as touchstones, and when they are not appreciated I know in what esteem I hold such persons." [73] "O! Richardson, if you did not, during your life, earn all the praise that you deserved, how great will be your fame among our descendants when they see you at the distance that we see Homer. Who will then dare to erase a line from your sublime work?" [74] When a lady criticized Clarissa, whose chief gift in her opinion was the making of fine phrases, Diderot became indignant. "I must confess that I think it is a great curse to think and feel thus: so great, that I would rather my daughter should presently die in my arms than know that she could thus be afflicted. My daughter—yes I say it deliberately and will not retract." [75] This seems today sheer madness of "sensibility." We can more easily understand why Diderot should have seen "sparks of sublime beauties" in Lillo's *London Merchant* and should have liked Moore's *Gamester,* and, when he saw it in French translation, should have praised Lessing's *Miss Sara Sampson.*

As we survey Diderot's critical work it is hard not to be unjust to the richness of its suggestions and the multitude of its interesting passages, ideas, and *aperçus,* because one cannot help seeing that Diderot is a man situated between two worlds, unable to choose between them. One can read into him anticipations of 19th-century bourgeois naturalism; one can see, in a few passages, anticipations of symbolist conceptions of poetry. The emotional romanticism and sentimentalism can hardly be denied, but surprisingly some of his finest criticism comes when he turns back to the past and seizes firmly on certain truths of the neoclassical creed, the impersonality of the artist, the inner ideal, the "interior model," the deliberate shaping of the artist's work. In this respect Diderot's development parallels that of the two great Germans, Goethe and Schiller, who also, after a youth of romantic emotionalism, restated the neoclassical creed in terms free from the old dogmatism.

THE TWO most significant figures of literary criticism and theory in France during the second half of the 18th century were obviously Voltaire and Diderot. The third most famous writer, Jean-Jacques Rousseau (1712–78), though enormously important in the general history of literature and ideas, was hardly a literary critic in the strict sense. His one formal piece of literary criticism, the *Lettre à d'Alembert sur les spectacles* (1758), is an attack on d'Alembert's proposal to allow a theater in Geneva. It is a highly moralistic piece, in which Rousseau tries to argue that drama may be good for the corrupt Parisians but would spoil the pure Genevans. He draws on the whole arsenal of the antistage controversy carried on for centuries by Puritans, whether Catholic or Calvinist, and excitedly declaims on the dissolute manners of actresses, the bad economic consequences of the sale of theater tickets, the spread of luxury and display, and so on. The whole argument seems of little relevance or even interest today. The famous criticism of Molière's *Misanthrope,* in which Rousseau takes the side of Alceste, proposes a complete rewriting of the play. Rousseau obviously sees himself as the misanthrope and wants Molière to justify him at every point. It is bad criticism, which confuses life and art, Molière's Alceste with a hypothetical human type. Logically Rousseau's rigid moralism is contradicted by his own frequent recognition that each society has the art it wants and needs. "An author," says Rousseau, "who wanted to injure the general taste would soon write only for himself." [1] Sophocles would fail on the French stage because "we cannot put ourselves in the place of people who don't resemble us." Drama "reenforces the national character, augments the natural inclinations, and gives a new energy to all our passions." [2] Besides, Rousseau also combats his own conclusion by minimizing the emotional and moral effect of the theater. He doubts that the passions may be purged in any other way than by reason, and objects to the idea that only specific passions can be aroused by a play. "Don't they know that all passions are sisters, that one suffices to excite thousands, and that to fight one by another is only a means of making the heart more susceptible to all?" [3] He decries the pity excited by the stage, particularly by the 18th-century sentimental drama. "It is passing and useless emotion, which lasts no longer than the illusion which produced it. It is a sterile pity, which has never caused the least act of humanity." [4] But then, of course, his indignation at d'Alembert's proposal seems out of proportion: Geneva, though it has a theater, is no sink of iniquity.

Rousseau's own proposal to encourage outdoor spectacles where the spectators would be actors has been hailed by Romain Rolland as an anticipation of his Theater of the People. [5] Actually Rousseau offers only naive suggestions about May-day celebrations, gymnastic competitions, boat races, solemn public balls, and reunions of citizens scattered abroad: all meetings where any artistic activity or purpose is lost sight of. He wanted to facilitate marriages, reduce clandestine courtships, and increase respect for the aged, not encourage art.

Rousseau's importance for literary criticism is in neither his puritanical horror of the stage nor his recognition of the relativity of taste nor his disparagement of sentimentalism in the drama, but in the general impulse he gave to the primitivistic view of poetry and to the whole "conjectural" history of society. The *Essai sur l'origine des langues* (1749) in particular contains echoes of views common since Vico and Blackwell on the metaphorical nature of early poetry and on the primacy of poetry over prose.* To define what Rousseau contributed to criticism by his attack on civilization, his exaltation of individuality, imagination, and revery, and his insight into the connection between man and nature would be an almost impossible task, merging into the general history of ideas.

Quite apart from the three *philosophes* stands the naturalist

---

* Esp. chs. 3 and 4, in *Œuvres complètes* (Paris, 1824), 2, 424 f. Fausto Nicolini, "La teoria del linguaggio in Giambattista Vico e Giangiacomo Rousseau," *Revue de littérature comparée, 10* (1930), 292–8, tries to show that Rousseau could have known Vico's *Scienza nuova,* but the main ideas could have come from any number of sources, e.g. Blackwell, Warburton, Condillac.

Buffon (George Louis Le Clerc, Comte de Buffon, 1707–88), who will always be remembered in the history of criticism for his *Discours sur le style* (1753). It is the plea of a scientist for things, ideas, reasons, something which would not merely strike the ear and occupy the eyes but also act on the soul and touch the heart in speaking to the mind. Buffon apparently wants matter, not manner or rhetoric. One must possess one's subject to write well. Good writing is good thinking. But the emphasis seems to shift when Buffon reflects that only well-written works pass on to posterity as new discoveries and new facts make most scientific books soon obsolete. "These things are outside man, the style is the man himself" is the passage which is frequently quoted both wrongly and out of context.[6] It does not imply a justification of individuality of style nor even of a physiognomy of style; it does not mean that the total man is expressed in style. Rather, style is a purely intellectual virtue to Buffon; it is order, continuity, reasoned development; it is the human element, man's mind ordering and communicating ideas. Buffon's ideal is the one great sublime style, universal, generalized, impersonal. He is a late representative of the Cartesian ideal rather than a writer recommending personality.[7]

Voltaire had definite adherents and followers in literary criticism. Two of these were extremely influential codifiers and popularizers of the taste of the time and are sufficiently distinct to merit separate treatment: Jean-François Marmontel (1723–99) and J. F. La Harpe. Marmontel wrote a two-volume *Poétique française* (1763) and contributed most of the articles on literary theory to the *Encyclopédie*. They were collected as *Éléments de littérature* (1787) and were often reprinted, even in the 19th century. Ostolopov's valuable Russian *Dictionary of Poetry* (1821) still draws heavily on Marmontel.[8] Marmontel aims at an alliance between poetics and science. He proclaims his poetics to be inductive and historical, an application of the methods of Bacon and Descartes to literature.[9] Actually his appeal to reason, experience, and nature is hardly different from that commonly found in the whole Stoic tradition of generalized nature and universal man. The decision that "the philosophic and the poetic spirit are one and the same," that the "more a poet is a philosopher, the more he is a poet," is not really carried out in practice, as Marmontel also talks about

genius, imagination, sensibility, enthusiasm, taste; and at the same
time he accepts many, even completely arbitrary, rules if they were
established *de facto*.[10] Marmontel has many rationalistic traits: he
distrusts verse and considers only rhythm essential to poetry; he
distrusts metaphor as associated with the savage state. "The less
civilized the poetry, the more figurative." [11] At times he seems to
think of poetry as a mere contrivance. Speaking of the epic, he calls
it a building, a machine contrived to produce a common movement, in which the characters function as wheels, the plot as
chain.[12] But this is hardly thought through, for he can also compare
the plot of the *Iliad* to a polyp, whose every cut-off part is a living
organic polyp in itself.[13] Unity is for him not only the three unities,
but also unity of design, unity of tone, and unity of style. The rules
are acknowledged side by side with genius and the gift of creation,
imagination, sensibility, taste. He can say that the one and only
rule of poetry is to be born a poet.[14]

While in Marmontel's poetic theory contradictory elements lie
next to each other unreconciled and unexamined, he made a real
effort to apply science to the history of literature. He would like to
"consider poetry as a plant and discover why, indigenous in certain climates, it rises and flowers as of itself; why in other climates
it flourishes only by cultivation; and in others cannot be made
to bloom in spite of all efforts; and why, even in the same climate,
it has sometimes flowered and borne fruit and sometimes with-
ered." [15] He would like to give a social and physical explanation of
the revolutions of the arts. But this grandiose plan, suggested by
Dubos and Montesquieu, is hardly realized in detail. The history
of poetry is largely made to celebrate the Greeks and the French
of the 17th century when social and moral circumstances combined to create great periods of literary excellence. The historical
explanation is, however, halfhearted: the Greeks are national but
the great French are universal, like the empire of passions.[16] Marmontel's taste is, in practice, Voltaire's; he shares Voltaire's horror
for Shakespeare's and Milton's "deformities." Richardson and the
English Augustans he praises as examples of the salutary influence
of the French.[17] The compliments to genius, even to "original"
genius, do not mean any sympathy with art outside of the Latin
tradition. Genius is merely the inventive faculty, while the actual
composition of a work of art is due to talent and taste and to the

observance of the rules. Virgil is much more tasteful than Homer, the French more than the ancients.[18] But even Marmontel's emphasis on taste and his frequent disapproval of Boileau are deceptive if we interpret them as mitigating the basic rationalism. Marmontel distinguishes between a taste of speculation and a taste of sentiment, with the taste of speculation representing "love for real beauty" and the "taste of sentiment" love for novelty. Love for novelty is the cause of decadence in this present age of sensationalism and sentimentalism. At the same time he introduces a somewhat different distinction between "natural" and "conventional" taste. Natural taste (hardly, one would think, the equivalent of speculative taste) is ascribed to antiquity and even to the savage, while conventional taste is assigned to the modern age. The two double concepts of taste do not match and are not reconciled: Marmontel wants to "naturalize" art, return it to a simple, severe, classical taste. Taste is to be Greek and natural, yet still rational and speculative.[19] As often at that time, fire and water were declared the same.

In general Marmontel represents an eclectic, loosely articulated view of literature, in which many current motifs of literary theory are juxtaposed: rationalism, neoclassicism, the new historical sense, the cult of taste and genius. Unfortunately his historical knowledge was too slight, his insight too dim to make a success of a history of literature in terms of the physical and social milieu. Still, he anticipates Madame de Staël, who herself did only a little better with the subject.

Jean-François de la Harpe (1739–1803), in his youth a protégé of old Voltaire, was the most influential codifier of French taste. He was a well-established poet, dramatist, translator, and critic when in 1786 he began a long series of lectures at the Lycée, a newly founded literary society in Paris supported by the nobility and ladies. His lectures were interrupted by the Revolution, and although he had been an ardent adherent of its principles he was imprisoned during the Terror but escaped execution through the timely fall of Robespierre. While in prison in 1794 La Harpe underwent a conversion. When he resumed his lectures in 1796 his religion and politics had changed, but not his critical outlook. In 1799 the lectures began to appear in book form as *Cours de littérature ancienne et moderne,* and reached sixteen volumes two years after his death. The *Lycée,* as it was frequently called, proved enormously popular, especially after the Restoration; deep into the 19th century it served as a kind of summary of the old French taste.[20]

La Harpe, in the Preface to *Lycée,* boasts of writing "a systematic history of all the arts of the spirit and the imagination from Homer to the present day," [21] including all times and all nations, and declares that he is absolutely the first, not only in France, to accomplish such an undertaking. Actually the volumes are confined to classical antiquity and to French literature of the 17th and 18th centuries. Only one lecture attempts a very cursory survey of the Middle Ages and the Renaissance, paying some attention to Marot and Ronsard.[22] Modern foreign literatures are not discussed in the course of the lectures at all, except in occasional remarks and in a few reviews which were inserted to fill the glaring gaps. These reviews discuss Ossian, Milton, Pope, and Goethe's *Werther* very critically.[23] Elsewhere there is praise for Fielding's *Tom Jones,* "the first novel in the world." [24] We must add an early and very Voltairian essay on Shakespeare (1778) and remember that La Harpe translated Camões' *Lusiads* (1776), parts of Tasso, and the *Psalms* (1798). La Harpe thus shares the growing interest in other foreign literatures.

His basic point of view, however, is a slightly liberalized version of French neoclassicism. One can observe a slow change from the early dogmatism of rules toward a more emotional conception of literature. Yet the belief in the neoclassical code persists and exists side by side with a recognition of something beyond it. La Harpe insists that there are eternal principles of literature, valid for all times and nations, that the rules are true guides, the feeling of beauty "reduced to method," that the critic's task is to make an "exact summary of the beauties and defects of every author." [25] He has no doubt that "our stage is superior to all others." [26] In discussing Dante, Milton, and Shakespeare he makes no concession to the view that there are "graces beyond the reach of art." He admits that there are beautiful passages in these poets, but they must have been executed according to principles. What is good in them is due to "art." What is bad is due to violation of the rules, which results in a lack of "conception of the whole." [27] The view of the French translator and admirer of Shakespeare, Le Tourneur, that Shakespeare despised taste, is simply ridiculous.[28] There can be no contradiction between genius and taste: taste is an essential part of genius. Sophocles, Demosthenes, Cicero, Virgil, Horace, Fénelon, Racine, Boileau, and Voltaire all prove this unity.[29] Shakespeare lacks taste and hence has neither truth nor nature. In the early essay La Harpe ridicules him with weapons drawn from Voltaire's armory: he quotes some clowning, quibbling, and coarse passages from the *Tempest* and *Othello,* insisting that he criticizes Shakespeare not for violation of the three unities or any rules about plot structure but for transgressions against good sense and good manners.[30] He quotes passages from *Othello* translated into French prose and confronts them with speeches from *Zaïre,* never dreaming that anybody could prefer Shakespeare's "unintelligible gibberish" to the fine verse of Voltaire.[31] Later he admitted that Shakespeare had some "natural talent," and even preferred him to Lope de Vega and Calderón. But none of the three is comparable to the great geniuses of the Age of Louis.[32]

La Harpe, in his *Cours de littérature,* describes and criticizes the French classics in great detail. His highest admiration is reserved for Racine; the sections on his plays, which expound their beauties at length and refute objections while admitting some blemishes, are still a good introduction to what a whole society was looking for and finding in French classical tragedy. Molière is also exalted as the first of the philosopher-moralists, and Boileau's *L'Art poétique* is eulogized as "a perfect legislation, whose application is found just in every case, an indefeasible code whose decision will serve forever to distinguish what should be condemned and what should be applauded." [33] Voltaire is the central figure of the 18th century; even the *Henriade* is defended at length, and two whole volumes are devoted to the tragedies. He is called "the most tragic of all poets," and even *Œdipe* is shown to be preferable to Sophocles' original play.[34]

Nevertheless this impression of complete acceptance of neoclassical taste, the endorsement of Boileau included, is somewhat deceptive. It cannot be said that La Harpe is merely eulogistic and that his praise is indiscriminate. Within the limits of his taste and critical equipment he knows how to criticize plot, character drawing, probability, and so on, often with severity and even acidity. Many minor figures and minor works of great writers are ill treated, discussed in a tone of pontifical self-confidence with elegant and somewhat facile oratory. The ideal of good style, of correct French, is a frequent measuring stick by which Corneille and many older writers are found wanting.

Like Voltaire, La Harpe is by no means a dry rationalist in his judgment of poetry. He severely disapproves of the pedantries of D'Aubignac and Le Bossu and attacks the early 18th-century rationalists, Fontenelle, La Motte, and Trublet, for their disparagement of poetry and preference for prose.[35] Poetry, he argues, is an art of the "mind, the ear, and the imagination"; it has its special "logic of passions" which must not be suppressed by the "spirit of system."[36] Long before his conversion La Harpe was touched by the emotionalism of the time. Poetry needs an inner warmth, needs *verve*. The French drama is praised for having introduced the theme of unhappy love, unknown to the ancients. The relief of tears is called "the ultimate effort of art, the most beautiful triumph of tragedy," and pity, not the purging of pity, is considered the aim of tragedy.[37] After his conversion, in the introduction to his translation of the Psalms (1798), La Harpe comes nearest to a new view of poetry in saying that everything in the Psalms is "image, emblem, allegory" and that "motion, images, sentiments, figures, are undoubtedly the essence of all poetry." We must read the Psalms with our heart.[38] But in a nonreligious context La Harpe usually tempered his emotionalism. Poetry, he says, is "the language of imagination guided by reason and taste."[39] He condemns the frequency and the boldness of metaphors in early 17th-century poetry, saying that the true principles of style have been fixed forever.[40] Style, in isolation, is even made to be the discriminating trait of French drama as compared to ancient drama, which is centered on plot.[41] The noble, pathetic style of Racine and Voltaire is the high point of all art. But style, of course, is not merely linguistic: it means a specific kind of sentiments and ideas. In a remarkable page criticizing the older Crébillon, La Harpe asserts that "there is a natural and almost infallible link between the manner of thinking and feeling, and that of expression." In general, "the man who writes badly has thought badly, and what one would like to let pass as a simple fault of taste in style is a fault of the mind, a lack of justness, clarity, truth, and force in ideas and sentiments."[42]

Occasionally La Harpe recognizes the value of the historical point of view. He applied it when he defended the Psalms by drawing on Lowth's *Lectures on Hebrew Poetry*.[43] He even asserts a "secret and necessary interdependence between the principles at the basis of a social order and the arts which adorn it." [44] There are numerous references to the different stage conditions of the Greek drama and to the social advances, such as the improved status of women, in modern France.[45] But the general approach is not historical at all. The French classics are held up as eternal models, beauty is declared to be the same in all ages, and in practice each author is criticized directly, text in hand, with no historical perspective. To claim for La Harpe the position of a founder of literary history and historical criticism seems quite mistaken.[46] Though professedly a history of literature, arranged in chronological order, La Harpe's *Cours de littérature* conveys no sense of evolution, not even of a history of genres or the development of a single author. Much in the later volumes is ideological polemics, written after the Revolution. La Harpe attacks Helvétius and Diderot for their atheism, and Rousseau is called a "vile charlatan." [47] On religion and such matters as the poetry of the Bible La Harpe definitely broke with his master Voltaire, but otherwise he must be considered as an exponent of Voltaire's taste, which was the taste of a whole society, of a strong literary and social tradition, and which remained fairly intact up to the fall of Napoleon.

While the followers of Voltaire dominated literary theory and taste, Diderot influenced some contemporaries very strongly. Unfortunately it was not the most original in Diderot which affected his time; it was rather his dramatic theories, his defense of the middle-class drama, his emphasis on emotional effect, and his sentimentalism which found an echo in many breasts. His closest friend and follower was Friedrich Melchior Grimm (1723–1807), a German by birth and training, who came to Paris in 1749. Sainte-Beuve has praised Grimm as "one of our [i.e., French] most distinguished critics," in a class above La Harpe and Marmontel.[48] Edmond Scherer, no mean critic himself, devoted a long book to him in which he hails Grimm as the "true precursor of criticism as it is understood today [i.e., in 1887], a criticism which is not content to analyze and quote, but which judges the works, explains the appreciations, discusses the doctrines, connects reflections with the books, and makes sometimes an original work out of an article." [49] But all this seems quite extravagant. Between 1753–63 Grimm wrote most of the *Correspondance littéraire,* a miscellaneous informative sheet sent to a very limited number of subscribers that included mostly German princes and princesses but also Catherine the Great, the King of Poland, and the Queen of Sweden.[50] It was published only in 1812 and thus could not have directly affected earlier critical writing. It is journalism: a treasure trove for the student of the history of French civilization, most important because it preserved the text of Diderot's novels and *Salons.* But Grimm's literary criticism, scattered throughout, seems far from distinguished. Compared to Diderot he is more balanced, more sensible, but also far more colorless and ordinary. He has nothing new to offer in theory. The dramatic criticism, which takes up a great deal of space, is very much determined by Diderot's ideas.* Grimm criticizes French classical tragedy as artificial and cold, dislikes the French alexandrine, and shows no ear for French poetry. What he recommends is an emotional realism: he praises Diderot's two plays to the skies; he would like to see more action on the stage, e.g., see Mariamne die, and, like Diderot, he even advocates a tragic pantomime.[51] His standard of judgment is always that of emotional effect, though he is much more sober than his master. Corneille seems to him dry and dull, Shakespeare is only vaguely recommended, with the usual reservations based on the standards of French taste. Still, although Grimm did not understand the performance of *Romeo and Juliet* which he saw in London in 1772, he liked the balcony scene and the huge funeral procession as pure spectacle.[52] He can praise the naturalness of the English stage and admire *The Beggar's Opera.*[53] Surprisingly, he has no use for Beaumarchais, whose *Eugénie* he judged harshly, predicting that he "will never do anything, not even anything mediocre." [54]

It fits in with this standard of emotional realism that Grimm

* Smiley, *Diderot's Relations to Grimm,* pp. 56 ff., argues that Grimm first developed the dramatic theories expounded by Diderot in the introduction to *Le Fils naturel* (1757). While one need not assume that Grimm could not have contributed to Diderot's theories, the case seems unproved in view of Diderot's discussion in *Les Bijoux indiscrets* (1748).

should praise the 18th-century English novelists Richardson and
Fielding. He disapproved of Marivaux and thought it astonishing
that such a bad writer could have stimulated the development of
the English novel, so superior to his own works.[55] For personal and
ideological reasons it is obvious that Grimm would ridicule Rousseau's novel, and even *Candide* is judged severely as being without
"design, plan, or wisdom." [56] Voltaire seems to Grimm old fashioned, not materialistic and atheistic enough, though he deplored
the bad taste of Voltaire's attacks on the Bible. In every way
Grimm is Diderot's disciple: he calls him his master [57] and shares
his general outlook, though he seems more pessimistic about human nature, less sanguine, less artistic, duller and drier. The conception of Grimm as an important intermediary between Germany
and France is not supported by evidence: in criticism he was originally a pupil of Gottsched, but Gottsched himself was only an
echo of French neoclassicism. Grimm's two early articles on German literature for the *Mercure* (1750–51) make very modest claims
and merely express hope for the future flowering of German literature.* Later he praised the idylls of Gessner extravagantly, but he
had no contact with the new German literature. Whatever nebu-
lous German characteristics can be found in his temperament, in-
tellectually, in his criticism at least, he is part of the French tradition.

Among the propagandists of emotional realism, a much more
original note was struck by Sébastien Mercier (1740–1814). Mercier was also an advocate of the sentimental bourgeois drama, as
before him was Beaumarchais himself in the Preface to *Eugénie*
(1767). But Mercier's book, *Du Théâtre, ou nouvel essai sur l'art
dramatique* (1773), is far more radical than even the romantics of
1830 in its rejection of the classical system. Mercier is definitely
inspired by a democratic hatred for this "ghost dressed up in
scarlet and gold," without soul, life, or simplicity.[58] Molière is condemned for ridiculing virtue and making vice attractive. Only
Tartuffe, as anticlerical, finds favor in Mercier's eyes. The unities

* Cf. Richard Mahrenholz, "Grimm als Vermittler des deutschen
Geistes in Frankreich," *Archiv für das Studium der neueren Sprachen,
82* (1889), 291–302. Louis Reynaud, in *L'Influence allemande en
France* (Paris, 1922) argues that Grimm was sent out by Gottsched to
Paris as a sinister propagandist of German literature.

of time and place are declared completely useless. The walls which separate the genres are themselves called upon to crumble.[59] The new middle-class drama is recommended: it must be moving, must draw tears, all in the interest of a new democratic solidarity. Mercier sounds almost like Tolstoy or Wordsworth when he wants art to "serve in linking men by the victorious sentiment of compassion and pity." We must judge "the soul of every man by the degree of emotion he displays in the theater." [60] Mercier wants a new political, patriotic tragedy, addressed to all people. It would not be afraid to depict extreme suffering and poverty, and it could set its scene in a hospital or a house of correction. The effect aimed at is always the same: "I weep, and I feel with pleasure that I am a man." [61] The theater is the masterpiece of society: sanguinely Mercier expects that a good tragedy could change the bad constitution of a kingdom and implies that it could bring about a political revolution.[62]

Mercier is a diffuse and declamatory writer who rejects all poetics and all system. In a collection of short essays, *Mon bonnet de nuit* (1784), all rules and critics are condemned as "the scourge of the arts, the real assassins of genius." We must start out alone and rely on genius; for there is no theory in the arts of taste. Boileau is called "dry, cold, minute," a mere pedant.[63] Poetry is the art of moving. At the same time Mercier's sentimentalism is highly and even prudishly moralistic. He writes indignant pages against the *Iliad* condemning its cruelty and grossness, against *Georges Dandin* as a licentious play which encourages adultery, and against the shocking morals of *Phèdre*.[64] He seems a representative of a new social type: the lower bourgeois, resentful of all upper-class art, sentimental, expansive, and yet rigidly puritanical in his rejection of the rococo society around him. It is not surprising that Mercier appealed to the young German *Stürmer und Dränger*, or that Heinrich Leopold Wagner translated his book (1776). Goethe contributed an appendix, "Aus Goethes Brieftasche," in which he endorsed the rejection of the conventions of French tragedy but warned that there is something like an "inner form." [65]

Mercier was by no means alone in his time, even in France. There was an enthusiastic, even mystical, group of writers who are today almost completely forgotten but represent a striking parallel

to the German Sturm und Drang.* One can collect many passages
from these writers praising genius and enthusiasm, sublimity, and
immediate feeling, and condemning good taste, the rules, the unities, and all "art." The enormous vogue of Ossian in France, the
growing appreciation of Shakespeare, at least on the stage, the admiration for the Bible as poetry—all this presages a new conception of poetry and, in principle, anticipates almost everything that
the later French romantics proclaimed as a new gospel. But these
anti-philosophes and anticlassicists were not able to give a clear
theoretical account of their loves and hatreds. The mystic Saint-
Martin's piece, "De la poésie prophétique, épique et lyrique," †
and the weird effusions of Jean-Marie Chassaignon, called *Catar-
actes de l'imagination, déluge de la scribomanie, vomissement littéraire, hémorrhagie encyclopédique, monstre des monstres* (1779),
have remained almost unknown. They serve to show that France
was not as homogeneously neoclassical before Hugo as is often
assumed.

One must realize that poetic emotionalism was supported also
from the opposite side of the mystics: by the dogmatic sensualism
of the Abbé Condillac (1714–80). His one book which belongs to
literary criticism, *L'Art d'écrire* (1775), is a rather elementary
textbook of rhetoric written for his pupil Ferdinand, the son of the
Duke of Parma. It contains a remarkable chapter on poetic style ‡
in which Condillac stresses the impossibility of fixing rules for

* Kurt Wais, *Das antiphilosophische Weltbild des französischen
Sturm und Drang* (Berlin, 1934), seems to exaggerate the coherence of
a group and to overrate the literary importance of the authors he discusses.

† In *Œuvres posthumes* (Tours, 1807), 2, 271 ff. Saint-Martin proclaims prophetic poetry the only genuine poetry. The true object of
poetry is to depict the "supreme facts" which can inspire us with a
divine fire (p. 276).

‡ Condillac was tutor in Parma from 1758–67. The textbooks (13
vols.) ran into trouble with censorship and could be published only in
1775 with the fictitious imprint Deux-Ponts. Condillac says that the
chapter on poetic style was added much later (p. 317 of 1782 ed.). I
cannot share Gustave Lanson's estimate of Condillac's literary ideas (in
Études d'histoire littéraire, Paris, 1929). The distinction between a universal philosophy and a national poetry is neither so novel nor so important as he claims.

poetic style, since there are as many species as there are men of
genius. Poetry varies extremely with every language, nation, and
time. It uses images and is thus local, national, tied to the languages, while philosophy on the other hand uses analysis and is
thus universal. Nothing is more contrary to taste than the philosophic spirit. Even rules and genres are variable. "The names of
epic, tragedy, comedy have been preserved, but the ideas connected
with them are not at all the same: and every people has assigned
different styles, different traits to each different species of poem." [66]
There are in poetry and in prose as many "natures" as there are
"genres." The nature of poetry and of each species is purely conventional, differing too much to be defined. The only advice
Condillac can give is: "One feels it, and that is enough." Reasoning is no use: "The better one reasons about beauty the less one
feels it." [67] Actually Condillac is primarily interested in speculative
psychology and "conjectural" history. He works out a scheme of
infancy, progress, and decadence, and in his other writings speculated like Rousseau on the origins of language and poetry as due
to man's need for self-expression and for emotional release.[68] Still,
he is enough of a rationalist and *philosophe* to argue that French
literature is the best because it combines the universal philosophical spirit, the "greatest connection of ideas," with the poetic spirit.

Thus from many different philosophical positions, from Rousseau's, Diderot's, Condillac's, and Saint-Martin's, the emotional
conception of poetry was established. The reasons why it did not become completely effective long before 1830 seem somewhat obscure.
No doubt these were partly that no really great poet and dramatist carried out the theories, partly that many propounders of even
the boldest theories kept a timid practical taste and made many concessions and compromises, and partly that the French Revolution
appealed again to classical antiquity. Napoleon, though he carried
Ossian and *Werther* in his pocket to Egypt, reinstalled neoclassicism as an official creed, and even the Bourbons, after the Restoration, did not change the official line.

There is something fresh and novel, however, in two figures of
the late 18th century: André Chénier (1762–94) and Antoine
Rivarol (1753–1801). Chénier remained unknown and unprinted
in his own lifetime and was discovered only in 1819. He wrote a
poem, "L'Invention," which upholds the slightly paradoxical posi-

tion that what is needed is invention or creation, but also, at the same time, imitation of the ancients. The famous verse

Sur des pensers nouveaux faisons des vers antiques,[69]

suggests a rather simple dualism of content and form. Chénier recommends a new content for poetry: modern science. He sees in Torricelli, Newton, Kepler, and Galileo a treasure open to the new Virgil. He himself attempted such a scientific poem, "Hermès," but simultaneously recommended adherence to the design and form of the ancients, stated sharply the demand for complete purity of the genres and for rigid preservation of decorum and good sense, and alluded unfavorably to the English as violators of truth and reason.[70]

Chénier's literary opinions become clearer from the fragments of an *Essai sur les causes et les effets de la perfection et de la décadence des lettres et des arts* which would have been, if finished, the kind of sociological history of literature later sketched in Madame de Staël's *De la Littérature*.[71] Chénier wanted to discuss the causes which favor literature—climate, laws, manners and customs, local and momentary circumstances, the influence of good literature— which were to contrast with the causes unfavorable to literature— coteries, court influence, bad literature, etc. What has been pre- served is only a series of notes which show that Chénier intended to praise naiveté and the simplicity of the Greeks, who always fol- lowed nature and truth. He disparages the barbaric convulsions of Shakespeare and the mad despair of Young, attacks both Voltaire and Pascal, and asserts the fierce independence of the poet against courts, rulers, and academies. Chénier himself points out the simi- larities of these views to those of his friend Alfieri.[72]

But more original than this worship of the Greeks or the exalta- tion of the poet's freedom are Chénier's occasional glimpses of an allegorical or symbolical concept of poetry. The "great movements of the soul inspire sublime expressions," ardor requires metaphori- cal language, allegory is a language of the mind. In his plan for "Hermès" he wanted to represent "the earth under the metaphori- cal emblem of a great animal that lives, moves, is subject to changes, revolutions, fevers, disorders in the circulation of its blood." [73] But when Chénier's poems were published they appealed chiefly as sensual or political poetry, whose versification pointed the way to romantic innovations. His great intellectual ambitions were disclosed only much later.[74]

Chénier perished by the guillotine. Rivarol died in exile in Berlin, almost forgotten. Today he is best known for his *Discours sur l'universalité de la langue française* (1784), a prize-winning answer to a question proposed by the Berlin Academy. This is a most interesting document on the dominant position of French language and literature late in the 18th century. It is also a reasoned and well-informed survey of the main European languages and their historical role. It culminates in a comparison between French and English which is frequently rash in its generalizations but has the merit of formulating the ideal of French clarity in strong terms. "What is not clear is not French." [75] There is some simple literary criticism in Rivarol's sketch of the history of French, in his emphasis on prose, and in his sharp rejection of the figurative when it is not strictly illustrative of meaning.

The translation of Dante's *Inferno* (1785) into prose must, however, be mentioned not only as a sign of changing taste but also for the introductory essay by Rivarol, who, though still full of reservations, shows a genuine taste for the sublime and terrible in Dante. He describes his style as "keeping on its feet by the sheer force of noun and verb, without the help of a single epithet." His verses are "at the same time thought, image, and sentiment. They are real polyps, alive in the whole, and alive in every part." [76]

But Rivarol's main claim to be remembered in a history of criticism is his book *De l'Homme intellectuel et moral* (1797), which begins with a discussion of language in general. It contains a psychology and anthropology of considerable originality.[77] It also contains some reflections on aesthetic problems. Rivarol distinguishes between an active creative imagination and a merely passive faculty. He defines genius as the creative faculty, distinguishing between a genius of ideas, which is the summit of the spirit, and a genius of expression, which is the summit of talent. Genius, then, is what engenders and procreates; it is the gift of invention.[78] In discussing criticism as a spirit of order, Rivarol distinguishes between particular and general criticism and stresses the need for judging both by masses and by detail.[79]

His friend Chênedollé has reported conversations with him held in Hamburg in 1795, which contain many striking remarks. "The poet is nothing but a very ingenious and animated savage, in whom all ideas present themselves as images. Both the savage and the poet . . . speak only in hieroglyphics." [80] This sounds like a good brief summary of some of the insights of Diderot, still new in France when the conversations were first printed. But it is hard to see why Sainte-Beuve said that Rivarol "could have been a great literary critic" and that there is a "French Hazlitt" in him.[81] His opinions on specific authors, quoted by Chênedollé, are mostly *boutades,* and much else he wrote on literary matters, such as the *Petit almanach de nos grands hommes* (1788), is merely a series of satirical squibs against most of his contemporaries. Rousseau and the French Academy are the particular butts of his satire, but he also attacks Voltaire and the early writings of Madame de Staël. Rivarol's view of Shakespeare is nonetheless substantially that of Voltaire. His taste is still the conventional sort: he did, however, welcome Chateaubriand and glimpse something of Dante's greatness. Though his speculations are groping toward a new conception of the mind and thus of poetry, in temperament and in practical taste Rivarol remained a Frenchman of the 18th century, witty, rationalistic, and cut off from the sources of great poetry. He represents the dilemma of the time: insight into the new, and yet deep involvement in the entrenched tradition.

5 : DR. JOHNSON

SAMUEL JOHNSON (1709–84) cannot be considered simply as a representative of English neoclassicism. He does, it is true, hold to many of its commonplaces and share most of its tastes. But he differs clearly from the neoclassical creed on some important issues. In him certain of its elements have overgrown all others and led to consequences which are destructive of its very essence. Dr. Johnson is, of course, no romanticist or even unconscious forerunner of romanticism: he is rather one of the first great critics who have almost ceased to understand the nature of art, and who, in central passages, treats art as life. He has lost faith in art as the classicists understood it and has not found the romantic faith. He paves the way for a view which makes art really superfluous, a mere vehicle for the communication of moral or psychological truth. Art is no longer judged as art but as a piece or slice of life. This new view comes out very clearly in Johnson's famous *Preface* to his edition of Shakespeare (1765).

> This therefore, is the praise of Shakespeare, that his drama is the mirror of life; that he who has mazed his imagination, in following the phantoms which other writers raise up before him, may here be cured of his delirious extasies, by reading human sentiments in human language, by scenes from which a hermit may estimate the transactions of the world, and a confessor predict the progress of the passions. . . . Shakespeare has no heroes; his scenes are occupied by men, who act and speak as the reader thinks he should himself have spoken or acted on the same occasion. . . . The dialogue of this author is often so evidently determined by the incident which produces it, and is pursued with so much ease and simplicity, that it seems scarcely to claim the merit of fiction, but to have been gleaned by diligent selection out of common conversation, and common occurrences.[1]

79

This view, that literature is "a just representation of things really existing and actions really performed," [2] that the "legitimate end of fiction is the conveyance of truth," [3] that the novelists should be "just copiers of human manners," [4] recurs again and again. There runs through Johnson a deep suspicion of all fiction and all art. According to Hawkins he "could at any time be talked into a disapprobation of all fictitious relations, of which he would frequently say they took no hold of the mind." [5] "The rejection and contempt of fiction is rational and manly" is another of his sayings.[6] We can see this preference for truth running through all Johnson's judgments. It comes out with ludicrous violence in a story, also told by Hawkins: "Talking with some persons about allegorical painting, he said: 'I had rather see the portrait of a dog I know, than all the allegorical painting, they can show me in the world.' " [7] It comes out even more strikingly in his preference for domestic tragedy: "What is nearest touches us most. The passions rise higher at domestic than at imperial tragedies." [8] *Timon of Athens* is a "domestic tragedy, and therefore strongly fastens on the attention of the reader." [9] A pathetic and moving scene in *Henry VIII* (IV. ii), in which Catharine of Aragon hears of the death of Wolsey and speaks of her own last wishes, was to Johnson "above any other part of Shakespeare's tragedies, and perhaps above any scene of any other poet, tender and pathetic, without gods, or furies, or poisons, or precipices, without the help of romantic circumstances, without improbable sallies of poetical lamentation, and without any throes of tumultuous misery." [10]

This emphasis on truth and suspicion of fiction is at the basis of some of Dr. Johnson's most striking and well-known literary opinions. He disliked Milton's *Lycidas* for many reasons, but one was "insincerity" of emotion. "It is not to be considered as the effusion of real passion; for passion runs not after remote allusions and obscure opinions. Passion plucks no berries from myrtle and ivy, nor calls upon Arethuse and Mincius, nor tells of 'rough satyrs and fauns with cloven heel.' Where there is leisure for fiction there is little grief." [11] Johnson does not realize that the requirement of sincere grief in the poet himself, though justifiable by Horatian or even Aristotelian precepts, does away with three-quarters of the world's literature and introduces the standard of

the individual experience of the author, which is both indetermin-
able and aesthetically false.

Johnson's discussion of Cowley's erotic verses is another instance.
He ascribes the fashion for amorous verse to the model of Petrarch
and continues: "But the basis of all excellence is truth: he that professes love ought to feel its power. Petrarch was a real lover, and
Laura doubtless deserved his tenderness. Of Cowley we are told by
Barnes . . . that, whatever he may talk of his own inflammability
and the variety of characters by which his heart was divided, he in
reality was in love but once, and then never had resolution to tell
his passion." On the basis of this most unlikely anecdote, Johnson
tells us that "no man needs to be so burthened with life as to
squander it in voluntary dreams of fictitious occurrences," and ridicules "him who praises beauty whom he never saw, complains of
jealousy which he never felt, supposes himself sometimes invited
and sometimes forsaken, fatigues his fancy, and ransacks his memory, for images which may exhibit the gaiety of hope or the gloomi-
ness of despair, and dresses his imaginary Chloris or Phyllis sometimes in flowers fading as her beauty, and sometimes in gems as
lasting as her virtues." [12]

Or take the curious reason for which Johnson singles out Pope's
Eloisa and Abelard for special praise, as "one of the most happy
productions of human wit." "The heart naturally loves truth. The
adventures and misfortunes of this illustrious pair are known from
undisputed history." "So new and so affecting is their story that
it supersedes invention, and imagination ranges in full liberty
without straggling into scenes of fables." [13] Actually *Eloisa* is based
on a highly sentimentalized and fictionalized version of the letters
by Bussy de Rabutin (1697) in an English translation by John
Hughes, and thus is at several removes from historical truth.

The same attitude can be seen almost anywhere: it is at the basis
of Johnson's dislike of ancient mythology because it simply is not
true. Discussing a tragedy by Edmund Smith, *Phaedra and Hip-
politus,* he says: "The fable is mythological, a story which we are
accustomed to reject as false, and the manners are so distant from
our own that we know them not from sympathy, but by study: the
ignorant do not understand the action, the learned reject it as a
school-boy's tale; *incredulus odi.* What I cannot for a moment

believe, I cannot for a moment behold with interest or anxiety." [14]
It is hard to see why the same criticism would not be applicable to
Racine's *Phèdre,* though Smith's tragedy may be as bad as Johnson
says it is. The condemnation of mythology extends, of course, also
to the "puerilities of obsolete [that is, Welsh] mythology" in Gray's
"Bard," [15] and to the allegorical figures in Aeschylus' *Prometheus* or Euripides' *Alcestis,* as well as to the allegory of Sin and
Death in *Paradise Lost.*[16] All allegories which are active agents are
absurd: they are only approved if they are mere figurative discourse, pleasing vehicles of instruction, such as Johnson himself
composed for the *Rambler* and *Idler* in dull profusion. The famous
objections to all pastorals are motivated in the same manner. Of
Lycidas he said, "Its form is that of a pastoral, easy, vulgar, and
therefore disgusting." [17] He has good fun in saying that "we know
they [Milton and Edward King] never drove afield, and they had no
flocks to batten." [18] "Nothing can less display knowledge or less
exercise invention than to tell how a shepherd has lost his com-
panion and must now feed his flocks alone, without any judge of
his skill in piping; and how one god asks another god what is become of Lycidas, and how neither god can tell. He who thus grieves
will excite no sympathy; he who thus praises will confer no
honor." [19] Two *Ramblers* (Nos. 42 and 46) are devoted to a satire
on the ideal rural life portrayed by pastoral writers, and *Idler* No.
77 shows how Dick Shifter discovered that rustic simplicity is not
what pastoral writings had led him to expect. Of Lyttelton's "Progress of Love" Johnson says curtly: "It is sufficient blame to say
that it is pastoral." [20] Though Johnson may have read through the
romance *Felixmarte of Hircania,* he disapproved of romances both
medieval and modern as well as of most novels, with the exception
of Fanny Burney's *Evelina,* which he admired, if we can trust Miss
Burney, for its "knowledge of life and manners" and "accuracy of
observation." [21]

The second great principle of Dr. Johnson's criticism after "reality" is, of course, "moral truth," morality. Didacticism has a vener-
able tradition in criticism, and I am not disposed to dispute its
rights if they are properly limited. In Johnson they are not always
properly limited. Instead, his didactic criterion often becomes a
demand for mere moralizing, for a selection from nature which
frequently runs counter to his own principle of reality. In *Rambler*

No. 4 he discusses modern fiction and begins by saying: "It is justly considered as the greatest excellency of art, to imitate nature; but it is necessary to distinguish those parts of nature, which are most proper for imitation: greater care is still required in presenting life, which is so often discolored by passion, or deformed by wickedness." He draws the conclusion that "many characters ought never to be drawn." The purpose of novels is "to teach the means of avoiding the snares which are laid by Treachery for Innocence . . . to give the power of counteracting fraud, without the temptation to practice it; to initiate youth by mock encounters in the art of necessary defence, and to increase prudence without impairing virtue." Perfect heroes are not objectionable, and "vice, for vice is necessary to be shewn, should always disgust." Johnson also frequently required poetical justice. He sides with the general public in preferring a happy ending for *King Lear*. "I was many years ago so shocked by Cordelia's death, that I know not whether I ever endured to read again the last scenes of the play till I undertook to revise them as an editor." [22] Johnson feels "some indignation" that Angelo in *Measure for Measure* is not punished. He even endorses Iago's warning to Othello ("She did deceive her father, marrying you"), solemnly moralizing on deceit and falsehood as "obstacles to happiness." He thought that "perhaps Shakespeare meant to punish Juliet's hypocrisy" when she asked to be left alone:

For I have need of many orisons.[23]

But Johnson's concept of poetic justice is not always so obtusely literal minded.

In the *Lives* there is a passage which admits that "since wickedness often prospers in real life, the poet is certainly at liberty to give it prosperity on the stage. For if poetry is an imitation of reality, how are its laws broken by exhibiting the world in its true form? The stage may sometimes gratify our wishes, but if it be truly the mirror of life, it ought to shew us sometimes what we are to expect." [24] The demand for reality here triumphs over the demand for morality with the argument that reality is instructive and hence moral. But more frequently the moralist is dominant, to the exclusion and even detriment of the critic. Johnson preferred Richardson to Fielding for moral and political reasons; he condemned *Tom Jones* as a "vicious book" [25] and Fielding as a "barren rascal." [26]

He despised Sterne for his impiety and obscenity. In spite of his admiration he had strong moral reservations against Swift; and of course Johnson is the most famous of those critics who, like Tolstoy and Shaw, complain of Shakespeare's lack of morality.

> He sacrifices virtue to convenience, and is so much more careful to please than to instruct, that he seems to write without any moral purpose. . . . He makes no just distribution of good or evil, nor is always careful to show in the virtuous a disapprobation of the wicked; he carries his persons indifferently through right and wrong, and at the close dismisses them without further care, and leaves their examples to operate by chance. This is a fault the barbarity of his age cannot extenuate; for it is always a writer's duty to make the world better, and justice is a virtue independent on time and place.[27]

Johnson has been widely admired for this type of pronouncement, for his sturdy common sense, for his attitude of "no nonsense." At the same time, therefore, he has been dismissed—especially on the Continent—as a "British superstition." It seems hard to deny that in Johnson we can observe a slipping of the grasp on the nature of art and an anticipation of standards of realism and moralism which will make art really as superfluous as it seemed to many Englishmen of the 19th century. It must have become so to Johnson, who in his later years felt that his conversation did as much good as his writings.

But it is impossible to dismiss him as a mere moralist or expounder of a realistic view which confounds art and life. For Johnson moralism and realism combine with a strong and emphatic exposition of many of the central neoclassical tenets, especially the basic rationalistic view of art, and with a trained and self-conscious taste which worked with remarkable sureness within the body of accessible literature. That Johnson is not a narrow authoritarian is obvious; he condemns the imitation of ancient authors. "No man ever yet became great by imitation," he says in *Rambler* No. 154, and repeats it in *Rasselas*. On the other hand Johnson recognizes the greatness of many ancients and the importance of the argument based on tradition and general agreement. "What mankind has long possessed they have often examined and compared; and if they persist to value the possession, it is because frequent comparisons have confirmed opinion in its favor." "What has been longest known has been most considered, and what is most considered is best understood." [28]

Literature is thus not imitation of ancient writers, but representations of general nature, of "general manners or common life," [29] as "reason and nature are uniform and inflexible" [30] and "human nature is always the same." [31] Realism, Dr. Johnson frequently recognizes, is thus not accurate copying nor is it merely selection by moral criteria; it is rather the depiction of the general, the universal, the typical. There is, I think, a certain undeniable contradiction between Johnson's many purely realist or moralist pronouncements and this abstractionism. There is a contradiction between his constant recommendations of the abstract, the generalized and universal, and his actual practical love of life, of its concrete particularity. The abstract neoclassicism clashes with the new realism; but the former, while deplorable in its desiccated abstractness, did something for Johnson: it gave him a hold on art, some view of the nature and function of art which would not simply identify it with a slice of life, selected and judged by moral standards.

He recognizes that realism is not enough. "If the world be promiscuously described, I cannot see of what use it can be to read the account: or why it may not be as safe to turn the eye immediately upon mankind as upon a mirror which shows all that presents itself without discrimination." [32] His usual remedy is moral selection. But this moral selection is assumed to proceed to "general and transcendental truths." Thus Johnson arrives at his condemnation of the particular, the local and transient, a thesis which he formulated possibly more sharply than any other critic of high repute. In the tenth chapter of *Rasselas* is the famous passage: "The business of a poet is to examine, not the individual, but the species; to remark general properties and large appearances: he does not number the streaks of the tulip, or describe the different shades in the verdure of the forest." [33] "Poetry," he says, discussing the pastoral, "cannot dwell upon the minuter distinctions, by which one species differs from another, without departing from that simplicity of grandeur which fills the imagination; nor dissect the latent qualities of things, without losing its general power of gratifying every mind by recalling its conceptions." [34] This view appears quite frequently. Thus Shakespeare is praised as the "poet of nature," a term which is, to a modern reader, surprisingly explained by what follows:

> His characters are not modified by the customs of particular places . . . by the peculiarities of studies or professions . . . or by the accidents of transient fashions or temporary opinions; they are the genuine progeny of common humanity . . . His persons act and speak by the influence of those general passions and principles by which all minds are agitated, and the whole system of life is continued in motion. In the writings of other poets a character is too often an individual, in those of Shakespeare it is commonly a species.[35]

The same view underlies the discussion of the metaphysical poets. Johnson objects to their failure to reach the sublime. "Sublimity is produced by aggregation, and littleness by dispersion. Great thoughts are always general, and consist in positions not limited by exceptions, and in descriptions not descending to minuteness." [36] We find this criterion again and again: Butler's *Hudibras* cannot last, because it is full of allusions comprehensible only at a particular time; a poem by Casimir (Sarbieski) expresses a thought "more generally, and therefore more poetically" than a poem by Cowley; Edgar's speech in *King Lear* describing the cliff of Dover is censured for "its observations of particulars, its attention to distinct objects," choughs and crows, the samphire gatherer and the fishermen. Johnson feels that the "one great and dreadful image of irresistible destruction" is "dissipated and enfeebled" by these details.[37] On the other hand, Gray's "Elegy" "abounds with images which find a mirror in every mind, and with sentiments to which every bosom returns an echo." [38]

Practically all critical theory since Johnson has run in the opposite direction. Bergson asserts that "art always aims at what is individual . . . what the poet sings of is a certain mood which was his, and his alone, and will never return." [39] Croce says the same in more philosophical terms. The view was not unknown to the 18th century, and we shall describe the trend toward particularity in Joseph Warton, George Campbell, and others.[40] The judgments of Johnson will surprise us: we are likely to think it is the highest praise of Shakespeare that he carefully individualized his characters, and might agree with Bergson that "nothing could be more unique than the character of Hamlet." [41]

Johnson's view has a very respectable ancestry in neo-Platonic aesthetics. It was common in the theory of fine arts during the 17th and 18th centuries: in Bellori, in Du Fresnoy, translated by Dryden,[42] in Shaftesbury, and very prominently in Reynolds' *Discourses,* which Johnson was unjustly suspected to have written himself. It seems to survive today chiefly in theories defending abstract sculpture. It certainly contains a germ of truth: all art must be in some way general in order not to be completely incomprehensible or uninteresting. The very nature of language is to work by generalizations. Dr. Johnson was pushing the extreme of generality, while we are apt to stress the opposite. He does seem, however, to acknowledge the value of particularity in places, and he certainly did show a passionate interest in what today would be called the "local detail" of poetry. He censured the plays of Nicolas Rowe because they do not show "any deep search into nature, any accurate discriminations of kindred qualities, or nice display of passion in its progress; all is general and undefined." [43] He complained about the general praise bestowed indiscriminately by epitaphs, and once he attacks the problem of relevance of detail. Shakespeare, "instead of dilating his thoughts into generalities and expressing incidents with poetical latitude, often combines circumstances unnecessary to his main design, only because he happened to find them together." [44]

Dr. Johnson's criticism, however, is not defeated by the conflicting theories of realism, moralism, and what is here called abstractionism. The three strands were no doubt reconcilable in his own mind. When he says "Nothing can please many, and please long, but just representations of general nature," [45] the term "just" means both true and moral. The three motifs here analyzed are kept in balance and stressed according to context, alternating by turns, apparently without a clear consciousness that these criteria lead to very different conclusions about the nature of art and the value of particular works of art. Johnson wrote valuable analyses of many critical questions from one or several of these points of view and enjoyed a positive appreciation of a whole body of literature accessible to him within the limits of his taste.

Historically most important was Johnson's attack on the rules.

He follows partly the usual line of recognizing that genius is above rules, that there "is always an appeal open from criticism to nature." [46] But this would be little but giving up the question. More frequently and more consistently he recognizes that it is the aim of criticism "to establish principles: to improve opinion into knowledge," [47] to discover "principles of judgment on unalterable and evident truth," [48] to use rules as "instruments of mental vision." [49] These basic principles must be distinguished from arbitrary local prescriptions: "The accidental prescriptions of authority, when time has procured them veneration, are often confounded with the laws of nature." [50] Some laws of criticism are to be considered "fundamental and indispensable, others only as useful and convenient; some as dictated by reason and necessity, others as enacted by despotic antiquity; some as invincibly supported by their conformity to the order of nature and operations of the intellect; others as formed by accident, or instituted by example, and therefore always liable to dispute and alteration." [51] This is, in itself, a fairly widespread idea accepted by Voltaire among others, but the dividing line between nature and custom drawn by Johnson involved a rejection of the rigid unities of time and place, and a defense of tragicomedy. In practice this was especially a defense of Shakespeare as a great English classic.

Johnson criticizes the unity of space with a recognition of the falsity of the usual neoclassical assumption of delusion.

> The objection arising from the impossibility of passing the first hour at Alexandria, and the next at Rome, supposes, that when the play opens, the spectator really imagines himself at Alexandria, and believes his walk to the theater has been a voyage to Egypt, and that he lives in the days of Antony and Cleopatra. Surely he that imagines this may imagine more. . . . The truth is, that the spectators are always in their senses, and know, from the first act to the last, that the stage is only a stage, and that the players are only players. . . . Where is the absurdity of allowing that space to represent Athens, and then Sicily, which was always known to be neither Sicily nor Athens, but a modern theater? [52]

The same argument holds good with respect to the unity of time. Johnson concedes that "probability requires that the time of

action should approach somewhat nearly to that of exhibition.
. . . But since it will frequently happen that some delusion must
be admitted, I know not where the limits of imagination can be
fixed." [53] Especially the interval between acts can be imagined as
long as the author thinks fit. Thus nothing is essential but the
unity of action. In these arguments Johnson correctly grasps what
modern aestheticians would call "aesthetic distance."

Tragicomedy is defended by Johnson with fundamentally realistic arguments. "The connexion of important with trivial incidents,
since it is not only common but perpetual in the world, may
surely be allowed upon the stage, which pretends only to be the
mirror of life." [54] Specifically Johnson defends Shakespeare's mixture of tragedy and comedy by going so far as to deny the distinctions of genres in him. "Shakespeare's plays are not in the rigorous
and critical sense either tragedies or comedies, but compositions
of a distinct kind; exhibiting the real state of sublunary nature,
which partakes of good and evil, joy and sorrow, mingled with end-
less variety of proportion and innumerable modes of combinations; and expressing the course of the world, in which the loss
of one is the gain of another." [55] "When Shakespeare's plan is
understood, most of the criticisms of Rymer and Voltaire vanish
away. The play of *Hamlet* is opened, without impropriety, by two
sentinels; Iago bellows at Brabantio's window, without injury to
the scheme of the play, though in terms which a modern audience
would not easily endure; the character of Polonius is seasonable
and useful; and the grave-diggers themselves may be heard with
applause." [56] Johnson accepts Menenius, the clownish senator in
Coriolanus, and defends the fact that King Claudius, a king, is
represented as a drunkard in *Hamlet.* Shakespeare "always makes
nature predominant over accident."

> His story requires Romans or kings, but he thinks only on
> men. He knew that Rome, like every other city, had men of
> all dispositions; and wanting a buffoon, he went into the
> Senate-house for that which the Senate-house would certainly
> have afforded him. He was inclined to shew a usurper and a
> murderer not only odious, but despicable: he therefore added
> drunkenness to his other qualities, knowing that kings love
> wine like other men, and that wine exerts its natural powers

upon kings. . . . A poet overlooks the casual distinction of country and conditions, as a painter, satisfied with the figure, neglects the drapery.[57]

One sees that in this example "nature" does not mean mere abstract man but men fully equipped with personal characteristics, whose characterization, however, may not observe the decorum of rank or historical accuracy.

While Johnson is thus liberal in the matter of decorum in characterization, he holds firmly to neoclassical views about decorum in language. His own theory and practice of style leans in the direction of the abstract, the grandiose, the ornamental. In *Adventurer* No. 115 he distinguishes a plain style, "clear, pure, nervous and expressive," which is used in the discussion of science and demonstration, but argues that if the "topics be probable and persuasory, the author must recommend them by the superaddition of elegance and imagery, to display the colors of varied diction, and pour forth the music of modulated periods." Elsewhere he says: "The pebble must be polished with care, which hopes to be valued as a diamond; and words ought surely to be labored, when they are intended to stand for things." [58]

Yet in his criticisms of Shakespeare and other writers Johnson does not stand very strictly by the ideal of splendid diction. Shakespeare is praised especially for his comic dialogue, which seems to Johnson a "style which never becomes obsolete, a conversation above grossness, and below refinement where propriety resides." [59] Many times Shakespeare is censured for his "disproportionate pomp of diction," his "tumor" [60] and even bombast. Gray's odes excite Johnson's dislike, partly for the "cumbrous splendor" of their diction.[61] We may be surprised, in view of a general similarity of Johnson's own style with that of Jeremy Taylor or Sir Thomas Browne, to see how severely he censured Browne's style as "rugged, pedantic, obscure, harsh, uncouth." [62] Much of this can be explained by the traditional rhetorical theories of levels of style and by Johnson's own interest in the stabilization and purification of the English language. Johnson devoted years of his life to the *Dictionary,* which is not merely a descriptive thesaurus of the English language but a work which aims to prescribe good usage and to censure words. It includes words such as "abstrude," "adjugate," "advesperate," and "agriculation," but either excludes many other words as obsolete or colloquial or lists them with notes stating that they are "low," "improper," "corrupt," "barbarous," "unauthorized," or "lacking in etymology." ("Punch," for example, is of a lower order than the Arabic "sherbet.") We thus can hardly be surprised that Johnson did not like "low" diction in a tragic context and devoted a whole number of the *Rambler* (No. 168) to a discussion of Lady Macbeth's speech (I, v, 51ff.):

> Come, thick night!
> And pall thee in the dunnest smoke of hell,
> That my keen knife see not the wound it makes;
> Nor heav'n peep through the blanket of the dark,
> To cry: Hold, hold!

"Dun" is criticized as an epithet "now seldom heard but in the stable," and "knife" as the "name of an instrument used by butchers and cooks in the meanest employments." "Who does not, from the habit of connecting a knife with sordid offices, feel aversion rather than terror?" Johnson can hardly "check his risibility" when he thinks of the two unfortunate words "peep" and "blanket." There are elsewhere censures of "studied barbarity" in Spenser's *Shepheardes Calender* [63] and of mean diction used by kings in *Henry V* or *Richard II*. But on the whole Johnson's views of diction are moderate and carefully graduated according to genre and context. He condemns technical terms derived from sailing in Dryden's *Annus Mirabilis* because "all appropriated terms of art should be sunk in general expressions, because poetry is to speak an universal language." [64] Although he always objects to Gallicisms, he is sensibly aware that "every author does not write for every reader." [65] He defends hard words in their proper context, but, like his time in general, is totally unappreciative of puns and ambiguities. *Samson Agonistes* affords examples of "all meanness that has least to plead, which is produced by mere verbal conceits," [66] and Shakespeare's quibbles are inexcusable. "A quibble was to him the fatal Cleopatra for which he lost the world, and was content to lose it." [67] Though Johnson has praised Shakespeare's style, especially in the comedies, he can elsewhere generalize so extravagantly as to speak of it as "ungrammatical, perplexed and obscure." He even says that Shakespeare "has corrupted language by every mode of depravation." [68] Johnson judges past diction and style by the ideals of his own time.

His attitude toward versification is somewhat different. Even more than in the matter of diction, Johnson was convinced that his own time had achieved the pinnacle of perfection. English versification is a "science" which excludes "all casualty" and aspires to "constancy." [69] Thus, once established, it cannot and should not be changed. After Pope, "to attempt any further improvement of versification will be dangerous." A whole *Rambler* essay (No. 86) is devoted to the distinction between "pure" and "mixed" measure in English heroic pentameters. By "pure" Johnson means lines which fulfill the metrical patterns exactly. He admits only grudgingly the necessity of "mixed" measures, i.e. those which allow "substitution," especially in the first measure. The possibility of using more unaccented syllables than two in a measure is not even mentioned, and triplets and alexandrines, while admitted as necessary, are condemned. Dr. Johnson's ear must have been early attuned only to the heroic couplet, whose niceties and differences he was obviously very well able to perceive and to describe. But he had considerable difficulties even with blank verse, a meter sanctioned in his eyes by the precedents of Shakespeare and Milton. In discussing Milton's arguments against rhyme, he professes to see a strong difference between English and the classical languages which can do without rhyme. "The music of the English heroic line strikes the ear so faintly that it is easily lost, unless all the syllables of every line cooperate together; this cooperation can be only obtained by the preservation of every verse unmingled with another as a distinct system of sounds, and this distinctness is obtained and preserved by the artifice of rhyme." [70] "Blank verse left merely to its numbers has little operation either on the ear or mind: it can hardly support itself without bold figures and striking images." [71] Thus the sublime Milton is admitted: also Young's *Night Thoughts* and Akenside's *Pleasures of Imagination;* but most of the contemporary blank verse, especially in didactic or burlesque subjects, excites Johnson's disfavor. "But it is blank verse" suffices to condemn a poem by David Mallet.[72]

Johnson was even more hostile to and apparently simply incapable of reading lyrical measures of greater complexity and diversity. He dislikes the "Pindaric madness" of Cowley, observing that the "great pleasure of verse arises from the known measure of the lines and uniform structure of the stanzas." [73] Dryden's and Pope's "Odes for St. Cecilia's Day" are similarly said to "want the essential constituent of metrical compositions, the stated recurrence of settled numbers." [74] Most famous, of course, are Johnson's strictures upon the minor poems of Milton: even the songs of *Comus* are "not very musical in their numbers," and *Lycidas* is written in "unpleasing numbers." [75] Thus his highest praise goes out to Pope. If we can believe Boswell, Johnson said that "a thousand years may elapse before there shall appear another man with a power of versification equal to that of Pope." [76]

Johnson is thus firmly rooted and even enclosed in the taste of his own age. He seems hardly touched by two of the new motifs of 18th-century criticism: aesthetics and cosmopolitanism.

There is hardly any discussion of beauty in Johnson's writings. The discussion which introduces No. 92 of the *Rambler* (1751) seems to come to relativistic conclusions. Beauty is "merely relative and comparative," and Johnson seems to grant that it is "little subject to the examinations of reason." But then he takes away this concession to skepticism by an appeal to the verdict of the ages, the common sense of humanity. The long continuance of the reputation of certain writings "proves that they are adequate to our faculties, and agreeable to nature." He announces the possibility of "reducing some regions of literature under the dominance of science" and enters into a discussion of the relation of sound and sense in verse. Beauty, in literature, seems to Johnson to be largely confined to beauty of language and versification, the sonority of sound, the regular recurrence of meter. Now and then, apparently under the influence of his friend Edmund Burke's *Inquiry into the Origin of Our Ideas of the Sublime and the Beautiful* (1756), Johnson distinguishes between the beautiful and the sublime, between attention to the vast and to the minute. Milton is characterized in terms of sublimity or "gigantic loftiness." [77] "Sublimity is the general and prevailing quality of this poem [*Paradise Lost*]; sublimity variously modified, sometimes descriptive, sometimes argumentative." [78]

Johnson resists, however, a tendency of current aesthetics, which we have met also in Diderot, to identify the sublime and the pathetic. *Paradise Lost* is sublime, but there is little opportunity in it for the pathetic, the passions being moved on only one occasion. In it sublimity goes with a "want of human interest." [79] Shakespeare, on the other hand, is pathetic, moves the passions, subdues the heart. Johnson prefers the moving and even tearful to the grandiose. He can praise Rowe's *Tragedy of Jane Shore,* "consisting chiefly of domestic scenes and private distress," for laying hold upon the heart. "The wife is forgiven because she repents, and the husband is honored because he forgives. This therefore is one of those pieces which we still welcome on the stage." [80] There is in Johnson a streak of 18th-century sentimentality which comes out in his literary tastes only fitfully, but is constantly present in his private *Prayers and Meditations* and in his letters to his wife and Miss Boothby.

The metaphysicals are criticized by Johnson partly for disappointing the expectations of emotional satisfaction. "They were not successful in representing or moving the affections." "They had no regard to that uniformity of sentiment which enables us to conceive and to excite the pains and the pleasure of other minds: they never enquired what on any occasion they should have said or done, but wrote rather as beholders than partakers of human nature; as beings looking upon good and evil, impassive and at leisure." [81] Johnson dislikes what we would call their ironic detachment, their lack of uniform sentiment, their refusal to allow the reader to identify himself emotionally with the speaker. He felt their qualifications and reservations, their rich and complex "local detail" as offending his demands both for the abstract and for the emotional. The "grandeur of generality" could be found in Milton, though he was deficient in humanity. Domestic tragedy, Richardson, the pathetic passages in Shakespeare—all these satisfied Johnson's desire for "uniform" sentiment, but the metaphysicals were neither sublime nor moving and did not, of course, live up to demands for smoothness of versification and beauty of sound which Johnson admired in Pope. The only good Johnson can find in them is some intellectual labor, learning, and ingenuity.

Apparently Johnson was not interested in the current widespread speculations about the reader's response and about taste. But he does show some awareness of the debate in which men like Burke and Hume took a prominent part. A passage in the life of Congreve parallels exactly the much earlier discussion of beauty in the *Rambler*. Johnson seems to endorse the relativity of taste. In referring to Congreve's dedication defending the *Double Dealer*, he says: "These apologies are always useless, *de gustibus non est disputandum;* men may be convinced, but they cannot be pleased, against their will," an argument already used by Dryden and Voltaire. But then again he offsets this concession to relativism by an appeal to universal common sense and the verdict of time. "Though taste is obstinate, it is very variable, and time often prevails when arguments have failed." To works of literature "no other test can be applied than length of duration and continuance of esteem." [82] The famous much misunderstood "common reader" is the representative of this universal common sense. "Uncorrupted by literary prejudices, after all the refinements of subtilty and the dogmatism of learning," he will "finally decide all claim to poetical honors." [83] The common reader is surely not the average man nor the common man in any sense of low social status, but the universal man in the neoclassical sense which put such hope in the uniformity of human nature. The critic and the scholar as such are not excluded (as Virginia Woolf would have it in her use of the term),[84] but only the critic corrupted by prejudices and the scholar hidebound by dogmatism. But Johnson does not pursue this trust in the "common reader" to its consequences. He does not analyze the reader's response or the nature of the audience or the processes by which an author established his fame. Though reliance on posterity might imply skepticism as to the durability and truth of one's own insights, Johnson rarely relents in his self-assurance. There are passages which show his suspicion of excessive rationalism, but just the theory of the "common reader" is merely a time-honored device to identify the critic with the audience, his voice with the verdict of the ages.

Nor did Johnson rely on the psychology of the artist. He certainly shows little interest in speculations about genius and imagination. Not that he never uses these terms: he always recognizes the necessity of genius in a poet, i.e. the necessity of his having some innate gift of nature. In describing the genius of Pope, he enumerates the standard qualities: invention, imagination, judgment.[85] He would say that "the highest praise of genius is original invention." [86] Discussing Shakespeare, Johnson can praise invention as the "first and most valuable" power of the poet and understand it as "that which is able to produce a series of events," to "strike out the first hint of a new fable: hence to introduce a set of characters and to wind up the whole in a pleasing catastrophe." [87] But "genius" has none of the romantic connotations. It is simply *ingenium,* "a mind of large general powers, accidentally determined to some particular direction." [88] In a conversation Johnson went so far as to say that "had Sir Isaac Newton applied himself to poetry, he would have made a very fine epic poem. I could as easily apply to law as to tragic poetry." Boswell objected, "Yet, sir, you *did* apply to tragic poetry, not to law." Johnson answered, "Because, sir, I had not money to study law. Sir, the man who has vigor, may walk to the east, just as well as to the west, if he happens to turn his head that way." [89] The implication that any man of parts could be a poet if he wills so, that there is no difference between the gifts for poetry, law, or mathematics, does not disturb Johnson, as he wanted the poet to be assimilated to man in general.

Thus Johnson cannot show any interest in the new theory of creative imagination. It is not, however, a sufficient demonstration of his distrust of imagination to point to Imlac's discourse in *Rasselas* (ch. 43) on the "Dangerous Prevalence of Imagination" or the 89th *Rambler* on "Luxury of Vain Imagination." Johnson there disapproves of day dreaming, escapism, and, as other passages in *Prayers and Meditations* show, simply of "sensual images and loose thoughts." "Imagination" is understood as the power of visualizing absent things, the common use of the 18th century. "Imagination selects ideas from the treasures of remembrance, and produces novelty only by varied combinations." [90] In purely literary contexts Johnson accepts imagination as part of the poet's equipment. He would say about Pope: "He had Imagination, which strongly impresses on the writer's mind and enables him to convey to the reader the various forms of nature, incidents of life, and energies of passion, as in his *Eloisa, Windsor Forest,* and the *Ethic Epistles.*" The inclusion of the *Ethic Epistles,* which we could hardly call "imaginative," is enough to show that "imagination" here is used merely as the power of representation. The term "invention" seems to come nearer to imagination in the modern sense, when Johnson praises Pope's invention in the *Rape of the Lock* as displaying "new trains of events and new scenes of imagery." On the other hand he couples the *Rape of the Lock* and the *Essay on Criticism* as having a kind of invention "by which extrinsic and adventitious embellishments and illustrations are connected with a known subject." [91] Invention here is little more than inventiveness, ingenuity in finding rhetorical ornaments. Mostly Johnson expresses his distrust of imagination as a "licentious and vagrant faculty, unsusceptible of limitations, and impatient of restraint." [92] In speaking of Young's *Night Thoughts* he refers to "the greatest ebullitions of imagination," "the wild diffusion of the sentiments and the digressive sallies of imagination." [93] He disapproved of his friend Goldsmith's *Vicar of Wakefield* as "having no real life in it, and very little of nature. It is mere fanciful performance." [94] He is not entirely unsympathetic to the marvelous in Shakespeare, but makes no issue of it as later the romantics did and as Joseph Warton and Mrs. Montagu did even long before the romantics. Johnson praises *The Tempest* for its "boundless invention": but *Midsummer Night's Dream* is called "wild and fantastical." Usually he gives a historical justification of the marvelous. The witches in *Macbeth* and the fairies in *Midsummer Night's Dream* are excused as contemporary superstitions. It is impossible to deny that Johnson did not like or understand highly fantastic art unless he could reinterpret it as a picture of truth. It was his settled conviction that "the mind can only repose on the stability of truth." [95]

The same attitude comes out in Johnson's discussions of imagery, simile, metaphor, and symbolism. Johnson can be very amusingly literal-minded in criticizing metaphors, of which he requires perfect consistency and rational progression. He censures, for instance, the first stanza of Gray's "Progress of Poetry" for "confounding the images of 'spreading sound' and 'running water,' " [96] or shows a surprising incomprehension of ordinary metaphorical expression when he comments on the conclusion of Gray's "Ode on a Cat": "If what glistered had been 'gold,' the cat would not have gone into the water; and, if she had, would not less have been drowned." [97] In close succession two figures by Addison are ridiculed for mixed or "broken" metaphor, *catachresis*. [98] Johnson is also opposed to figures drawn from art to illustrate nature. " 'Idalia's velvet-green' has something of cant. An epithet or metaphor drawn from Nature ennobles Art; an epithet or metaphor drawn from Art degrades Nature." [99] This is a common rhetorical theory which seems to be based on a theological view of the inferiority of man's work to God's, but which, applied rigorously, would make short work of much of the metaphorical wealth of poetry today and during the Renaissance.

Johnson considers simile an ornament which serves only as "illustration" or rhetorical heightening, "ennobling the subject." [100] And metaphor is defined in the *Dictionary* as a simile "comprized in a word." Denham's well-known lines expressing the wish that his style would flow like the river Thames are praised for the way "the particulars of resemblance are so perspicaciously collected and the different parts of the sentence are so accurately adjusted," but are censured because "most of the words thus artfully opposed are to be understood simply on one side of the comparison, and metaphorically on the other; and if there be any language which does not express intellectual operations by material images, into that language they cannot be translated." [101] This curious demand for translatability into an imaginary, purely rational, abstract language (something like the *characteristica* of Leibniz or modern symbolic logic) seems to say that language, even in poetry, should express intellectual operations without any material images. Johnson wants to hear about style but not about the stream, and he objects that the desired qualities of the style could not be found literally in the river, even though he recognizes that they are ingeniously matched.[102]

The same rationalistic conception underlies Johnson's most elaborate analysis of the metaphors in the metaphysical poets. The term "metaphysical" comes originally from Dryden but was made a matter of common acceptance only through Johnson's *Life of Cowley* (1780). It meant to Johnson not "concerned with metaphysics," but "metaphysical," "beyond nature," or really "unnatural," the opposite of "natural" in the neoclassical sense of the universal. "They neither copied nature nor life; neither painted the forms of matter nor represented the operations of intellect." [103] Their imagery or "wit" is well described by Johnson as *discordia concors:* "a combination of dissimilar images, or discovery of occult resemblances in things apparently unlike." "The most heterogeneous ideas are yoked by violence together." "Their attempts are always analytic: they broke every image into fragments." [104] This is still good characterization, and Johnson's skillful *florilegium* of metaphysical conceits is worth reading. But in this analysis it is not very clear why ideas must not be "yoked by violence together," what would be meant by nonviolent combinations, nor what is bad about analytic poetry, the breaking of images into fragments. In discussing simile elsewhere, Johnson seems to hold the opposite view. "A simile," he says, "may be compared to lines converging at a point and is more excellent as the lines approach from a greater distance: an exemplification may be considered as two parallel lines which run together without approximation, never far separated, and never joined." [105] But apparently even when a simile is drawn from the most remote and opposite parts of the universe, the tenor and the vehicle should remain neatly separated and not "yoked by violence together," whatever "violence" may mean to Johnson. Analytic poetry is bad because it does not allow a uniform sentiment and a unity of tone, and fragmentation of images requires a close attention, which has the effect of dispersal, ambiguity, and irony, things which we seem to love today. The fact that Johnson thought Cowley "undoubtedly the best" of the meta-physicals [106] and that he totally ignored their actual qualities shows the strength of his rationalistic prejudices against anything which seemed to him a special taste, a fashion rather than the assertion of universal truth. One of the most special tastes the world has ever seen—abstract neoclassicism—was erected into the only standard of art and poetry.

Johnson's incomprehension of the centrally metaphorical character of poetry illuminates and is in turn illuminated by his attitude toward religious poetry. In many contexts Johnson condemns religious poetry. In discussing Cowley's *Davideis* he shows that he thinks poetry and imagery as "amplification" (of sacred history) are "frivolous and vain: all addition to that which is already sufficient for the purposes of religion seems not only useless, but in some degree profane." [107] Speaking of Waller's sacred poems, Johnson explains again that "poetical devotion cannot often please." He allows that doctrines of religion may be defended in a didactic poem and that the beauties of nature may be praised in a descriptive poem. The subject of the description "is not God, but the works of God." But "contemplative piety, or the intercourse between God and the human soul, cannot be poetical. Man admitted to implore the mercy of his Creator and plead the merits of his

Redeemer is already in a higher state than poetry can confer."
This can be interpreted as meaning that prayer is a higher state
than poetic contemplation, and one apparently excludes the other.
"The essence of poetry is invention; such invention as, by producing something unexpected, surprises and delights. The topics of
devotion are few, and being few are universally known; but, few
as they are, they can be made no more; they can receive no grace
from novelty of sentiment, and very little from novelty of expression." ("Grace" here means adornment, ornament; "sentiment"
the content, the subject matter; "expression" the rhetorical
form.) * "Omnipotence cannot be exalted; Infinity cannot be am-
plified; Perfection cannot be improved." [108] Exactly the same ideas
underlie the criticism of *Paradise Lost:* "The good and evil of
Eternity are too ponderous for the wings of wit." [109] *Paradise Lost*
is vitiated by a constant confusion of spirit and matter, especially
in the narration of the war in heaven.[110] Isaac Watts's devotional
poetry is also unsatisfactory. "The paucity of its topics enforces
perpetual repetition, and the sanctity of the matter rejects the
ornaments of figurative diction." [111] It seems surprising to be told
so, in view of the Bible's figurative diction so recently described by
Bishop Lowth. But one must recognize that Johnson here joins in
an old critical debate in which Boileau had taken the side Johnson
accepted: the Christian marvelous was condemned. Johnson takes
this side in the controversy for deep personal reasons: religion is
for him completely divided from fiction, the gulf between God
and man being almost as great as in Calvinistic doctrines. Though
he was an Anglican he was incapable of sharing the older view of
a Chain of Being, the gradual ascent from nature to God,† the
whole metaphorical view of the universe, its correspondences and
relations among which poetry as well as religion weaves a web.

Johnson was also untouched by the new cosmopolitanism. He
did, of course, read some French and Italian literature. But his
critical writings contain only the most perfunctory references to

* This explanation seems needed, as Allen Tate has misunderstood
these words, taking "grace" to mean "supernatural grace." Cf. "Johnson
on the Metaphysicals," *Kenyon Review, 11* (1949), 384.

† Cf. Johnson's review of Soame Jenyns, *Free Enquiry into the Nature and Origin of Evil* (1757), in *Works, 11,* 276 ff. The ridicule of the
social implications of Jenyns' "cosmic Toryism" seems richly deserved.

modern foreign authors: occasional praise for La Bruyère's *Characters* or Cervantes are the high points. "Corneille," he said to Mrs. Piozzi, "is to Shakespeare as a clipped hedge is to a forest." [112] Boileau's "Tenth Satire" is inferior to Pope's "Characters of Women," though "he surely is no mean writer to whom Boileau shall be found inferior." "As to original literature the French have a couple of tragic poets who go round the world, Racine and Corneille, and one comic poet, Molière." Fénelon's *Télémaque* is "pretty well." Voltaire has not stood his trial yet and nobody reads Bossuet.[113] It will not surprise us that Rousseau excited his contempt. "I think him one of the worst of men; a rascal who ought to be hunted out of society. . . . I would sooner sign a sentence for his transportation, than that of any felon who has gone from the Old Bailey these many years. Yes, I should like to have him work in the plantations." [114] But this is hardly literary criticism, and we must not forget that Johnson was needling Boswell, who made a pilgrimage to Switzerland to see Rousseau. There is nothing beyond the bare names in Johnson concerning Dante, Petrarch, or Boccaccio. Tasso's *Aminta* is condemned specifically as a pastoral, and *Orlando Furioso* is criticized for the enchanted wood to which we follow "Rinaldo with more curiosity than terror." [115]

But Johnson was not only touched but deeply involved in the general awakening of the historical sense and specifically in the revived interest in early English literature and in literary antiquarianism and historiography. There is, of course, the evidence of his *Dictionary*, which shows that he had read in practically every earlier English writer, though it may be difficult in some cases to distinguish between real reading and mere sampling by him or an amanuensis. There is the Introduction to the *Dictionary*, which is a history of the English language, and in which, incidentally, Johnson has something to say about early English literature. He quotes specimens of Anglo-Saxon and Middle English from Hickes's *Thesaurus*, and remarks, with an unusual suspension of judgment, that "our ignorance of the laws of their metre and the quantities of their syllables excludes us from that pleasure which the old bards undoubtedly gave to their contemporaries." [116] Johnson wanted to edit Chaucer. His edition was to contain "remarks on his language, and the change it had undergone from the earliest times to his age, and from his to the present, with notes explana-

tory of customs, etc. and references to Boccace, and other authors
from whom he has borrowed, with an account of the liberties he
has taken in telling the stories." [117] Yet Johnson could not have
appreciated Chaucer highly. He says, of Dryden's retelling the
"Nun's Priest's Tale," that the "Tale" seems "hardly worth revival," and he censures Dryden's praise of the "Knight's Tale" as
"hyperbolical." [118] Johnson smiled at some of the excesses of antiquarianism: in *Rambler* No. 177 he ridicules an antiquary proudly
displaying "a copy of the *Children in the Wood,* which he firmly
believed to be of the first edition." "Chevy Chase" is condemned
for "chill and lifeless imbecility." [119] Medieval mysteries are "wild
dramas." [120] But for linguistic reasons Johnson read some of the
romances, dipped even into Lydgate, and, of course, prepared
his great edition of Shakespeare, which, besides its critical preface
and comments on the individual plays and passages, is also a work
of textual criticism and historical elucidation. Johnson's *Proposals
for Printing the Dramatic Works of William Shakespeare* (1756)
expounds a very full program for interpreting Shakespeare's allusions, language, and relation to his sources; and Johnson at least
partially fulfilled this plan in his edition. He hoped, by "compar-
ing the works of Shakespeare with those of writers who lived at
the same time, immediately preceded, or immediately followed
him, to be able to ascertain his ambiguities, disentangle his intrica-
cies, and recover the meaning of words now lost in the darkness of
antiquity." [121] Johnson wrote a commendatory preface to Mrs.
Charlotte Lennox's *Shakespear Illustrated* (1753), a first collection of Shakespeare's sources, and used the information in his notes
to the edition without, it seems, adding anything of his own.[122]

   We get Johnson's nearest approach to a literary history of England in the *Lives of the Poets* (1779–81), which are of course primarily biography and straight criticism, but which contain an implicit scheme of the history of English poetry of the preceding century. The choice of lives was prescribed by the booksellers who
ordered them, and thus from the outset Johnson was limited to the
living tradition of poetry, from Cowley to Gray. He himself seems
to have urged only the inclusion of minor poets such as Blackmore,
Watts, Pomfret, and Yalden. Nothing came of a suggestion made
by George III that Spenser should have been included.[123] In the
Life of Cowley Johnson starts with a discussion of the metaphysi-

cals as background and foil to the tradition he is about to treat in full, and he stresses everywhere the anticipations and steps which led to its establishment. The reform begins with Waller and Denham, who "traced the new scheme of poetry." [124] The actual founder of the new style was Dryden: "To him we owe the improvement, perhaps the completion of our metre, the refinement of our language, and much of the correctness of our sentiments." [125] Before the time of Dryden "there was no poetical diction: no system of words at once refined from the grossness of domestic use and free from the harshness of terms appropriated to particular arts." [126] Johnson always points out either relapses from or approximations to this ideal norm. Addison "debased rather than refined" the versification which he had learned from Dryden.[127] And Pope, of course, is the summit of perfection.

This view of a progress of English poetry toward an ideal technical norm attained especially by Pope is curiously enough combined in Johnson with a constant recognition of the historical point of view and pleadings for some relativity of standards. He recognized that wit "has its changes and fashions, and at different times takes different forms." [128] He explicitly states that "to judge rightly of an author we must transport ourselves to his time, and examine what were the wants of his contemporaries, and what were his means of supplying them." [129] As early as the *Observations on Macbeth* (1745), Johnson had stated that "in order to make a true estimate of the abilities and merit of a writer, it is always necessary to examine the genius of his age and the opinions of his contemporaries." However, he uses the historical argument largely as an apology for shortcomings and mistakes in older literature. Thus Dryden's "Threnodia Augustalis" has the "irregularity of meter, to which the ears of that age however were accustomed"; [130] Milton's verse was "harmonious, in proportion to the general state of our metre in Milton's age"; [131] Waller's poem "On the Danger of the Prince on the Coast of Spain" may be "justly praised, without much allowance for the state of our poetry and language at that time." [132]

Once, in Johnson's defense of Pope's translation of Homer, the historical argument is prominent and effective. "Time and place will always enforce regard. In estimating this translation consideration must be had of the nature of our language, the form of our meter, and, above all, of the change which two thousand years have made in the modes of life and the habits of thought" since Pope "wrote for his own age and his own nation." [133] But the historical argument which seems to Johnson valid in case of an adaptation of a work of remote antiquity did not affect his central view of English literature as one continuous effort toward the establishment of a timeless norm, that of Pope and Dryden. Johnson certainly believed in progress (despite all personal pessimism as to the possibility of human happiness). He rejected the view that the world "was in its decay" and that "souls partake of the general degeneracy." [134] "Every age," he thought, "improves in elegance. One refinement always makes way for another." [135] But the new dispensation seems firmly established. Since Dryden, English poetry has had "no tendency to relapse to its former savageness." [136] This faith or hope may help explain Johnson's acrimonious criticism of Gray's and Collins' attempts to revive what he considered an obsolete and essentially superseded diction and versification. It explains in part the harshness of his comments on Milton's early poems, which he knew were not only highly valued by his contemporaries but had also become the models of a new Miltonic school of which he disapproved as of any archaism. He did not and could not very well see that he himself stood almost at the end of a great tradition. The stirring of the new seemed to him only the odd, perverse, and, at the most, partially successful revival of old and worn-out things. His own critical work is certainly varied enough, unified without being monotonous, strongly rooted in the tradition but still far from merely dogmatic in its acceptance of it. Johnson, while holding firm to the main tenets of the tradition of neoclassical criticism, constantly reinterprets them in a spirit for which it is difficult to avoid a term he would have hated: liberal.

6: *THE MINOR ENGLISH AND SCOTTISH CRITICS*

THE FIGURE of Dr. Johnson looms large on the English scene of the later 18th century. Yet all around Johnson a great activity was being carried on which proved exceedingly influential in both England and abroad, and which finally became destructive of the position of neoclassicism everywhere in the Western world. The ideas propounded in England and Scotland were not peculiarly English or Scottish: they could be paralleled in France and Italy, and they were certainly carried further and elaborated more systematically and radically in Germany. Still, the English and Scottish body of thought was, at least in its early stages, more coherent than anything comparable on the Continent. Modern subjective aesthetics and a historical conception of the development of literature were formulated in England and Scotland first, whatever the scattered anticipations elsewhere.

It is now the fashion to deny the existence of preromanticism and to minimize the revolutionary elements in these critics. One may admit that the older interpretations drew the issues far too crudely. Neoclassicism in England was rarely a narrow, rigid creed, and certain critics who have been called precursors of romanticism held basic neoclassical positions. A praise of Homer and Shakespeare and a mere rejection of the authority of Aristotle and of the three unities in the drama are not, in themselves, indications of romanticism, and in practice they were perfectly compatible with a strong hold on neoclassical tenets. The first reaction against neoclassicism was hardly conscious, certainly not organized, and thus not describable as a "movement." In any case, it did not move in one direction.

A strong naturalistic tendency is obvious even in so classical a figure as Johnson, and emotionalist concepts flourished long before one can speak of anything as romantic or even preromantic taste. Such concepts were strongly encouraged by ideas revived from ancient rhetoric with its emphasis on effects, and by the growing taste for the pathetic, the moving, and the downright sentimental. Anticipations of the imaginative and symbolist concepts of poetry later to be adopted by the great English romantic poets were rare. One must grant that there was a real break in the English critical tradition when Coleridge and Shelley revived Platonic ideas or imported similar German concepts.

Whatever the arguments for caution in speaking of preromanticism and however justified may be the dissatisfaction of some scholars with the multiple meanings of the term "romanticism," it seems impossible to deny that we are confronted with the problem of the dissolution of neoclassicism and its replacement by new and different theories. The problem should not be ignored and obscured by exclusive insistence on the undeniable survivals, the compromises, and the open contradictions of individual authors. What mattered were frequently short striking pronouncements in texts whose general import may have been quite conventional. It has been the privilege of every age to pull sentences out of context, to fasten on what is new and fertile and meets its own demands for change.[1]

When we look at the criticism produced in the second half of the century in England and Scotland, we must come to the conclusion that the achievement in literary theory and practical criticism was not impressive. No individual critic can compare with Dr. Johnson. Among attempts at a general theory of literature, Lord Kames's *Elements of Criticism* (1762) seems the only independent and systematic synthesis. Compared with it, Hugh Blair's widely known *Lectures on Rhetoric and Belles Lettres* (1782) is only an unoriginal textbook. But what the age lacked in strictly literary theory was amply made up in two related disciplines which profoundly influenced literary criticism: aesthetics and literary historiography. We shall have to discuss these disciplines if we are to understand the further development of criticism.

There is no need to enter into detail about the early history of British aesthetics. It has, roughly speaking, two fairly well-defined traditions: one empiricist and mechanistic, which goes back to Hobbes; the other Platonic or rather neo-Platonic, for which, in the 18th century, Shaftesbury was the main source. Hobbes's influence was frequently modified and mollified by Locke's. Shaftesbury's was also far from clear-cut, since he was a loose thinker who eclectically combined elements from Stoicism, neo-Platonism, and the new empiricism. His aesthetic ideas were soon amalgamated with the Lockean tradition by his main disciple, Francis Hutcheson.

In Shaftesbury beauty is form, proportion, eternal harmony. We can learn to perceive it correctly. But this beauty is not necessarily physical proportion and form. The higher stages of beauty reveal an "inward form," "interior numbers," a secret invisible measure and harmony, a design or "idea" which at times is conceived as residing in the mind of the artist, in his inner vision, and at times is conceived of as a reflection of the light of God.* Shaftesbury thus condemns mere liking, capricious individual taste. He thinks of the act of valuing as an intuitive judgment of something objective, be it beauty or virtue. Hutcheson, who wrote the first formal treatise on aesthetics in English, *An Inquiry into the Original of Our Ideas of Beauty and Virtue* (1725), though professing to "explain and defend the principles of the late Earl of Shaftesbury," actually translates his ideas into very different terms.[2] Taste to him is an "inner sense." Though this sense still recognizes a world of objects characterized by unity in variety, attention is shifted to the aesthetic response. Divergences of taste are explained by the interference of personal, purely individual associations.

David Hume discarded the survivals of Platonic ontology when in his essay "Of the Standard of Taste" (1757) he came to apply radical empiricism to the question. "All sentiment is right," he asserts boldly. "Beauty is no quality in things themselves. It exists merely in the mind which contemplates them." Taste and literary opinions, one might conclude, are purely subjective. But Hume rejects this consequence immediately, appealing to the uniformity of human nature, the verdict of the ages, the universal principles

* Shaftesbury probably did not read Plotinus himself, but he read the Cambridge Platonists, Platonizing Italians such as Bellori, and Maximus Tyrius, a peripatetic philosopher under Emperor Commodus, from whom he drew a central quotation; see *Characteristics* (3d ed. London, 1723), 2, 295. Shaftesbury here refers to an "ancient philologist" who, I believe, has never before been identified.

of association. These principles are used to justify such neoclassical doctrines as the purity of genre and the unity of action in tragedy. Hume does not see that he is appealing to the taste of a small group at a particular time and place and that he identifies this group with humanity. One of his examples gives the argument away: "Whoever would assert an equality of genius and elegance between Ogilby and Milton, or Bunyan and Addison, would be thought to defend no less an extravagance, than if he had maintained a mole-hill to be as high as Teneriffe, or a pond as extensive as the ocean." [3] Many today would feel no qualms in preferring Bunyan's genius to Addison's (if not his elegance), though Ogilby, a 17th-century translator of Homer, has not found modern defenders. In Hume the identity of his own taste or that of his class with that of humanity is merely asserted as a fact.

In Edmund Burke's discussion of taste, added in 1758 to his *Philosophical Inquiry into the Origin of our Ideas of the Sublime and Beautiful* (1757), the problem is solved by dividing taste into two kinds. Burke grants the subjectivity of taste as far as it is imaginative and sensuous, but at the same time argues that "the cause of a wrong taste is a defect of judgment," that taste concerns questions of disposition, decorum, congruity, and that therefore understanding operates with it.[4] Taste, in a wider sense, includes judgment.

This solution, which reintroduces rationalism or at least the function of reason into the problem of aesthetic response, is also the solution of the most elaborate and most scholastic treatise of the time on the subject, Alexander Gerard's *Essay on Taste* (1759). Gerard analyzes taste into a number of "simple senses": novelty, sublimity, imitation, beauty, harmony, wit and ridicule, and virtue. This incongruous list does not help him, however, to escape from the empiricist predicament. At first he tries hard by postulating a standard of cooperation or union among these different "senses," [5] but then he himself recognizes that this does not allow him to get beyond individual taste, and he is forced to abandon his doctrinaire empiricism: he must again appeal to judgment validated by tradition and the verdict of the ages. With Gerard taste, by including virtue, has ceased to be distinctly aesthetic.

Kames seems to have been the only writer during the period who explicitly recognized what was implied by an appeal to universal human nature. He expounds a theory of taste very similar to Hume's but concludes that we must exclude several classes of men from the standard of taste: "Those who depend for food on bodily labor, are totally void of taste, of such a taste at least as can be of use in the fine arts. This consideration bars the greater part of mankind; and of the remaining part, many by a corrupted taste are unqualified for voting. The common sense of mankind must then be confined to the few that fall not under these exceptions." Though he admits that the "exclusion of classes so many and numerous, reduces within a narrow compass those who are qualified to be judges in the fine arts," he still preserves his faith in a "wonderful uniformity in the emotions and feelings of the different races of men." [6] He does not see any contradiction in arguing for a universal standard which may be appreciated by only a very few. Thus the discussion of taste arrives at an impasse. Yet at least it poses the antinomies of Kant's *Critique of Judgment* and resolutely raises the problem of criticism as such. Actually it is a criticism of criticism.

The discussion of taste in the 18th century is paralleled by a discussion of the equipment of the poet, his genius and his imagination. This too leads to a complete impasse, to a leveling and obliteration of the creative act, just as taste by identifying itself with moral judgment had done. "Imagination" as conceived in the Renaissance is the creative imagination of the poet: the term recurs again in the 18th century in Shaftesbury and others, and means there the inventive, spontaneously creative power of the poet. It is frequently used as a defense of the "marvelous" in poetry, of the "fairy way of writing," of supernatural machinery such as the sylphs in Pope's *Rape of the Lock,* or it justifies allegories and personifications. Imagination is also associated with genius and originality. Shaftesbury especially, with his emphasis on genius, on the poet as "a second maker, a just Prometheus, under Jove, who like that sovereign artist or universal Nature forms a whole, coherent and proportioned in itself," revives Platonic motifs which later proved very influential in Germany.[7]

Edward Young's *Conjectures on Original Composition* (1759) takes up the same ideas, though emphasizing more the "individuality" and "originality" of the great poet. Young asserts that all men are born "originals," that "no two faces, no two minds are just alike." Antiquity must not be imitated. "The less we copy the renowned ancients" the more we shall resemble them. Genius, which at one time meant little more than *ingenium,* great gifts or talents, with Young assumes the ancient connotation of religious inspiration, of supernatural magic. "With regard to the moral world, conscience, with regard to the intellectual, genius, is that god within," he says, apparently alluding to the Socratic demon. "A genius differs from a good understanding, as a magician from a good architect." What original genius makes is then no longer an artifact, a work of design and labor. It "may be said to be of vegetable nature; it rises spontaneously from the vital root of genius; it grows, it is not made." [8] Biological analogy has replaced the analogy from physics or handicraft. The work of art has become the result of an unconscious act or process, something like procreation or growing. The poet's imagination ceases to be a constructive combinatory faculty and becomes the creator of a second world. The radicalism of these statements cannot be obscured by Young's diverse *caveats* (one inserted by Richardson) or his pious commonplaces. But Young remains isolated in the England of his time.

Late in the century, in William Blake, we can find again such assertions of the power of imagination. In Blake imagination becomes so exalted that it ceases to be an artistic or even a human faculty. Imagination is "the real and eternal world of which this vegetable universe is but a faint shadow." "Vision or Imagination is a Representation of what eternally exists, really and unchangeably." Blake considers the external world as the "dirt upon his feet," because he wants to "look through" the eye and "not with it." In his violent annotations to Sir Joshua Reynolds' *Discourses* he attacks Reynolds' disparagement of inspiration and originality. "Man brings all that he has or can have into the world with him." "Taste and Genius are not teachable or acquirable, but are born with us." "Man is all Imagination. God is man and exists in us and we in Him." In annotating Wordsworth's *Poems* Blake asserts that "one power alone makes a poet: Imagination, the Divine Vision." It has nothing to do with memory, it is only hindered by natural objects. Nature itself is imagination, is a spiritual sensation. Blake wants an all-pervading symbolism, "addressed to the intellectual powers, while it is altogether hidden from the corporeal understanding." But it would be a mistake to press his concept of the imagination into literary or even aesthetic terms: it hardly flows from the tradition of aesthetic thinking but rather from mystical theories of knowledge and interpretation. Blake stands quite alone and almost unknown in his time. Some of the pronouncements just quoted, though not perhaps datable with accuracy, are very late: as late as the 20's of the 19th century, and thus may reflect the new romantic atmosphere. Certainly Blake's conception of the imagination is neither the usual 18th-century idea nor the romantic. His poet is a visionary without pride, a "literalist of the imagination" who takes down what is dictated to him by the "authors in Eternity." [9]

The general 18th-century development of the concept of imagination went rather in an opposite direction—toward identifying imagination, at first simply with the power of visualization, as in Addison's papers "On the Pleasures of Imagination," and then increasingly toward the power of evoking associations, especially emotive ones, the power of entering sympathetically into other people's feelings. Scholars who have hailed every 18th-century expression of concern with imagination as romantic are certainly mistaken. In the 18th century imagination becomes so broadly conceived that it cannot define the creation or contemplation of art or even distinguish it from any kind of recall of a touching event or picturesque scene, or from the reading of a physiognomy, or from the intuitive insight into character from gestures or words. The sympathetic imagination of the 18th-century aestheticians is indistinguishable from the "sympathy" of Hume or Adam Smith, which had become with them the only organ of morality.

The shift away from Addison's meaning of imagination as visualization seems first accomplished in Edmund Burke's *Philosophical Inquiry into the Origin of Our Ideas of the Sublime and Beautiful.* Burke argues against the necessity to visualize in the verbal arts. A particular effort, he says, is required in order to visualize metaphors. Implicitly, at least, Burke rejects the 18th-century emphasis on description, and he uses the example, later exploited in Lessing's *Laokoon,* of the impression Helen made on the old men of Troy, which Homer conveys without any description of her beauty. Burke concludes that "poetry and rhetoric do not succeed in exact description so well as painting does; their business is, to affect rather by sympathy than imitation; to display rather the effect of things on the mind of the speaker, or of others, than to present a clear idea of the things themselves." [10] In a chapter ("Of Sympathy") in his *Essays on Poetry and Music* (1776), James Beattie drew the contrast between this faculty and the comic, which he saw as the intellectual and hence unimaginative and unsympathetic view of the world.[11] The comic writer has the cold, detached view of a spectator. As Blair formulates it, the tragic writer has the power of entering "deeply into the characters which he draws; of becoming for a moment the very person whom he exhibits, and of assuming all his feelings." [12]

With Beattie and other followers of Adam Smith sympathy is active and is, of course, a moral asset. It characterizes both the great poet and the connoisseur of the arts. With the strict associationist, however, sympathy can, at least in theory, become passive, the mere result of a "train of emotions." Archibald Alison, in his *Essays on the Nature and Principles of Taste* (1790), holds that it is in "this powerless state of reverie, when we are carried on by our conceptions, not guiding them, that the deepest emotions of beauty or sublimity are felt, that our hearts swell with feelings which language is too weak to express, and that in the depth of silence and astonishment we pay to the charm that enthrals us, the most flattering mark of our applause." [13] Alison quotes Rousseau's *Rêveries*. Yet he uses the principle of association, deterministic as it is, to defend uniformity of effect and tone as a requirement of art. He even objects to tragicomedy on the grounds of its irregularity and appreciates Corneille for his "uniform character of dignity." [14] (Beattie had drawn the opposite conclusion from the principle of sympathy. He had argued that Shakespeare's tragedies would be insupportable if not relieved by comic interludes such as the porter scene in *Macbeth* and the gravediggers in *Hamlet*.[15]) The consequences of this view of imagination as sympathy were only drawn in the early 19th century by Jeffrey, Hazlitt, and Keats.

The same process of the dissolution of ancient concepts occurs in another central question of aesthetics: that concerning the object and method of imitation. During the later 18th century in England the traditional view was best formulated not by a literary critic but by the painter, Sir Joshua Reynolds, in his *Discourses* before the Royal Academy (1769–90). The third discourse (1770) especially makes a general statement which is also applicable to literary theory. Simple copying of nature is rejected in favor of representing ideal beauty, the perfect state of nature, superior to all singular forms, local customs, particularities, and details of every kind. Imitation is not of anything supernatural (as in the Platonic theory upheld by Shaftesbury), nor of any inner vision, nor does it demand an irrational genius or inspiration. "This great perfection and beauty are not to be sought in the heavens, but upon earth. They are about us, and upon every side of us." The artist does not depict the individual, but represents the class, the "common idea and central form," the species.[16] At times Reynolds thinks of this common idea as an average, a means arrived at by empirical observation. In general he restates the Aristotelian view which had been applied to the fine arts at least since the time of Cicero, the view that the object of imitation lies in the general nature of man, in what is characteristic of a species, of humanity as such. Yet on occasion he leans, though cautiously, to the neo-Platonic view, which postulates an "image of perfect beauty" in the mind of the artist. Idealization, with Reynolds, may even mean simple indulgence, escape into a dream world. "The object and intention of all the arts is to supply the natural imperfection of things, and often to gratify the mind by realizing and embodying what never existed but in the imagination." [17] One suspects that Reynolds is not quite clear about these distinctions: the very looseness of his phrasing allows him to praise both Michelangelo and Correggio. He recommends both the "grand style," historical painting, which he equates with poetical painting, and the portrait, which must, however, be generalized to escape the danger of mere naturalism.[18] "Imitation" and "idea," as before in history, serve to justify quite diverse kinds of art.

Belief in the theory of imitation nevertheless remained very strong. It was, moreover, fostered by the contemporary victory of philosophical empiricism with its emphasis on sense experience. The theory of imitation underlies the many recommendations of particularity, vividness, and concreteness which appear during the century. These are associated with the concept of imagination as visualization and with the prevailing interest in description and descriptive poetry. Quintilian is the classical authority for particularity, followed by a whole group of the mid-century critics.

Joseph Warton wants "clear, complete, and circumstantial images" and expressly objects to the growing taste for generalities, alluding to the style of Johnson.[19] Kames wants us to "avoid as much as possible abstract and general terms" and recognizes that "images, which are the life of poetry, cannot be raised in any perfection but by introducing particular objects." [20] Campbell in his *Philosophy of Rhetoric* (1776) devotes much space to "specialty," advising "not only to particularize, but even to individuate the object presented to the mind." [21] To this trend we owe not only the minute descriptive poetry which is characteristic of the period but also the numerous treatises devoted to the "picturesque." The two best known books, William Gilpin's and Sir Uvedale Price's, have, however, little to say of literature.[22] William Blake, who in his manner of painting stands quite apart from this particularizing trend, expressed his opposition to classical generality when he annotated Reynolds' *Discourses*. "To generalize is to be an idiot. To particularize is the alone distinction of merit." [23]

But both these rival theories, that recommending the general and that recommending the particular, were undermined in the 18th century by the emotionalist concept of art, which minimizes the object of imitation completely in favor of the effect of that object on the mind. This was not a theory of emotional expression, of romantic subjectivity. It was rather a result of the turn to pathos and rhetoric, and of the whole empiricist logic which ceased to be able to account for abstraction. Burke, in his *Sublime and Beautiful* (1757), cuts off poetry from representation and imitation. He cannot understand that words are symbols and must conclude that their effect is merely emotional, sympathetic, touching, with a resultant emphasis on the vague, the obscure, or what he calls "the sublime." The sublime, which had originally been a rhetorical name for the elevated style, becomes with Burke and many contemporaries a synonym for the dark and terrible, for the occult fears of man, rather than for any determinate aesthetic object or style. The whole world of objects is relegated to an inferior province of "beauty." Beauty with Burke is social, sexual, little, pretty, smooth, weak, in short typically rococo. He even tries to give a physiological explanation of the contrast between the sublime and beautiful. Beauty acts by "relaxing the solids of the whole system." The sublime, as fear and terror, increases tension.[24] Poetry, which affects the emotions, "cannot," he concludes logically, "with strict propriety be called an art of imitation." [25] The theory of imitation was undermined also from other sides: several writers excluded music from the imitative arts.[26] Sir William Jones, in his "Essay on the Arts, commonly called Imitative" (1772), proclaimed boldly that neither music nor poetry belongs to the arts of imitation.[27]

One can well observe the different strains of aesthetic speculation as they apply to literature in Lord Kames's *Elements of Criticism*. Kames lays an elaborate groundwork in association psychology before applying his observations about emotions and passions to literature. He feels that he is an innovator, a pioneer: "To reduce the science of criticism to any regular form, has never once been attempted." [28] To some extent he makes good his extravagant claim by complex psychological explanations of sound symbolism, metrics, and imagery, a detailed classification of figures of speech, and an analysis of the principles of composition and the unities. Kames uses the Hobbesian term of "ideas in a train" rather than association, but works with a scheme based on resemblance, contiguity, and causation in order to account for simplicity, contrast, variety, motion, grandeur, and other aesthetic ideas. Poetry is always communication of emotion achieved by what he calls "ideal presence," illusion.[29] Kames's exemplifications of the effect of sound and meter and his attempts at a new classification of figures are often purely scholastic and sterile. His personal taste is very conventional and he disparages the witty and paradoxical. He has strong prejudices in favor of real experience which lead him constantly into awkward confusions between art and life. Thus he declares that a man like York in *Henry VI,* "spent and disspirited after losing a battle, is not disposed to heighten or illustrate his discourse by similes"; that hyperbole is never prompted by sorrow, and that "in expressing any severe passion that wholly occupies the mind, metaphor is improper." [30] Kames's standards are always those of concrete vivacity and emotional impact. The two collaborate so closely as to be almost identical for him. A man of sixty-six when his book was published, he remained quite conservative in his defense of the main neoclassical conventions. True, he recognized that the genre theories are untenable in their rigidity. "Literary compositions run into each other, precisely like colors: in their strong tints they are easily distinguished; but are susceptible of so much variety, and so many different forms, that we never can say where one species ends and another begins." [31] But he does not draw the legitimate consequences from that empirical observation. He points the way toward a theory of poetry as communication of emotion, with all the difficulties implicit in it: in distinguishing between art and life or between poetry and oratory, in defining genres, and classifying works of art.

Most critics of that time seem not to have perceived the problem of genres at all but simply to have accepted the inherited conceptions of their hierarchy and ideal purity. Hugh Blair's *Lectures on Rhetoric and Belles Lettres* has a series of chapters on the principal genres, but no introductory discussion of kinds in general or principles of literary classification. Nor do the kinds he selects have any methodological or other consistency. First Blair has a chapter on pastoral and lyric poetry, then one on didactic and descriptive poetry, which is followed by the one on the "Poetry of the Hebrews," which is scarcely a genre. Later he takes up the two highest kinds of poetic writings, the epic and the dramatic, while the novel, which is treated with unusual sympathy, appears not among the poetic genres but as "fictitious history" in the same class with historical writings, dialogues, and letters.[32] There is no system, no defense of the kinds, not even any awareness of the problem.

The bulk of 18th-century criticism moved in the well-worn grooves of the kinds and their particular traditional problems. Most attention was still given to the highest genres, though the successes of the age were not in tragedy or the epic. The theory of tragedy remained that of the Aristotelian system as modified by the French, though during the 18th century significant changes began to take place. The rules, which had been attacked even in the 17th century, were combated much more effectively and successfully in the second half of the 18th. The influence of Shakespeare, whose fame grew in spite of the rules by leaps and bounds, proved decisive. At first the arguments either excused Shakespeare's violation of the rules on grounds of ignorance, or maintained that, despite his success, he would have done even better had he observed the rules. Or it was said that what is good in Shakespeare follows the rules if they are properly interpreted. The distinction between eternal and temporary rules was drawn by Dryden. More and more often it was said that Shakespeare violated only the rules which were merely the fashion of the 18th century. Later the view emerged that Shakespeare established his own kind of art. Thomas Percy, for instance, said that the histories are neither tragedies nor comedies, but simply plays.[33] Finally, Shakespeare was glorified as the wild genius who was right by virtue of his genius. "Whatever Shakespeare wrote is right" seems the slogan of the cult. Shades of these opinions need illustration only in a history of Shakespeare criticism.

Disparagement of the unities went along with a shift from interest in plot and structure to interest in character drawing and in Shakespeare's knowledge and depiction of human nature. During the 18th century, almost from its beginning, a large body of criticism was devoted to the discussion of Shakespeare's dramatic characters, often quite independently of the plays themselves. Joseph Warton's essays in the *Adventurer* (1753–54) on the *Tempest* and *King Lear,* which characterize Ariel and Caliban and give a running commentary on the progress of Lear's feelings, are good examples of a kind of criticism which Warton himself felt to be new: namely, if I may use a term unknown to Warton, "psychological."[34] Henry Mackenzie's essays on Hamlet in the *Mirror* (1780) anticipate Goethe's sympathetic interpretation of Hamlet's weakness. Other books, like those by William Richardson, use Shakespeare largely as a text for disquisitions on morals.[35]

The most self-conscious and original of 18th-century essays on Shakespeare is Maurice Morgann's *Essay on the Dramatic Character of John Falstaff* (1777). This professes to refute the usual labeling of Falstaff as a coward and braggart. Morgann defends a method of "looking to the spirit rather than the letter of what is uttered, and relying at last only on a combination of the whole," and of distinguishing between a real and an apparent character. He seems to have been the first to speak of a "certain roundness and integrity in the forms of Shakespeare, which gives them an independence," and the first to argue that Shakespeare, in "unfolding" his characters from within, must himself have felt every varied situation. Shakespeare's art is something hidden, a "felt propriety and truth from causes unseen." Criticism has the task of "entering into the inward soul of [Shakespeare's] compositions." The characters are totalities, wholes. The poet "gives to every particular part a relish of the whole, and of the whole to every particular part." [36] Morgann has a vague feeling for Shakespeare's art, for the *Gestalt,* the wholeness of his characters, for a central principle conceived in almost biological terms. But in his argument he constantly runs the risk of confusing fiction and reality, of treating his dramatic character as a historical person, of pressing a thesis about Falstaff's lack of cowardice while only half believing in it. He echoes too the current ideas on sympathetic imagination, the view that poetry is justified by its effect, that it is, as Young implies, "magic." Though it seems difficult to prove direct influence, Morgann anticipates the methods of Lamb, Coleridge, and Hazlitt. A. C. Bradley complimented the distant originator of his own method when he wrote of Morgann's essay that "there is no better piece of Shakespeare criticism in the world." [37]

Almost as important as the 18th-century breakdown of the unities and the shift to character analysis were the new conceptions of the effects of tragedy. The Aristotelian version of *catharsis* seems not to have been understood except by specialists. What interested the time was the question of why we derive pleasure from tragedy, joy from grief. The purgation of pity and fear was talked about, but interpreted not to mean purgation at all and not to refer to both pity *and* fear. Tragedy was increasingly considered simply a means of arousing pity. Blair said bluntly that the "intention of tragedy is to improve our virtuous sensibility," and George Campbell wanted to "include under the name of pity all the emotions excited by tragedy." [38] Burke shifts the emphasis to irrational feeling even more radically. Our sympathy is "antecedent to any reasoning, by an instinct that works to its own purposes without our concurrence." Since Burke cannot distinguish between a work of art and real life, he concludes that it would be the triumph of real sympathy if, at the announcement of an execution in the adjoining square, everybody left the theater to see it. He does not face the objection that the theater might also be emptied by a coronation or any other rare spectacle, or that viewing an execution might be an indulgence in cruelty and not in sympathy. He thus concludes that "the nearer a tragedy approaches the reality, and the further it removes us from all idea of fiction, the more perfect is its power." [39] Implicitly Burke justifies middle-class tragedy, naturalistic in technique, emotionally harrowing. Questions of structure and even meaning become irrelevant: the drama as drama is destroyed.

Kames tries a compromise between tradition and the new experiments by recognizing two types of tragedy: moral and pathetic. He clearly prefers the second type for its appeal to sympathy, and shows an amazing coolness toward Greek tragedy. Greek tragedies, he tells us, are "more active than sentimental," that is, contain more action than feeling. They have "no sentiments except of the plainest kind . . . no intricate or delicate situation to occasion any singular passion: no gradual swelling and subsiding of passion: no conflict between different passions." [40] Shakespeare satisfies Kames's requirements on these counts: he quotes numerous instances of Shakespeare's psychological penetration and truth to life. Still, he disapproves of tragicomedy because "discordant emotions are unpleasant when jumbled together," [41] and he slights the unities of space and time as merely contributory to the one obligatory unity, that of action. Kames's standard is always that of emotional effect, which can be achieved only by illusion, an impression of reality, as if we were spectators of a real event. "Any interruption annihilates that impression, by rousing the spectator out of his waking dream, and unhappily restoring him to his senses." [42] Johnson must have had this passage in mind when he argued that the spectator is always in his senses.

Hume, somewhat surprisingly in view of his ethics of sympathy, was one of the few who saw that tragedy cannot be reduced to pity. If sympathy were the effect of tragedy, he says tellingly, "an hospital would be a more entertaining place than a ball." [43] He himself propounded, in his essay *Of Tragedy* (1757), a complex theory of tragic pleasure, according to which the dominant pleasure, that of imitation, is reinforced by the subordinate unpleasant feeling of pain, just as love is supposed to be strengthened by jealousy.[44] But this view remained without influence.

Only very much later the concept of tragedy as pitiful gives way to a return of the Stoic idea that in tragedy we are to feel sentiments of heroic magnanimity. In 1805 Richard Payne Knight expounded this view, which had again found favor in Germany with Schiller.[45]

Compared to tragedy, the theory of comedy was given little attention during the 18th century. The old commonplaces about its salutary effect on morals and its ridicule of vice were repeated *ad nauseam*. Sentimental comedy, which flourished on the stage, seemed hardly to have any defenders among critics, though Hurd says grudgingly that he does not "dispute the propriety of serious or even affecting comedies." [46] More important for the future were the general discussions of the comic and laughter. These, although not literary in themselves, do reflect a shift from the early meaning of humor as oddity to the new meaning of sympathy, laughter through tears. But Kames and Beattie, who discuss comic theory most fully and with many literary examples, are not yet aware of this change. They refute Hobbes's view of laughter as "sudden glory" and argue mostly for incongruity as a general explanation of the comic.[47]

Developments in epic theory parallel those in dramatic. Le Bossu's extremely rationalistic definition of the epic was never accepted in England.[48] Milton's fame in itself combated the view that the "Christian marvelous" should be excluded from the epic as Boileau had demanded. Pope, in *Peri Bathous,* had parodied "a receipt to make an epic poem." Two new elements, however, enter epic theory in the 18th century. Homer was increasingly interpreted as a primitive bard, especially after Thomas Blackwell's *Enquiry into the Life and Writings of Homer* (1735). This was (if we ignore the unknown Vico) the first attempt to see Homer independently of the tradition of epic rules, as a representative of his age and society. The "discovery" of Ossian further hastened the breakdown of the old ideas on the epic, or at least the recognition of a special type of primitive epic. Hugh Blair, in his influential *Critical Dissertation on the Poems of Ossian* (1763), had argued that "in strength of imagination, in grandeur of sentiment, in native majesty of passion" Ossian is the equal of Homer and Virgil, though he granted that Ossian has not "the regular dignity of narration" which we find in them. Although Blair took the precaution of showing that *Fingal* fulfills all the essential demands made by Aristotle on the epic, his positive stress was on the poet of the heart who makes his readers "glow, and tremble, and weep." [49] Blair's comparative restraint was soon thrown to the winds by many enthusiasts for Ossian who exalted him above Homer and his lyrical looseness above the time-honored epic conceptions.

While primitivistic conceptions of Homer and Ossian offered one alternative to the classical epic tradition, another was offered in a cult of the Italian "romantic" epic poets, Ariosto, Tasso, and their English follower, Spenser. Admiration for Ariosto and Tasso had never completely disappeared. About the middle of the century the theoretical defense of the structure and machinery of their poems, which had been undertaken in the Renaissance by many Italian and French critics, was revived in England, largely because of the need to defend the *Faerie Queene*.* Thomas Warton's first book, *Observations on the Fairie Queene* (1754), a loose collection of notes on sources, the history of allegory in England, chivalry, and so on, surrendered the cause of Spenser's "regularity" in order to argue that "the faculties of creative imagination delight us, because they are unassisted and unrestrained by those of deliberate judgment. . . . Though in the *Fairie Queene* we are not satisfied as critics, yet we are transported as readers." [50] Warton thus admits the validity of a criticism based on the classical canon of composition, but evades it by pleading for an aesthetics of effect, a "grace beyond the reach of art." Ariosto and Spenser "did not live in an age of planning" and must not be judged by "precepts they did not attend to." [51]

Richard Hurd, in his *Letters on Chivalry and Romance* (1762), is much bolder. He does not concede any lack of decorum in the *Faerie Queene*. He argues that the poem should be "read and criticized under this idea of a Gothic, not classical poem," [52] and that there is a unity of design, if not of action, in the whole. Hurd plays down plot and composition and emphasizes description and manners. He praises Tasso as an "original painter of the world of magic and enchantments." [53] He asserts the "preeminence of the Gothic manners and fictions, as adapted to the ends of poetry, above the classic," and has a good word to say even for medieval romances. He had hardly read real medieval romances and would

---

* Hurd knew Sir John Harington's "Apologie of Poetrie," prefixed to his translation of *Orlando Furioso* (1591); see entry in his commonplace book, quoted in Edwine Montague, "Bishop Hurd as Critic," unpublished dissertation, Yale University (1939), p. 124. He also knew defenses of Italian poetry by 18th-century Italians: Scipione Maffei, Baretti, etc. He may have read Jean Chapelain's "Dialogue de la lecture des vieux Romans" (1646), first printed in 1728. *Opuscules critiques*, ed. Alfred C. Hunter (Paris, 1936), p. 206. See Victor M. Hamm, "A Seventeenth Century French Source for Hurd's *Letters on Chivalry and Romance*," *PMLA*, 52 (1937), 820–8.

not have admired them as works of art. "The tales of fairy," he says, "are exploded, as fantastic and incredible. They would merit this contempt, if presented on the stage," but they have their place in the epic. The gallantry of feudal times seems to him more poetical than the "simple and uncontrolled barbarity" of the Greeks, and the enchanters and witches more "sublime, more terrible, more alarming than those of the classic fablers." [54] Folklore and romance motifs are justified by the new emotionalist theory of poetic effect, not by medievalism, if we mean by that sympathy for the Middle Ages. Percy was the first real student of medieval romances in England, and he tried laboriously to find traces of classical composition in one romance of the Gawain cycle, *Libius Disconius*.[55] Later in the century romances began to be studied seriously by Thomas Warton and Joseph Ritson: but even they treated them largely as pictures of manners, as documents, and at most as occasions for speculations on the migrations of folklore themes. Did these come from the Orient through the Arabs, or from Brittany or Wales or Scandinavia, or did they arise independently in all countries? [56]

The 18th-century decline of interest in conventional epic theory is also reflected by a growing interest in the novel as an art form. The novel labored under the suspicion of being a mere waste of time, a frivolous and even pernicious amusement. Many critics are definitely embarrassed in dealing with it. Hurd calls novels "hasty, imperfect, and abortive poems." [57] Henry Fielding, as a practicing novelist, tried to combat this attitude by arguing that the novel is an epic in prose. *Tom Jones* closely parodies devices and procedures of the Homeric convention. Fielding's excellent plotting and Richardson's sentimental morality helped to raise the novel in critical consideration. Late in the century Blair, Beattie, Mrs. Clara Reeve, and John Moore sketched its history and showed its continuity with the romances.[58] Classical epic theory more and more became a purely academic subject.

Similar shifts can be observed during the period in the theory of lyrical poetry. In neoclassical theory the lyric itself had excited little attention. Bacon and Hobbes, who considered plot as central for poetry, excluded the lyric completely: generally it was rated among the minor genres. Yet the great ode, because of its elevation of style and solemn subject matter, was classed among the higher

genres. In England Dryden's *Alexander's Feast* was admired as the
height of the sublime. The Pindaric ode, in practice a vehicle for
frigid and stilted rhetoric, became in theory the focus of many new
ideas. The ode was declared the oldest and most primitive genre
of poetry, for it was thought to preserve its original characteristics:
lively metaphorical language, deep feeling, pathos, rapture, a loose
composition, and a musical verse. In Collins and Gray the ode
assumes central place. Joseph Warton thought Gray's "Bard" truly
sublime, superior to anything in Pope.[59] Gray tried in his odes to
recapture the "oriental," elevated, sublime, metaphorical style
which was supposed to be nearest to the language of the heart and
thus to the poetry of unspoiled natural man. Figurative language,
which had always been recognized as particularly poetic, was newly
recommended by the belief that it was the original language of
man and the sign of a fiery imagination.[60] Lowth's *De sacra poesi
Hebraeorum* (1753) is a repertory of illustrations drawn from the
Bible. Daniel Webb tried to explain why imagery is the language
of passion, suggesting that imagination is literally heated with the
animal spirits. He commented at length and with considerable
subtlety on Shakespeare's similes, metaphors, and figures.[61] The
shift of emphasis to the expression of feeling in poetry and the
growing interest in world-wide folk poetry brought about at last,
late in the century, a definite dethronement of the drama and epic
in favor of the lyric. Sir William Jones, the distinguished oriental-
ist, repudiated imitation precisely because poetry was to him
mainly lyrical poetry. "The finest parts of poetry, music and painting, are expressive of the passions, and operate on our minds by
sympathy. The inferior parts of them are descriptive of natural
objects, and affect us chiefly by substitution." [62] Jones was an exception in England: no English writer went to the lengths of
Herder or Leopardi in installing the lyric as the center of poetry.

Still, a great revolution in the concept of poetry was prepared in
the second half of the century: feeling in neoclassical theory had
often been perhaps somewhat less than feeling, in that it was
broadly generalized and its character fully prescribed. But feeling
was soon to be translated into personal emotion, "sincerity," even
autobiographical confession. In England this view was completely
victorious only in the 19th century. During the 18th century metaphor, which had always been the proper ornament of a poem, be-

came its central principle, and vividness and particularity replaced generality as the main demand made on poetry. The emotional effect which had always been the aim of rhetoric and of some poetry became, under the influence of sentimentalism, the *sine qua non* of all poetry, even of all literature. Romantic subjectivism was only a step away.

The shift to the emotionalist conception of poetry was generally European, as Diderot and Herder testify. But the new historicism was at first mainly an English contribution, though it was later developed more fully by the Germans. It was no accident that the new historicism arose in England, where modern aesthetics also first arose. Aesthetics meant a turn to individuality, to the concrete response of the individual: it prepared the way to a true understanding of history, not as something dead and schematic, but as a living process. This new historicism first gave increasing attention to the setting and conditions of poetry. It amounted to a plea (which had many precedents) that we can "never completely relish, or adequately understand, any author, especially any ancient, except we constantly keep in our eye, his climate, his country and his age." [63] This is not, as is often asserted, the historical method in the full meaning of the word. This only intensifies the classical recommendation of a proper regard for decorum and circumstance. But a natural consequence of this awareness of the influence of environment was an increased skepticism as to the permanence of critical standards. Goldsmith, for instance, demanded that "English taste, like English liberty should be restrained only by laws of its own promoting." Criticism must "understand the nature of the climate and country &c. before it gives rules to direct taste. In other words, every country should have a national system of criticism." [64] Such broadmindedness led to greater and greater tolerance for different types of art and finally, in the 19th century, to a paralyzing relativism.

The emphasis on environment became especially significant when the "manners" which determine a work of art were analyzed in detail. At first the most remote explanation was the most widely favored. Sir William Temple's theory about the connection between the variable English weather and the odd humor of Englishmen [65] was one of the earliest instances of the explanation of literature by climatic conditions. Later the older idea that poetry—

especially highly imaginative poetry—flourished best in the South received a rude shock from the "discovery" of the northerner Ossian. Gray admitted that "imagination dwelt many hundred years ago in all her pomp on the cold and barren mountains of Scotland" and thus could not be the result of heat.[66] But Hume and Kames became quite skeptical of the whole business of explaining poetry by climatic conditions.[67]

The climate theory becomes much more acceptable when it is reinterpreted to include geographical conditions. Bishop Lowth's *De sacra poesi Hebraeorum* tried to explain the particular character of Hebrew poetry by the influence of the surrounding objects of nature: he traces Palestinian landscape in the imagery of the Bible. Robert Wood traveled in the Near East and, in *An Essay on the Original Genius and Writings of Homer* (1769), studied the topography of the site of Troy, concluding that Homer was "the most constant and faithful copier after nature." [68]

Political conditions too were invoked to explain literature. The ancient association of liberty and letters was firmly implanted in the minds of Englishmen during their own Glorious Revolution. In the later 18th century Kames observes that "taste could not long flourish in a despotic government." [69] The whole time is full of unfavorable comparisons between Italy, Spain and France, and free England in respect to all aspects of civilization, including literature. Yet Hume and a few others saw that the simple equation of liberty and letters is refuted by history. The greatness of the ages of Louis XIV or Leo X can hardly be ascribed to freedom.[70]

But mostly the history of literature was explained by a theory which is usually, though somewhat misleadingly, called "primitivism." It assumes that "simple manners foster poetry," that poetry thus flourished best in early societies and that it has since inevitably declined. The conception of this simple society varies considerably with individual authors. Among writers in English, Blackwell's book on *Homer* (1735) was the fountainhead of the view that Homer was a primitive bard, but Blackwell suggested that Homer's society was not at all savage but rather in a state of transition, when manners were passing from the stage of rudeness to the polite stage.[71] This golden moment of the emergence of man from the primitive was found by others in the Elizabethan age. Hurd's dialogue "On the Golden Age of Queen Elizabeth" (1759) describes it in these terms, and Thomas Warton takes over Hurd's ideas. The defenders of Ossian were naturally more enthusiastic about more primitive times. Blair thought that the "times which we call barbarous are most favorable to the poetical spirit," and that "imagination is most glowing and animated in the first ages of society." [72] William Duff, another Scottish enthusiast for Ossian and Homer, went to greater extremes in praising the "early and uncultivated periods of society" as "peculiarly favorable to the display of original poetical genius." [73] Robert Wood, in trying to account for the greatness of Homer, drew upon his observations in North Africa to offer Arab society as an analogy for the Homeric.

What is most striking to a modern observer is the complete confusion about the states of society supposed to be primitive. The early stages of Greek civilization, the society depicted in the Old Testament, contemporary Arabian society, the feudal Middle Ages, and the dim time in which Ossian was supposed to have lived are all considered the same. This sociological simplification is matched by the crudity of the 18th-century dichotomy between natural poetry and art poetry. This contrast dates back to the Renaissance, but only in the 18th century was natural poetry identified with a universal folk poetry in which everything which deviates from the Latin-French tradition was lumped together: the Bible, Homer, Ossian, the Welsh bards, the few Lapland and Indian songs known at the time, the Scottish ballads, and even chivalric romances. Thomas Percy seems to have been the first to entertain the explicit conception of primitive poetry as a whole. He planned a collection of *Specimens of the Ancient Poetry of Different Nations,* and his lifework consisted in various attempts to carry out this plan. His translations from the Chinese and from Runic poetry, his paraphrase of the Song of Songs as a "sample of Hebrew poetry," his *Reliques of Ancient English Poetry* (1765), which contains not only ballads but many Elizabethan lyrics and scenes from Shakespeare, his specimens of "Moorish" romances, his transcriptions of chivalric romances, and the planned edition of Surrey [74]—all point to this conception of a substantial identity of primitive poetry. His dissertations on the *Ancient English Minstrels,* the *Origin of the English Stage,* and the *Ancient Met-*

rical Romances are all contributions to a history of such poetry, however halfhearted and cautious his own taste remained and however apologetic he felt toward his work.[75]

The same conception underlies Gray's antiquarian and critical activity. Gray planned a history of English poetry which would have provided a wide background in primitive poetry. Gaelic (Welsh and possibly Erse) and Gothic (Scandinavian and Anglo-Saxon) poetry was to be discussed at length.[76] Gray was rather an antiquary than a critic. He studied the history of versification closely and tried to show that rhyme came from the Welsh, though later he suggested that it "might begin among the common people, and be applied only to the meaner species of poetry." [77] He made some attempt to set parts of his history down on paper. We have a descriptive piece on Lydgate and another on Samuel Daniel, but the whole remained only a plan.[78] Gray pronounced often on his reading and made many criticisms of the poetry of his friends in his fine letters, yet he knew that he was not a critic. "You know I do not love, much less pique myself on criticism and think even a bad verse as good a thing or better, than the best observation, that ever was made upon it." [79]

But if poetry was originally primitive, some attempt had to be made to account for its evolution. Most writers assumed a process of inevitable decline of imagination with the growth of civilization. John Brown attempted quite systematically to give a "conjectural" history of poetry in his *Dissertation on the Rise, Union and Power, the Progressions, Separations and Corruptions of Poetry and Music* (1763). Brown collects examples for primitive poetry from all over the world, from Greece, Ossianic Scotland, Bardic Ireland, Scaldic Iceland, Peru, India, China, and America. Among all nations, Brown declares, there obtained an original "union of song, dance and poetry." Verse came before prose because the "natural passion for melody and dance throws necessarily the accompanying song into a correspondent rhythm." With the advance of civilization the arts break up into their several kinds. At first they "lie confused, in a sort of undistinguished mass, mingled in the same composition." The original union of poet, musician, and legislator would, however, dissolve, and the individual arts arise. Poetry would at first be the confusion of all genres, a "rapturous mixture of hymn, history, fable and mythology." Then the individual kinds would arise: first lyrical poetry, odes and hymns, because "these in their simple stage, are but a kind of rapturous exclamations of joy, grief, triumph, or exultation." Then the epic would come, and finally the drama. The later process is again one of fission, specialization, and, in Brown's eyes, degeneration caused by the general corruption of manners. Obviously Brown derives his history of the genres from the study of Greek poetry, from the sequence of Orphic hymns, Homeric epics, and Attic tragedies. But he looks for confirmation elsewhere and tries to fit Hebrew poetry and Ossian into the same scheme. The Renaissance must be condemned on Brown's terms. During that period the three greater kinds of poetry were divorced from music: tragedy became "the languid amusement of the closet," odes were written "that cannot be sung," epics which can now only be read and not recited. The whole history of poetry appears as a single process of disintegration and a gradual dissolution of the original ideal union of the arts. Brown himself hoped to reverse the course of events and therefore traced the several modern attempts to reunite poetry and music: the song, the opera, the motet, and the oratorio. But he condemns them all as imperfect and sees hope only in odes in the style of Dryden, with musical accompaniment, supplying a dreary example of such an ode himself.[80]

Brown's scheme, certainly influenced by Rousseau, was varied by many other writers of the time: for instance, Adam Ferguson, who in an *Essay on the History of Civil Society* (1767) described the history of literature as a progressive division of labor. Brown and Ferguson with their speculative schemes anticipate the evolutionary historians of the 19th century, Brunetière and John Addington Symonds. But their concrete knowledge of literary history was weak. While grasping evolution and change in relation to society, they lost all hold on individuality. Literature is handled by them as a mass seen from afar, an almost anonymous lump.

Similar schemes also underlie the works of the best practical critics of the time: the Wartons and Richard Hurd. Joseph Warton's *Essay on Pope* (1756, 1782) combines a theory of history which assumes a decline of imagination into prose, with a parallel theory of genres and a classification of human faculties. Warton has a strong feeling that poetry must and cannot help but express the real sentiments of an age, and that it must be personally, even autobiographically, sincere. He thus thinks that Pope could not have written an epic or that his projected *Brutus* would have been a failure because Pope is "disqualified for representing the ages of heroism, and that simple life, which alone epic poetry can gracefully describe." Modern poets in general are handicapped by the unheroic age in which they live and would do better to "treat of things, not men," to "deliver doctrines, not display events." [81] Didactic and descriptive poetry is justified as a necessity of the time, as a result of the necessary decline of imagination. Pope is the poet of a late prosaic time, though he is unsurpassed in the kind of poetry now possible. This historical scheme presupposes a ranking of poetry according to the faculty to which it is addressed and by which it is presumably produced, and a hierarchy of genres which basically is the ancient one, exalting epic and tragedy. The greatest English poets are Shakespeare, Milton, and Spenser, because they wrote tragedies and epics, are sublime and pathetic, and appeal to the heroic and imaginative in man. "The sublime and the pathetic are the two chief nerves of all genuine poesy." Pope belongs to a second class of poets, the "men of wit and sense." "What is there transcendentally sublime and pathetic in Pope?" asks Warton, and his answer is almost entirely in the negative. *Eloisa to Abelard* and the *Elegy to the Memory of an Unfortunate Lady* are praised as pathetic; but on the whole, Warton argues, Pope's "grand characteristical talent is satiric or moral poetry," and "wit and satire are transitory and perishable, but nature and passion are eternal." Pope's admirers must be content to consider him "the great poet of reason, the first of ethical authors in verse." [82] Warton is far from disparaging Pope: one could argue that it is hardly possible to give him a higher rank, just below the greatest. Still, the general effect of the book was to widen the gulf between the poet of imagination and the poet of sense, between what Warton calls (very differently from our use) "pure poetry" and satirical and moral poetry. The whole book constitutes a defense and reassertion of Warton's early preface to his own *Odes* (1746). There he complained that the fashion of "moralizing in verse has been carried too far," and he announced that "invention and imagination are the chief faculties of a poet" and that the *Odes* are "an attempt to bring back poetry into its right channel." [83] Warton, like John Brown, did not worry over the fact that, according to his own concept of history, his attempt was foredoomed to failure.

Hurd's *Letters on Chivalry and Romance* is based on an identical historical scheme. Like Warton, Hurd is far from subverting the accepted hierarchy of genres, as is obvious from his other writings, e.g., his "Dissertation on the Provinces of the Drama" (1753). He is firmly neoclassical in his treatment of imitation and kinds, and by temperament he is more systematic and scholastic than his close associates. Yet the *Letters* fit the defense of Spenser, Ariosto, and Tasso into the new historical scheme: the decline of imagination with the growth of civilization. "What we have gotten by this revolution . . . is a great deal of good sense. . . . What we have lost, is a world of fine fabling." [84] Hurd somewhat nostalgically looks back into the poetical past, but he does not, and on his principles cannot, advocate a return to it. He wants to extend the range of feeling, to justify his own intense admiration for Spenser and his Italian models. He closely paraphrases Joseph Warton when he makes the contrast between "the greater, and what may be called pure poetry" of Spenser and Milton and the "humbler sorts of poetry, chiefly satiric and ethic" of Dryden and Pope.[85] Bishop Hurd is a man of his age, proud of its accomplishments and progress, but at the same time he deplores the decay of imagination and would like to restore the appreciation of the "romantic" Italian poets. Like many in his time he could not escape an unreconciled dualism between head and heart. He wrote much criticism which accepts the reigning system and he never ceased to enjoy and admire Dryden and Pope, but on the other hand he recognized something which eluded the system: a greater imaginative poetry in the past.

Hurd influenced Thomas Warton, whose *History of English Poetry* (1774–81) could be described as an exemplification of the same historical scheme and of the same division in the mind of its author. It has some unique merits: it is the first history of English literature of any scope and it combines historical sense with a critical regard for the individual work, at least in theory and ambition. Warton was somewhat overwhelmed by his materials, floundering in a mass of quotations from manuscripts, out-of-the-way books, and information on bibliography and biography. His *History* is loosely organized. Yet it has a basic scheme and conception which is the best elaboration of the double allegiance we have described in his brother and in Hurd. Warton believes in progress, from "rudeness to elegance." He asserts that we "look back on the savage conditions of our ancestors" with a "triumph of superiority." [86] He constantly traces an advance in versification toward the ideal of regularity of his own time. He disparages the grotesque, the fantastic, and the tasteless, and deplores the absence in older times of canons of composition, correctness, selection, and discrimination.[87] There was thus no insincerity or later conversion in Warton's "Verses on Sir Joshua's Painted Window at New College," written in the year (1782) after publication of the third volume of the *History*. Warton sings of being brought "back to truth again,"

> To truth, by no peculiar taste confined,
> Whose universal pattern strikes mankind:
> To truth, whose bold and unresisted aim
> Checks frail caprice, and fashion's fickle claim.[88]

But, side by side with this belief in progress and universal truth (a progress toward the universal truth of classicism), Warton had a genuine taste for the curious and wild, the strange and imaginative, the Gothic and extravagant. His admiration for Chaucer, the Scottish Chaucerians, much in the chivalric romances, Dante (with some reservations), Spenser, and Milton's minor poems was genuine and deep. Believing in progress, he accepts the view of the decline of imagination since the early stages of society. "Ignorance and superstition, so opposite to the real interests of human society, are the parents of imagination." Echoing Hurd's *Letters*, Warton recognized that the modern world had gained "much good sense, good taste, and good criticism." "But, in the mean time, we have lost a set of manners, and a system of machinery, more suitable to the purposes of poetry than those which have been adopted in their place. We have parted with extravagancies that are above propriety, with incredibilities that are more acceptable than truth, and with fictions that are more valuable than reality." [89] Warton did not really prefer fiction to reality, but he wanted to argue as Hurd had done that a certain kind of fiction is more valuable than reality for the uses of poetry. He shared his brother's and Hurd's regret that chivalry and folk mythology could not be used by modern poets because they no longer carried conviction.

This double point of view allows Warton a glorification of the age of Queen Elizabeth as the age which successfully combined imagination and reason. Despite the degree of civilization that age enjoyed, there was still alive a "degree of superstition sufficient for the purposes of poetry, and the adoption of the machineries of romance." [90] Criticism did not yet restrain imagination, satire did not curb the flights of fancy, science had not yet blighted all illusions.

In Warton's view English poetry (and presumably all poetry) passed through three stages: imagination, imagination and reason synthesized, and judgment and correctness, which seemed to him beneficial from the point of view of the social advance of humanity even though it might spell death to imagination and poetry.

Still Warton had not lost hope for poetry. In spite of his rigid scheme with its fear of a further decline in imagination as a result of the further growth of civilization, he hoped that the process might be reversed. He looked upon the contemporary Miltonic revival as a "visible revolution," an attempt to reintroduce "fiction and fancy, picturesque description, and romantic imagery" without sacrificing the "selection and discrimination, address and judgment" which seemed to him the gains of modernity.[91] Somewhat uneasily Warton and his associates kept a double point of view: trust in the progress of modern civilization and even of modern good taste, and yet regret for the "world of fine fabling."

Only on the Continent, in the German *Sturm und Drang*, were the consequences understood and the compromise rejected. From a present-day point of view, however, the English compromise will appear not without its attraction or even rational justification. It is animated by a truly historical spirit of tolerance and a recognition of the impossibility of a return to the conditions which produced early poetry. In a different situation and in different terms we are apt to share this compromise today. Our historicism, which countenances the most diverse kinds of art, from prehistoric cave paintings to Picasso, from Homer to Eliot, from plain chant to Stravinsky, is an all-embracing eclecticism. It has the same implications of sterility which we feel in the antiquarian critics of the 18th century. Today they rightly elicit great sympathy and interest, for they represent the beginnings of an attitude which seems to have become almost universal in the academic world of our time.

ITALY plays a large and significant part in the history of criticism: in the Renaissance, in the early 18th century, and again later in the 19th (De Sanctis) and early 20th century (Croce). But in the later 18th century its role seems to be comparatively minor.

Gian Vincenzo Gravina's *Della ragion poetica* (1708) is one of the best formulations of the neoclassical doctrine. Poetry is truth disguised in a popular semblance, a science in which the abstract is expressed in concrete form. "Poetry is a sorcerer, but a salutary one, and a delirium which dissipates our follies."[1] Gravina opposed slavish adherence to the rules and deplored the extreme intellectualism of some of the French Cartesians. In an early piece, *Discorso sopra l' Endimione* (1691), he even pronounced against the concept of genre, though later he wrote on the theory of tragedy.* On the whole it is difficult to see how he could have been hailed as a forerunner of romanticism. He was a jurist, basically a rationalist, who saw in the poet a man who gives body to concepts and uses the sweetness of song to civilize men.[2]

His contemporaries, such as the learned scholar Ludovico Antonio Muratori (1672–1750), belong roughly to the same tradition, which attempted to revive Renaissance poetics after what seemed to them the aberrations of the baroque. They talk about good taste as did the French, defend the marvelous, and uphold imagination: i.e., the power of invention, the right of fiction, of visual representation, of making the improbable probable—positions

---

* "Discorso sopra l'Endimione di Alessandro Guidi," in *Prose*, pp. 249 ff., esp. pp. 260–1. Croce, in *Estetica*, Eng. trans., pp. 444–5, and M. Fubini, "Genesi e storia dei generi letterari," in *Tecnica e teoria letteraria*, ed. A. Momigliano (Milan, 1948), pp. 189 ff., make much of this passage, but it seems to me little more than a plea for exceptions and novelty. Later, Gravina wrote "Della tragedia" (1715), *Prose*, pp. 150 ff., without qualms.

which had been defended by all good neoclassicists. They hardly
differed from the more liberal defenders of the neoclassical creed
abroad and they did not exercise a distinct influence outside of
Italy. The one very tenuous contact was the reception given to
Pietro di Calepio by Bodmer, the Swiss critic, for his little treatise,
Paragone della poesia tragica d'Italia con quella di Francia (1732).
Calepio anticipated some of Lessing's arguments against the
French stage, not appealing, of course, to romantic freedom, but to
the text and true meaning of Aristotle against the French rules.[3]

But while the neoclassical tradition was re-established in Italy,
there lived and wrote in Naples a philosopher, Giambattista Vico
(1668–1744), who expounded a very different concept of poetry and
literary history in his *Scienza nuova* (1725). Poetry is resolutely
opposed to the intellect, associated with the senses, identified with
imagination and myth. Poets belong to the early heroic ages of
mankind when people spoke a language of metaphor, of real signs.
Vico, apparently for the first time, taught that poetry is a necessity
of nature, the first operation of the human mind.[4] Homer, who
is only a name for the Greek nation telling its history in song, and
Dante, the Homer of the new barbarism of the Middle Ages, are
the representatives of the poetic ages, while modern times can only
produce rhetoricians, *literati*, philosophers.[5] Nature, not art—
imagination, not reason—seems to sum up Vico's theory.

This astonishingly novel and radical concept of poetry and its
history is intricately woven into a stupendous speculative scheme
of a philosophy of history and mankind: its significance was not
recognized until Benedetto Croce expounded it in his *Estetica*
(1902). Croce, who sees in Vico his immediate spiritual ancestor
and the founder of aesthetics, emphasizes what he considers the
fruitful motifs and consistently minimizes or ignores other elements which make Vico's doctrines far less clear-cut than they
appear in his brilliant exposition.[6] Vico was actually unable to
distinguish between poetry and myth, and his "poetic wisdom" is
not Croce's intuition but simply inferior knowledge. In practice,
his conception of poetry is not so distant from that of his com-
patriot Gravina as it would appear. "Fantastic truth" is an inferior
kind of truth available to primitive societies, and poetry is by no
means autonomous but was the main educative force leading men
out of barbarism.[7]

Granting the Crocean interpretation, one may still have one's doubts as to whether the complete divorce of poetry from the intellect and the identification of poetry with language are such merits. One must accept Croce's own system to see in Vico the founder of aesthetics. To a non-Crocean Vico is rather a philosopher of history, even a sociologist who attempts to construct a scheme of historical evolution. His grasp of concrete literature seems weak: Homer and Dante are treated only as symbols for the heroic ages he was studying. Vico's interpretation of Dante, which brushed aside theology and allegory and saw the sublimity of his imagination, was, while limited and debatable, Vico's most important insight into a work of art.[8]

In discussing Vico in a history of criticism, we cannot ignore the fact that he had little recognition or influence in his own century.[9] This surely does not lessen his greatness, yet it does lessen his historical role. There are some echoes of Vico in Italian 18th-century criticism, but they are faint and never show any grasp of his revolutionary importance. The attempts to prove his influence in France, England, and Germany during the 18th century, especially in aesthetics, have all failed. There is not a shred of evidence that he was read by any Englishman before Coleridge, who was lent a copy of *Scienza nuova* by Dr. Prati in 1825.[10] Yet even Coleridge did not see his full significance for aesthetics and literary theory. There seems to be no evidence that Condillac or Rousseau could have drawn directly on Vico. In Germany Vico's influence also comes very late: Hamann ordered a copy of the *Scienza nuova* in 1777, when his ideas had all been formulated. Goethe got a copy in Naples in 1787 but seems not to have read it. Herder vaguely refers to Vico as late as 1797 and 1800 as a "very sensible philosopher of humanity." [11] No argument or proof can be produced that Vico was understood abroad in his century: his difficult, crabbed style, the obscure plan, and the whole air of 17th-century obsolete erudition were forbidding.

The similarities which can be found between Vico's teachings and those of several contemporaries must be explained by common antecedents and by a common situation. Nobody reproduced the peculiar pattern of his thought, but individual ideas, which seem characteristically Vichian, were well known before. The distinction between the poetry of art and the poetry of nature goes back to the Renaissance. It is, for instance, fully elaborated in Francesco Patrizzi's *La deca disputata* (1586). Puttenham and Samuel Daniel assume it and it was constantly debated in the 17th century. Fontenelle's *Traité de la poésie en générale* is an exact counterpart to Vico's historical scheme, though with opposite evaluation. Fontenelle hails the end of the age of "fabulous and material images," the end of inspiration and talent, and hopes for a future poetry of the intellect.[12] Vico's conception of Homer, which completely dissolves his personality, is not paralleled elsewhere; still, the idea of Homer as a primitive poet has its sources in antiquity and was commonplace enough at that time for Englishmen, such as Richard Bentley and Henry Felton, to refer in 1713 to Homer's "loose songs" and "strings of ballads." [13] Vico's influence on aesthetics and criticism in the 18th century was nonexistent.

Italian criticism of the second half of the 18th century must be described as largely derivative, not so much from its own tradition as from the French and English criticism of the time. Whenever it emancipates itself from the doctrines of Gravina, it does so only to absorb the ideas of English empiricism and French sensualism. Late in the century the German revival of neo-Platonic aesthetics, by Winckelmann and the painter Rafael Mengs, began also to affect Italy.

The most prominent poets of the second half of the century, Parini and Alfieri, are of little importance as critics. Giuseppe Parini gave the lectures *Dei principi delle belle lettere* (1773-75), echoing the commonplaces of the time: good sense and reason, pleasure and taste, the motivation of poetry in boredom, its end in moral elevation and social utility, its means as touching and moving the reader. Parini was apparently one of the first Italians to abandon rationalism, to appeal to the pleasure principle and sensuous impression, and to speak of sincere emotion. But that was news only in Italy. Basically Parini was still a moralist who believed in "the natural sentiment of men, common to all and not subject to any change." [14]

Vittorio Alfieri, the great tragedian, propounded views on the role of literature which are hardly very new yet are surprising for their fervent tone and almost prophetic rapture. *Del principe e delle lettere* (1788) is really a dithyramb or diatribe (one is not sure which) in favor of the old identification of liberty and letters. Alfieri contrasts the Prince, the ruler, with the man of letters, and wants no dealings whatever between them. Any court literature, any acceptance of patronage, any subservience to authority is treason, "la trahison des clercs," as we would say with Julien Benda. Alfieri reviews the history of literature from this single point of view: Virgil, Horace, Tasso, Ariosto, and Racine all had patrons and were thus corrupt; only Dante (and, we understand, Alfieri) were really and totally free. Alfieri's glorification of the passionate genius, of natural impulse, seems to have romantic overtones, but actually it is rather the survival of aristocratic pride, humanist aloofness, a last hymn to the vainglory of the *vates* thirsting for eternal fame.[15]

The more professional poetics and criticism of the time were largely traditional or variations of the new empirical theories. Thus Cesare Beccaria's *Ricerche intorno alla natura dello stile* (1770) is based on the view that all our ideas are derived from sensations, and that therefore the best style will be the one which evokes the most pleasurable sensation.[16] It is an argument in favor of a vivid concrete style and against the abstract rhetorical tradition inherited from the Renaissance. The opposite tendency toward an aesthetics of the ideal was revived late in the century largely by theoreticians of the fine arts such as Milizia, who was under the influence of Winckelmann and Mengs. A little known Abbé, Giuseppe Spalletti, presented in a small *Saggio sopra la bellezza* (1765) a version of the theory of ideal beauty, but admitted, in a subordinate position, the "characteristic," the peculiar, the individual.[17] The term "characteristic," known since Shaftesbury, found much favor in Germany with Sulzer (who seems to have picked it up from Spalletti), Hirth, Heinrich Meyer, Goethe, and finally with Friedrich Schlegel and Hazlitt. Bosanquet even calls it "the central idea of modern aesthetic," [18] though in itself it seems only a new term for the main problem of imitation.

The same struggle between the old classicism and the new empiricism can be illustrated in the practical criticism of the time. The literary polemics reflect, as everywhere, the emergence of a new taste. Saverio Bettinelli, in his *Lettere virgiliane* (1757), criticized Dante according to the taste and general arguments of Voltaire. The *Divine Comedy* is a poem "without action, of goings and comings," full of bad taste, with a few fine passages.[19] Virgil,

Petrarch, and Racine are his heroes: a new modern literature is to emerge free from what Bettinelli considered the dead hand of the past. Gasparo Gozzi's *Difesa di Dante* (1758) rehearses the arguments for Dante's sublimity, for his "gallery of pictures," and tries to find the unity of the poem in the person of the poet: if the *Commedia* had been called *Danteide,* the neoclassical consciousness of Gozzi would have been satisfied.[20] The *Difesa* is no revolutionary document: it seems characteristic that Pope's *Essay on Criticism* appears in Italian translation as an appendix.

Only two critics stand out as real personalities and innovators: Melchiorre Cesarotti and Giuseppe Baretti. Cesarotti (1730–1808) has been called the Italian Herder, and at first sight his position is not dissimilar. Cesarotti translated, or rather adapted, Ossian in Italian unrhymed verse, which recently has again found fervent admirers.[21] A letter Cesarotti wrote to Macpherson shows his preference for the "poetry of nature and sentiment" over the "poetry of reflection and mind." [22] The notes to Ossian praise him as a genius of wild nature and quote Vico that "rough and passionate men singularize and speak by sentiments," calling this the most essential quality of poetic language.[23] Like Herder, Cesarotti was acutely conscious of the diversities of national taste and the need for a philosophical history of literature.

But actually Cesarotti is not comparable to Herder, either in range or achievement or for his historical position. Though his translation of Ossian shows a new sensibility, Cesarotti never broke with the basic 18th-century concepts of poetry. He remained a man of the Enlightenment, similar in outlook to the Scots and English who prepare the way for Herder—Blair, Percy, Warton. He was not so much of a primitivist as Blair was in his praise of Ossian. Even the taste for Ossian is a taste for the civilized, the refined and delicate, which Cesarotti was delighted to find in the midst of barbarism. Though he had his misgivings about the complete authenticity of Macpherson's version, he could prefer Ossian to Homer, asserting that Homer is inferior to Ossian in humanity.[24] Cesarotti's own adaptation of the *Iliad, La morte di Ettore* (1789–94), is quite rationalistic and moralistic. Helen voices remorse for her betrayal of Menelaus, Hector is punished for his connivance at the passion of his brother Paris. Cesarotti was an anti-Greek modernist of some violence and even rancor. Though—or perhaps because—he was a professor of Greek and lectured extensively on the literature, he pronounces Lucian the only Greek author worth translation in extenso, and he has nothing but contempt for Greek philosophy.[25]

Cesarotti was not a primitivist and had no feeling for folk poetry, but he admired and liked the pathetic, the grandly emotional. Metastasio seems to him the greatest poet, and late in his life he was highly impressed, though deeply disturbed, by Foscolo's *Jacopo Ortis*.[26] Dante is chaotic, English tragedy irregular and sanguinary.[27] There is no contradiction between his translating three of Voltaire's tragedies and Ossian and his admiring Metastasio. They are all pathetic.

In his literary theories Cesarotti was likewise unusual only in the Italian context. Substantially he holds the views of Gravina, whom he praised fervently and often.[28] He rejects Vico's view of Homer, recognizing that in Vico primitive poetry is the "natural speech of men" and that his Homer is not that of the ancient and modern masters at all.[29] Similarly, late in his life he argued against the Wolfian theories of Homeric origins.

In an acute essay on the theory of tragedy, *Ragionamento sopra il diletto della tragedia* (1762), Cesarotti criticizes Dubos and Hume as well as Aristotle. Tragedy, he argues, causes real emotion and intermittently complete illusion. The fact that we know the events are unreal can only decrease our feeling of horror and pain but cannot change them into delight. The good effect of tragedy comes only from its moral, its plot. We seek it out because it is a "mirror of our dangers." [30] Cesarotti remained unsatisfied with the current psychological discussion which ignored the plot of tragedy and argued on the pleasure-pain principle. Though he violently disparages purgation and Aristotle's *Poetics,* he is more of an Aristotelian than he knew.

Cesarotti has other merits: his *Saggio sulla filosofia delle lingue* (1785) gives a liberal interpretation of linguistic change sorely needed in an Italy still worshiping archaic imitation for its own sake. In *Saggio sulla filosofia del gusto* (1785) Cesarotti impressively formulates the requirements of good taste: "a harmonized ear, an awakened fancy, a heart ready to respond with an instantaneous tremor to the smallest vibrations of sentiment, a readiness to transport oneself into the situation of the author, a quickness in seizing hidden signs and elusive flashes of expression," all of which he wants to see combined with discipline and knowledge and a "spirit superior to the miserable prejudices of the age, the nation, and the school." [31] There is merit also in the posthumous *Saggio sul bello* (1809), which shows in its scholastic classifications the new taste for the sublime and the terrible. Demosthenes, Tacitus, Bossuet, and Ossian are the examples of the grand and pathetic: [32] an incongruous list to our minds but congenial to the emotional eclecticism of the time.

Though Cesarotti's merits in a history of Italian criticism are high, he cannot be ranked among the great in the general European context. He was no genuine innovator or synthesizer but a man of compromise, of the middle road, and such men, however sensible, are never long remembered.

The one Italian critic of the later 18th century who is known, even today, in the English-speaking world is Giuseppe Baretti (1719–89). His long and close association with Dr. Johnson, his many compilations useful for the study of Italian language and literature (dictionaries and anthologies) make his name familiar to students of the 18th century. But few realize that Baretti has acquired or regained a great Italian reputation, largely for his periodical *La frusta letteraria* (*The Literary Whip*, 1763–65). He is at present being praised as "the critic," the critic of genius, and is newly edited, reprinted, anthologized, and much debated. Undoubtedly Baretti, in his Italian context, has great historical merits: he attacked, with satirical skill and moral fervor, the ruling literary and poetic fashions of the time—Arcadian pastoral poetry and its mummery, the orotund bookish prose derived from the imitation of Boccaccio, the pedantic inert learning of the academicians and Jesuits, the whole Italian literary decadence. His standards, though rarely formulated theoretically, are always those of "life," of common sense, utility, simplicity, truth, good morals. At his best Baretti was a writer of power and edge: he had a popular journalist's feeling for the urgent and useful; he had a gift for grotesque, racy, ebullient language. He created, in the wake of the English periodicals modeled on the *Spectator,* a fictional speaker, the rough soldier Aristarco Scannabue, behind whose mask he could speak his mind freely and frankly. His methods are those of a constant appeal to common sense, clarity, and simplicity. He takes a piece of conventional poetry and subjects it to questioning: how is it that the year is old and "white-haired" in December, presumably because it snows, while in January it is in its childhood though snow is still falling? [33] What is all this fuss about "laughing roses of sweet lips," "arrows from the quiver of Cupid," etc., etc? [34] How is it that the hero of Goldoni's comedy, *La bottega del caffé,* though a simple servant, displays medical learning, talks high-flown morals, and indulges in obscene allusions all at the same time? [35] What can one say for Goldoni's *Pamela,* where the humble peasant father of the girl turns out to be a Scottish peer and the English ladies drink rum in their tea? [36] It is all nonsense; it has nothing to do with real life. Even Dante, though admired in parts, "cannot be read rapidly and with pleasure"; it requires a "good dose of resolution and patience" to get through him.[37] Petrarch has false Platonic ideas about love and also needs to be studied to be well understood.[38] Boccaccio is immoral, "dirty," and besides, he initiated the vicious Latinized Italian which Baretti wants to replace with a living language.[39] Baretti rediscovered Cellini's autobiography and was one of the first to praise its "most vivid and picturesque" style.[40] *La frusta letteraria* thus belongs to the Enlightenment, which preached "things" instead of "words." Though Baretti's social and political outlook was conservative and extremely hostile to French philosophy—to Voltaire and Rousseau—he believes in utility, the common man, and a realism which is hardly able to distinguish between art and life.

All this was most important in the Italy of his time, but it is difficult to see Baretti's greatness as a critic in a general European context. What he says on theoretical questions was simple and common at that time: poetry must be inspired, genuinely felt, a critic must have some poetic feeling himself; poetry is "saying natural things, beautiful things, great things, many things, with simplicity, with energy, with enthusiasm." [41] Where he goes beyond such declarations, he is derivative and even copies Johnson: thus he takes the specific objections to pastoral poetry from Johnson and argues exactly in his terms against literal theatrical illusion and the unities of place and time.[42] He follows Johnson's *Preface* so closely that the claims made for the *Discours sur Shake-*

speare (1777), witty and telling as it is, as a "work of genius," seem grossly exaggerated.* It comes too late, after Johnson, Lessing, and even Herder, to add anything new to the arguments directed against the French system.

Nor can one say that Baretti's practical criticism is particularly well defined or fully argued. His innate realism and moralism is clear enough; but side by side there is his admiration for Ariosto, whom he considers the greatest Italian poet, for Berni and the whole burlesque tradition, and, most incongruously, for Metastasio.[43] Metastasio is praised for the "clarity and precision of his thought" and for his depiction of subtle "sentiments which even Locke or Addison could hardly express in prose." [44] No wonder that Baretti also praises many minor poets and poetasters of the time and does not see what is new and great in Goldoni because he dislikes his skepticism and morality.

Baretti, through the vicissitudes of his life, his travels to France, Spain and Portugal, his two long stays in England (1751–60, 1766–89), became a man of wide interests in other literatures than Italian. One of his first works was a translation of Corneille (1747), whom he continued to admire as the greatest of the French tragedians, the "poet for men," while he disparaged Racine as a "poet for the ladies." [45] Two of his publications, the English *Dissertation upon Italian Poetry* (1753) and the French *Discours sur Shakespeare* (1777), are polemics directed against Voltaire. In the early piece Baretti, rather timidly, defends Dante and Tasso against Voltaire's *Essay on the Epic Poetry,* showing that Voltaire knew little Italian and had no right to judge Baretti's compatriots. In the later pamphlet he attacks Voltaire for his judgment of Shakespeare. He again shows that Voltaire does not know much English, that he translates wrongly and maliciously, and that his opinion is of no value. He proves to his satisfaction Voltaire's "insolence, malignity, brutality and stupidity," but elsewhere admits that he is (after Johnson) the greatest writer of the century.[46] He had less patience with Rousseau: *Émile* seemed to him mere sophistry.[47] But he knows his French and French literature, within the limits of his age and his hatred of the *esprit philosophique.*

* Fubini and Binni praise Baretti far beyond his merits. Fubini, *Dal Muratori al Baretti,* p. 145: "il più audace e geniale scritto del nostro autore, il *Discours sur Shakespeare.*"

Baretti also knew much about Spanish literature and gave one of the first accounts of it in English. He described Calderón and Lope de Vega sympathetically, though with many neoclassical reservations.[48] Many English authors, including Shakespeare, Milton, Dryden, Pope, and Addison, were familiar to him. His conception of Shakespeare is clearly Johnson's. Shakespeare is praised for his profound knowledge of human nature, for his characters, which are not individuals but species, for his popular appeal.[49] But Baretti says little of the others, even of the admired and revered Dr. Johnson, whom he quotes in his *Frusta* and introduces in the disguise of Diogene Mastigoforo as the master of his Aristarco.[50] Much of Baretti's work in England was devoted to an exposition and description of Italian literature: there he wrote the *Dissertation upon Italian Poetry* (1753), for which he translated passages from Marino and Dante, a *History of the Italian Tongue* (1757), and other works. But his point of view was not that of 18th-century cosmopolitism: he rather thinks in terms familiar to Goldsmith and Herder, of national systems of literature and taste which are, will, and should remain different. "Since there have been two nations in the world, each speaking its own language, it has been impossible to find a taste common to the two." [51] He is content with this variety and delights in it, explaining the difficulties of translating, the divergences of meanings between the languages he knows. All of this, of course, does not prevent him from scolding Voltaire for upholding his special French taste, for he was a good Italian patriot, after all, and admired his Shakespeare.

Baretti, who is still untouched by primitivism and the love of folk poetry, presents thus an intermediate stage on the way to literary nationalism and its presumed synthesis in a conception of a varied world literature, as it was then being achieved in Germany by Herder. Besides, he represents in Italy the same turn toward realism and common sense which Johnson represents in England. But he is greatly inferior to Johnson in range, learning, and theoretical awareness. He will remain interesting rather as a character, a temperament, a readable lively polemist, amusing even when he indulges in clumsy verbal gambols and vindictive abuse.

THE DEVELOPMENT of literary criticism and theory in Germany differed in many respects from that of other Western countries. A long tradition of Renaissance and Baroque poetics died out in the early 18th century.[1] Johann Christoph Gottsched (1700–66), the commanding literary figure of the 30's and 40's, established a ponderous and pedantic local version of French neoclassicism with his *Kritische Dichtkunst* (1730). The older German literature had become either unknown or rejected as obsolete. No body of poetic texts was canonical as in France or demanded admission imperiously as did Shakespeare and Milton in England. Thus poetic theory remained an abstract academic exercise. Lessing was the first German critic of high standing, and even his importance was mainly at the level of theory.

The comparative isolation of German critics from concrete literature goes a long way to account for their intense preoccupation with general aesthetics. A new theory of literature was to bring about a new flowering of poetry. The main source of inspiration was the philosophy of Leibniz, which, in a watered-down version by Christian Wolff, dominated the German universities and effectively immunized them against the extremes of both Cartesian rationalism and Lockean empiricism. The very term "aesthetics" was invented in Germany during this period. Alexander Gottlieb Baumgarten (1714–62), in his *Meditationes philosophicae de nonullis ad poema pertinentibus* (1735), a small dissertation in crabbed Latin, suggested that there should be a "science of perception," an "aesthetic" (from the Greek *aisthanesthai*), and in 1750 he put the term *Aesthetica* on the title of the first volume of his system of the new science. The term is today accepted so completely and used so widely to designate almost anything that has to do with art that Baumgarten's specific meaning and theory have been lost sight of. This is due in part to the extreme rarity and in-

accessibility of these Latin writings (*Aesthetica* has never been
translated into any modern language) and in part to the scholastic
method of presentation and the sharply defined theoretical framework in which Baumgarten was clumsily moving, as if in heavy
armor. Baumgarten, however, has not only the merit of inventing
an important term. More definitely than anybody before him with
the possible exception of Vico, he distinguished the realm of art
from the realms of philosophy, morality, and pleasure. Aesthetics
is to him a "science of sensuous cognition." [2] Art and poetry are
"cognition," but not thought; they are nonintellectual knowledge,
"perception." Thus art does not convey theoretical or moral
truths; its knowledge precedes that of intellect. But it is not sensuous pleasure either, because it is a form of knowledge. If aesthetics,
as Baumgarten argues, were merely a science of perception, it
would have little to do with actual works of art. There are passages
in the *Aesthetica* which show that he conceived of his science as a
kind of general inductive logic; he treats of telescopes, barometers,
and thermometers as instruments of perception. He brings in actual works of art by defining a poem as a "perfect sensuous discourse." [3] Discourse, language, is the material of poetic art, and
perfection means, as Baumgarten explains in detail, two things:
clarity (which must not be confused with logical distinctness) or
vividness of representation, and what we would call organization,
totality, wholeness. Both of these requirements are pushed very
far, further than in any other theory of the time. The emphasis
on sensuous vividness and concreteness is so strong that we might
be tempted to consider Baumgarten's ideal of poetry almost
imagistic, and certainly it is, in part, a defense of descriptive
poetry, of the doctrine *ut pictura poesis*.[4] Baumgarten is simply following the logic of his reasoning when he finds personifications,
exemplifications, and especially proper names the most concrete
and hence the most poetic of all terms. He praises the catalogue of
ships in the second book of the *Iliad* as particularly poetic. His
emphasis on the concrete and individual is combined with a view
that the "interconnection is that which is poetic," that the poet is
like a maker or a creator, that a poem ought to be like a world—
ideas which seem to take up the praise of the creator-poet in Scaliger and Shaftesbury. But Baumgarten sharply distinguishes between "heterocosmic" or probable fictions and "utopian" or im-

probable fictions. "Heterocosmic" is another word for coherent, self-consistent, for any fiction which displays a "lucid order" and fulfills the demands of Aristotelian probability.[5] His formulas sound bolder today than they actually were.

Unfortunately Baumgarten was not able to hold to his central insight that art is neither *utile* nor *dulce*, neither instruction nor pleasure. The Leibnizian scheme of the mind, with its emphasis on the law of continuity and its hierarchy of faculties with reason as the highest, forced on Baumgarten the view that aesthetic knowledge is, after all, only an inferior form of logical knowledge: poetry, in many of his pronouncements, becomes only a preparation for philosophy; aesthetic knowledge an *analogon rationis, gnosologia inferior.*[6] Intellectualism won out.

A totally different tradition of aesthetic thought is represented by Baumgarten's contemporary, Johann Elias Schlegel (1719–49), an uncle of the two celebrated romantic critics. He was a clumsy writer and still very conventional in his taste. His comparison between Shakespeare and Andreas Gryphius (1741) shows a knowledge of only *Julius Caesar,* which is criticized for "cold scenes," violation of the unities, "low" words, and bombast. It is praised only for good characterization. But as a theoretician Schlegel had an unusual grasp of the difference between art and reality. In several papers he speculated on imitation, much more subtly than any of his contemporaries. Image and model, he argued, must be dissimilar. What is decisive is the effect, the emotional impact, and not the resemblance to reality. He attacks the notion of art as deceptive illusion and declares that we are never deceived in the theater. The French neoclassicists had defended the unities of time and place with naturalistic arguments. Schlegel defends them on the different ground that they allow concentration on action, on characters, on the passions. They support the "rapture" induced by a work of art.[7]

Neither Baumgarten nor Schlegel had much influence in his time. They were both still untouched by British empirical aesthetics. Baumgarten moves in the framework of Wolffian faculty psychology, Schlegel emerged slowly from the tutelage of Gottsched's pseudo-Aristotelianism. Neither had much to say about actual literary texts. Both seem hardly affected by the contemporary turn toward literary history.

The influx into Germany of two new critical motifs, empirical
aesthetics and historicism, was accomplished largely by Johann
Jakob Bodmer (1698–1783) of Zurich, who was the first of the great
Swiss intermediaries among the European nations; he brought the
form of the *Spectator* essay into German and translated *Paradise
Lost,* Homer, the old English ballads, *Hudibras,* and the *Dunciad.*
He was the first to defend Dante in Germany with historical arguments. He was the discoverer of German medieval literature: of
Wolfram's *Parzival* (1754), the *Nibelungenlied* (1757), the great
Minnesänger manuscript (1758–59). Though his editions and versions were shockingly inaccurate and incomplete by modern standards (he published at first only the second part of the *Nibelungenlied*), Bodmer had more than the antiquary's interest in unearthing
the past. He had a real appreciation of what he thought was the
fresh spontaneity of the *Minnesang,* the Homeric sublimity of the
Nibelungenlied, and even the scholastic metaphysics of Dante,
"without which Dante would not be Dante." [8] He represents a
new taste and, in Germany, the first lively feeling for history.

In literary theory Bodmer appeared as the bitter opponent of
Gottsched, and with his friend Johann Jakob Breitinger (1701–76)
composed a rival *Kritische Dichtkunst* (1740). Bodmer, whose
main role was that of an importer of ideas, thought of himself as a
useful merchant; [9] he adopted and expounded Addison's concept
of the pleasures of imagination, he introduced Blackwell's idea of
original metaphorical poetry, he learned something of Italian
aesthetics from his friend Pietro di Calepio,[10] he read Batteux and
Dubos. But he was more than a mere eclectic or middleman: he
assimilated Western theories of imagination to Leibnizian philosophy and thus made a bold defense of imaginative poetry. The
poet, according to Bodmer, is not an imitator of nature. Rather,
"he imitates the powers of nature in transferring the possible into
the condition of reality." [11] "Poetry always prefers to take the material of imitation from the possible rather than from the existing
world." [12] Leibniz' possible worlds become here an argument in
defense of "heterocosmic" poetry, which is not merely, as in Baumgarten, "probable poetry," but poetry using the Christian marvelous and even the "fairy way of writing." Like Blackwell, Bodmer
stresses the metaphorical character of poetic language: the whole
system of poetry must agree exactly in all its figurative connections;

the poet creates a whole in which all parts hang together. There should be a center to every work of art.[13] But these strikingly radical pronouncements, which show Leibnizian and Platonic elements and revive the ancient parallel between microcosm and macrocosm, are, in Bodmer's text, heavily modified by other traditional survivals. His recommendation of imaginative poetry remains in the service of Christian doctrine, of a religious didacticism which wants to defend the angels and devils in Milton and in Klopstock. The emphasis on wholeness, on metaphorical truth, is compromised by Bodmer's frequent surrender to mere allegory: he admires the didactic fable. His stodgy middle-class morality constantly warps his imaginative insights. In the context of German criticism he was a great precursor, an initiator.

The ideas of these three critics—Baumgarten, Schlegel, and Bodmer—seem to combine in the writings of Moses Mendelssohn (1729–86). Mendelssohn, his friend Lessing, and a third author, Friedrich Nicolai (1733–1811), created German periodical criticism and concentrated it in the new intellectual center, Berlin. Nicolai surveyed the state of German literature in 1755 with a severe eye. In 1759 he founded both a *Bibliothek der schönen Wissenschaften und freien Künste,* which lasted till 1805, and *Briefe, die neueste Literatur betreffend* (1759–65), where Lessing and Mendelssohn were the main contributors. Nicolai later acquired a bad reputation for his parody on *Werther* and his constant attacks on the German classics. Mendelssohn was a distinguished reviewer, though largely of learned publications rather than of imaginative literature. He was one of the early admirers of Shakespeare in Germany, but as a practical critic he usually kept to a middle road, disapproving of sentimentalism and *Sturm und Drang* as well as of old-style academic neoclassicism. The review of Rousseau's *Nouvelle Héloïse* [14] shows his distaste for emotional extravagance and artistic incoherence. But Mendelssohn's strength is in theory rather than in practical criticism. He picks up ideas from everywhere: from Baumgarten, from Dubos, from Kames; his emphasis is always psychological and moralistic. He tries to sketch a system of the arts [15] based on a distinction between arbitrary and natural signs, which he derives from Dubos. Poetry is a time-art, using arbitrary signs. Mere word painting, onomatopoeia, is childish. But the arts can combine—music with poetry and so on. What is common to the arts is the aim of "presenting perfection sensuously." Here the terms are derived from Baumgarten. But Mendelssohn speculates also on taste, on the beautiful and the sublime, on the pleasures of tragedy. He combines Leibnizian and neo-Platonic ideas with the empiricism he has learned from the French and English. His ideas on taste as a "faculty of approval," and of beauty as inducing a "quiet liking," remote from the desire to possess or utilize the object, prepare the way for Kant's views, at least terminologically.[16] His concept of genius also anticipates Kant's, as he stresses the need, in genius, of all faculties collaborating in perfection toward one single aim.[17] In strictly literary theory he discussed illusion in a way that was to prove fruitful. Coleridge's "willing suspension of disbelief" formulates strikingly what Mendelssohn had argued. "A certain capability is needed to surrender to illusion and to resign the consciousness of the present in its favor." "If we carry with us the intention to let ourselves be deceived in an agreeable manner, sensuous knowledge will do its usual job; from the signs of passion, from the signs of free actions we shall draw inferences as to intention and motivation and shall thus become interested in nonexistent persons. We take a real part in unreal actions and feelings because, for the sake of being pleased, we abstract intentionally from their unreality." [18] Here Mendelssohn develops suggestions made by Schlegel. In his theory of tragedy he was almost Lessing's collaborator.

Before we can approach Lessing himself, we must add Winckelmann to our roster of authors who make his background comprehensible. Johann Joachim Winckelmann (1717–68) was no literary critic or theorist, but his importance in the history of aesthetics is such that he influences all literary theory after him. It is not mainly the content of his doctrines but rather his total exaltation of the Greeks at the expense of the Romans and the Latin tradition, his tone, his fervor, and his style which color the whole course of German classicism. Herder and Goethe, quite justly, erected "monuments" in prose to his memory. Lessing begins his *Laokoon* with a saying by Winckelmann. Schiller is full of Winckelmann. Seen purely in terms of a history of ideas, Winckelmann can be described as reviving neo-Platonic aesthetics as he found it in Shaftesbury and in the Italian aestheticians of the 17th century. Beauty is divine: it is reflected in the beautiful minds, bodies, and statues of the Greeks and the best paintings of Italians such as Raphael. This beauty is ideal in the many senses available to Platonizing aesthetics: it had been an ideal realized in ancient Greece, under a serene sky, in a free society, where men and women could develop perfect bodies and harmonious minds. It is "ideal" in the sense that the artist concentrates what is found only rarely in reality, and it is ideal as an image in the mind of the artist, an inner vision, an idea. It is the ideal of "noble simplicity and quiet grandeur," [19] which inspired the paintings of David and the sculptures of Canova and Thorwaldsen. Winckelmann stands at the fountainhead of this movement,[20] which seems to us today rather dreary in its worship of abstract classical form. Winckelmann wrote a great deal about the pure, colorless, "indeterminate" ideal, and even indulged in speculations and recommendations concerning recondite allegories.[21] Yet both as a writer and as a person Winckelmann was really quite remote from all that. He was deeply influenced by sensualism: his experience of Greek statues was sensual, even sexual. His friendships with men were of the highly emotional "Platonic" variety, and he finally fell victim to a homosexual murderer. His whole experience of the classic is concrete, vital, organic. The way he described statues (however conventional the same statues may seem to us) is ecstatic and expressionistic. It is an evocation of emotional states which, transferred to literary criticism by Herder, changed the whole tenor of German writing on literature. To Winckelmann's sensualism we must add his genuine historicism: he had a feeling for and insight into the concrete reality of antiquity which went far beyond any merely antiquarian humanism. His *Geschichte der Kunst des Altertums* (1764), though very limited in its knowledge of genuine Greek sculptures, was the first internal history of any art, and by its method and conception it profoundly influenced the writing of literary history. Both Herder and Friedrich Schlegel wanted to become the Winckelmanns of literary history. In the *History of Ancient Art* Winckelmann not only describes and evokes individual works, not only tries to account by historical conditions for the unique greatness of Greek art, but quite consciously attempts to write an internal evolutionary history of style. The account of the styles of Greek sculpture,[22] while hardly more than sketching and guesswork, elaborates a parallel with the course of human life—its rise, maturing, decline, and end. He distinguishes four periods of Greek sculpture: the grand and high style of the earliest time, the beautiful of the Periclean climax, the decline with its imitators, and the end with the late Hellenistic mannerists.

Winckelmann's achievement is extraordinarily complex and openly contradictory. Platonizing neoclassicism with its ideal of quiet beauty, strong sensualism, and a new historicism struggle for supremacy in a body of work which anticipates many later German developments. The neoclassicism was to be developed in Lessing, Goethe, and Schiller, the sensualism in Herder and in such a crude but vigorous worshiper of the body as the novelist Wilhelm Heinse, the historicism in Herder and the Schlegels.

All the authors surveyed briefly in the present chapter precede the great flowering of literary theory in Germany. The first great literary critic, in a narrow sense, was undoubtedly Lessing.

Gotthold Ephraim Lessing (1729–81) has an enormous reputation as a literary critic, but a clear account of the reasons for his prominence in a history of European criticism is hard to find. There is no difficulty in accounting for his importance in the development of German literature, and Germans have constantly stressed his historical merits. He was, after all, the first great man of letters Germany produced in modern times: he has been called the founder of modern German literature and its liberator (i.e. the liberator from the dominance of French neoclassicism as represented by the mediocre Gottsched). Lessing certainly was a dramatist of considerable power, though hardly of enduring greatness. He was also a theologian and semiphilosopher who, especially in his last writings, formulated an important version of the optimistic philosophy of the Enlightenment, with surprising touches of mysticism and what the 18th century called "enthusiasm," in his *Education of the Human Race.* He was also a classical philologist and an archaeologist of great erudition, though this phase of his work is inevitably obsolete today. He was, besides, an aesthetician who, in the *Laokoon,* speculated importantly on the limits of the arts and the differences between poetry and painting. And finally he was a literary theorist and critic. All these varied activities are held together by the power of an obviously straightforward honest personality and an individual style of wonderful clarity and sobriety which is a joy to meet in reading German. Lessing's criticism is frequently encumbered by a heavy ballast of classical learning, and is sometimes marred by the demands of an existence absorbed in literary journalism and thus in the necessity of writing on ephemeral topics of the day and also by the acerbities and brutalities of contemporary polemical manners. But on occasions, and they are luckily not rare, he rises above these handicaps, suddenly breaking into a striking simile or a dignified assertion of his superiority to the times and his opponents. "Why do I detain myself with these chatterers? I will go my way and persist regardless of what the grasshoppers chirp by the roadside. Even a step aside to crush them is too much honor. The end of their summer is not long to await." [23]

Thus it is not easy to isolate Lessing's literary criticism from his manifold activities and its permanent value from its merely historical merit. One can understand George Saintsbury's feeling of disappointment in Lessing's criticism, especially since Saintsbury always wants pure literary criticism and means by it a body of literary judgments on specific authors. "There is nearly always something that Lessing prefers to literature, constantly as he was occupied with books. Now it is the theater; now it is art;—especially art viewed from the side of archeology; now it is classical scholarship of the minuter kind; now philosophy or theology; now it is morals; not unfrequently it is more, or fewer, or all of these things together, which engage his attention while literature is left out in the cold." [24]

It is true that we get in Lessing little practical literary criticism of important authors. There is a good deal of minute discussion of specific plays in the *Hamburgische Dramaturgie,* but, with very few exceptions, even those who are widely read have not and would not care to read the plays in question. The only exceptions are the plays of Voltaire and one play (*Rodogune*) by Corneille, and even they have few admirers today. In the *Laokoon* there is detailed criticism of Homer and Sophocles which is still of interest, and there are the scattered passages on Shakespeare, which are, however, quite disappointing if we judge them as criticism of Shakespeare. They merely echo the passage in Dryden on Shakespeare as the "poet of nature": Lessing had translated Dryden's *Essay of Dramatic Poesy* for one of his early collections, *Theatra-*

lische Bibliothek (1754–59). The famous 17th *Literaturbrief* (February 16, 1759) attacks Gottsched's introduction of a Frenchified theater into Germany with the claim that "we Germans rather fall in with the taste of the English than of the French"; prints the fragment of a scene from a supposedly ancient German tragedy of *Faust;* and advances the claim, astonishing for the time and place, that "Shakespeare is a much greater tragic poet than Corneille, though Corneille knew the ancients very well and Shakespeare scarcely at all." Corneille rivals the ancients in "mechanical contrivance" (*mechanische Einrichtung*), but Shakespeare in the "essential" (*das Wesentliche*). But beyond the statement that Shakespeare's plays have more power over our passions than any others except Sophocles' *Oedipus,* no reason is given for the superiority of the former, and even in the *Hamburgische Dramaturgie* no plays of Shakespeare are discussed. Lessing seems to have known *King Lear, Richard III, Othello, Hamlet,* and *Romeo and Juliet,* but he never goes beyond saying that *Othello* is "the most complete text book of this sad madness, jealousy" [25] and that *Romeo and Juliet* is "the only tragedy in which Love itself has collaborated," [26] whatever that may mean. The only more specific criticism of Shakespeare in Lessing is the comparison he makes between the ghost in Voltaire's *Semiramis* and the ghost in *Hamlet,*[27] and this is rather a discussion of poetic belief than practical criticism, and in its praise of the effect of the ghost it is derivative of Addison rather than an independent discussion. The praise of Shakespeare is mostly in rhetorical hyperboles, as in the famous passage where Lessing denies that it is possible to commit plagiarism on Shakespeare. "What has been said of Homer, that it would be easier to deprive Hercules of his club [i.e. by Donatus in *Vita Vergilii*] than him of a verse, can be as truly said of Shakespeare. There is an impress upon the least of his beauties which at once exclaims to all the world: I am Shakespeare's—and woe to the foreign beauty which has the self-confidence to place itself beside it." [28]

There is little more concrete criticism in his other discussions of English authors: something is said about Ben Jonson in connection with a discussion of the meaning of the English term "humor." *Every Man Out of His Humour* is described as "play without fable, where a crowd of the oddest fools appear one after

another, one does not know either how or why." [29] Once Lessing
quotes a fantastic scene about the hunger of some shipwrecked
people in Beaumont and Fletcher's *Sea Voyage*.[30] In order to disparage Thomas Corneille's tragedy of Essex, Lessing describes an
English play on the same subject by John Banks, *The Earl of Essex*
(1682), translating passages very freely into prose and pruning the
diction, which he considers "too vulgar or too precious, too creep-
ing or too bombastic." [31] This is, I believe, all the knowledge Lessing shows of the earlier English drama. He undoubtedly knew
more about the contemporary stage: there are references to Addison's *Cato*, which he liked only mildly—he would have rather
written Lillo's *Merchant of London*.[32] He was obviously acquainted with many English comedies like those of Colman and
Farquhar, and with bourgeois tragedies, but we have no extended
criticism of a single one. His extremely favorable introduction to
the translation of James Thomson's *Tragedies* (1756), which today
are rightly forgotten, is practically a translation from the English,
at least in regard to the judgments on the plays.[33]

Nor is an examination of Lessing's criticism of English poetry
more fruitful. There is an extended account of Pope's *Eloisa to
Abelard* in *Kritische Nachrichten* (1751), praising its tenderness,
and there is, of course, the famous answer by Lessing and Mendelssohn to the Berlin Academy's prize question on the metaphysics
of Pope. *Pope—ein Metaphysiker!* (1755) is a brilliant attack on
the claims made for intellectual coherence in Pope's *Essay on Man*,
and an analysis which sharply points to the difference between
Pope's eclecticism and Leibniz' metaphysical system. There are, in
the course of the *Laokoon*, references to Dryden's "musical painting" in the "Ode in Honour of St. Cecilia's Day" and—most interesting in view of T.S. Eliot's discussion—there are remarks on
Milton's *Paradise Lost* as an example of the nonvisual imagination,
or rather of the right kind of "progressive paintings," which are
not merely static descriptions. A note on Milton's blindness tries
to show that it had an effect on the way Milton described some
scenes—that the poet would, to use a modern term, "compensate"
for his lack of sight by elaborating on visual subjects.[34]

Lessing's criticism of English prose is not extensive or important. Like so many of his contemporaries, he thought very highly
of Richardson, while he disparaged Smollett's *Roderick Random* [35]

as being far below Lesage. There is a review highly praising Johnson's *Rambler* [36] without, however, mentioning his name. We must not forget that Lessing translated such books as Francis Hutcheson's *System of Moral Philosophy* (1756) and William Law's *Serious Call* (1756), and that he had a wide acquaintance with English critical and aesthetic literature. A study of his dramas reveals many English sources in the comedies (Farquhar) and bourgeois tragedies (Lillo), though the source hunting has obviously been overdone. But there is little literary criticism in the strict sense.

It would be easy to show this with respect to the other literatures too. It seems significant that Lessing, though he devoted much of his efforts to an attack on French drama, wrote no real discussion of either Racine or Molière. The references to Molière are quite unimportant, and when, in the *Hamburgische Dramaturgie,* Lessing had an opportunity to discuss *L'École des femmes* he merely repeated some information from a French source.[37] He seems to have preferred Destouches (of whom he compiled a *Life* early in his career) and Marivaux, and they certainly are the models of his own early comedies. He admired Diderot as a critic and playwright, but there is no extended discussion of the plays. Corneille and Voltaire draw Lessing's whole fire.

There is little on Italian literature: the Ugolino episode in Dante's *Inferno* aroused Lessing's disgust.[38] Ariosto's description of the fay Alcina is singled out in the *Laokoon* as an example of ineffective description of female beauty.[39] There is also an elaborate analysis of Maffei's tragedy *Merope,*[40] which aims to show the dependence of Voltaire's own tragedy on it and the absurdities of Voltaire's deviations. Maffei is treated with respect but hardly with great interest. Lessing has nothing to say on Gozzi or Goldoni, though he once started to translate one of the latter's plays.

He shows some interest in Spanish literature; he certainly knew, through a French translation, Lope de Vega's *Arte nuevo de hacer comedias,* and in the *Hamburgische Dramaturgie* he gives an elaborate description, with a very free and loose translation, of a 17th-century Spanish play, *El Conde de Sex,* by Antonio Coello (1652), which interested him as a contrast to Thomas Corneille's French and John Banks's English tragedies on Essex. Lessing also knew something of Cervantes and Calderón, but his Spanish was meager and faulty and his information mostly secondhand and inaccurate. One cannot speak of any criticism of Spanish literature or say that Lessing prepared the way for the Schlegels' appreciation of the Spanish drama.[41]

We expect more of Lessing's literary criticism of classical writers, but are hardly rewarded, though there are frequent discussions of philological points and many references. Lessing obviously admired Homer beyond any other author and uses him in the *Laokoon* as a constant illustration of what poetry can and should do: how he describes Helen by her effect on the old men, how he singles out one trait in an object by a single adjective, how he builds up an elaborate description like that of the shield of Achilles by telling of its manufacture. The praise of Homer is always generous, and the consideration, though never directed at the totality of either the *Iliad* or the *Odyssey*, is certainly literary in its attention to descriptive technique. The discussion of Greek tragedy is, however, disappointing as such. Aeschylus is hardly mentioned, and then Lessing commits the gross error of referring to the poet's *Perserinnen*, a confusion of the sex of the chorus which seems derived from D'Aubignac.[42] Sophocles fares somewhat better: Lessing compiled a very learned *Life of Sophocles*,[43] which has, however, no critical content; in the *Laokoon* he uses *Philoctetes* and the *Trachinians* as illustrations for the treatment of bodily pain in drama. The *Hamburgische Dramaturgie* contains, in different contexts, speculations on some of the lost plays of Euripides and on the reasons why Aristotle called him "the most tragic of all the tragedians." [44] But there is no extensive discussion of Greek tragedy. As for comedy, Aristophanes is totally ignored, if we disregard the passage in which Lessing objects to the view that Aristophanes drew the caricature of an individual in the Socrates of the *Clouds*.[45] Roman comedy obviously interested him more: we have from him a fine analysis of Terence's *Adelphi*, especially of the intrigue and the main character, Demea.[46] Among Lessing's early writings is a *Life of Plautus*, a translation of his *Captivi* and a discussion of its merits [47] which has some critical interest. There is plenty of other evidence to show his wide acquaintance with classical antiquity and its literature: a defense of Horace against charges of immorality; a condemnation of Seneca as an ancestor of Corneille.[48] But there is not much that could be called literary discussion.

Most of Lessing's literary criticism, of course, concerns German literature, and much of it is now of no interest except to specialists. He did not know anything of older German literature, though late in his life he looked at Bodmer's garbled edition of the *Nibelungenlied,* and his own antiquarian studies led him to a study of German fables of the 15th century, on which he published a small discovery of authorship and date: "Über die sogenannten Fabeln aus den Zeiten der Minnesinger" (1773). Lessing showed some interest, mainly of a theological or philological nature, in some of the literature of the German Reformation and Humanism, and he edited the epigrams of a 17th-century German poet, Friedrich Logau: thus he is touched by the new spirit of patriotic antiquarianism.

But mostly Lessing wrote about his immediate elders or his contemporaries. He is implacable in his condemnation of Gottsched. Surveying the contemporary German stage, he criticizes many minor authors whose very names are forgotten. This was part of his duty as the Hamburg *Dramaturge.* He constantly attacked the young Wieland both for his shoddy didactic poems and for his imitative dramas, though later he defended Wieland's translation of Shakespeare and called *Agathon* the "work of the century." [49] He admired Klopstock, mainly as a master of diction and verse, though he recognized his lack of epic talent and the dangers of his pietistic sentimentality.[50]

Lessing did not live long enough to see the new Storm and Stress movement as a unity. His opinions of his younger contemporaries were either barely crystallized or not recorded. He liked Leisewitz's *Julius von Tarent* [51] and admired the art of Gerstenberg's *Ugolino* as "nourished on the spirit of Shakespeare," [52] but in a long letter to the author he disapproved of its main theme— passive, innocent suffering—as undramatic.[53] Lessing's attitude toward the early Goethe is ambiguous: he calls him a genius,[54] but in the same context disapproves of his "silly" and "malicious attack" on Euripides' *Alcestis.*[55] *Goetz* seems to be alluded to in Lessing's condemnation of plays in which "the poet puts the biography of a man into dialogue and pretends that the thing is drama"; [56] and *Werther* is criticized for moral reasons and, doubt-less, because Lessing knew the model of Werther, Karl Wilhelm Jerusalem, and respected his intellect and memory. "Do you be-lieve that a Roman or Greek youth would have taken his life in this way and for that reason? Certainly not. They knew how to guard themselves quite differently against the extravagance of love . . . Only Christian education succeeded in producing such big-little, disdainfully worthy originals, as it knows how to turn a physical need so beautifully into a spiritual perfection. So, dear Goethe, I want a little chapter added at the end, and the more cynical the better." [57] Like most professional critics, he could not really relish the taste of a new generation.

Thus the individual critical pronouncements of Lessing do not add up to a corpus of sensitive evaluation or close discussion of great works. But it is impossible to overrate his importance in the raising of the general level of German criticism. Negatively his attack on the French classical tragedy must have meant a great deal; and positively his recommendation of Shakespeare was im-portant for the time, though he had precursors such as Gersten-berg even in Germany. There were, besides, traces in Lessing even of interest in folk poetry: in *Briefe die neueste Literatur betreffend* (No. 33) he praises a Lapland song and a Latvian *dainos* (a kind of elegy) for their "native spirit and charming simplicity," conclud-ing that "poets are born under any climate, and vivid sentiments are not the privilege of civilized nations." [58] This opinion is all the more striking since Lessing obviously cared little for lyrical poetry: his interests were in the drama, the epic, and such semididactic genres as the fable and the epigram. On these last Lessing wrote learned theoretical and historical dissertations full of overly ingen-ious distinctions and subdivisions.

If Lessing had left us only a body of special pronouncements and criticisms of plays forgotten in many cases, he would have merely a historical importance: only historians of German literature would make the effort to read his dissections of German and French plays, even though they are always done with great shrewdness and dialectical power. But Lessing is, of course, far more than just a practical critic. He is a theorist of literature, on the borderline of aesthetics. He cannot be relegated to general philosophical aesthet-ics with Kant: there are hardly any general speculations on beauty or taste as such in Lessing. Rather he takes up very concrete problems of literary theory, and even those not in any systematic fashion. The *Laokoon* was originally to bear the name of *Hermaea*,[59] and it is described as "collectanea for a book." The *Hamburgische Dramaturgie* by its very plan lent itself to casual discussion, and when Lessing got involved in an abstract problem like that of generality he could break off and say: "I here remind my readers that these sheets are to contain anything rather than a dramatic system. I am therefore not bound to resolve all the difficulties I raise. My thoughts may seem less and less connected, may even seem to contradict themselves. What matter? If only they are thoughts amid which may be found food for independent thinking. I only want here to scatter *fermenta cognitionis*." [60] But in spite of this lack of system we get close discussions of several problems: in the *Laokoon* of the relations between poetry and painting, in the *Hamburgische Dramaturgie* of the function of tragedy, the meaning of pity and fear, purgation, problems which Lessing had discussed years before in an extensive correspondence with Mendelssohn and Nicolai.[61] Besides, in these writings and even scattered through the letters there are many pronouncements on basic problems of 18th-century criticism: on the rules, on genius, on the nature of poetry. Thus something like a picture of Lessing's literary theory can be pieced together.

Laokoon oder über die Grenzen der Malerei und Poesie (1766) starts with an empirical problem suggested by the statue of Laocoon, the Trojan priest, depicted as two huge snakes attack him and his two sons at the bidding of Apollo, who punished him for his warnings against the taking of the wooden horse into Troy. This marble group was found in Rome in 1506 and was quickly identified as the work referred to by Pliny,[62] who mentions its sculptors, Hagesandros, Polydoros, and Athenodoros of Rhodes. The statue was admired throughout the 16th and 17th centuries as one of the foremost known works of classical sculpture: a Latin poem composed in the year of its discovery by Giacopo Sadoleto bears witness that the group was admired for its violent expression, its naturalistic depiction of horrible pain. In their exaggerated stress on muscles, 17th-century copies show the cult of anatomy and the baroque taste for horror which the group seems to have satisfied. But J. J. Winckelmann, in his *Gedanken über die*

Nachahmung der griechischen Werke in der Malerei und Bild-hauerkunst (1755), challenged the current interpretation. Laocoon to him shows "a great and composed soul despite all passions . . . this pain does not reveal itself with any fury either in the face or in the whole posture." The Laocoon of the statue "does not intone a fearful shout, as Virgil sings of his Laocoon. The opening of the mouth does not allow it; it is rather an anxious and oppressed groan. The pain of the body and the greatness of the soul are distributed and, so to speak, balanced throughout the entire frame of the figure with equal strength. Laocoon suffers, but he suffers like the Philoctetes of Sophocles. His misery touches our soul, but we would wish to be able to bear misery like this great man." [63] Thus Laocoon confirms Winckelmann's generalization about Greek art, its "noble simplicity and calm grandeur." [64] Lessing accepts Winckelmann's description of the statue, but objects to the comparison with Philoctetes and to the generalization about Greek art and literature. Philoctetes shouts, laments, curses, groans, and howls. Venus, though only scratched, screams in Homer. Mars roars, the dying Hercules cries and bellows with pain. Lessing concludes his first chapter saying: "If it be true that a cry at the sensation of bodily pain, particularly according to the ancient Greek way of thinking, is quite compatible with greatness of soul, it cannot have been for the sake of expressing such greatness that the artist avoided imitating this shriek in marble." [65] Rather, sculpture and painting were limited to the depiction of beautiful bodies. Beauty (and here this obviously means physical beauty) was the highest law of the plastic arts. In an ancient picture of the sacrifice of Iphigenia, Agamemnon is shown hiding his face, and the sculptor of the Laocoon likewise had to reduce the pain. "He must soften the shrieks to sighs, not because a shriek would have betrayed an ignoble soul, but because it would have produced a hideous contortion of the countenance." [66] Virgil can tell us of Laocoon shrieking: it does not occur to anybody that a wide-open mouth is necessary for shouting and that a big mouth is ugly.[67] Slowly Lessing works up to a theoretical statement:

> If it is true that painting and poetry in their imitations make use of entirely different means or signs . . . if these signs in-

disputably require an adequate relation to the thing signified
. . . then it is clear that signs arranged in juxtaposition can
only express subjects of which the wholes or parts exist in
juxtaposition; while consecutive signs can only express subjects of which the wholes or parts are themselves consecutive.
Subjects whose wholes or parts exist in juxtaposition are called
bodies. Bodies with their visible properties are the peculiar
subjects of painting. Subjects whose wholes or parts are consecutive are called actions. Actions are the peculiar subject of
poetry. Still, bodies do not exist in space only but also in time.
They endure, and in each moment of their duration may assume a different appearance, or stand in different combination. Each of these momentary appearances and combinations
is the effect of a preceding one, may be the cause of a subse-
quent one, and is therefore, as it were, the center of an action.
Consequently, painting too can imitate actions, but only indicatively, by means of bodies. On the other hand, actions
cannot exist by themselves, they must depend on certain
beings. So far, therefore, as these beings are bodies, or are
regarded as such, poetry depicts bodies, but only indicatively,
by means of actions. Painting can only make use of a single
instant of the action, and must therefore choose the one which
is the most pregnant . . . Poetry in its progressive imitations
is confined to the use of a single property of bodies, and must
therefore choose that which calls up the most sensuous image
of the body . . .[68]

This central distinction has practical consequences of considerable importance. For painting, it means the condemnation of allegory and of much of what the time considered the highest genre
of painting, history painting, as well as sequences of scenes in one
picture, which Lessing calls "an intrusion of the painter into the
realm of the poet which good taste will never approve of." [69] It
leads to speculations about the fruitful, the most pregnant moment. In literature it leads to a condemnation of enumerative description and implicitly of the descriptive poetry of the time, which
had flourished since the enormous success of Thomson's *Seasons*
in Germany with such imitators as Brockes, Haller, and Ewald von

Kleist. The Horatian saying *ut pictura poesis,* which had served for centuries as the basis for comparison of the arts, is thus rejected both for painting and for poetry. Lessing is also arguing here against theories widely held at the time. Joseph Spence's *Polymetis* is specifically condemned, because Spence had stated that "scarce anything can be good in a poetical description which would appear absurd if represented in a statue or a picture." [70] The Comte Caylus had argued in his *Tableaux tirés de l'Iliade* (1757) that the more a poem furnishes images and actions which can be painted the greater it is as a poem, and he had gone through the *Iliad,* the *Odyssey,* and the *Aeneid* making suggestions for paintings. Thus Lessing was not tilting at windmills. He quotes a descriptive passage from Albrecht von Haller's *Alpen* enumerating plants and flowers, and insists that unless we have seen them before we cannot get any kind of visual image from it.[71] He quotes Ariosto's description of the fay Alcina [72] to prove that we cannot visualize her, even though the author describes her hair, her forehead, her eyebrows, her lips, her teeth, her neck, and her breasts in great detail. Such enumerative description is contrasted with the method employed by Homer to suggest beauty. Helen appears in the assembly of the Trojan elders, and the elders speak to each other: "Nobody should blame the Trojans and Achaeans for suffering misery so long for such a woman." [73] "What Homer could not describe by its constituent parts he lets us acknowledge in its effect. Paint for us, you poets, the delight, the affection, the love, the rapture, which beauty produces, and you have painted beauty itself." [74] The poet, beside showing the effects of beauty, can also show us beauty in motion, namely charm. Poetry, unlike painting, can also afford to depict extreme ugliness, thus to arouse mixed feelings of laughter and terror, as for Thersites in Homer or Richard III in Shakespeare. Yet Lessing condemns the repulsive and disgusting both in painting and poetry, quoting for poetry descriptions of hunger from Dante (Ugolino) and from Beaumont and Fletcher (*The Sea Voyage*). The last chapters of the *Laokoon* are taken up with archaeological points, e.g., an argument against Winckelmann's view that the statue of Laocoon belongs to the time of Alexander the Great. Lessing is anxious to date it after Virgil's *Aeneid* and puts it as late as the reign of Emperor Titus. Modern archaeological research has found inscriptions in Rhodes which show that the

sculptors must have worked about the year 50 B.C., thus preceding
the *Aeneid*.*

One must acknowledge the high importance of Lessing's central
problem: the differences and limits of the arts. It is impossible to
agree with Croce, who refuses to recognize any classification of the
arts, putting artistic creation purely in the mental act of the artist,
which is assumed to be unaffected by the medium. Lessing himself
in *Emilia Galotti* seems to endorse the view that "Raphael would
have been the greatest genius among painters, even if he had unfortunately been born without hands." [75] But Lessing's whole theory runs counter to this view: it can even be said that he seems
uninterested in or vague about the question: what is the common
element in all the arts? Lessing's main distinction between the arts
of space and time, though debatable, is basically sound. His objections to static descriptions in literature were not only salutary
in their time, but, if properly qualified, are applicable even today:
most of us skip the formal descriptions in the novels of Scott or
Balzac. Lessing is certainly putting his finger on the issue when he
points to the difficulty of our forming a whole from an accumulation of traits, and he is also right in opposing the stress on visualization in literature, which in the 18th century was favored by the
current interpretation of the term "imagination" as practically
identical with visual imagination. Literature does not evoke sensuous images, or if it does, does so only incidentally, occasionally, and
intermittently. Even in the depiction of a fictional character the
writer need not suggest visual images at all. We can scarcely visualize most of Dostoevsky's or Henry James's characters, while we
know their states of mind, their motivations, evaluations, attitudes,
and desires very completely. Lessing stresses characterization by
the single trait, by the one Homeric epithet, the method which is
substantially that of Tolstoy or Thomas Mann.

Lessing formulates his view best in one of the notes for the con-
tinuation of the *Laokoon*. "I assert that only that can be the aim
of an art to which it is uniquely and alone fitted, and not that
which the other arts can do just as well or even better. I find a
simile in Plutarch which illustrates this very well. A person, he

* Published after Virgil's death in 17 B.C. Thus neither Winckelmann nor Lessing was right. Winckelmann dated the group far too
early, Lessing slightly too late.

says, who tries to chop wood with a key and open a door with an
axe, not only spoils both tools, but deprives himself of the use of
both tools." [76] Purity of effect is what we sympathize with if we
dislike literary painting, program music, poetic architecture, and
similar mixtures of the arts. Yet Lessing's conception of what is
peculiarly literary will not strike us as convincing. It is, in effect,
the view that drama is the highest and the central genre of literature. Part of this is simply due to his equation of action (*Handlung*) with drama, though he recognizes that action in poetry is
not necessarily outward, external motion. And part must be due
to the insensitivity of Lessing and his contemporaries to the lyric,
which to modern readers seems the center of poetry. Part again is
due to Lessing's preoccupation with a form which was his own
field of creative endeavor and to the central position drama held
in the Aristotelian theory of poetry. Lessing's own view is most
clearly stated in a letter to Nicolai (May 26, 1769), which comments
on a review of the *Laokoon* by Garve. Lessing recognized that his
book does not answer all questions; after all, a sequel was planned,
and the *Laokoon* was called Part I. He admits that the view expounded in the text needs qualification: painting is not actually
confined to natural signs, poetry is not confined to arbitrary signs.
But it is certain that "the more painting gets away from natural
signs, or mixes natural signs with arbitrary signs, the more it gets
away from its highest point of perfection; while poetry approaches
perfection the more nearly, the more its arbitrary signs approxi-
mate natural signs. Thus the higher painting is that which uses only
natural signs in space and the higher poetry that which uses only
natural signs in time." Lessing does not deny the effects of historical
and allegorical painting, but they seem to him impure.

> Poetry must try to raise its arbitrary signs to natural signs:
> that is how it differs from prose and becomes poetry. The
> means by which this is accomplished are the tone of words,
> the position of words, measure, figures and tropes, similes, etc.
> All these make arbitrary signs more like natural signs, but
> they don't actually change them into natural signs; conse-
> quently all genres that use only these means must be looked
> upon as lower kinds of poetry; and the highest kind of poetry
> will be that which transforms the arbitrary signs completely

into natural signs. That is dramatic poetry; for in it words
cease to be arbitrary signs, and become natural signs of arbitrary objects. Aristotle said that dramatic poetry is the highest, even the only, poetry, and he assigns second place to the
epic only insofar as it is for the most part dramatic or can be
dramatic.[77]

This is an extremely revealing letter. It needs some interpretation:
certainly the term "natural signs," derived from Dubos, is used
here strangely and very broadly. The passage just quoted mentions onomatopoeia, the use of language as directly imitating an
object; it mentions meter, which is natural because physical in its
effect; and it also mentions, curiously enough, metaphors, which
are considered (as a discarded draft shows) a device to raise arbitrary signs to the value of natural signs. "As the power of natural
signs consists in their similarity with things, metaphor introduces,
instead of such a similarity, which words do not have, another
similarity, which the thing referred to has with still another, the
concept of which can be renewed more easily and more vividly." [78]
A simile is nothing but an extended metaphor. This is a strange
theory of imagery which would reduce metaphor to the comparisons of unfamiliar with more familiar objects, and even with this
restriction the theory seems incapable of establishing the claim
that metaphorical language is natural and not arbitrary. Lessing's
view is closely related to the common 18th-century view of primitive, natural, poetic language as metaphorical. But he appears to
look on such language as merely a makeshift for the employment
of natural signs in the drama. There, if I understand Lessing
rightly, language is natural because it is spoken *by* characters and
in character, with gestures and expressions of the face as in real
life, and thus it loses the fatal quality of conventionality which
inheres in all other uses of language; spoken language is the natural language of emotion and thus can communicate the emotions
of sympathy and pity, the highest object of the drama. Thus the
Laokoon is not unrelated to *Hamburgische Dramaturgie:* we pass
logically from one to the other.

Lessing's conception of the fine arts is undoubtedly far more
narrow than his conception of literature, which argues precisely
for a latitude of emotional effects. In the fine arts he holds to a

very abstract ideal of physical beauty to which expression is strictly subordinated. Even his interpretation of the Laocoon group seems mistaken: good modern photographs show that Laocoon's face is distorted by violent pain. "He draws in air through the slightly opened mouth, draws in his abdomen, thus pushing up his breast, and throws his head back upon the nape of his neck." [79] The whole group seems rather a crass example of Hellenic "baroque" than of classical repose. Lessing in any case confines the plastic arts to the depiction of physical beauty so narrowly that he totally obliterates the distinction between sculpture and painting. He discusses sculpture in a way which assumes that what he says of it applies to painting, and thus he creates a confusion of two arts which runs counter to his avowed purpose of differentiation. In painting itself, Lessing obviously preferred mere design and did not recognize composition by color. Design would be confined to human figures, because the "highest bodily beauty exists only in man and even in him only by virtue of the ideal." [80] The painting of animals, flowers, and landscapes is rejected because these are not capable of the ideal.[81] Here Lessing seems to share the Renaissance view of painting as a liberal art which must tell a story of human significance. But at the same time he explicitly rejects history painting, along with still-life and landscape. He is thus left with the mere depiction of physical bodies, which, according to the theory of the pregnant moment, may convey a human meaning by suggestion. It is not surprising that Lessing should ask "whether one would not wish that the art of oil painting had never been invented." [82] This is a dreary ideal which even the best designs by Flaxman, David, or Ingres do not make attractive. It sacrifices the humanistic values of the old *ut pictura poesis* theory without replacing it by a new ideal of pure painterly values.

A good deal of evidence has been accumulated to show that Lessing's ideas were not entirely new. It is obviously true that many of his questions and some of his solutions had been suggested before. In Shaftesbury, for instance, there is an elaborate discussion of the "fruitful moment," and there are numerous anticipations of Lessing's distinctions between the fine arts and poetry in Dubos, James Harris, Diderot, and, especially, in Edmund Burke.[83] But scattered anticipations can be found of almost any idea. Lessing certainly formulated his main argument strikingly and persuasively.

The influence of the *Laokoon,* in Germany especially, was profound, and not only in arresting the vogue of descriptive poetry. Herder, we shall see, started his critical theory in reaction to the *Laokoon,* Goethe in his autobiography paid generous tribute to its revelations and wrote his own piece on Laocoon (1798). German poetry quite consciously turned to drama, and even in the lyric it required movement, motion, dynamism at any price.

But the *Laokoon* is only part of Lessing's critical work. The theory of tragedy and the interpretation of Aristotle expounded in the later sections of the *Hamburgische Dramaturgie* were almost equally influential. Some of its central views are anticipated in his 17th *Literaturbrief* and in his correspondence with Mendelssohn and Nicolai in 1756–57. A close study would have to define the differences between these early discussions and the mature views in the *Dramaturgie.* Lessing, in the correspondence, is still fumbling. He defines the aim of tragedy merely as the arousing of pity: "It must extend our capacity for feeling pity. The most compassionate man is the best man . . . and he who makes us compassionate, makes us better and more virtuous." [84] Dramas which arouse only admiration for sufferings heroically borne, as do those of Corneille, are not really tragic. On this evidence Lessing would emerge as a defender of domestic tragedy, even of the view that tragedy must be judged by the degree of emotion it evokes, the number of tears it draws. His polemics would merely be directed against "admiration" for the Cornelian Stoic hero, whom we cannot pity but rather must envy and emulate as if he were the hero of an epic.[85] In the *Laokoon* Lessing gives the example of the Roman gladiator who had to suffer silently, because if he had excited compassion the games would have been stopped. The existence of these gladiatorial games proves to Lessing that the Romans could not have had true tragedy. Senecan tragic heroes are nothing but pugilists (*Klopffechter*) [86] on buskins.

The *Hamburgische Dramaturgie* resumes this argument but fortunately goes far beyond it. The reason that the *Dramaturgie* is in many ways a disappointing book may be understood in terms of its genesis. Lessing was invited in 1767 to become the dramatist of a newly founded National Theater in Hamburg. As he did not wish to be obliged to supply a stated number of plays, the idea was accepted that he would write a kind of theatrical journal which would comment on the plays performed, thus fulfilling an advertising function, helping to influence the taste of the public, and advising the actors who owned the theater. Lessing actually began by reviewing plays regularly twice a week, also criticizing the performances of the actors. But the journal soon ran into trouble, and he abandoned criticism of the acting because he had caused bad blood among his employers. He also fell considerably behind in his commentaries on the plays. The numbers were reprinted piratically, which caused financial losses. Thus after No. 32 the pretense of periodical publication was abandoned: Lessing more and more gave up following the repertory. After No. 52 he discussed only seven plays and felt far freer to indulge in general reflections on the nature of tragedy, the meaning of Aristotle's *Poetics,* and similar topics. The journal came to an end with Nos. 100–4, dated April 19, 1768, which nominally discussed a performance given in the preceding July. The theater itself failed within a year. As Lessing reflects in the concluding number, "What a guileless idea, to establish a National Theater for us Germans, when we Germans are not yet a nation. I am not speaking about political constitution, but only about the moral character. One could almost say we have none. We are still the inveterate imitators of everything foreign." [87]

Thus the *Dramaturgie* must be judged as originally designed for day-by-day reviewing of plays on whose selection Lessing had no influence. This alone explains the choice of Corneille's *Rodogune* and the emphasis on Voltaire. They were produced and Racine was not. This explains the attention to French and German plays now totally forgotten; it also explains the general polemical undercurrent against the French drama, from whose fetters Lessing wants the Germans to be freed. The arguments against the French stage are not merely nationalistic, though Lessing challenges his readers: "Mention any play of the great Corneille which I would not improve upon ["besser machen" must mean "write a better play on the subject" and not merely "improve"]. What will you bet?" [88] They are based on a different conception of the nature of tragedy and a different interpretation of Aristotle (which undoubt-

edly is nearer the meaning of the text than Corneille's). What is
new and surprising in Germany, and has led to the error of identifying Lessing simply with neoclassicism, is his stress on Aristotle
as the master. "I don't hesitate to admit (even if I should be therefore laughed to scorn in these enlightened times) that I consider
the work [the *Poetics*] as infallible as the *Elements* of Euclid . . .
I would venture to prove incontrovertibly, that tragedy cannot de-
part a step from the plumb line of Aristotle, without departing
thus far from its own perfection." [89] This, of course, is not au-
thoritarianism but trust in absolute truth. "I would dispose of his
authority," Lessing says elsewhere,[90] "easily enough if I could only
dispose of his reasons." He describes his procedure thus:

> In this conviction I set myself the task of judging in detail
> some of the most celebrated models of the French stage. For
> this stage is said to be formed quite in accordance with the
> rules of Aristotle, and the attempt has been made particularly
> to persuade us Germans that only by these rules have the
> French attained to the degree of perfection from which they
> can look down on all the stages of modern peoples. We have
> so long firmly believed this that our poets regarded imitating
> the French the same as working according to the rules of the
> ancients. But this prejudice could not eternally survive against
> our feelings. These were fortunately roused from their slum-
> bers by some English plays, and we at last realized that tragedy
> was capable of another effect, quite different from that
> achieved by Corneille and Racine. Then, dazzled by this sud-
> den ray of truth, we rebounded to the brink of another abyss.

An opinion arose that there was no need of any rules; Germans
were on the point of "wantonly throwing away the experience of
all past times" and demanding from the poet that "each one
should discover the art anew." Lessing hopes to have checked this
"fermentation of taste" by combating the delusion of the regularity of the French stage. "No nation has more misapprehended the
rules of ancient drama than the French." [91] This seeming paradox
underlies the arguments against the rules. He constantly disparages the mechanical rules: in the discussion of Voltaire's *Merope*
an elaborate attempt is made to show that his preservation of the
unity of place, time, and action leads really to improbabilities and

even absurdities. "As far as I am concerned Voltaire's *Merope* and Maffei's *Merope* may extend over eight days and the scene may be laid in seven places in Greece, if only they had the beauties to make me forget these pedantries." [92] But Lessing's argument is not the common one that genius can transcend the rules or that rules are narrow. He would occasionally say something which sounds deceptively romantic: "Genius laughs at all the boundary lines of criticism." [93] "Genius is permitted not to know a thousand things that every schoolboy knows. Not the accumulated stores of his memory, but that which he can produce out of himself, out of his own feelings, constitutes his riches." [94] But most commonly he stresses the compatibility of genius and the rules, of imagination and judgment.

> We have now, thank heaven, a generation of critics whose highest criticism consists in making all criticism suspicious. They vociferate: "Genius! Genius!" "Genius transcends all rules." "What genius produces is rules." Thus they flatter genius, in order, I fancy, that they also may be held geniuses. But they too evidently betray that they do not feel a spark of it in themselves, when they add in one and the same breath: "Rules oppress genius." As if genius could be oppressed by anything in the world, and furthermore by something that, as they themselves admit, is deduced from it. Not every critic is a genius, but every genius is a born critic. He has the proof of all rules within himself.[95]

"Whoever reasons rightly, invents too, and whoever wants to invent, must be able to reason." [96] Thus Lessing develops the view that the poet acts with purpose and must create a world which is also purposeful and coherent.

The mechanical rules do not matter. Nor does even the purity of genres, as one surprising passage states:

> In our textbooks it is right that we should separate them from one another as carefully as possible, but if a genius, for higher purposes, amalgamates several of them in one and the same work, let us forget our textbook and only examine whether he has attained these higher purposes. Why should I care whether a play of Euripides is neither wholly a narrative nor

wholly a drama. Call it a hybrid; it is enough that this hybrid
pleases me more, edifies me more, than the most lawful births
of our correct Racines or whatever else they may be called.
Because the mule is neither a horse nor an ass, is it therefore
the less one of the most useful beasts of burden? [97]

What matters is the coherence of the poet's world, its probability
and the purity and specificity of its effect. Lessing constantly repeats that an action must have its logical course. "Genius can bother
only with events that are rooted in one another, with chains of cause
and effect: to reduce the latter to the former, to weigh the latter
against the former, everywhere to exclude chance, to cause everything to occur so that it could not have happened otherwise, this
is the business of genius." [98] There must be no miracle in the
drama, not even mere historical accuracy, because there are many
historical events which are entirely inexplicable, incomprehensible, and incoherent. Tragedy is not "history put into dialogue." [99]
This is a point which Lessing argues at great length in connection
with Thomas Corneille's *Essex* and Voltaire's historical objections
to that play. Where the poet is confronted with improbable events,
such as Cleopatra's murdering her husband and two sons in Corneille's *Rodogune,* he must invent a series of causes and effects by
which these improbable events can be made to seem necessary.
"Not satisfied with resting their probability on historical authority,
he will endeavor so to construct the characters of his personages, so
to necessitate, one from another, the events that place these characters in action, so to define the passions of each character, and to
lead these passions through such gradual stages, that we shall everywhere see nothing but the most natural and common course of
events." [100] The poet must develop the "hidden organization" of
his plot [101] because he needs this "inner probability" [102] to achieve
that identification with the character which is the ground of pity
and hence of the effect of tragedy. We must recognize that a
"similar stream might also have carried us away to do deeds which
in cold blood we believe far removed from us." [103]

Thus the question of the effect of tragedy, of purgation through
pity and fear, is tied in with the question of the structure of tragedy. Lessing has now discovered that it is impossible to define the
tragic effect as mere pity or compassion. He interprets the crucial

passage in Aristotle to mean "pity with fear" in a situation where
fear is a necessary concomitant of pity. The fear is not terror, but
fear which "arises for us from our similarity with the suffering
person . . . the fear that we ourselves could become this object
of pity"; [104] we must pity the hero if the hero is "of the same wheat
and chaff," [105] is "one of us" [106] and thus is not above or below
common humanity. The martyrs and monsters of Corneille are
not pitiful and therefore not tragic, just as Richard III is not
tragic. Such tragic pity with fear must be distinguished from what
Lessing calls "philanthropy," the compassion which, as men, we
would extend even to the worst criminal, though we could not fear
for ourselves in witnessing his fate. But what is meant by "purgation" of such pity and fear? The term "catharsis" has given rise to
the most diverse interpretations: to some it has meant inuring,
hardening our minds against the feeling of pity and fear. To others
it has meant almost the opposite: a tempering, a purification, a
cleansing of pity and fear, or even an increase in these feelings. By
modern Aristotelians such as Bernays [107] it has been convincingly
interpreted in medical terms as a homeopathic cure. The *mind* is
to be purged of pity and fear. Catharsis is a process of healing.
Lessing has his own interpretation, which hardly commends itself
as historically correct but fits into his own scheme: he equates purgation with the right mean of the passions as taught by the *Nico-
machean Ethics*. "Purification consists in nothing else than the
transformation of passions into virtuous habits." [108] We must
achieve the golden mean of pity and fear: those who feel too much
must learn to feel less, those who feel too little must learn to feel
more. Tragedy is thus a "school of the moral world." [109] This, of
course, is basic to the neoclassical view of all literature. "All species
of poetry are intended to improve us"; it is lamentable "that there
are poets who doubt even this." [110]

All genres exist for the purpose of improving us. Tragedy, however, has this specific means of improvement: the purgation of pity
and fear. Lessing insists—in apparent contradiction to the passage
where he admits a mixture of kinds—that "all genres of poetry
cannot improve all things, at least not every genre so perfectly as
another; but what each can improve most perfectly, and better
than any other genre—that alone is its peculiar aim." [111] He becomes quite indignant at the view that the theater needs only to

amuse by telling a story. "To what end the hard work of dramatic
form? Why build a theater, disguise men and women, torture their
memories, invite the whole town to assemble in one place, if I
intend to produce nothing more with my work and its representation than some of those emotions that would be produced about
as well by any good story that everybody could read by his chimney
corner at home?" [112] This strange complaint overlooks the existence and attraction of comedy, and ignores the simple fact that
actors don't torture their memories but like to learn their roles and
that people love to disguise themselves and to assemble in one
place.

But it is not possible to dismiss Lessing's theory of tragedy as
simple didacticism or even as reducible to the balancing of pity
and fear which he interprets as "purgation." Tragedy achieves all
this because it creates a world analogous to the real one. The
world of drama is

> another world, a world whose chance events may be connected
> in a different order, but must still be connected logically as
> they are here: a world in which cause and effect may follow in
> different order but yet lead to the general effect of good; in
> short a world of a genius, who (if I may be permitted to desig-
> nate the creator, without naming him, by his most noble crea-
> tion) in order to imitate the highest genius in miniature,
> transposes, reduces, increases the particles of the present world
> in order to form a whole therefrom that shall harmonize with
> his own aims and ends.[113]

Tragedy, it appears, is thus a justification of God, a theodicy, a
world inherently ethical, just as God's created cosmos is good even
though we may not see the ultimate goodness of any individual
evil. In history there may be monsters such as Richard III, and
there may be innocent suffering. But then history

> has its good reason in the eternal and infinite connection of
> all things. In history all is wisdom and goodness, though it
> may appear to us that there is blind fate and cruelty in the
> few links picked out by the poet. Out of these few links the
> poet ought to make a whole, rounded in itself and complete,
> fully explained in itself, where no difficulty arises to which a

solution is not found in his plan. We ought not to be forced
to seek a reason outside, in the general plan of things. The
whole fashioned by this mortal creator [the poet] should be
a silhouette of the whole of the eternal Creator. It should ac-
custom us to the thought that as in it all things are resolved
for the best, so also will it be on earth. The poet forgets his
most noble calling when he forces into a narrow circle the incomprehensible ways of Providence and deliberately awakens
our shudder thereat . . . To what end this sad emotion?
To teach us submission? Cool reason alone could teach us
this, and if the teachings of reason are to have any hold on us,
if we for all our submission are to retain confidence and joy-
ful courage, it is most necessary that we should be reminded
as little as possible of perplexing examples, of unmerited terrible fates. Away with them from the stage, away with them,
if possible, from all books! [114]

Drama then shows us the world rational, transparent to the ethical
will, subservient to it. There must be no innocent suffering on the
stage because reason and religion should have convinced us that
the very idea of human beings as wretched because of no guilt of
their own is "as false as it is blasphemous." [115] Tragedy has the high
function of revealing the order of the universe. Lessing, with the
optimism of the 18th century and its peculiar kind of belief in a
benevolent God and His universe, dissolves the conception of
tragedy: in his tragedy there can be no free will, no conflict between man and God or fate or the universe.

Lessing's conception of tragedy is a deeply ethical one. It agrees
with Butcher's later interpretation of Aristotle, according to which
"the dramatic action must be so significant, and its meaning capable of such extension, that through it we can discern the higher
laws which rule the world." [116] But unfortunately Lessing betrays
the limitations of his temper and his time in his conception of
these higher laws. His is the 18th-century universe of a benevolent
God, a benevolent Nature, and a basically good man. Tragedy is
deprived of its connection with sacrifice, with the grandly heroic,
the marvelous and divine, the *mysterium tremendum,* and is reduced to an object lesson in humanitarianism. Lessing's emphasis
on the coherence and wholeness of the world of drama, its inner

probability, actually justifies any art which is psychologically true and consistent, which is a fully motivated portrayal of life even though it be not tragic or even dramatic at all. The hero is reduced in stature: he cannot be either a martyr or a criminal; he must be a middling man, whose guilt is only an understandable failure, a mistake committed under mitigating circumstances of strain or ignorance. His pathos is that of mere suffering. The auditor is conceived as a virtuoso of pity, a man who has to exercise his humanity and train it in virtuous habits, not a man who is to be either shaken up and torn by tragedy or healed to Stoic endurance and indifference. Thus Lessing illustrates the same failure of his age to grasp the nature of art which we found in Dr. Johnson and in Diderot. Along with them, he prepares the conception of literature underlying the psychological and social realism of the 19th century.

Lessing tried to restate the neoclassical creed by abandoning its French version and substituting a liberalized interpretation of Aristotle which allowed him to satisfy his desire for an ethical realism. He thus upheld the basic principle of mimesis, the concept of rules (however much he wanted to change them), and the view that literary creation is a work of judgment as well as talent.

But this revised neoclassicism soon proved unacceptable in Germany. The reaction against French taste and the Enlightenment imported from France became more and more radical, until in the early 1770's it broke out in a movement known as Storm and Stress. The group of writers associated with this title of a play can hardly be described as critics. Their ideas are all substantially derived from the French sentimentalists and the British primitivists, though they reworded them much more sharply and pronounced them much more shrilly: the rules were completely rejected by . Lenz; [1] Bürger preached popular poetry; [2] Stolberg glorified divine poetry as "streaming from the fullness of the heart." [3] "Genius" became a slogan in which complete rejection of discipline and tradition was linked with belief in creative spontaneity. [4] Nature now meant raw nature, naturalness, naturalism. The tone, the violence, even the shriek do not make criticism: a body of thought, a new taste, a philosophy of literature was not formulated until Herder.

The English preromantic view was introduced into Germany by Heinrich Wilhelm Gerstenberg (1737–1823) who, however, restated it much more radically. His *Briefe über Merkwürdigkeiten der Litteratur* (1766), almost at the very beginning, report on Warton's *Observations on the Fairie Queene,* ridiculing Warton for his timidity, his admission of Spenser's faults, and his whole hesitating attitude toward the demand for unity of composition. Spenser, according to Gerstenberg, must not be judged by such irrelevant standards: he had no other intention than to give us an anthology of romantic adventures. Spenser pleases by "graces beyond the reach of art," he carries us away by the marvelous power of creative imagination.[5] In recommending Shakespeare to the Germans in a series of letters beginning with a criticism of Wieland's prose version, Gerstenberg, with a typical *salto mortale* into opposite extremes, brushes aside all questions of genre, rules, and composition. "Away with the classification of the drama"; "call them *plays,* history, tragedy, tragicomedy, comedy, what you will: I call them living pictures of moral nature." [6] Gerstenberg rejects the idea of considering catharsis, or even the moving of the emotions pity and fear. *Lear, Macbeth, Hamlet, Richard III, Romeo,* and *Othello* are rather character plays than tragic fables.[7] This does not mean that Shakespeare is artless or savage: just the other way: "I see everywhere a certain whole, beginning, middle and end, proportion, intentions, contrasting characters and groups." [8] There is picturesque unity of intention and composition, a "poetical illusion," which to Gerstenberg is totally untheatrical, even antitheatrical. "Tragedy," meaning French tragedy and its imitations, "is not poetry." [9] Shakespeare, he tries to show in a series of quotations illustrating his art of characterizing speakers according to their age, is a master of psychological portraiture, not a playwright.[10]

Gerstenberg added Nordic poetry to Shakespeare and Spenser. He lived in Denmark, knew Danish, and thus was able to describe the Danish folk ballads (*Kaempe Viser*) collected in the 16th century, and to translate something from the *Edda.* What he quotes seems to him truly Pindaric, highly metaphorical like early poetry and Shakespeare, whose puns he was one of the first to defend.[11]

This poetry of nature is poetry of genius, contrasted with that of *bel esprit* or a witty mind. Genius is Gerstenberg's watchword as it was Hamann's: it is inspiration, imagination, fire, the creation of illusion, invention, novelty, originality.[12] Poetry is the higher epic (Homer) and the high ode (Pindar) not drama. "Among witty heads there are grades, but none among poetic geniuses. A poet without great genius is no poet." [13] All the new terms of the time are here assembled.

Yet Gerstenberg was not always as radical as these pronouncements sound. One could easily collect from his scattered writings, which include a long series of reviews for the *Hamburgische Neue Zeitung* (1767–71), opinions favorable to Dryden, Pope, Johnson (he admired the *Rambler*), Richardson, Sterne, Goldoni, and even Wieland.[14] They show that Gerstenberg's taste was eclectic and that he also liked, besides Homer, Shakespeare, Spenser, and Cervantes, realism, sentiment, and rococo playfulness. But all these uncertainties should not obscure the glowing passages on Shakespeare and genius which proved to be most influential. They suggested the curious image of Shakespeare which also became Herder's and the young Goethe's: Shakespeare as the poet, the character writer, divorced from the stage. The reflections on genius set the tone for the glorification of spontaneity, creativeness, and unreflecting fervor which the new generation expected from poetry.

Johann Georg Hamann (1730–88) is usually considered Herder's spiritual father. He differs profoundly from Herder, however, and must be discussed separately. Hamann was one of the first Germans to arrive at a complete rejection of the Enlightenment; this occurred after a religious conversion he experienced during a journey to London (1758). His theory of literature (insofar as he has one) is strictly part of a religious philosophy which implied a rejection of the whole of modern civilization. Hamann thus cannot be judged as a literary critic or even as a man of letters; he was and wanted to be a religious prophet. Culturally he belongs in the company of Jakob Böhme and similar Renaissance mystics. He combined, in a weird mixture, elements derived from gnosticism, neo-Platonism, etc., with a strong dose of Lutheran pietism, and added to them something of recent sensualism. His writings, as published by himself, were merely a series of small pamphlets, sometimes issued anonymously in a few copies, which therefore could not have reached a wider audience. They present no continuous arguments but usually are only a series of aphorisms or jocular and grotesque polemics, full of the most local and temporal allusions and the most abstruse, often Greek and Hebrew, quotations. Hamann's reputation in his time was purely personal, even legendary, yet his influence was profound, as Herder was his pupil and Goethe and Jacobi learned from him. Not until long after his death, when in 1821–25 Friedrich Roth published a collected edition, could Hamann's writings be read and studied. Then slowly his position in Protestant theology became established and

he acquired a group of enthusiastic followers who studied his
works as if they were the Bible. This limited cult has only in this
century been replaced by an objective study of Hamann's historical
role and thought. But it has led to the magnifying of his position
into the *magnus parens* of the whole great age of German literature.
Goethe's saying that he was the greatest man of the century is
again taken seriously.[15]

Whatever his importance as a religious thinker may be, we must
pronounce on his role in a history of criticism. It can be considered only that of an inciter. His remarks on poetry could be
collected in two pages, though it is possible to add a good many
opinions on specific writers which, however, are never developed
or substantiated. Thus Shakespeare, though highly admired, remains in Hamann's writings hardly more than a synonym for
genius.[16] The two pages of sayings, largely in the "Aesthetica in
nuce," a section of *Kreuzzüge des Philologen* (*Crusades of the Philologist*, 1762), are, however, startling. The whole world is the
language of God and poetry is therefore nothing but the imitation
of this language. *Logos* is Reason, but also the Word and Christ.
Thus "all our knowledge is sensuous, figurative." [17] Poetry speaks
only in images. "Senses and passions speak and understand nothing
but images. In images is the whole treasure of human knowledge
and happiness." [18] Poetry, historically, is one with human knowledge, religion, and myth. "Poetry is the mother tongue of the human race; just as gardening is older than agriculture, painting than
writing, singing than declamation, similes than syllogisms, barter
than commerce." [19] "*Mythos*, fable and invention, always seems to
precede *pathos* and the rush of sentiment." [20] "Epic and fable are
the beginning, and besides them nothing but ode and song." [21]
Poetry is thus the same as religion, it *is* original religion, a "natural
kind of prophesying." [22] All poetry is sacred; the Bible is not only
the Word of God but also the highest poetry. Hamann preaches
what he calls "salvation by the Jews," "pilgrimages to *Arabia felix*,
crusades to the East," for "Nature and the Holy Writ are the materials of the beautiful creating imitating spirit." [23] Thus Oriental
poetry and the Bible, together with Homer and Shakespeare, are
the great models. They are all parabolic poetry, not folk poetry as
Herder later proclaimed them. In Hamann there is only a passing
glance at Latvian folk songs which points in this direction.[24]

Lowth, with his *Lectures on Hebrew Poetry* and Bacon and his interpretation of ancient myths, are referred to, but not Percy or Ossian.[25]

Hamann thus can condemn imitation of nature, probability, *la belle nature,* and all the assumptions of neoclassicism. Voltaire he calls the *"Lucifer* of the century." [26] He condemns the new interpretation of the Bible that seeks only one meaning in a text; he believes in allegories and parables, as all nature is one great parable of God's power.[27] "The summary of the newest aesthetics, as of the oldest, is: 'Fear God and render Him homage.' " [28]

This world view, with its identification of reason and language, implies the exaltation of genius, and of all of Hamann's literary ideas proved most influential in his time. His idea of genius is all feeling, imagination, fire, inspiration, originality, creativeness. "My coarse imagination has never been able to imagine a creative genius without genitals." [29] But sensualism and emotionalism are combined with mysticism. Hamann's genius is also the Socratic *daimon* and its "ignorance." "Genius plumbs all things, even the profound things of God." [30] Genius is almost the same as prophet and inspired fool. For literature it means the rejection of the rules. "What makes up in Homer for his ignorance of the rules which an Aristotle thought out after him, and what in a Shakespeare makes up for the ignorance or transgression of those critical laws? Genius is the unanimous answer." [31] "Those who want to deprive the arts of caprice and fancy are assassins that attack their very honor and life." [32]

These are the main motifs of Hamann's thought that are of literary interest. In their radical anti-intellectualism they seem the fountainhead of much that immediately followed in Germany. Hamann links a dim past of mysticism, neo-Platonism, and pietism with German Romanticism. Goethe wanted to edit Hamann and gave him a prominent place in his description of the literary situation of his youth.[33] Hegel reviewed him with reservations, but admiringly.[34] Kierkegaard was one of his most assiduous readers.[35] Still, one should not overlook the profound differences between Hamann and later critical thought. Even his pupil Herder differed from him on important points: with Herder the lyric, not myth, is at the origin of poetry, and it is surely a symptom of their basic disagreement that Hamann violently attacked Herder for denying the divine origin of language.[36] Hamann criticized Kant's *Critique of Pure Reason* with arguments which, in themselves, suffice to exclude him from any understanding of German idealistic philosophy.[37] He remained a mystic, a strict supernatural dualist, for whom anguish, as for Kierkegaard, is the only proof of our double nature, without which there would be no homesickness for heaven.[38] This mystical world view is necessarily static and unhistorical. There are in Hamann pronouncements to the effect that an author should be interpreted in the spirit of his age (as Pope and many other good 18th-century minds recommended), but he has no real interest in development or in historical change.[39] Poetry is religion and myth; it was so at the beginning of creation and should be now. "All aesthetic juggling cannot replace immediate feeling." [40] Hamann thus disclaimed being a critic, though he wrote numerous reviews, did translations, and was a learned, widely read student of literature.[41] Like everybody who wanted to be a real reformer of criticism or the propounder of a new philosophy of literature, Herder had to tread different paths and look for other ancestors.

Though the name of Johann Gottfried Herder (1744–1803) was not mentioned in my account of the late 18th-century English and Scottish critics, they provide the background for Herder's ideas and, in combination, represent almost the totality of his critical thought. There is scarcely any idea in Herder which could not be traced back to Blackwell or Harris, Shaftesbury or Brown, Blair or Percy, Warton or Young. Herder read them all, and of course he read his German predecessors and contemporaries, especially Lessing, Hamann, and Winckelmann. He sat at Hamann's feet and felt himself to be his personal disciple. He read the French—Rousseau, of whom he disapproved for a time,[42] Diderot, and many others; and echoes of Vico's thought seem to have come to him through Cesarotti's notes to Ossian, which he read in the German translation by Michael Denis.[43]

But it would be a mistake to consider Herder merely the synthesizer of what could be vaguely called preromantic criticism in Europe. He is not only a synthesizer whom none of his predecessors can approach in sweep and scope, he is also the first who sharply breaks with the neoclassical past, who abandons that curious double point of view which we found in writers such as Warton or

Hurd. The whole scale of values is completely reversed, though even in Herder we can, of course, find survivals and accommodations to the older views. Herder differs from all other critics of the century not only in his radicalism but also in his method of presentation and argument. In his writings there is a new fervid, shrill, enthusiastic tone, an emotional heightening, a style which uses rhetorical questions, exclamations, passages marked by dashes in wearisome profusion, a style full of metaphors and similes, a composition which often abandons any pretense at argument and chain of reasoning. It is that of a lyrical address, of constant questions, cumulative intensifying adjectives, verbs of motion, of metaphors drawn from the movement of water, light, flame, and the growth of plants and animals. There is a constantly shifting use of terminology in which ancient words lose their original meaning, in which "drama," "ode," "elegy" may mean almost anything the author wants them to mean in his context. There is hardly a real book among the thirty-three volumes of Herder's *Collected Works*. Many of them are called quite rightly *Fragmente, Torso, Wälder, Briefe, Zerstreute Blätter, Ideen zur* . . . ; or they have fancy titles such as *Adrastea, Kalligone, Terpsichore,* which often conceal an extremely miscellaneous content. With the exception of a few treatises definitely devoted to theology, it is not safe to ignore any of his writings in a study of his literary criticism. Opinions and pronouncements on literary questions can occur in any context. Besides, Herder constantly rewrote what he had written: the second edition of the *Fragmente* differs profoundly from the first, and materials are often moved from one book to another. The exclamatory style, the shifting terminology, the fragmentariness of the arguments, the constant oscillation and flitting from one topic to another are extremely irritating and justify Saintsbury's charge of "fearful wooliness," [44] but they do not justify a neglect of Herder. Saintsbury dismisses him without proper examination, obviously having read not more than a few pages, and discussing him after Sainte-Beuve and Hugo, Wordsworth and Coleridge.

Not only is Herder of considerable intrinsic interest and, in spite of his incoherent style, of great inner intellectual cohesion and simplicity, but he has been enormously influential: the effect of his contact with the young Goethe in the winter of 1770–71 in Strasbourg is very well known; it is obvious that Herder's ideas were

the great quarry for the German romantics, for Jean Paul, for Novalis, and especially for the two Schlegels. It seems to me an ex-
aggeration to claim that Herder was the first modern historian of
literature and the first man with historical sense: but he is certainly
the one who has most clearly been the fountainhead of universal
literary history. He has also undoubtedly been the most influential force for stimulating interest in folk poetry and in establishing
it as the ideal of poetry, though he himself was, of course, stimulated by the halfhearted Percy and the much more fervid Scottish
primitivists. Herder's influence on the whole revival of folk poetry
—its collecting and imitating, its interpretation and evaluation—
is immeasurable, especially in the Slavic and Scandinavian countries. His influence was often indirect and anonymous, combined
with that of predecessors, contemporaries, and followers; it is
almost underground, for reasons which are in part due to the characteristics of Herder's writings and in part to extraneous circumstances such as the intermittent hostility of Goethe and Schiller.
While his influence was obscured in the early 19th century, he has
again been studied intensively in recent decades, especially in Germany, and has been played up as a sort of counterweight to Goethe
and Schiller. The revival of Herder, which came originally from
historians with religious interests (Nadler and Unger), was later
taken up by the Nazis, who saw in him a source of German nationalism, of a national conception of literature and of the "blood and
soil" ideology. They conveniently ignored or minimized his central teaching of *Humanität*. From the very nature of Herder's
manner of thinking it is almost impossible to isolate his literary
criticism and theory from the general body of his thought, from
his philosophy of history, his theology, psychology, linguistic speculations, and aesthetic. We shall try, however, to do so, paying only
minimal attention to the background and implications of his
literary ideas for a general philosophy or *Weltanschauung*.

What has been said before suggests that Herder's conception of
the aim of criticism differs from that of the main neoclassicists, the
whole tradition which attempted to build up a rational structure
of coherent and systematic literary theory and of immutable standards of judgment. Herder conceives of criticism mainly as a process
of empathy, of identification, of something intuitive and sub-
rational. He constantly rejects theories, systems, faultfinding. In

an early piece, the preliminary discourse to the second collection
of *Fragmente über die neuere deutsche Literatur* (1767), he describes his views of the function of criticism: the critic should be a
"servant of the author, his friend, his impartial judge. He should
try to get acquainted with him, make a thorough study of him as
a master, not seek to be your own master. . . . It is difficult but
reasonable that the critic should transfer himself into the thoughts
of his author and read him in the spirit in which he wrote." [45] In
praising Gerstenberg's *Ugolino* (1770) he says that "we do not
criticize from Hedelin [= D'Aubignac] or Racine, but from our
feeling." [46] What matters is to "live in the spirit of an author, to
make one's own his manner of speaking, to be informed, so to say,
of the plan and aim of his work out of his own soul." [47] No wonder
that Herder quotes Leibniz with approval. Leibniz says that he has
little "censorious spirit. It is strange. But I like most things I
read. I always like to seek out and note what is praiseworthy
rather than what is blameworthy." [48] In Herder we have the criticism of beauties rather than faults of which Chateaubriand is supposed to be the originator. It is actually not so much criticism as
understanding, empathy (*Einfühlung*), submission to the author.
"If there need be criticism of poets, then criticism which traces the
steps of the original, which feels after it is the best." [49] Herder has
glimpses of a science of interpretation, *hermeneutics,* as it had
been developed especially in Protestant theology. He constantly
asks for "living reading," for a "divination of the soul of an
author," for a consideration of every book as the imprint of a living human soul. "Such reading is emulation, *heuristics* . . . the
more we *know* a living author and have lived with him, the more
vital will be our contact." [50] Thus "criticism without genius is
nothing. Only a genius can judge and teach another." [51] These
were important sayings, salutary in their time for their stress on
understanding, but they also contain the germs of much that is
bad in criticism since Herder's time: mere impressionism, the idea
of "creative" criticism with its pretensions to duplicating a work
of art by another work of art, the critical errors of excessive attention to biography and the intention of the author, mere appreciation, and complete relativism.

This empathic conception of criticism is closely related to
Herder's historical sense, his insistence that every work of litera-

ture needs to be seen and interpreted in its historical setting. "Every sound critic in the whole world says that, in order to understand and interpret a piece of literature, it is necessary to put oneself . . . in the spirit of the piece itself." [52] "The most indispensable explanation especially of a poet is the explanation of the customs of his age and nation." [53] In the late *Briefe zur Beförderung der Humanität* (1796) Herder expressly discusses methods of literary study. He rejects classification by genres and finds division into types such as "subjective" and "objective" (in Schiller) vague and unprofitable. The correct method is the "natural method, which leaves each flower in its place, and contemplates it there just as it is, according to time and kind, from the root to the crown. The most humble genius hates ranking and comparison. He would rather be the first in a village, than the second after Caesar. Lichen, moss, fern, and the richest scented flower: each blooms in its place in God's order." [54] The natural method is Herder's own, the historical method, which sees each work as part and parcel of its milieu and hence feels that each is in its place, fulfills its temporary function, and thus really needs no criticism. Everything had to be the way it has been: there is no need of judging, no need of standards, as all ages are equal. In *Auch eine Philosophie der Geschichte zur Bildung der Menschheit* (1774) he defended the Middle Ages and rejected the idea of uniform progress. "Nothing in the whole kingdom of God is . . . a means only —everything is means and end at the same time, and certainly also these centuries," [55] a saying which anticipates Ranke's famous phrase that every age is "immediate to God." Luckily Herder did not develop the full consequences of his historical relativism, though his sympathies and taste were catholic beyond those of any critic of the 18th century.

We can describe his conception and ideal of poetry quite concretely. Herder's aesthetic is curiously sensualistic: he tried to deduce the individual arts from their respective senses, distinguishing sharply between painting—the art of the eye, music—the art of the ear, and sculpture—the art of touch. The last idea, later developed in a little work on *Plastik* (1778), was especially new at the time. At first Herder saw no way of reducing poetry to one of the senses and did not even classify it with the arts. Later he concluded that poetry has a special position in being the art of imagination, the "only fine art immediate for the soul," the "music of the soul" [56] which "affects the inner sense, not the external eye of the artist." [57] This view is effectively used in Herder's attempt at a refutation of the *Laokoon*, in the first *Kritisches Wäldchen* (1769), which, though diffuse, is one of his most impressive and coherent performances. He argues that Lessing's contrast between painting as an art of space and poetry as an art of time is specious. The mere succession in time is not central to the effect of poetry. Succession in time he assigns, unconvincingly, to music, forgetting about harmony and ignoring the fact that his arguments on poetry apply also to the forms of music. Sounds in poetry and language have meaning or soul. Poetry differs from the other arts by being energy, not work, a distinction Herder drew from James Harris' *Three Treatises* and ultimately from Aristotle (*energeia* vs. *ergon*). Herder's spontaneous energy is an obscure idea which removes poetry from the other arts, each correlated to a sense, merely on the analogy of the triad "time, space, and energy." [58] He seems to mean an organizing power, a coherence of imaginative ideas,[59] which makes it possible for poetry to express not only actions in succession but also bodies, images, pictures. "I learn from Homer that the effect of poetry is never that of sound upon the ear, nor is it upon the memory, however long I can retain any particular detail out of the whole succession of details, but upon my imagination. . . . I thus oppose it to painting, and regret that Mr. Lessing has not paid attention to this central point of the nature of poetry, this 'effect on our soul, or energy.' " [60]

Herder never gave up the view that poetry stands apart as the art of emotion, expression, and energy, appealing to the imagination. Nevertheless he recognized more and more its basis in language and in the sound of language. He asks us to read a poet (Jakob Balde) "not with the eyes alone." "Hear him simultaneously, or, as far as possible, read him aloud to somebody else. Lyrical poems should be read that way. . . . With the sound emerges their spirit, movement, life." [61] He can advise a friend to whom he has sent his translations of Shakespeare's lyrics: "You must only sing, not read." [62] He constantly stresses the sound and meter of poetry, and criticizes the inappropriate meter of Denis' German translation of Ossian. His own numerous verse translations all attempt first to imitate the sound, the tone, and the meter. Such a conception of poetry is, of course, lyrical. "Lyrical poetry is the perfect expression of an emotion or representation in the highest euphony of language." [63] This is a late definition, but even among the earliest fragments of Herder we find two sketches for a history of the ode and the lyric. The ode is "the firstborn child of emotion, the origin of poetry, the germ of its life." [64] This view is associated with the view that there was an original unity of poetry and music, that poetry was never more powerful than when it was combined with music, that the poet and the composer were originally the same: all ideas suggested by John Brown and known to anybody who had studied the Greek drama. Herder would say even that the "Greek theater was song," [65] and would refer to the tragedy of Sophocles as "heroic opera." [66]

Language is associated in Herder's mind with literature from the very beginning. The first collection of the *Fragmente* opens with the statement that the "genius of a language is also the genius of the literature of the nation." [67] Hence the origins of poetry and of language are one and the same. Herder's treatise *Über den Ursprung der Sprache* (1772) is thus a speculative history not only of language but also of poetry. The first language was nothing but a collection of elements of poetry. A "dictionary of the soul, it was at the same time mythology and a marvelous epic of the actions and speeches of all beings—thus a constant fable with passion and interest," song, poetry, and music all rolled into one.[68] Herder here rejects both the divine origin of language and the old rationalistic compact theory, at the same time improving on Condillac's sensualistic theory which derived language from cries. Man, according to Herder, invented language "from the tones of living nature [and made them] signs of his governing reason." [69] Consciousness (*Besonnenheit*) made signs out of cries. Thus poetry is not merely a lyrical cry but also fable and myth, and is shot through and through with metaphor. In Herder's theory of knowledge [70] the role of imagery and analogy is central. "What we know, we know from analogy, from creature to us and from us to the creator." There is no other key to the interior of things than imagery, analogy. "I am not ashamed . . . of running after images, similarities, after laws of agreement with the One, because I know no other play of my thinking powers (if we must think at all) and because I believe that Homer and Sophocles, Dante, Shakespeare, and Klopstock have furnished more matter to psychology and the knowledge of man than even the Aristotles and Leibnizes of all nations and times." [71] A late piece, "Über Bild, Dichtung und Fabel" (1786), expounds this in some detail. "Our whole life is, so to speak, a poetics. We do not see, we create images ourselves." [72] Poetry is naturally metaphorical and allegorical (Herder, it seems, does not distinguish between allegory and symbolism). Primitive man thinks in symbols, allegories, and metaphors, and their combinations make fables and myths. Thus poetry is not an imitation of nature but an "imitation of the creating, naming Godhead." [73] The poet is a "second creator, *poietes,* maker," [74] a saying which associates the poet with Prometheus and which comes from Shaftesbury. The poet is an original, an individual, and in Herder's mind this is not incompatible with his creating unconsciously and intuitively: Shakespeare "paints passion to its deepest abysses without his knowing" of it and describes Hamlet "unconsciously" up to his hair.[75] Later Herder became disgusted with the excesses of the *Sturm und Drang* cult of pure genius and began to reaffirm the role of reason and judgment, but he never gave up his view that genius is mainly instinctive, even sensuous. In long-winded and often quibbling polemics directed against Kant's conception of genius in the *Kritik der Urteilskraft,* Herder reaffirms his view that genius is inborn, that it expresses itself and possesses not merely imagination and reason but also a "disposition of sensuous sensibilities as well as that divine urge, that quiet mental warmth which is enthusiasm but not rapture." [76]

It is no chance, of course, that the concept of poetry and the poet here expounded is seen in terms of a history of poetry in which the origins of poetry describe its nature. Herder is convinced that "it is absolutely impossible to have a philosophical theory of the beautiful in all arts and sciences without history." [77] The concepts of a theory of literature "grow out of manifold concrete things, in many kinds and phenomena, in which genesis is the All-in-All." [78] "If we want ever to achieve a philosophical poetics or a history of poetry, then we must begin with the individual genres and trace them back to their origins." [79] He would say that as the "tree from the root, so must the progress and the flowering of an art be deduced from its origin. It contains the whole being of its product just as a whole plant is hidden with all its parts in a grain of

seed." [80] "Origins show the nature of a thing." [81] This is the doctrine which the 19th century was to push to the extreme of neglect-
ing the problems of description and evaluation in contemporary
terms in favor of explanation by remote prehistory. It was to lead
to an emphasis on Sanskrit and Proto-Indo-European rather than
the study of contemporary speech, of Anglo-Saxon literature as
compared to the study of the literature of our own time.

This evolution of literature is conceived of by Herder as literal
evolution, as the growing of a germ, on a completely biological
analogy. In describing the followers of Homer in Greece Herder
says, "where an epigenesis, i.e., a living additional growth in regular form or powers and limbs, should occur, there must be, as the
whole of nature shows, a living germ, a shape of nature and art,
whose growth all elements joyously favor. Homer planted such a
germ, an epic art form. His family, the school of the Homerids,
brought up the tree." [82] Though this biological parallel permeates
all of Herder's writings on literary history and history in general,
he does not quite draw the fatalistic conclusions which are implied
in any view of the growing, maturing, and aging of poetry. Actually Herder does not believe in uniform degeneration from the
glories of the age of poetry, though there are many passages [83] in
his writings which would suggest this view, common at that time.
It was argued that there used to be an age of imagination, that we
have now entered an age of reason and are thus fatally committed
to further progress and hence to the drying up of the sources of
imagination. We found this view in Vico and Fontenelle's *Traité
de la poésie en général*. To Vico and Herder poetry belongs to the
past, since it requires contact with nature, emotion, and spontaneity, which modern civilization stifles and kills.[84]

The biological view of the evolution of poetry should logically
produce resignation to an inevitable development. Poetry is the
language of primitive man, of the childhood of mankind, and no
return is possible since none of us can become young again. But
Herder's view is not logical: first of all, he has recourse to the
theory of cycles. Humanity is not conceived of as a single individual—there are as many humanities as there are nations. After
the decline of Rome, there came the new flowering of the Middle
Ages; after the degeneracy of the Renaissance and its artificial
literature, there may come a new flowering of the imagination.

Moreover, Herder frequently forgets the implications of his deterministic biological point of view and simply appeals to the will to change the direction of development, asking for a return to the age of poetry. "Let us return to the oldest human nature and everything else will be all right." [85] In this view the Germans have a peculiar position. They seem to him in the greatest danger of losing their individuality and forgetting the treasures of their past. "Now," he shouts, mixing his metaphors more than usually, "Now! The remnants of all living folkways are rolling with a last hurried plunge into the abyss of oblivion. The light of so-called culture corrodes everything like a cancer." [86] "We are at the very edge of the abyss: another half a century and it is too late." [87] Herder, after all, was a practical critic, a reformer who wanted to change the direction of literature and influence his time. It could not be done by resigned fatalism. The whole argument of the *Fragmente,* his first important publication, is directed against imitation, especially that of French and Latin literature. There also, for the first time, he publicly points to the regenerative power of folk poetry and recommends collecting it, not only in Germany but among "Scyths and Slavs, Wends and Bohemians, Russians, Swedes, and Poles." [88] Thus a turn in the development of literature is possible if we return to our own past and to the past of humanity which lies all around us, in folk poetry, songs, legends, and myths, even in superstitions and in the character of the language. Herder is one of those who believe that the German language is somehow peculiarly aboriginal because it is not derived from the Latin and is not a mixture of Latin and Germanic as is English. Thus Germans should cultivate its peculiarities, its idioms, its wealth of synonyms, its inversions, all its illogicalities, which are a source of poetry compared to the clarity, straightforwardness, poverty, and shallowness of the French language.

Throughout Herder's activity there runs this messianic desire to be a reformer and restorer of German poetry, and one must recognize that the advent of Goethe, who was Herder's personal pupil, seemed to justify his optimism and prophecy. One can understand how bitter was his disappointment when Goethe, and with him Schiller, turned to what Herder considered sterile classicism and aestheticism, thus denying all his teachings of a return to the folk and the national past.[89] Herder had constantly condemned the

Latin influence in the Middle Ages and Renaissance and the French influence in the 17th and 18th centuries: "O the cursed word: Classic! It has made Cicero a classic orator; Horace and Virgil classic school poets, Caesar a pedant, and Livy a word-monger." [90] He had argued that the Germans were worse afflicted than the English with the disease of the artificial. This is the point of a remarkable paper, "Von Ähnlichkeit der mittleren englischen und deutschen Dichtkunst" (1777), which tries to explain why Germany had no Shakespeare.[91] According to Herder, English civilization remained national and even managed to assimilate the Renaissance. Shakespeare is to him a popular writer who draws his materials from folk songs, ballads, romances, and popular chronicles.[92] Shakespeare always looms in the background of English poetry, and the English have never lost touch with their national past. Herder constantly praises the efforts of the English antiquaries and sees them as superior to those of their German colleagues. "If we consider the learned industry which the English have lavished on their old poets, e.g., Warton on Spenser, Tyrwhitt on Chaucer, Percy on the ballads, and so many, many of their best read men on their Shakespeare and their old drama: and then consider ourselves—what shall we say?" [93] The Germans were overwhelmed by humanism, handicapped by a lack of a national state, torn by the wars of religion.

> Thus, from ancient times we have absolutely no living poetic literature upon which our modern poetry might have grown, as a branch upon the national stem; whereas other nations have progressed with the centuries, and have shaped themselves upon their own soil, from native products, upon the belief and taste of the people, from the remains of the past. In that way their literature and language have become national, the voice of the people has been used and cherished. They have secured far more of a public in these matters than we Germans have. We poor Germans have been destined from the start never to remain ourselves.[94]

Thus Herder's theoretical historicism is offset by his practical patriotism, by his belief that the Germans need to be saved from the blight of civilization and returned to the wellsprings of their power.

But it would be a mistake to think of Herder merely as a Teutonizing nationalist: his whole conception of the nation was that of a steppingstone toward "humanity." From a literary point of view the German nation was inferior to those which had preserved their individuality better and longer. Thus Herder constantly held up the example of other nations, and tirelessly translated, collected, and described the wealth of the world's literature. His *Volkslieder* (1777–78), now best known under the title given to them after Herder's death, *Stimmen der Völker in Liedern,* is the first comprehensive anthology of world literature, animated by a conception of folk poetry which was extremely broad and included much which we would not today think of calling by this term. Folk poetry is to Herder the fullest and most cherished embodiment of a people's soul. "Unless we have a folk," he says, "we lack also a public, a nation, a language, and a literature that are ours, that live and work in us. We write eternally for desk students and squeamish critics . . . we write romances, odes, heroic epics, church and kitchen songs, which no one understands, no one desires, no one feels. Our classical literature is a bird of paradise, gaily colored, very pretty, all flight, all elevation, but never with a foot on German earth." [95] Herder thus does not confuse the folk with the lower classes. "Folk does not mean the rabble on the streets which never sings and creates, but roars and mutilates." [96] Folk poetry is a highly inclusive concept: it includes Genesis, the Song of Songs, the Book of Job, the Psalms, in fact nearly all of the Old Testament. It includes Homer, Hesiod, Aeschylus and Sophocles, Sappho and the *Greek Anthology,* Chaucer, Spenser, Shakespeare, and the contents of Percy's *Reliques* (not only English and Scottish ballads but Elizabethan songs). It includes medieval romances, the German *Heldenbuch,* the troubadours, the *Minnesang,* Bürger's ballads, and Klopstock, whom Herder admired beyond any of the German poets. It includes even Dante [97] and of course Ossian.

Ossian crystallized Herder's conception of folk poetry. The reputation of these monotonous, melancholy, sentimental rhythmic compositions by James Macpherson was tremendous all over Europe. Herder first read them in the hexameter translation by Denis, turning also to Hugh Blair's *Dissertation on the Poems of Ossian* (1763), which gave him all the materials for the comparison

with Homer. He read, besides, the notes supplied by Denis, reproducing those of the Italian translation by Cesarotti. There he could
read that "Imagination was the first philosophy of nations. Here
one must look for the origin of myth. One must agree with Vico
when he says: Raw nature produces poets." [98] Herder, without as
yet knowing the original English, condemned the artificial translation of Denis and created for himself the image of a natural poet
through the mist of what he considered the translation of a translation. He himself adopted passages from Denis, translating them
into a style which he fancied that of folk poetry, a style much
more abrupt, more obscure, halting, and "wild" than the fluid and
placid *Ossian* of Macpherson.[99] When Herder saw the originals at
last, he experienced a disappointment he laid to Macpherson's
"translation." But his suspicions began to be aroused by contact
with an eccentric Scotchman, Baron de Harold. In the *Volkslieder*
Ossian is represented only by three specimens, and in the prefaces
he is passed over with surprising silence. Herder never quite gave
up the view that Macpherson was not an inventor but a reworker,
a collector, and did not live to see the full evidence which demonstrated on how slender a basis Macpherson had constructed his edi-
fice of supposedly third-century Gaelic epics. Herder's astonishing
enthusiasm for Ossian was the basis for his conception of folk and
national song. Even the Creation story in the Book of Genesis he
thought of as developed out of a number of primitive folk songs.[100]

This conception of folk poetry is most conspicuous and most one-
sided in Herder's view of Shakespeare. A paper entitled "Shakespeare" was contributed by Herder to a collection called *Von
deutscher Art und Kunst* (1773), which included Goethe's lyrical
address on the Strasbourg cathedral: "Von deutscher Baukunst."
The Shakespeare piece is a most characteristic performance, a
lyrical rhapsody rather than a piece of criticism. It begins with a
vision of Shakespeare sitting high on the summit of a rock, at his
feet storm, thunder, and the roaring of the sea, but with his head
in the rays of heaven. The question of the unities is then brushed
aside by the historical argument: in Greece the drama arose in a
way in which it could not arise in the North. Nordic drama cannot be the same as Greek. The drama of Sophocles and that of
Shakespeare are two separate things, which from a certain point
of view should hardly have the name in common. The unities

were necessary in Greece from their origin in the chorus. The whole French tragedy is a "glittering classic thing," "without nature," "absurd," "disgusting." Shakespeare did not find a chorus, he found puppet shows and chronicle plays before him. His dramas are "dark little symbols of an outline for a theodicy" (an allusion to Lessing's conception of tragedy). *Lear, Othello,* and *Macbeth* are described by evoking their setting: e.g. the heath with lightning and thunder, the swallows nesting in Macbeth's castle. In each play there is, according to Herder, a pervading mood which permeates it like the soul of the world. "Take the soil, the sap, and the energy from this plant, and you have planted it in air: take away place, time, individual status from these men, and you have taken away their breath and soul." How absurd is the question of the unity of time! What must be the illusion experienced by a man who after every scene will look at his watch to see whether it could have happened in the time elapsed. For a poet, a creator, a "dramatic God" no clock strikes on spire or temple: he has to make his own measures of space and time to produce a world which will move the audience. How Shakespeare has transformed a miserable romance, novel, or fabulous history into a living whole is the question Herder would consider the heart of the investigation. But he does not really attempt it and ends with a suggestion on the classification of Shakespeare's plays. They are all "history in the widest sense," the "greatly portentous happening of a world event, of a human fate." [101] The view that Shakespeare's plays are dramatizations of ballad materials was, of course, not Herder's only. There are many suggestions along these lines in English 18th-century editions. Even Johnson thought that Shakespeare took the story of King Lear "perhaps immediately from an old historical ballad." The *Reliques* of Percy contained a whole section on "Ballads That Illustrate Shakespeare." Both in Percy and in Herder's *Volkslieder* Shakespeare is represented by scenes such as the Willow Song from *Othello* or the songs of Ophelia in *Hamlet.* One sees what further motive there was in Herder's call for a collection of German folk songs. Such a collection, he must have felt, might stimulate the new German Shakespeare. That is why he urged Goethe to collect folk songs in Alsace. That is why he hailed *Goetz von Berlichingen,* based on an ancient chronicle, and *Faust,* which is drawn from a puppet play and includes songs, one of them imitated from *Ham-let.*

It would be easy to criticize Herder's conception of folk poetry, or rather of nature poetry. The overrating of Ossian seems the most incomprehensible: "There will be times," he prophesied, "that will say: let us close Homer, Virgil, and Milton, and judge from Ossian." [102] The view that poets such as Chaucer or Dante were in any way popular seems to us totally mistaken. Herder certainly has a very one-sided conception of Shakespeare or Homer: he overrated or started the overrating of all kinds of folklore without being able to distinguish genuine productions from artificial derivatives and even fakes such as Ossian. His criticism of much neoclassical literature seems to us grossly unjust. His conception is too indulgent toward the purely naive, the mere lyrical cry, the merely spontaneous, and too inimical to great art, which may be intellectual, sophisticated, ironical, grotesque. But we must realize that Herder was struck with the novelty of his discoveries, which were fresh and appealing against the background of a decaying neoclassicism, while we are inured to many romantic charms by a century and a half of their vulgarization. We must not underrate the historical importance of Herder's conception of poetry, which certainly widened the horizon immeasurably and brushed aside many narrow or false conceptions of the neoclassical creed: its stress on the unities, its preoccupation with pure genres, its limitation to upper-class literature. In spite of the excesses of his primitivism and lyricism, Herder had a clearer and truer conception of poetry than all the critics we have discussed hitherto. His conception of poetry is centrally true: he is right in his stress on the role of metaphor, symbol, and myth, on poetry's essential function in a healthy society.

But Herder's importance lies not merely in his new conception of poetry or even in his general scheme of its origins. He is also, in many ways, the first modern historian of literature who has clearly conceived of the ideal of universal literary history, sketched out its methods, and written outlines of its development which are not merely an accumulation of antiquarian research, as the works of Warton and Tiraboschi, or the *Histoire littéraire de la France* tended to be. Herder certainly raised a great many of the problems of literary history and suggested what should be done and what questions should be answered. Literary history should trace the "origins, the growth, the changes and the decay [of literature] according to the different styles of the regions, times, and poets." [103] "How has the spirit of literature changed in the different languages into which it entered? What did it take along from all the places and regions which it deserted? . . . What kind of a thing arose from the mixture and fermentation of such diverse matter?" [104] Herder rejects the ordinary literary history, which, "laden with learning, paces through nations and times in the quiet step of a miller's animal, with its eyes too close to the ground to see any of the visions that hover even a little above it." [105] He wants to grasp the spirit of literature and wishes the historian to hold "time against time, country against country, and genius against genius." [106] Literary history thus will "ennoble the desecrated phrases *histoire de l'esprit humain* and 'History of the Human Mind.' " [107] In theory, then, Herder's literary history is cultural history in the broadest sense. One sees its aim when he describes the procedure. In reading Dante or Petrarch, Ariosto or Cervantes he first sees only the poet, as a unique person; then he sees everything which has contributed to his formation or misformation.

> The whole world of poetry before and after him disappeared from my eye: I saw only him. But soon I was reminded of the whole course of the ages which came before him and after him. He learned and taught, he followed others, others followed him. His language, his ways of thought, his passions, were ties which connected him at first with a few other poets and in the end with all others. Because he was a *man,* he wrote for *men.* Thus unawares we are led to investigate how each poet stands in relation to those similar to him in his nation and outside of it, while his nation is compared to theirs both before and afterwards; and thus an indivisible chain pulls us into *pandemonium,* the realm of spirits.[108]

Literary history is thus conceived of primarily in sociological terms. There are impressionistic analyses of works of literature scattered through Herder's writings. The evocation of Sophocles' *Philoctetes* in the argument against Lessing is very suggestive and sensitive. *Vom Geist der ebräischen Poesie* (1782–83) contains many penetrating, but also many fantastic, interpretations of the Old Testament. Elsewhere there are comments on the odes of Horace. The taste and sensitivity of Herder could be most amply demonstrated and investigated by an examination of his numerous poetic translations, which are, on the whole, extremely successful, though he suffered from a lack of access to the originals or from inadequate philological knowledge. But there is nowhere in Herder an attempt to interpret a work of art as a total organism, to analyze its structure or composition. His literary history is one of broad vistas, wide sweeps, bold generalizations.

He has been considered a forerunner of Taine in his stress on milieu. There is in Herder much about climate (hot, cold, and temperate),[109] landscape, race (nations), customs, and even political conditions such as Athenian democracy in their relations to literature. One of his prize essays, called *Über die Wirkung der Dichtkunst auf die Sitten der Völker in alten und neuen Zeiten* (1778), is a survey of the history of literature with stress on its educative and civilizing function. But Herder rarely analyzes the environmental factors and never brings them into close relationship with the actual literature. He constantly argues in a circle: i.e., he explains a work of literature by history and then utilizes the work to throw light on history. In the case of Ossian, for instance, since there exist no early documents about ancient Scottish history, Herder derived all the information about the social setting from the poems, and that was extremely vague and baffling. He uses such criteria as climate and landscape very loosely, and even the racial point of view amounts to little more than the old contrast between North and South, the Germanic and the Latin nations. In a paper on Homer and Ossian, Herder tries to derive the poetic differences between the two from differences in climate and national stock.[110] But "Nordic," as often at that time, is a vague grandiose conception which includes not only the Germans but also the Celts and the English. We ought not to forget that Herder praised the Slavs as the great new peace-loving nation for which he prophesied a glorious future and which seemed to him still original and spontaneous.[111] Instead of climate, race, and concrete social conditions, Herder mostly operates with terms such as "spirit of the time," "spirit of a nation." He would say that "each age has its own tone, its color," and that it gives us "peculiar pleasure to characterize it correctly in contrast to other times." [112] He would generalize recklessly about the national taste of every one of the great European nations. "The Italian sings; the French prose-poetry reasons and narrates; the English thinks in his most un-musical language." [113]

But whatever the shortcomings of Herder's method—which to us, after 150 years of unparalleled accumulation of information and research, must appear dilettantish, arbitrary, and indiscrimi-nate—the value for the times of his sketches of literary history can-not be doubted. What was needed was a premature synthesis, an asking of questions, without which literary history would have been totally swamped by antiquarianism. Indeed, the bold sketches of the Schlegels are directly inspired by Herder. One of the best of Herder's outlines is in the 7th and 8th collections of *Briefe zur Beförderung der Humanität* (1796). He starts with the reasons for the decay of Greece and Rome and thus of Greek and Roman poetry, gives an enthusiastic account of Latin Christian hymns such as "Dies irae," sketchily describes Nordic sagas and myth-ology, and then, in some detail, Provençal poetry and the Minne-sang. The description of medieval poetry, with its stress on love, courage, and piety, and the suggestion of a connection between courtly love and the cult of the Virgin Mary, was certainly highly important for the romantic conception of the Middle Ages which only a few years later was in full bloom in Novalis' *Christenheit oder Europa*. Much is then made of the good and evil influence of the invention of printing, the Reformation, and humanism. Shakespeare is again explained as coming at the right moment be-tween the age of imagination and the age of reason, a "dramatic minstrel." [114] "Poetry of reflection" was soon to replace the "poetry of pure fable." Milton is to Herder the first and greatest of the poets of reflection, who created his own artificial language and wrote in a heroic measure, "monotonous, pompous, and noble." [115] Cowley is condemned because of his Pindarics, Pope's poetry is mildly praised as versified common sense, successful in satire and the burlesque. Young is rejected as a forced and strained hyper-bolical author, and even the praise of Thomson is only lukewarm. The treatment of English prose, of Swift, Richardson, and Field-ing, though laudatory, is only perfunctory and could not be sub-stantially supplemented from Herder's other writings.

Herder has been acclaimed as the father of Germanistics. But his

several attempts at histories of German literature are hardly systematic and well informed, even for the time. He begins a history
of German poetry with the *Edda* and reflections on the loss of
ancient German poetry. He translated the *Ludwigslied* and
strangely enough thought Otfried was writing in Bardic meter. But
his knowledge of Old High German and Middle High German
literature was apparently quite scanty. Once he examined the
famous Jena manuscript of the *Minnesänger* and transcribed
rather badly some poems of Henry VI, King Conrad, and Duke
Henry of Breslau. He was still untouched by the enthusiasm for
the *Nibelungen* and the German court epic, and did not know
Walther von der Vogelweide. His main interest was in the didactic
literature of the later Middle Ages and in *Reineke Fuchs,* which he
extravagantly praised as a German Homer. Among Reformation
forms of literature Herder lavishly praises German church song,
and among 17th-century authors he took an especial liking to a
Jesuit writing in Latin, Jakob Balde, whom he translated and
recommended late in his life. This is Herder's one close contact
with a writer whom today we would call baroque, but an examination of his translations shows how much he shared the prejudice
of his time against the wit and conceit of Jesuit poetry. It is no
chance that he endorsed Johnson's discussion of the metaphysicals
and went out of his way to condemn Cowley's Pindarics, calling
them a "Gothic building, incoherent and obscure in its details, exaggerated in its metaphors, overladen with ornament." [116] There
are many survivals of 18th-century taste in Herder's predilection
for didactic and moralistic poetry. For instance the taste for Metastasio, the "poetic masterwork of his nation," is surprising.[117]

Herder is, of course, most disappointing when he discusses the
French, for here his national and literary prejudices are greatest.
He could not have known much of the French Middle Ages: he is
obviously full of disgust for the "pomp" and "show" of the French
drama of the 17th and 18th centuries. For the *Pucelle d'Orléans*
Voltaire is praised only as a witty storyteller. Diderot, whom
Herder met in Paris as a youth (1769), remained one of his favorite
authors, and late in life he planned a translation of his writings
which apparently would have extended to some of the novels, such
as *Jacques le Fataliste.* Among the French writers Herder singles
out for praise La Fontaine, as their "most original genius, whose
charm will never become obsolete, as long as the French language

lasts." [118] Herder seems not to have known anything about the
Spanish drama; but his last work, shortly before his death, was a
free translation of the Cid romances, which unfortunately was
based on a collection of late Spanish poetical versions and a French
prose rendering.

This survey of Herder's literary opinions serves to illustrate
more concretely his conceptions of literary history and poetry. It
also serves, if we add what we have said before about his ideas
about Shakespeare and folk poetry, to point up the radical revalua-
tion of the past in which he was engaged and to exemplify the shift
of sensibility which had occurred in Germany around the year
1770: the turn toward the individual, the characteristic, the lyrical,
and the popular. In Herder the poetics of neoclassicism is, if not
dissolved completely, in the process of dissolution. He rejects all
its main tenets: the imitation of nature, decorum, the unities,
probability, propriety, clarity of style, purity of genre. Though he
speculates a good deal on genre and of course uses the names of the
genres, they constantly melt into one another in his discussions:
epic, drama, and lyric are almost the same to him. Herder obviously was not much interested in Aristotle, whom he called once
"a stiff man of bones like a skeleton: nothing but disposition, nothing but order." [119] Aristotle's theory of tragedy he considered a
mere deduction from the practice of the Greek theater, of no
validity whatever for later times. Only very late in his life, in
Adrastea, does Herder discuss catharsis, and then apparently just
to attack the drama of Goethe and Schiller with a new argument.[120] On the whole, he endorses Lessing's view of Aristotle, for
didacticism was apparently the strongest neoclassical conception
(and incidentally the strongest religious preconception) surviving
in Herder. In him we see then the ruins of neoclassical poetics: he
himself began to build a new romantic poetics on the conception of
a natural poetry, sensuous, metaphorical, imaginative, spontaneous, with a standard of judgment based on historical relativism and
an implicit distaste for the poetry of statement, reasoning, or reflection. But Herder's terminology is very loose: his concepts are
shifting, his language is emotional and rhapsodical. While he was
the great initiator, he left to others the task of formulating a new,
coherent, systematic theory of poetry and literature. His first disciple was, Goethe, who proved an unfaithful one.

GOETHE (1749–1832) wrote a whole library, and an even larger library has been written about him. It is thus surprising to discover that there is no extended systematic discussion of his literary criticism, though Sainte-Beuve called him the "greatest critic of all ages" and Matthew Arnold "the supreme critic." [1] The reasons for this failure of Goethe scholarship are not far to seek: the mere bulk of his production, the fact that his literary pronouncements are rarely stated in a systematic context, the difficulty of isolating his strictly literary criticism from his speculations on the plastic arts and on art and nature in general, and finally the span of his life, the constant shifts and changes in his views, are obstacles which could be overcome only by long study and meditation. A full treatment would require a volume in itself. To be methodologically sound it would have to proceed on chronological lines, carefully distinguishing between the time before his arrival in Weimar (1775), the time in Weimar before the Italian journey (1786–88), the Italian journey itself, the period after the return to Weimar before the association with Schiller (1794), the friendship with Schiller to the time of Schiller's death (1805), and the last years, in which one could again discover several stages. A monographic treatment would make a distinction between Goethe's formal pronouncements in works such as *Dichtung und Wahrheit,* his more occasional journalistic writings, his private letters and diaries, and finally his conversations, among which those reported by Eckermann hold a special place because of their substantial accuracy. As we do not have the space to make these distinctions, we shall discuss Goethe first before his journey to Italy and then as the mature writer, without much regard to chronology or source of information.

The young Goethe, after he had freed himself from the conventional rococo taste of his student years at Leipzig, was converted by

Herder during their association in Strasbourg in the winter of
1770–71. Goethe completely adopted the Herderian point of view.
He collected and imitated folk songs, shared Herder's enthusiasm
for Ossian and a primitive Homer, was carried away by Rousseau,
and adored Shakespeare. In the speech *Zum Schakspears Tag*
(1771) he made a fervent profession of personal indebtedness.

> The first page I read of him made me his own for life, and
> when I had finished the first play I stood there like a man born
> blind to whom a miraculous hand had given sight in an
> instant. . . . I did not doubt for a moment that I must give
> up the regular theater. The unity of place seemed to me nar-
> row as a prison, the unities of time and action obnoxious
> chains for our imagination. . . . Shakespeare's theater is a
> beautiful peepshow, in which the history of the world passes
> by our eyes on the invisible thread of time. His plots are, to
> speak in the vulgar style, no plots, but his plays all revolve
> around the hidden point (which no philosopher has seen and
> defined) in which the specific quality of our ego, the assumed
> freedom of our will clashes with the necessary course of the
> whole.

Echoing the praise heaped upon Shakespeare since Dryden, Goethe
rapturously exclaims, "Nature, Nature! Nothing is as much
Nature as Shakespeare's men. . . . He competes with Prometheus,
he forms his men after him trait by trait, only in colossal size." Behind Shakespeare looms Greek tragedy: "Originally an intermezzo
in the cult of the god, then solemnly civic, the tragedy presented
to the people certain great actions of their forefathers with the
pure simplicity of perfection, and stirred whole, great emotions
in their souls, for it was itself whole and great." Shakespeare and
this religious, national drama written for Greek souls (and what
souls!) dwarf French tragedy which Goethe had hitherto admired.
"Little Frenchman, what do you want with the Greek armor? It is
too big and heavy for you." It would be easier for a marquis to
imitate Alcibiades than for Corneille to follow Sophocles. "Arise,
Gentlemen!" Goethe concludes his exhortation: "trumpet all noble
souls out of the paradise of so-called good taste!" [2]

The agreement with Herder's piece on Shakespeare is obvious.
There is the same emphasis on Shakespeare as a "historian" of

humanity. Like Herder, Goethe always sees in Shakespeare's plays some hidden unity, some prevailing tone. Among the excesses of the *Sturm und Drang* Goethe preserves a feeling for form, both in his writings and in his literary theory. When commenting on Heinrich Leopold Wagner's translation of Mercier, he says that "it is at last time to stop talking about the form of dramatic plays, their length and shortness, their unities, their beginning, their middle and end." He would rather have a confused play than a cold one. But he sees that nothing much is achieved by stretching every tragic event to a drama, by compressing every novel to a play, as his friends and contemporaries were doing. An "inner form" is required: and if "form, even the most felt form, has something untrue to it, still it is, once for all, the burning glass, through which we draw the holy rays of scattered nature to the heart of men in a fiery focus." [3]

The term "inner form," derived from Shaftesbury, only hints at the problem with which the young Goethe was faced: if we reject the system of neoclassicism what is there to replace it? In the meantime he could say only: let us have feeling, inspiration, genius, "adoration for the creative man," [4] nature in the sense of simplicity and truth, even naturalism. Goethe then defends the Dutch peasant women representing Madonnas in Rembrandt's pictures and wants to leave Rubens his fleshy women, because they are *his* women.[5] Generality is empty, "characteristic art is the only true art," says Goethe in his ecstatic praise of Strasbourg cathedral, which defies all 18th-century scorn for the Gothic.[6] Aesthetics mean little to the young Goethe. Theory, he asserts, blocks the way to true enjoyment.[7] In reviewing one of the works of Sulzer, Goethe rejects the concept of *la belle nature*, didacticism, and the whole psychological approach to the response of the audience. "What does the gaping audience matter?" The only function of theory is to "free the energies of the artist, to make air for his natural fire that it may spread and be active." [8]

The ten-odd reviews which Goethe wrote for the *Frankfurter Gelehrte Anzeigen* (1772–73) are the most formal pronouncements of his early years on literature: [9] they are all either satirical squibs or lyrical meditations rather than critical analyses. They all assert his dislike of the rationalistic, rococo civilization around him, and contrast the artificial with the natural and genuine, the greatness of the past with the littleness of the present. Sulzer is ridiculed for an adaptation of Shakespeare's *Cymbeline*. "Shakespeare, who felt the worth of several centuries in his breast, through whose soul the life of whole centuries was stirring!—and here—comedians in silk and buckram and daubed scene painting!" [10] An imitation of Sterne's *Sentimental Journey* by J. G. Schummel is judged by the criterion of spontaneity and sincerity. "Yorick felt, and this one sat down to feel: Yorick was seized by a mood, cried and laughed in a minute, and through the magic of sympathy we laugh and cry with him: but here stands somebody and reflects: how do I laugh and cry? What will the people say when I laugh and cry? What will the reviewers say?" [11] Sterne, one of the most histrionic, self-conscious writers of the time, becomes the model of genuine feeling and sincerity; so in Werther's heart the contrivances of Ossian expel Homer, and the sentimentalities of *The Vicar of Wakefield* transfigure Goethe's love for the rector's daughter of Sesenheim.* But amidst this cult of feeling Goethe preserves some critical sense and a feeling for form. In a review of Gessner's idylls he applies the standard of totality effectively; in Gessner "the spirit is lacking which weaves together the pieces so that each could become an essential part of the whole. Gessner cannot fuse scene, action and feeling." He remains in the land of ideas, of the shadows of abstract beauty.[12]

This standard of totality and wholeness conceived on the analogy of nature is also the most remarkable feature of the famous discussion of *Hamlet* in *Wilhelm Meister*. As *Wilhelm Meisters Lehrjahre* was published as late as 1795, these passages are usually considered the work of the mature Goethe. But a practically identical discussion is in the earlier version, *Wilhelm Meisters Theatralische Sendung,* composed between 1778 and 1785, the years in Weimar before the Italian journey.[13] It shows the beginnings of the change in Goethe's literary views. The unity of action is recognized as necessary and there is praise for Corneille, his "noble soul," his "great vein." [14] But what is said about Shakespeare is still in the tone of the early years. Through the mouth of his hero

---

* See Goethe's famous account in *Dichtung und Wahrheit,* Bk. 10, and the praise of Goldsmith in a letter to Zelter, Dec. 25, 1829. Weimar, Pt. 4, *46,* 193–4. Goethe classed Goldsmith with Shakespeare and Sterne. Cf. Eckermann, 2, Dec. 16, 1828; Houben, p. 239.

Goethe describes the effect of Shakespeare on himself. The plays
"are not fictions. You would think while reading them that you
stood before the open enormous Books of Fate, while the whirl-
wind of the most impassioned life was howling through the leaves
and tossing them to and fro." [15] The echo in style and conception
of Herder's rhapsody is as clear as in the speech for Shakespeare's
birthday.

The famous characterization of *Hamlet* is closely interwoven
with the action but must be assumed to represent Goethe's own
views. Meister, who is to play Hamlet on the stage, tries to interpret his role by distinguishing what Hamlet's character might have
been before the news of his father's death. This young man is then
confronted with the task of avenging his father. It is laid "upon a
soul unfit for the performance of it . . . An oak tree is here planted
in a costly jar, which should have borne only pleasant
flowers in its bosom: the roots expand, the jar is shivered. A
lovely, pure, noble, and most moral nature, without the strength
of nerve which forms a hero, sinks beneath a burden it cannot
bear and must not cast away. All duties are holy to him: this one
is too heavy." [16] The active Hamlet who talks bawdry and daggers,
kills Polonius like a rat, and sends Rosenkranz and Guildenstern
to their death is forgotten. Hamlet has become an 18th-century
melancholiac.

Meister (or rather Goethe) wants to defend every detail of the
play: acceptance, sympathetic criticism designed to "penetrate the
sense and the intentions of the author," [17] is Goethe's as it was
Herder's aim. We must understand why Ophelia sings lascivious
songs: "When her self-command is altogether gone, when the
secrets of her heart are hovering on her tongue, that tongue betrays her: and in the innocence of insanity she solaces herself,
unmindful of king or queen, with the echo of her loose and well-
beloved songs." [18] The director's suggestion to combine Rosenkranz and Guildenstern into one character is rejected.

> What these two persons are and do it is impossible to repre-
> sent by one. It is in such small matters that we discover
> Shakespeare's greatness. These soft approaches, this smirking
> and bowing, this assenting, wheedling, flattering, this whisk-
> ing agility, this wagging of the tail, this allness and emptiness,

this legal knavery, this ineptitude and insipidity—how can they be represented by a single man? There ought to be at least a dozen of these people, if they could be had: for it is only in society that they are anything; they are society itself; and Shakespeare showed no little modesty and wisdom in bringing in only a pair of them.[19]

Meister also defends the composition of *Hamlet:* "I am very far from censuring the plan of *Hamlet:* on the contrary I believe there never was a grander one invented: nay it is not invented, it is so— the hero is without plan, but the play is full of plan." [20] When the director of the company suggests cutting the play, separating the wheat from the chaff, Wilhelm will not hear of it. "It is not wheat and chaff together, it is a trunk with boughs, twigs, leaves, buds, blossoms, and fruit. Is not the one there with the other, and by means of them?" [21] But while Meister would like to present an un- cut *Hamlet,* he recognizes the practical impossibility and suggests adaptations. He will have nothing to do with the happy ending which is currently being acted in Germany. "How can I keep Hamlet alive when the whole play is crushing him to death?" [22] But Meister distinguishes between external relations and the grand internal relations of the persons and events, and would cut the role of Fortinbras, the despatch of Hamlet to England, his capture by pirates, the death of the two courtiers by the letter, and so on.[23] Goethe (or Meister) as a stage manager would rid the play of all its business, all the survivals of the old story, and would almost reduce it to a psychological character study, a family tragedy. The way to the plan of an adaptation of 1811,[24] in which King Claudius in- stead of Polonius would be killed behind the arras and the last two acts be dropped entirely, is not so long as it may seem.

All Goethe's literary criticism before the trip to Italy is held together by standards of naturalness and spontaneity, by the whole concept of nature poetry codified by Herder. If we had only this much of Goethe's writings on literature we could not claim for him an important position in the history of criticism. Even the very influential discussion of *Hamlet* hardly goes beyond the char- acter writing of Henry Mackenzie and his companions in England and Scotland.

Goethe becomes important as a critic only later in his life, when

he has returned to classicism but reformulated it by assimilating
literary theory to a philosophy of nature which is also a theory of
symbolism. He comes back from Italy not only with his taste
changed but with a new theory developed under the influence of
the study of classical art and the reading of Winckelmann. But
Goethe does not merely restate neoclassicism, though for some
years at least, especially in the fine arts, he is a strict neoclassicist
recommending an art which we today would consider a dreary
academicism. Rather he uses the experience of his *Sturm und
Drang* period and the creed he has adopted from Herder to develop a theory which assimilates the basic tenets of classicism in
an original synthesis. Goethe never abandons his hold on the creativity of the poet, the experience of the artist's freedom, the autonomy of art. When he is praised as a master he declines the name
and prefers to be called "liberator." He claims only that he has
made the Germans aware that the "artist must always act from
inside, that do what he will he can only bring forth his individuality." [25] Goethe's sayings—that all his works are "fragments of a
great confession," [26] that all his poems are "occasional poems" [27]—
have been quoted over and over again to document his view that
poetry is self-expression. He speaks often of the personal release he
experiences in his art. *Werther* saved him from suicide, for in
writing it he overcame his own pathological condition.[28] Many
times Goethe describes the creative process as purely unconscious:
he wrote works like a sleepwalker, "instinctively, dreamily." [29]
Many times he asserts that "true creative power is in the unconscious," [30] that the "artist is born," that poetry is "inspiration . . .
genius." [31]

But these pronouncements must be interpreted in the light of
Goethe's new general outlook. Even the famous saying on "occasional poetry" means, if read in its context, something very different from personal poetry. It is rather poetry "occasioned by reality." Goethe always disapproved of mere subjectivity, which he
calls "the general disease of the age." [32] He always emphasizes that
the roots of poetry (particularly of his own) are in external reality.
He wants to give the "real a poetic form," [33] and he adopts with
pleasure the saying of Heinroth that his thinking is "objective." [34]
We might even conclude that his theory of art has become totally
extrovert, turned toward imitation of nature as all classicism was.

But Goethe has no difficulty in reconciling these apparent contradictions: his whole conception is based on a conviction of the profound identity of subject and object, mind and nature. In penetrating to the core of nature the artist expresses his innermost being; in surrendering to the deepest instincts of his mind he grasps the essence of things. When Goethe saw the great works of antiquity in Italy he felt that he had discovered this identity of man and nature, of the workings of the imagination and the laws of the universe. The Greek statues of the gods reveal the forces of the universe; they are at once poetry, nature, and art. "These noble works of art of the ancients are at the same time the noblest works of Nature, produced by men according to true and natural laws. Everything arbitrary, everything merely fanciful collapses; here is necessity, here is God." [35] The laws of art closely parallel the laws of nature: "they lie just as truly in the nature of creative genius, as the great universal nature preserves the organic laws in eternal activity." [36]

One of Goethe's first papers after the return from Italy, "Einfache Nachahmung, Manier, Stil" (1788) formulates his views most clearly. Style is the highest achievement of art. Simple imitation is the first stage, which is practiced by men of quiet, genuine, but limited nature. "Manner" arises when the artist expresses himself, gives an individual twist to representation. Style is above both the purely objective imitation and the purely subjective manner. When "art has acquired a clearer and clearer knowledge of the peculiarities of objects and their mode of being, oversees the classes of forms, and knows how to connect and imitate those that are distinct and characteristic—then style will reach the highest point it is capable of . . . style rests on the deepest foundations of knowledge, on the essence of things, so far as we are able to recognize it in visible and comprehensible forms." [37]

While such a term as the "essence of things" sounds like good classicism, it assumes its own Goethean coloring when he closely parallels the creation of nature and the creative process of the artist. The ideal artist must "succeed in penetrating into the depth of the objects as well as into the depth of his own mind, in order to produce something, in competition with nature, spiritual-organic, and to give his work of art such a content and form that it appears both natural and supernatural." [38] The artist must learn from na-

creates "a second nature," [39] another cosmos governed by the same
laws as nature. But how, we may ask, can the poet create according
to the laws of nature? One can see how Goethe could have found
such nature in Greek statues representing beautiful human bodies.
But is it possible to transfer the method of the sculptors to literature? Does it mean more than postulating the old Platonic ideal?

Still, Goethe tries to define his criteria of judgment, the descriptive terms by which a genuine work of art differs from a mere
exercise of technique or outpouring of sensibility. He adopts the
organism analogy, the concept of the wholeness, the totality of
every work of art. In abstracting the treatise of his friend Karl
Philipp Moritz, *Über die bildende Nachahmung der Natur* (1788),
he endorses the view that a work of art "is the miniature print of
the highest beauty of Nature." [40] It is thus the more beautiful the
more it mirrors this great whole. Moritz speaks of a "center," a
"focus" of a work of art, terms apparently drawn from perspective
and suggesting a central point of organization. A work of art is
complete, perfect in itself. "The beautiful in the fine arts arose,
without any regard for the good or ill it may cause, purely for its
own sake and the sake of its beauty." Any regard for the effect of
a work of art puts its focus outside, damages the quiet contemplation of it. About beauty one can say "nothing more sublime than
that *it is*." [41] A work of art must have a higher "inner form" which
in Goethe's mind excuses "imperfections of language and external
technique." [42]

Negatively the organism analogy is illustrated by Goethe's frequent rejection of analogies drawn from putting together, com-
posing, assembling. In talking of Mozart's *Don Juan* he becomes
quite indignant at the "vile" word "composition," which suggests
to him cooking, "as if [it] were a piece of cake made of eggs, flour
and sugar. It is a mental creation in every detail, and the whole is
of one spirit and act, permeated with the breath of one life." [43]
On the other hand, when Goethe wants to disapprove he also
speaks of works of literature in such biological analogies. Kleist's
version of *Amphitryon,* he asserts, "divorces the ancient and modern
rather than fusing it. If one brings together the opposite ends of
a living being by force, no new kind of organization results. At the
most it is a queer symbol, like the snake which bites its own tail." [44]
A bad work of art is often compared to a diseased body or plant.
In commenting on a "pathological" tragedy by a young poet

Goethe speaks of the "superfluity of sap bestowed on some parts which do not require it, and drawn out of those which stand in need of it. The subject is good, but the scenes which are expected are not there, while others which I did not expect were elaborated with assiduity and love." [45] Goethe similarly expresses his distaste for Heinrich von Kleist as "always exciting horror and disgust, like a body intended to be beautiful by nature which has been afflicted by an incurable disease." [46] Even in speaking of a writer rather than a work of art he says of Molière that he was "a pure man, with nothing crooked or deformed about him." [47]

This criterion of wholeness—haleness, health—is not used, however, to mean simply organic order, specificity, concreteness, or uniqueness. Occasional pronouncements might mislead us. Thus Goethe said of the younger romantics, Werner, Oehlenschläger, Arnim, Brentano, that they "all end in the formless and characterless. None will understand that the only and highest operation of nature and art is forming and specificity in the form, so that everything would become, be, and remain something particular and meaningful." [48] Actually Goethe sees the work of art always as a member of a species and beyond that as pointing to the totality of nature and art. At times he formulates this in the traditional terms of universality demanded of a work of art. "The poet should seize the particular, and he will, if it is something wholesome, make it general." [49] In his taste in the plastic arts, Goethe leans to the academic abstractionism of the time. He considers it a reason for special praise that Laocoon, in the famous sculpture, is not represented as a priest or a Trojan but simply as a father who defends his two sons against the attack of two dangerous animals.[50]

Later, however, Goethe becomes aware of the term "symbol," and rephrases the relation between the particular and the general more clearly. He is apparently the first to draw the distinction between symbol and allegory in the modern way. There are anticipations of the use before him, but in Winckelmann it seems to mean the same as an allegory or an arbitrary sign.[51] Goethe discovers the new meaning of the term in 1797 when he describes his impressions in revisiting Frankfurt am Main. He is struck with the peculiar feelings he experiences at the sight of some familiar objects which he now calls "symbolic." They are "eminent cases which are representative of many other cases, include a certain totality, require a certain order, excite something similar or strange in my mind and make claims both from outside and inside to a certain unity and totality."[52] A paper, "Über die Gegenstände der bildenden Kunst" (1797, not published until 1896) formulates the distinction somewhat obscurely. Symbolic objects seem to stand for themselves and still are significant because the ideal always implies the universal. Allegory signifies directly, symbol indirectly. A paper, with the same title, contributed by Goethe's close collaborator, Heinrich Meyer, to *Die Proplyäen* (1798) elaborates the distinction between allegorical and symbolical presentations: allegories transcend the limits of art. They must be clear, unambiguous even to a limited understanding, while in symbolic figures art elaborates its highest subjects, commands even ideas and concepts to appear in sensuous form and forces them to enter space, to assume human shape and to become visible to the eyes. The ancient gods, Christ, and the Madonna are such symbolic subjects.[53]

This discussion seems to have impressed Schelling and the Schlegels, who developed the distinction on their own before Goethe returned to it when he edited his correspondence with Schiller (1824). He has the contrast between himself and Schiller in mind when he comments: "There is a great difference, whether the poet seeks the particular for the general or sees the general in the particular. From the first procedure arises allegory, where the particular serves only as an example of the general; the second procedure, however, is really the nature of poetry: it expresses something particular, without thinking of the general or pointing to it." [54] Schiller would be an allegorist, not really a poet. Goethe stresses the concreteness of symbolism. "True symbolism is where the particular represents the more general, not as a dream or a shadow, but as a living momentary revelation of the Inscrutable." [55] Or, possibly most clearly and sharply, Goethe says that "allegory changes a phenomenon into a concept, a concept into an image, but in such a way that the concept is still limited and completely kept and held in the image and expressed by it," while symbolism "changes the phenomenon into the idea, the idea into the image, in such a way that the idea remains always infinitely active and unapproachable in the image, and will remain inexpressible even though expressed in all languages." [56] Myth, "great motifs, legends, ancient historical traditions" are at the center of Goethe's own poetry. He describes how these images

hovered around him for fifty years, how they were transformed by
his imagination and grew to a "purer form, a more decisive representation." [57] It would be hard to overrate the significance of classical myth in all its forms for his own poetic practice: we need
only recall the encyclopaedia of classical mythology in the second
part of *Faust*. With the romantics Goethe dreams of a poem which
would summarize the new philosophy of nature as Lucretius' *De
rerum natura* had done for antiquity. His own cycle of philosophical poems, "Gott und Welt" and the verse expositions of the
metamorphosis of the plants and animals are attempts of this sort.
But to develop this point fully would demand a discussion of
Goethe's entire poetic work. It is sufficient for our purposes to
realize that he remained aloof from romantic mythology and from
Creuzer, who wanted to "unify and transsubstantiate everything,"
and that he remained unconvinced by Schelling and Hegel.*

Goethe tends rather to identify the typical and the symbolic and
thus to keep his hold on the essentials of classicism. Only rarely
can we find expressions which point in the romantic direction.
Thus some sketches by Tischbein are praised because the "most
beautiful symbols are those which allow a multiple interpretation." [58] He complacently acknowledges that there is something
"totally incommensurable" in *Faust*.[59] But the workings of his
mind lead him always to a balance, to a genuine synthesis in which
both thesis and antithesis would be preserved. Art is the synthesis
of the universal and particular, the real and the rational, mind
and nature.

While Goethe's general preoccupations in aesthetics are clear
enough, it is harder to form a picture of his specifically *literary*
theory. Much of what has been quoted was written in general
terms, often with the plastic arts implicitly or expressly in mind.
It does not always seem clear that Goethe thinks of the arts as a
unity. On occasion, at least, he tried to divorce poetry from the
plastic arts. He tells us that there is "an enormous gulf" between

* To J. G. J. Hermann, Sept. 9, 1820; Weimar, Pt. 4, *33*, 143: "Alles
mit allem verknüpfen, vereinigen, ja transsubstanzieren." The complex relations to Schelling and Hegel would need detailed investigation. Note e.g. Goethe's criticism of a highly Hegelian interpretation
of *Antigone* by H. F. W. Hinrichs, in Eckermann, *3*, March 28, 1827;
Houben, pp. 476 ff.

them, so that it is difficult if not impossible to pass from the plastic arts to poetry and rhetoric.[60] He even denies that poetry is art or science. "It is conceived in the soul and should be called genius." [61] While Goethe works hard to know the techniques of painting, he thinks himself comparatively ignorant of those of poetry.[62] He often consults friends about metrical questions and meekly submits to technical corrections. I am not aware of any attempts on his part to define the nature of literature or poetry, though he describes its motives or effects: his ideas become concretely literary only when he speculates about the theory of genres.

Goethe, with his conception of organic growth, applies the instinct of a biologist to the different species of poetry. In a piece on the "Natural Forms of Poetry" he states that there are only three genuine natural forms of poetry: the "clearly telling," the "enthusiastically excited," and the "personally acting"—epic, lyric, and drama. They can occur together even in the smallest poem: e.g., in the best ballads. We see them also together in the oldest Greek tragedy; only after a certain lapse of time do they begin to separate. As long as the chorus is the main character of Greek tragedy, the lyric prevails. The Homeric poem is completely epic. The rhapsodist dominates and nobody is allowed to open his mouth who is not assigned a speech. Goethe recognizes the difficulty of such classification and speculates on the order of the three kinds. He suggests that one should arrange them in a circle and then look for examples of works in which the different elements (lyric, epic, dramatic) prevail. Then one could collect examples which would lean to this or that side until finally the union of all three would appear and the circle would be filled and closed. Such a scheme would also include the necessary inner origins in a comprehensible order.[63] It is difficult, however, to see how anything historical can come from such a circular chart. The principle implied is obviously that of Goethe's own metamorphosis of the plants: the view that there is an *Urpflanze,* of which all the other plants are merely variations. There was also an *Urpoesie,* out of which the three genres grew by separation.

Genre criticism is also Goethe's constant preoccupation in the correspondence with Schiller. Much of it revolves around attempts to define the distinctions between the epic and the drama. Goethe and Schiller finally agreed on a common document, "Über epische und dramatische Dichtung," in which they tried to define the differences between the two kinds by their origin in either rhapsodic or mimetic representation. The method is genetic but aims at abstract definitions which would hold true at all times. "An epic poet narrates an event as completely past, while the dramatic presents it as completely present." Epic presents activity, tragedy suffering. Epic characters act externally, e.g., in battles or travels; tragedy presents man as an internal agent and the action therefore requires little space. In the epic

> the rhapsodist as a higher being ought not to appear himself in the poem: he should read best of all behind a curtain, so that we may separate everything personal from his work, and may believe we are hearing only the voice of the Muses in general. The *mime*, the actor, represents the opposite. He presents himself as a distinct individuality; it is his desire to have us take an interest exclusively in him and his immediate surroundings, so that we may feel with him the sufferings of his soul and body, may share in his troubles and forget ourselves in him. The spectators must not rise to a contemplative frame of mind, but must follow eagerly; their imagination [used here as image-making reverie] must be completely silenced, no demands must be made upon it, and even what is narrated must be vividly brought before their eyes, as it were, in terms of action.[64]

Goethe thus strongly disapproves of the mixture of genres—"childish, barbarous, tasteless tendencies which the artist should resist with all his powers." He should separate a work of art from another "by an impenetrable magic circle, preserve each in its quality and peculiarities as the ancients did, for that made them such artists." Goethe also tries to account historically for the modern mixture of genres by the desire of his own age for naturalism. All the plastic arts want to approach the effects of oil painting because painting creates most illusion. The same is true of poetry; all genres try to approach the drama, the representation of the completely present. Goethe sees the same tendency in the contemporary vogue of the epistolary novel, which is completely dramatic and where one can insert formal dialogues as Richardson did.[65] While deploring the dissolution of the genres, Goethe recognizes the inevitability of the process. Later he even cites a new historical argument. "If the romantic tendency of uncivilized centuries had not brought the sublime into contact with the absurd, how could we have got *Hamlet, Lear, La Devoción de la Cruz, El Principe constante?"* [66]

The implications of these pronouncements are always a recognition of the existence of basic genres combined with a feeling for their continuous transformation, changes, and mixing in actual history. The discussion with Schiller seems by implication to rate the epic higher, because it is more removed from naturalistic art and nearer to "style" in Goethe's sense. As a manager of the Weimar theater, Goethe himself tries to revive the stylized drama and a conventionalized style of acting. He even adapts two of Voltaire's plays (*Mahomet* and *Tancrède*) for the stage (as Schiller did Racine's *Phèdre*). Though he can dismiss the unities as "a stupid law" even in old age,[67] on occasion he sees their point. "They mean nothing else than distributing a great subject with probability among a few characters and representing it." [68] He recognizes how strongly the observance of the rules is determined by social requirements. The French treat the genres as different social groups, in which a specific behavior is proper. They do not shrink from speaking of *convenances,* a word which really is valid only for the proprieties of society. In Goethe's view only the artist can and should make genre distinctions; since taste is innate in genius, he will make the right ones.[69] In the drama his taste, in spite of his own second *Faust,* becomes inimical even to a mixture of the comic and tragic. Goethe adapts *Romeo and Juliet* for the stage, dropping the nurse and Mercutio as "farcical intermezzists," "disharmonious allotria," [70] and he voices the opinion that Shakespeare belongs to a "history of poetry and appears only by chance in a history of the theater." [71] "He was no playwright; he had never thought of the stage; it was far too narrow for his great mind." [72] This was by no means to be regretted, however, since Shakespeare gained as a poet what he lost as a playwright: "Shakespeare is a great psychologist, and one learns from his plays how people feel inside.[73]

But while such pronouncements seem to suggest Goethe's preference for the closet drama which, after all, he himself cultivated, he frequently seems to take the opposite view. To excuse his shortcomings he uses the argument that Shakespeare is primarily a playwright: "[Shakespeare] saw his plays as something moving, living, which from the stage would very quickly flow by eyes and ears and which one could not hold fast and criticize in detail, as it only mattered that something should be effective and significant at a particular moment." [74] Goethe understood that Shakespeare worked scene by scene and did not bother about minor inconsistencies.* When confronted with plays by Kleist which he considered unsuited for the stage, he expresses his distaste for dramatists waiting for a theater of the future, "like a Jew who waits for the Messiah, a Christian who waits for the New Jerusalem, a Portuguese who waits for the return of Don Sebastian." He holds the model of Calderón before him. "In front of every wooden scaffolding, I would say to a truly theatrical genius, *Hic Rhodus, hic salta!* I would venture to cause pleasure at every fair, on planks laid on barrels, with Calderón's plays, *mutatis mutandis,* both to the educated and the uneducated public." [75]

But no doubt the drama on the stage seems to Goethe an inferior kind of art. He condemns all regard for the public. "What does not please is the right thing; the new art corrupts because it wants to please." [76] The true artist must ignore his public, just as the teacher disregards the whims of his children, the physician the desires of his patients, the judge the passions of the litigating parties.[77] It is best to pretend that there is no public, or at least to admit that the artist has only a small public of friends, addresses only a "community of saints." [78] But this is not only Goethe's sense of the artist's alienation from society, his opposition to the time in which "a true artist lives often alone and in despair." [79] It is also his theoretical conviction that art is man's necessary productivity, which is falsified by regard to its effect. *"We* struggle for the perfection of a work of art, in and by itself, *they* think of the effect outside, which does not concern the genuine artist at all, just as little as nature is concerned when it produces a lion or a hummingbird." [80] Goethe even defines the difference between ancient art and modern art in terms of a contrast between direct grasp of nature and striving for effect. "They portrayed the reality, we usu-

---

* Eckermann, *3,* April 1, 1827; Houben, pp. 495–6. But Goethe wrongly assumes a contradiction between Lady Macbeth's saying, "I have given suck" (I, 7), and Macduff's exclaiming, "he has no children" (IV, 3). Macduff is speaking to Ross and refers to Malcolm, who has told him to "be comforted" at the news of the murder of his wife and children.

ally its effect; they described terrible things, we describe terribly; they pleasant things, we pleasantly, and so on." [81]

This view appears most strikingly in Goethe's complete rejection of the Aristotelian theory of tragedy because it is based on a description of the effect of tragedy on the spectator. In "Nachlese zu Aristoteles Poetik" (1827) he argued that Aristotle, whose mind is always on the object (as Goethe prided himself on having it), must be concerned only with the construction of tragedy. Purgation can exist only in the tragedy itself: it is the reconciliation and expiation of the passions of the dramatic characters themselves. Catharsis is the reconciling rounding-off which is demanded of all drama, indeed of all works of poetry. This occurs in tragedy at the end of the play, through a kind of human sacrifice. Goethe admits only that

> if the poet has fulfilled this purpose and his duty on his side, tying together his knots of meaning and unraveling them again, the same process will pass before the mind of the spectator: the complications will perplex him, the solution enlighten him, but he will not go home any the better for it. He will be inclined perhaps, if he is given to reflection, to be amazed at the state of mind in which he finds himself at home again, just as frivolous, as obstinate, as zealous, as weak, as tender, or as cynical as he was when he went out.[82]

Goethe's doubts about catharsis are connected with his low estimate of the immediate moral effect of art. He expressly endorses Kant's isolation of the aesthetic as a great deed of liberation,[83] and condemns the "old prejudice" that a work of art need have a didactic purpose.[84] In a special article denying that didactic poetry can be ranked with the three main kinds, he lists it only as a hybrid between poetry and rhetoric, a difficult attempt "to weave something together from science and imagination, to combine two opposite elements into a living body." All poetry should be didactic, but unnoticeably so: "The reader must draw instruction from it himself, as he does from life." [85] Goethe knows that "a work of art can and will have moral consequences, but to ask moral purposes of an artist means to spoil his trade." [86] He even condones an "offensive" subject on a Greek bas-relief. "Here art appears completely independent even from morality, which for a noble

man will always remain the highest and most worthy of veneration. But if art wants to proclaim itself completely free, it must
pronounce its own laws decisively." [87] Goethe is convinced that
"art in itself is noble: that is why the artist does not fear the vulgar. By the mere act of its admission it is ennobled." [88]

It is hardly a contradiction that Goethe is pleased when his
works are praised for their morality. He himself likes to praise
authors as different as Sterne and the humble Nürnberg poet,
Grübel, for their good morals.[89] Young Meister claims that the
poet is, at the same time, "a teacher, prophet, friend of gods and
men," [90] and the old Goethe speaks even of the poet at the end
liking best "to use his talent for the praise and celebration of
God." [91] Though generalizing, he was referring to the mystical
Persian poet Jalálu'd-dín Rúmí.

The feeling that a work of art is part of nature, produced like
nature, is basic to Goethe's conception. It is further confirmed by
his strong sense for the setting of literature, its social and historical
evolution. It seems a common error to declare Goethe unhistorical
in his outlook because he shows frequent impatience with contemporary historiography and has a gloomy view of war and politics.[92]
Actually one of the most marked features of his criticism is his
stress on a genetic interpretation and study of literature. He would
say that "it is always in following the genesis of things that I have
best arrived at an intuitive insight," [93] or that "works of art, like
works of nature, cannot be known when they are completely
finished: one must surprise them in their formation in order to
understand them a little." [94] Goethe has a very 18th-century sense
of the importance of climate and landscape: he speculates on the
similarity of the poetry of two mountain people, the Serbs and the
Scotch.[95] He feels that in visiting Sicily he has learned much about
Homer. "His descriptions, comparisons, etc. seemed poetic: yet,
they are natural, to an unutterable degree. Only now has the word
Odyssey become a living word." [96] When interpreting Oriental
poetry, he tried to show how the prime metaphors about camel,
horse, and sheep grow out of what he calls "life relations." [97]

In discussing the problem of German classicism Goethe explains
its limitations almost purely in social terms. The Germans lack a
cultural center and are divided politically; they are not a happy
and unified nation, pervaded with a national spirit and with an

established literary tradition. Only from a real nation can a national writer of the highest order be expected. Characteristically Goethe, the conservative and Weimar patriot of 1795, reflects that "we do not wish for Germany those political revolutions which might prepare the way for classical works." French classicism with its centralization in Paris and Versailles is obviously in his mind, and he would rather put up with the imperfect individualism, the isolation from society, of the German writer even at the expense of perfection. He is content to see an "invisible school" of German writers such as Wieland, who by their example smooth the road for their younger contemporaries.[98]

Goethe is quite annoyed with Madame de Staël's discussion of his writings in *De l'Allemagne*. There his works appear "fragmentary," in isolation.[99] In contrast he praises the editors of *Le Globe*, especially J.-J. Ampère, who "knows his business thoroughly, shows the kinship of products with the producer and judges the poetic products as fruit of diverse epochs of the life of the poet." [100] In commenting on his German audience he praises those who "look for the author in the writings, who try to discover the gradual, step-by-step evolution of his intellectual education." [101] His autobiography, *Dichtung und Wahrheit,* is largely an effort to understand his own intellectual evolution by means of the time in which he grew up, of the interchange between his mind and his surroundings. The book falls somewhat short of its aim: the self-analysis seems insufficient and the emphasis is too strongly on the external and picturesque. But if we see it as a first attempt, quite different from completely external autobiographies such as Cellini's or purely subjective self-analyses such as Augustine's or Rousseau's *Confessions,* one can recognize its achievement. As Goethe writes to Humboldt in the last year of his life: "Everything becomes more and more historical to me . . . I myself appear more and more historical to myself." [102]

Goethe also prominently and constantly uses the historical period-concepts which the writers of his time elaborated, and he feels that he has contributed importantly to their development. He sees that Schiller invented his concept of the opposition between naive and sentimental poetry with the contrast of their methods in mind. "I laid down the maxim of objective treatment in poetry and would allow no other; but Schiller, who worked quite in the subjective way, deemed his own fashion the right one, and to defend himself against me wrote the treatise on *Naive and Sentimental Poetry*. The Schlegels took up this idea, and carried it farther, so that it has now been diffused over the whole world: and everyone talks about classicism and romanticism—of which nobody thought fifty years ago." [103] Goethe's history is not quite correct. He overrates Schiller's closeness to the Schlegels and interprets romantic-classic merely as a contrast between organic and inorganic art. Goethe always prefers Schiller's concept because it points to the relation between art and nature which is his own preoccupation. Shakespeare, Goethe declares, was naive, not romantic, because he lived in the present, in nature.[104] Goethe likes to reinterpret the contrast of the Schlegels to suit his own purposes. When he becomes quite antagonistic to the romantics he coins the famous definition that the classical is the healthy, the romantic the sickly. "In this sense, the *Nibelungenlied* is as classic as the *Iliad,* for both are vigorous and healthy. Most modern productions are romantic, not because they are new, but because they are weak, morbid, or sickly: and the ancient is classical, not because it is old, but because it is strong, fresh, joyous, and healthy." [105] At other times Goethe equates the unreal and impossible with the pathological and romantic.[106] Actually he reverses the distinction of the Schlegels, who thought of romantic form as organic, and classical, or rather pseudoclassical, as mechanical. With Goethe there is always only one standard: the standard of nature, reality, truth, health, which are all fundamentally identical.

Goethe's attempt in the article "Shakespeare und kein Ende" (1813) to set up a slightly different typology seems rather forced. Ancient and modern tragedy are contrasted by contraries such as natural—sentimental; pagan—Christian; classic—romantic; realistic—idealistic; necessity—freedom; duty (*Sollen*)—will (*Wollen*). In the ancient tragedies there is a disproportion between duty and achievement, in the modern between will and achievement.[107] Goethe's dichotomies assume Schiller's and the Schlegels' interpretation of Greek tragedy as a tragedy of fate contrasted with modern tragedy as a tragedy of character. They seem doubtful generalizations if we think of *Antigone* or *Romeo and Juliet*.

But such polarities are Goethe's natural way of thinking in all his sketches of literary history. Action and reaction are used to describe German literary history at the beginning of his own life. Expansion and narrowing, prolixity and conciseness in style, idealism and realism in the manner of acting are the alternations Goethe sees everywhere. Metaphors such as oscillation, polarity, systole and diastole (the contraction and expansion of the heart), the recurring cycle, and the spiral permeate his reflections on history and the fate of humanity.[108]

The term "world literature" is Goethe's invention. It suggests a historical scheme of the evolution of national literatures in which they will fuse and ultimately melt into a great synthesis. Today the term is used in a sense which was not in Goethe's mind. It means all literature from Iceland to New Zealand, or the classics which have become a common heritage of all nations. But when Goethe uses it for the first time, in a review of a French adaptation of his *Tasso* in 1827, he expresses his conviction that "there is being formed a universal world literature, in which an honorable role is reserved for us Germans." [109] This review is commented upon in the Paris *Globe,* and Goethe, in reproducing the comments, expresses a lively pleasure that "our western neighbors should have taken up the idea." He sees the reasons for increased literary intercourse among nations in the weariness of strife after the Napoleonic wars. World literature is being prepared by a constant interchange of ideas and forms; but this interchange is not world literature itself. It is rather an ideal of the unification of all literatures into one literature, where each nation would play its part in a universal concert. "Left to itself," Goethe argues, "every literature will exhaust its vitality if it is not refreshed by the interest and contribution of a foreign one." [110] But he is far too sensible not to see that one literature is a distant ideal. In commenting on the English periodicals the *Foreign Review* and the *Foreign Quarterly Review,* both newly founded, Goethe curbs his enthusiasm. "We repeat, the idea is not that the nations should think alike, but that they shall learn how to understand one another, and, if they do not care to love one another, at least they will learn to tolerate one another." [111] He sees that then as today not a single nation is willing to give up its individuality, literary or political, and he even reminds the Germans that they would lose most by such a change.[112] He apparently means by this somewhat cryptic remark that the Germans have the most individualistic, peculiar literature, which would lose its character in a world union.

Goethe's literary cosmopolitanism is not actually in contradiction to his frequent stress on national individuality and his interest in folk poetry, which includes German dialect poetry such as the Allemanic poems of J. P. Hebel. Goethe recommends Arnim and Brentano's *Des Knaben Wunderhorn* very warmly and is seriously interested in all German folk song and much local literature.[113] But his interest in folk poetry extends to Slavic, Modern Greek, and Oriental literature. He is impressed, for instance, by the supposedly Old Czech manuscripts of Králové Dvůr and Zelená Hora, and even starts to learn some Czech during his summer stays in Bohemia.[114] He translates from the French one of the best of the Serbian heroic songs, "The Lament of the Noble Women of Asan Aga," which proves to be the main impetus for the intense 19th-century interest in Yugoslav folk poetry, and he follows Fauriel's lead in studying modern Greek songs. His interest in Arabic and Persian poetry fits equally into the world-wide scheme inspired by Herder. Poetry is the natural speech of mankind—uniform, generally human, but also therefore local and national. "There is only one poetry, genuine poetry which does not belong either to the people or nobility, king or peasant: whoever feels himself a true man will exercise it: it appears irresistibly in a simple, even a rude people, but is not denied to a civilized, even a highly civilized nation." [115] But at other times he preserves his faith in the ancients as eternal models and suggests a double standard of judgment. "However much we value foreign literatures, we must not cling to one in particular and try to take one as our model. We must not think the Chinese, the Serbian, Calderón, or the *Nibelungen* can be that. When we are in need of a model, we must always go back to the ancient Greeks, in whose works the object of representation is always beautiful man. Everything else we must look at from a purely historical point of view, and take in what is good in it as far as we can." [116]

With the years Goethe's attitude becomes more and more tolerant. His criticism of books and men shows, even more pronouncedly and self-consciously, the benevolence, the desire for mediation* which friends had noticed early in his life. This is surely the reason why most of the criticism collected in the *Schriften über die Literatur* leaves us with a sense of disappointment. They are mostly short notices which show Goethe's wide interests, especially in foreign literature and in the reactions of foreigners to his own writings and to German literature. There is no attempt on his part to comment systematically on contemporary literature, and many of the most famous native and foreign names are missing. One must go to Goethe's private letters, notes, and conversations to get anything like a complete picture of his literary opinions. Many of his most striking judgments are made casually, when he feels free to speak his mind and can use a less formal tone. He dislikes polemics and avoids public pronouncements on his critics and enemies. There is little that is negative in his criticism, though there is sometimes an expression of distaste for the morbid, the unhealthy, the forced and tortured.

This tolerance is justified theoretically as well as temperamentally. The old Goethe describes Parnassus as Montserrat, a "jagged peak which allows settlements on many ledges." Everybody should try to find a place, either on the summits or in recesses.[117] He sees also that vices go with virtues. In describing the metaphors of Oriental poetry, many of which must have seemed in bad taste or at least farfetched and merely witty, Goethe recognizes that there is no boundary line between what is praiseworthy and blameworthy, and that their virtues are only the flowers of their faults.[118]

Criticism thus, we see, should be criticism only of beauties. Goethe distinguishes between destructive and what he calls "productive" criticism.

> The former is very easy: for one need only set up an imaginary standard, some model or other, however foolish it may be, and then boldly assert that the work of art under consideration does not measure up to that standard, and therefore is of no value. That settles the matter and one can without

* In *Dichtung und Wahrheit*, Bk. 18; *Werke*, 25, 67. Goethe tells of Merck resenting his "das ewige Geltenlassen." The figure of "Mittler" in *Wahlverwandschaften* is only one of Goethe's conciliators.

further ado declare that the poet has not come up to one's requirements. In this way the critic frees himself of all obligations of gratitude toward the artist. Productive criticism is much harder. It asks: what did the author set out to do? Was his plan reasonable and sensible, and how far did he succeed in carrying it out? If these questions are answered with discernment and sympathy, we may second the author's efforts in his later works.[119]

This attitude leads inevitably to an emphasis on good intention, and thus to critical relativism. Everything grows and thus is in its place and good in its place. Goethe seems to accept the most diverse types of art as given facts, as events fruitful in his own life at a specific stage. He expressly defends himself on this point. "Some of my well-wishing readers have told me for a long time that instead of expressing a judgment on books, I describe the influence which they have had on me. And at bottom this is the way all readers criticize, even if they do not communicate an opinion and formulate ideas about it to the public." [120] Subjectivity is here proclaimed the standard, though we must not, of course, think of it as caprice. In Goethe it always means a recognition of something existent, a discernment which separates the fruitful from the barren, health from sickness, life from death.

Thus a survey of Goethe's literary opinions hardly seems called for. It would be in effect a survey of the world's literature; and since many of Goethe's pronouncements are only obiter dicta, not analyses, they throw little light on principles. In surveying his views of German literature, it would be particularly difficult to isolate strictly literary opinions from his judgments on personalities and their relations to him. Goethe was in personal contact with many German writers for a long period of time, from Gottsched, of whom he had a glimpse in Leipzig, to such visitors of his last years as Immermann and Heine. He literally lived in close association with some of the greatest of his contemporaries: with Herder, with Schiller, with the Schlegels, and his attitude toward their works is hardly divorceable from literary politics, changes in personal feelings, and the influences of friends and family. Even Goethe's famous pronouncements on Byron, which contain some of his most sustained criticism, are not primarily literary: the reasons for his admiration are due only in part to an appreciation of Byron's poetry. He envied a lord who defied society, he was flattered by Byron's own attention to him, which led to the dedication of *Werner* to Goethe when an earlier "homage of a literary vassal to his liege Lord" [121] had not materialized. Goethe was genuinely pleased by evidence of the influence of *Faust* on *Manfred*. He admired *Cain* and *Heaven and Earth* and read *Don Juan* with admiration though with some puzzlement. He calls it a "work of infinite genius, misanthropic to the fiercest cruelty, philanthropic to the depth of sweetest love." But he thought it also "madder and grander" than any of the other poems.[122] He knew, however, the limitations of Byron, including his "hypochondriacal passion and ferocious self-hatred." He puts his finger on Byron's poetic deficiencies in calling his poems "suppressed parliamentary speeches," and on his intellectual limitations in saying that he is great only when he writes poetry. "As soon as he reflects, he is a child." [123]

The relationship to Scott remained politely distant. Increasingly Goethe admired his great talent, the diligence of his historical studies, and the great truth of detail, but he thought of him as only an entertainer. "I would always be amused by him, but could never learn anything from him. I have time only for the most excellent." [124] The standard of personal profit to be derived from another author is here complacently proclaimed: it seems to reject an objective ideal of criticism. One can understand that Saintsbury finds this calculus of profit "mighty disgusting" and "mighty dangerous," and can conclude that "Goethe, the critical Goethe, has too much the character of a superstition, now rather stale." [125] But Saintsbury could hardly have known or paid attention to the bulk of Goethe's theories: to his finely developed restatement of classicism, his theories of the symbol, his thinking about literary history and world literature. One must admit that there is a certain gap between Goethe's aesthetics and literary theory and his many pronouncements of practical taste. There is no actual contradiction, but there is no close integration between the two, and little that could be called systematic criticism. One will have to strike a medium between the extravagant admiration of Sainte-Beuve and Arnold on the one hand and the irritated depreciation of Saintsbury on the other, and then Goethe will appear an important link in the chain of German speculation on art and literature. But it seems impossible to accept his central doctrine: the conception of the work of art as a work of nature. It is inconceivable that an ideal existence can follow the same laws as a natural being and that, in practice, the artist or the critic can ever discover this presumed identity. Goethe's obiter dicta, his practical taste, will elicit admiration for their general sanity, restraint, and good sense, their universal tolerance. But by their very universality they expose the difficulties of all pantheistic optimism: an acceptance of the world as it is, a final relativism. It must be emphasized that Goethe had not yet reached these consequences: he had too strong a hold on a specific taste, too clear an intellect to surrender to the "natural idealism" he was trying to buttress. He achieved a delicate balance which may seem to us precarious and irretrievable.

LATE in the 18th century, mainly as an effect of the publication of Kant's *Critique of Judgment* (1790), Germany began to produce an unending stream of books on aesthetics and poetics. The movement found its provisional end and codification in the five bulky volumes of Friedrich Theodor Vischer's *Aesthetik* (1844–56). The greatest philosophers took part in this preoccupation with aesthetic ideas: Kant, Schelling, Schleiermacher, Hegel, and Schopenhauer. Each produced his system of aesthetics, or at least assigned to art a prominent part in his scheme of the world. Partly under the direct influence of the philosophers, poets and literary historians popularized, applied, and modified the ideas propounded by the great speculative minds. Schiller, Novalis, Tieck, Jean Paul —each and every one expounded his philosophy of art and literature. The contemporaneous historical movement fused with the aesthetic movement: for the first time history was written with critical and aesthetic principles, at first timidly by Bouterwek, then brilliantly and boldly by the Schlegels, Gervinus, and many others.

From our specific point of view—which is always focused on literature, the theory of literature, poetics, and criticism—much that was of central importance for the German aestheticians and poets seems only indirectly relevant. Such topics properly belong to the history of aesthetics. But even the more abstract aestheticians constantly raised questions basic for a theory of literature: the position of literature among the arts, the nature of poetry, the function of art in civilization, the psychology of the artist and the audience. Moreover, almost all German aestheticians were interested in the question of genres of poetry, for they thought of these distinctions as a philosophical problem, and almost all were occupied with the nature of tragedy. Aesthetics easily passed into poetics, and many questions of poetics—such as the crucial difference between classical and modern (romantic) art—led into questions of a philosophy of history, to historical poetics, and, inevitably, to the criticism of works of literature.

In this tremendous body of thought it seems especially difficult to draw the line between abstract, abstruse speculations on the nature of beauty and art on the one hand and literary criticism on the other. Books such as Schelling's *Philosophie der Kunst* or Hegel's *Vorlesungen über Aesthetik* provide both metaphysical speculation and quite detailed practical criticism, not in separation but in close integration. In studying these authors we become acutely aware how right Croce is in stressing that criticism is a part of aesthetics, *is* applied aesthetics. Still, just because much attention has been paid to this body of aesthetic thought as a philosophical discipline, it may be of some value to emphasize the interest these writers had in the more concrete questions of literary theory and criticism.

Our task would be comparatively simple if we could speak of this body of thought as a unified whole and if it were true (as many histories of philosophy tell us) that there was a logical development from Kant to Fichte and thence to Schelling and Hegel. But reality is much more complex; every one of these philosophers grew out of a different intellectual soil and passed through a different development. The poets and practical critics are not easily classified as simple adherents or popularizers of the philosophers. The question of priorities, of sources and influences, is hopelessly entangled, and in the absence of accurate detailed studies cannot be answered with assurance in many instances. One also has to recognize that for a time there was an actual "symphilosophizing," a community of thought and speculation which accounts for the wealth of crosscurrents and crossfertilization.

English readers will have an added difficulty in understanding these authors: the philosophical premises of many of them have become almost incomprehensible to many of our contemporaries who have grown up in a totally different intellectual atmosphere. Many will reject these speculations as mere card houses of scholastic verbalism or mystical illumination. Such a general impression will have some basis in fact: these Germans are frequently in acute danger of cloudy mysticism or scholastic, verbalistic ambiguities. They use words loosely, shift their meanings quickly and without warning, indulge in many equivocations and private

games of naming. We must be on constant guard against the tricks
of their language, though we should recognize that they would
have defended their practice by a contextual theory of language
and by the argument that philosophical creation is also linguistic.
We must constantly try to translate what they say into our idiom,
as mere reproduction would not fulfill our purpose of making
these authors understood and, when understood, laid open to use
and criticism.

Much writing about them, especially in German, proves singu-
larly unhelpful because it merely reproduces their vocabulary and
their proportions of emphasis, and has no principle of selection,
no reservations, no distance. Some English accounts are no more
helpful for a different reason: they seem not to have understood
the vocabulary and the basic assumptions and aims. For example,
it is easy to make nonsense of Hegel by assuming that *Begriff*
translates "concept" and to ascribe to him a "panlogism," the
monstrous belief that the philosopher creates the world by a chain
of reasoning.

Kant's *Critique of Judgment* (1790) must be the starting point
of any discussion, since its methods and problems proved enormously influential for all later thought on art in Germany. The
Critique of Judgment has nothing to say of individual authors
and only very little directly about literature or poetry. From
Kant's other writings, his lectures and letters, it would be possible
to collect his literary opinions and tendencies of his taste. He was
an avid reader not only of German but also of French and English
literature. But his literary criticism (which is not distinguished in
any way) is hardly of any relevance to the speculative position
established in the *Critique of Judgment*. In it, however, Kant did
most resolutely isolate the aesthetic realm from the realm of
science, morality, and utility by arguing that the aesthetic state of
mind differs profoundly from our perception of the pleasurable,
the useful, the true, and the good. Kant invented the famous definition: aesthetic pleasure is "disinterested satisfaction" ("interesse-
loses Wohlgefallen"), a term which, however, can be badly mis-
interpreted if it were taken to suggest some kind of art-for-art's
sake doctrine. "Disinterested" to Kant means the lack of interference from desire, the directness of our access to the work of art,
undisturbed, uninterfered with (*inter-esse*) by immediate utili-

tarian ends. Kant in no way denies the enormous role of art in society or, as we shall see, in metaphysics. He merely wants to distinguish the object of our investigation from morality, pleasure, truth, and utility.

This idea of the autonomy of art is not, of course, totally new with Kant: it was being prepared throughout the century by thinkers such as Hutcheson and Mendelssohn. But in Kant the argument was stated for the first time systematically by defending the distinction of the aesthetic realm against *all* sides: against sensualism and its reduction of art to pleasure, against moralism, intellectualism, and didacticism. Many attempts have been made to refute Kant's conclusions: certainly sensualism and intellectualism have still many adherents. But whatever the difficulties of Kant's solution, he has put his finger on the central issue of aesthetics. No science is possible which does not have its distinct object. If art is simply pleasure, communication, experience, or inferior reasoning, it ceases to be art and becomes a substitute for something else.

But other ideas besides this initial definition in the *Critique* proved equally influential. Kant, as many writers before and after him, was worried about the relativity of taste, its subjectivity. He grants the truth of subjectivity but retracts this concession by a theory of a "common sense" of all men. Each aesthetic judgment is a mere subjective feeling, but it *claims* universal validity and can do so justly because we must assume a common sense of mankind as an ideal norm.

Kant's view of genius is similarly based on a recognition of its basic irrationality, its source in the unconscious, with the claim of prescriptive, normative coherence for its products. Genius for Kant is innate, the "talent by which nature prescribes rules of art." [1] It is then unconscious: it cannot invent prescriptions for other works of art; it is always original genius. But there might, of course, be original nonsense (just as there can be nonsensical judgments of taste). The products of genius must be exemplary, prescriptive, just as true taste is prescriptive; i.e., works of art claim recognition.

But for the later development of German aesthetics, another idea of Kant's proved most important: art and nature are conceived by him as strict analogies. The work of art is a parallel to an organism, not only in a metaphorical sense which compares the

unity of a work of art to that of an organism, but because both art
and organic nature must be conceived of under the terms of "pur-
poseless purposiveness." Art and organic nature point to a final
overcoming of the deep dualism which is basic to Kant's philosophy. The world is divided into two realms: that of appearance (and
hence necessity), accessible to our mind by the senses and the categories of our understanding, and that of moral freedom, accessible
only in action. Kant glimpses in art a possibility of bridging the
gulf between necessity and freedom, the world of deterministic nature and the world of moral action. Art accomplishes a union of
the general and the particular, of intuition and thought, imagination and reason. It guarantees thus the existence of the "supersensuous," for only in art, through "intellectual intuition," do we
have access to what Kant calls the "intellectual archetype." But he
hesitates to come to this conclusion: the "supersensuous sub-
stratum of nature" [2] escapes any *theoretical* knowledge. As Hegel
was to complain: "It is the spirit of Kant's philosophy to have a
consciousness of this highest idea, but always to eradicate it
again." [3]

Poetry as such is hardly treated in the *Critique* except in the
classification of the arts, where it is listed as "art of speech" with
rhetoric and put first among the arts,[4] because it liberates imagination and raises itself to "ideas." "Idea" is one of Kant's most difficult terms: it is not, of course, identical with general idea or concept. An aesthetic idea is a representation of the imagination for
which no definite thought (i.e., concept) can be adequate. Ideas
are representations of the imagination which have the semblance
of reality. But what happens in art is precisely that "rational"
(speculative) ideas (i.e., those of invisible things, of the realm of
the blessed, of hell, eternity, creation, etc.) are made sensuous by
the poet. He can make sensuous death, envy (or any other vice),
love, or fame.[5] The term "idea" is near to the later term "symbol";
it points to the general problem of the *Critique:* to the union of
the general and particular, the abstract and the sensuous, achieved
in art.

Kant's theory of the sublime, though applied by him almost
exclusively to nature, proved extremely influential in the history
of aesthetics: Schiller and the Schlegels used it to interpret tragedy.
The sublime is described by Kant in terms of current 18th century

ideas: it is frightening, upsetting, even horrifying, but at the same time attractive. Man in the experience of the sublime in nature confronts either magnitude or power, both of which transcend the capabilities of his imagination. While beauty induces sensibility and understanding to collaborate harmoniously, sublimity causes a conflict between imagination and reason. Our imagination fails to grasp the infinity of the universe or the omnipotence of nature, displayed in storms, earthquakes, or other natural catastrophes. But while we experience our impotence before nature, we still assert our humanity, a sense of our freedom, of our supersensuous destiny. Thus the sublime proves to be another road to the super-sensuous, not, of course, grasped by reason, but glimpsed merely by imagination. If we apply the sublime to art (as Kant does not explicitly), we have found another way to give metaphysical and moral meaning to art. Kant himself hesitated to draw the consequences, but all his followers saw the implications much more clearly and freely. An aesthetics which starts out with the delimitation of the realm of the aesthetic became the justification of the boldest metaphysical and moral claims for art.

Kant's first and still cautious follower was the poet Friedrich Schiller (1759–1805). The sources of Schiller's literary theories are in the epistemology and aesthetics of Kant, but Schiller himself cannot be described as a mere disciple of Kant. He drew much of his terminology and some basic assumptions about man's double nature, sensuous and free, natural and moral, from Kant's teachings; but he sharply modified them. In some respects he picks up the thread of neo-Platonic aesthetics derived from Shaftesbury and the followers of Leibniz in Germany.* Schiller's theories proved to be the fountainhead of all later German critical theory. In a changed form, his method continues in the writings of the two Schlegels, in Schelling, and in Solger; it comes to England through

---

* This is a much debated, difficult historical question. For the stress on Leibniz cf. e.g. Robert Sommer, *Grundzüge einer Geschichte der deutschen Psychologie und Aesthetik* (Würzburg, 1892); for the stress on Shaftesbury cf. Ernst Cassirer, "Schiller und Shaftesbury," in *Publications of the English Goethe Society*, new ser., *40* (1935), 37–59. William Witte, *Schiller*, corrects this balance. The earlier literature is surveyed in Wilhelm Böhm's *Schiller's "Briefe über die aesthetische Erziehung des Menschen,"* Halle, 1927.

the mediation of Coleridge; and it culminates in Hegel, who in turn deeply influenced many later 19th-century critics such as Belinsky in Russia, De Sanctis in Italy, and Taine in France.

Schiller has been very widely discussed as an abstract aesthetician. Much of his writing is preoccupied with speculative questions of general aesthetics, the nature and function of beauty, aesthetic illusion, the relation of art and morality, art and philosophy, the "beautiful soul," grace and dignity in men and objects of nature, and so on. For our purposes it will suffice to allude briefly to some issues which will be important for literary theory. One can trace Schiller's complex evolution in his attitudes to these questions. He moved from a rather crude didacticism to a position which, under the influence of Kant's analysis, recognizes the distinctness and apartness of the aesthetic realm. In some of his formulations he seems to come near an art-for-art's-sake position, of which he has been claimed one of the main progenitors.* But this would be a gross misunderstanding of Schiller's actual point of view and of the unfortunate and misleading term "play-urge" (*Spieltrieb*), with which he characterized the free aesthetic activity. Play-urge has nothing to do with the lack of consequence, the frivolity and unreality of a child's game. It is a term which designates the artist's freedom from immediate practical purposes, from utilitarianism and moralism—his creativity, his "self-activity." In Schiller's conception the artist is the mediator between man and nature, between intellect and sense, between the *Stofftrieb* (the urge to assimilate the world of senses) and the *Formtrieb* (the urge to subdue the world to the moral law). Art thus assumes a tremendous civilizing role, described by Schiller in his *Letters on the Aesthetic Education of Man* (1795). It heals the wounds of civilization, the split between man and nature and between man's intellect and his senses. Art makes man whole again, reconciles him with the world and with himself.

Just as it would be a misunderstanding to consider Schiller an aesthete because he recognized the special nature of art and saw

* Cf. Rose Frances Egan, *The Genesis of the Theory of Art for Art's Sake in Germany and England*, 2 pts. Northampton, Mass., 1921, 1924. See also Irving Babbitt, "Schiller as Aesthetic Theorist," in *On Being Creative* (Boston, 1932), pp. 134–86, for a crude misinterpretation of Schiller's position on the basis of a few quotations.

it as a free activity, so would it be a gross misunderstanding to think of him as a formalist because he can say that "in a truly beautiful work of art the content should do nothing, the form everything . . . the special secret of the art of a master is to erase the matter by means of the form." [6] Form and matter are here used in the peculiar Kantian sense which assumes a dualism between mere unorganized sense data and the categories of man's mind. In general, however, Schiller formulates a theory of the strict reciprocity of form and content, of "an actual union and interpenetration of matter and form," [7] for which he uses the term "living shape." [8]

At first Schiller was irritated by an extravagant statement of the organistic theory. When he read Karl Philipp Moritz' treatise *On the Plastic Imitation of the Beautiful* (*Über die bildende Nachahmung des Schönen*, 1788), he was displeased by the "exaggerated assertion that every work from the realm of the beautiful must be a complete rounded whole; if a single radius were missing in this circle, it would sink below the useless. According to this pronouncement we don't have a single perfect work and cannot expect one soon." [9] But later, probably under the influence of Goethe, he would say that "every work of poetry—insofar as it is, if only *in hypothesi*, a whole organized in itself—must be judged by itself and not by general and therefore empty formulas." [10] In his critical practice, however, Schiller frequently falls back into a dichotomy of form and content, subject and treatment. He constantly discusses the choice of the theme, saying even that the "whole *cardo rei* in art lies in the invention of a poetic plot." [11] There is little discussion of technically formal questions in Schiller's writings, even when he goes into great details of his own or Goethe's processes of composition. In praising Aristotle's *Poetics*, which strangely enough he did not read until very late (1797) in his critical career, he calls him "the severest judge of everybody who would slavishly cling to external form or ignore form altogether." [12]

But these are questions of general aesthetics, important though they are for literary theory. Schiller's main significance for criticism must be sought rather in his reformulation of the old Ancient-Modern debate by a new dichotomy of "naive" and "sentimental" poetry which he broadens into a theory of both modern literature and the whole history of literature, and in his new theory of genres, which tries to replace the traditional classifications by new categories of "modes of feeling." Schiller was primarily a theorist of literature; yet he also exemplified his theory in a rather limited body of practical criticism which is not only illuminating for an understanding of his theory but has intrinsic value as criticism for a few, mostly contemporary, German authors: Goethe primarily, Bürger, Klopstock, and Schiller himself, for he analyzed and even publicly (though anonymously) reviewed his own work with great candor and detachment.

Schiller had expected a complete regeneration of his art from his speculations, but he came to judge of the practical and immediate value of theory for the artist quite negatively. "It is still the question whether the philosophy of art has anything to say to the artist," he wrote, admitting that he would give "all that I and others know about abstract aesthetics for a single empirical advantage, for a single trick of the craft." He complains that he himself has "applied the metaphysics of art too directly to objects and handled it as a practical tool for which it is not quite suitable," citing his own reviews of Bürger and Matthisson as examples.[13] When the *Maid of Orleans* became the object of a metaphysical analysis by one of Schelling's followers, Schiller complained that there is no "transition from general empty formulas to a particular case." "Philosophy and art have not yet comprehended each other and interpenetrated, and one misses more than ever an *organon* which would mediate between them." [14] This was precisely Schiller's own aim, which can hardly be considered utopian or unimportant.

Schiller's most important criticism is the treatise *On Naive and Sentimental Poetry* (*Über naive und sentimentalische Dichtung*, 1795–96). It is based on a deceptively simple contrast: "naive" poetry is "natural," written with an eye on the object—"imitation of nature," a fundamentally realistic, objective art, impersonal, plastic; while "sentimental" poetry is reflective, self-conscious, personal, and musical. The "sentimental" poet is confronted with the gulf between reality and the ideal. He has a choice of attitudes toward it. He can stress the distance between the ideal and the real, look down from the height of the ideal to reality and thus take the attitude of satire. He can mourn the loss of the ideal and write ele-

236 A HISTORY OF MODERN CRITICISM

gies. Or finally he can imagine the ideal in the past or future as real and write idylls. Schiller's classification wavered on this point: at first he ignored the idyll, then he admitted it only as a subspecies of the elegy, and finally he gave it an independent position. Still, the general theory is clear: it is a classification not by traditional genres but by modes of feeling, by attitudes toward reality: there can be an elegiac drama such as Goethe's *Tasso,* or a satirical tragedy such as Schiller's own *Robbers.* Milton's *Paradise Lost* and Thomson's *Seasons* could furnish illustrations of all three sentimental modes.[15]

This new theory of poetic modes, combined with a scheme of history and a theory of modern literature, proved a self-justification for Schiller in his rivalry with Goethe and became the starting point for the Schlegels, who reformulated Schiller's dichotomy as the opposition of classical and romantic literature. The difficulty of combining a typology of literature with a philosophy of its history and a concrete critical application to particular figures and ages was not completely overcome: there are inconsistencies in the formulation, shifts in the meaning of terms, and varying emphases in Schiller's evaluation. The types of subjective attitudes are too sharply distinguished or too closely identified with specific historical periods. The periods are characterized too much in terms of a few rather arbitrary criteria according to specific characteristics of individual authors. It is easy to point out that there never was a purely "naive" poet or a purely "naive" age, that Schiller thinks too much in terms of oppositions, pure types, and sharply set-off ages. But with these reservations, the theory gives a profound insight into the process of literature and the peculiar situation of modern literature.

"Naive" poetry is primarily that of antiquity—in practice the poetry of Homer; "sentimental" poetry is modern, of an age in which the poet is in conflict with his environment and is divided within himself. Intellect and feeling are divorced, the unity of apperception has been destroyed, the "dissociation of sensibility" (to use Eliot's term) accomplished. Schiller himself recognizes, however, that the historical distinction is not absolutely neat and clear cut. He knows that there were "sentimental" poets in antiquity, especially toward its close (e.g., Horace), and he admits the possibility, at least in isolated cases, of "naive" poets in modern "sentimental" times. His great example, whom he has in mind even when he does not name him, is Goethe, whose nearness to nature, spontaneity, realism, and objectivity were the constant objects of Schiller's admiration and envy. His attitude toward Goethe and his view of the possibility of "naive" poetry in modern times was, however, quite ambiguous. Partly he wants to account for Goethe, to put him in his place as a lucky survival, almost a freak of nature, in an age when he himself and his contemporaries are necessarily "sentimental"; and partly he wants to think of Goethe as a guarantee of the possibility of a rebirth of "naive" poetry, as the great example of the Greek German, the new classicist. On the one hand Schiller celebrates classical antiquity. He shares, to a large extent, the extravagant Hellenism of his friends: of Goethe, Humboldt, and Hölderlin. He sees the ideal of humanity realized in Greece and wants to restore it in his own age. But on the other hand, he recognizes that this is impossible, and that he himself, like his whole age, is irrevocably committed to the reflective, the self-critical, the divorce between head and heart, the "sentimental" in his own peculiar sense of the word.

Ultimately Schiller would want a reconciliation of the "naive" and the "sentimental," of antiquity and modernity, nature and art, sentiment and intellect, his own character with that of Goethe. Speaking of the objects of nature, Schiller says: "They are what we were; they are what we ought to be again some day. We were nature as they are: and our civilization must bring us back to nature by way of reason and freedom." [16] "This way," he explains, "which the modern poets take, is after all the same as that which man in general must follow. Nature makes him one with himself, art divides and separates him, through the ideal he returns to unity." [17] Nature, art, and ideal are the three stages which correspond to naive, sentimental, and "synthetic" poetry, which has no special term in Schiller.

We need not examine how far the concept of "naive" poetry actually agrees with a modern conception of the nature of Greek poetry and even of Homer. Already Friedrich Schlegel had begun to demolish this conception of the Greeks which, in Germany at least, derived mainly from Winckelmann's phrase about their "noble simplicity and calm grandeur." Burckhardt and Nietzsche have corrected the view of German classicism and possibly over-

stressed the "Dionysian," the chaotic, the "endangered" and sophisticated in the Greeks. But the historical accuracy of Schiller's image
of the Greeks matters little: we must recognize the skill and insight with which the type is construed. His "naive" poet is not, of
course, the primitive poet but the one who observes reality calmly,
lives in contact with nature, and makes friends with the cosmic
forces by transforming them into beautiful gods. His early poem
"The Gods of Greece" (1788) had found the classic formulation
for the contrast, worked out first by Lessing, between the skeleton
on Christian tombs and the beautiful young men extinguishing a
torch on the ancient sarcophagi. The Greeks differ from us in their
feeling for landscape and nature: they do not know the mechanistic view of the universe; they see nature animated and lived in;
they have, in Wordsworth's words, "glimpses that would make
me less forlorn." The Greeks are objective, unself-conscious, and
direct in their ethical relations. Schiller illustrates this contrast by
Homer's matter-of-fact relation of the meeting between Diomedes
and Glaucus on the battlefield before Troy. The enemies recognize each other as former guests, agree to avoid each other, and,
as a token, exchange their armor. Ariosto describes a similar scene
of two knights and rivals, Ferraù and Rinaldo, engaging in single
combat but then making peace and mounting one horse together
in order to pursue Angelica. "Ariosto, the citizen of a later and
morally less simple world, cannot hide his own surprise and emotion in relating this incident. He is overcome by the sense of the
distance between those manners and the manners of his own age.
He suddenly leaves off portraying the object and appears in his own
person addressing the 'magnanimity of ancient chivalry.' " [18]

But not only Homer is in Schiller's mind. Shakespeare is also
"naive" in his sense of the word. Schiller confesses that at first he
was "repelled by Shakespeare's coldness, by his indifference, which
permitted him to jest in the middle of the highest pathos, to let
the fool break in upon the heart-rending scenes in *Hamlet, King
Lear, Macbeth,* etc. I was not yet able to understand nature at first
hand." Shakespeare is "naive" because he is objective. "Like God
behind the structure of the universe, he stands behind his work.
He is his work and the work is he." [19]

By "naive imitation of nature" Schiller thus does not mean
naturalism. He shares the neoclassical distaste for the "Dutch," the

common, the grotesque. His ideal of "naive" art is good classicism, an art based on the eternal principles of nature. He consistently objects to naturalism and does so with increasing vehemence.

The "sentimental" poet is the modern one, the poet in the age of civilization, convention, and specialization—divided within himself, in conflict with society. Schiller has a feeling, extraordinary for his time, of the alienation of the artist from his age. He recognizes that naiveté is foreign to his age. "Poets of the naive type are out of place in an artificial age. They are hardly possible in it any more unless they run wild in their age and are saved by a lucky chance from its crippling influence. They can never come out of society, though they appear outside of it from time to time, but rather like strangers whom we gape at and as ill-mannered sons of nature who rouse our anger." [20] The "sentimental" poet who cannot imitate the base reality around him must strive for an ideal, must seek the "infinite," while the "naive" poet can be limited to the finite world in front of him. The "sentimental" poet will never be as perfect as the "naive," as he never can reach his aim, the ideal, fully. "Naive" poetry is the art of limitation; "sentimental," of the infinite.[21] Often Schiller thinks that there is something higher in this mere striving of the "sentimental" poet than in the contentment and achievement of the "naive." Occasionally he would become openly critical of Greek civilization. He objects to it as "merely aesthetic," [22] he voices his disappointment with the base and unideal attitude of the Greeks toward women,[23] and, in his review of Goethe's *Iphigenie,* in an elaborate comparison with the corresponding play by Euripides, he definitely prefers Goethe's humanitarian refinement to the Greek poet's cruelty. The soliloquy of Orestes in which he parts with the Furies in his mind (III. ii) seems to Schiller to demonstrate not only Goethe's superiority over Euripides but also the support the modern poet derives from the "progress of moral culture and the milder spirit of our times," "the more beautiful humanity of our modern manners." [24]

Most commonly Schiller is driven to prefer the "sentimental" on negative grounds. We simply cannot return to the naive. The pastoral dream is a mere illusion. We must live in our time and according to the way poets express contemporary humanity, for the highest concept of poetry is "to give the most complete expression to humanity." [25] Our highest aim is the return to nature, but it must be a conscious and voluntary return. Modern art, at its highest, has to unite the universal and the particular, the individual and the ideal, necessity and freedom.

Schiller develops the theory of the four modes of feeling with much ingenuity. In each case he also works out a criterion of value and shows the peculiar danger of aberration to which each of these "modes of feeling" is liable. The "naive" poet is in constant danger of slipping into the low, the trivial, the merely natural, because he is necessarily more dependent on nature, on his environment and society. To be a poet he needs a nature "rich in forms, a poetic world, a naive humanity," [26] and therefore he is much more likely to succumb to mere feeling, to a mere imitation of nature. Triviality and lowness can at times be found in Shakespeare, Molière, Goldoni, and Holberg, not to speak of Homer, Aristophanes, and Plautus.

This is the point of view from which Schiller judged Bürger in a review which has excited much unfavorable comment for its lack of charity and its display of intellectual condescension. But it is hard to see how he could help condemning the crude naturalism of Bürger's themes, the trivialities of his diction, and the sound-imitations common in his poems. There is also much justice in criticizing the direct expression, the mere spontaneity of feeling, the overflow of emotion on which Bürger prided himself. Schiller would have agreed with the *Paradoxe sur le comédien* by Diderot and with Wordsworth, who recommended "emotion recollected in tranquillity." * The poet must beware of singing "his pain in the midst of pain." He must write "from the milder and more distancing memory," never from present emotion. "He must become a stranger to himself; must extricate the object of his fervor from his individuality." [27] Impersonality, objectivity, the general and generally human are Schiller's ideal, as they are of every classicist.

In the review Schiller applies his point of view also to the problem of popular poetry. He recognizes the difficulty of becoming a popular poet in an age when a wide gulf had opened between the

* L. A. Willoughby has argued that Wordsworth derived his idea from Schiller and that he read the Bürger review. But it is possible to admit that Wordsworth's theory is based on his personal experience. See "Wordsworth and Germany," in *German Studies Presented to Professor H. G. Fiedler* (Oxford, 1938), pp. 432–58.

taste of the élite and that of the masses. The popular poet who would not pander to the taste of the masses must attempt the much more difficult task of satisfying the tastes of both the connoisseur and the people. He can achieve this only by being universally human, by raising the individual and local to the general. In Schiller's terms, this process is one of idealization also in the moral sense, an educational process of refining and maturing both the public and the poet. The poet "descends" to the people, but he himself must be a mature and cultured mind if he is to serve as an educator. "Only a calm and quiet soul can give birth to the perfect." Clearly this view did injustice to the vigorous and crude talent of unhappy Bürger, and it hardly copes with the problem of mass art. Schiller uncompromisingly condemns not only the low and obscene but also the purely personal and naturalistic. He was quite untouched by the preromantic fervor for the songlike and the primitive. There is nothing of Herder's *Volkspoesie* in his conception of "naive" poetry.

Later Schiller faced the problem of the audience for the modern poet. Surprisingly enough, he recognizes the need of the "tired businessman" (his exact term) [28] and the "dull scholar" for mere recreation and amusement in art. He also sees the other danger— that demands made on literature will require moral uplift and improvement in a way which does not take into account the nature of art and overrates its direct influence on morals. But Schiller is unable to solve the dilemma he must have been one of the first to see. He puts a hesitant hope in a "class of people who without work are active and can idealize without extravagance." "Only such a class can preserve the beautiful whole of human nature which is momentarily disturbed by any kind of work and completely destroyed by a working life, and can give by its feelings, rules to universal judgment in all things that are purely human." But Schiller concludes cautiously: "Whether such a class really exists, or rather whether the class now existing in similar external conditions answers to this conception internally, is another question with which I am not concerned." [29] His wholesale condemnation of labor as the destroyer of aesthetic civilization and his recognition of the soul-destroying forces of modern specialization and commercialization do not quite persuade Schiller to find his ideal audience in the aristocracy of his time, to which he must be alluding in the last words quoted. But the solution in an ideal élite of leisure and refinement reveals the limitations of Schiller's utopian idealism.

Goethe, we know, was Schiller's constant critical whetstone: the antipode of his own mind, the great Greek in a "sentimental" time. At first Schiller felt definitely repelled by him. Even after a friendly meeting Schiller reports that he does not wholly like Goethe's philosophy: "It draws too much from the world of sense, where I draw from the soul. On the whole, his mode of perception is too sensuous and he handles and fingers things too much." [30] But then Schiller broke the ice and wrote Goethe a long letter (August 24, 1794) which Goethe himself considered as "having summarized my existence." [31] It has become an important document in the history of Goethe criticism, with its description of his "observing eye," "right intuition," and method of "grasping nature as a totality." Goethe "creates after nature, penetrates into her hidden technique." Anticipating the ideas of the later treatise on *Naive and Sentimental Poetry*, Schiller speculates that Goethe, if he had been born a Greek or even an Italian and had been surrounded by a "select" nature and idealizing art, would have found his way without painful deviations. "Now since you were born a German, since your Greek spirit was cast into this Nordic world, you had no other choice than either to become a Nordic artist [a "sentimental" poet in Schiller's later terminology] or to supplement your imagination in what reality withheld from it with the aid of the power of thought, and so, as it were, from the inside out, and in a rational way, to give birth to a Greece." [32] The ideas of this famous letter are vague and even inconsistent. Creation on the analogy of nature is very general praise. It is even contradicted by Schiller's recognition of Goethe's concern for a conscious conquest of the classical, for the problem of translating concepts into intuitions, thoughts into feelings. Goethe, Schiller continued a little later, had successfully accomplished the transformation of the "thinking power into imagination, generalized his intuition, and made his emotion prescriptive," while Schiller's understanding merely symbolized, hovered "between concept and intuition, rule and emotion, the technical head and genius." [33] Here is the germ of Schiller's later typology and the

contrast between the unified "naive" poet and the divided "sentimental" poet.

Schiller also devoted quite specific critical attention to several of
Goethe's works. The correspondence with Goethe contains a careful, step-by-step, "genetic" review of *Wilhelm Meister,* which he
read in manuscript installments. He characterizes *Wilhelm Meister*
convincingly: Goethe's attitude of detachment and irony, the general drift of the action, the motivation of the events and characters.
He always presses for more clarity in the economy of the whole, for
a reduction of the purely "novelistic" and "epic machinery," and
for a pointing up of the moral and philosophy. In rereading the
complete *Meister* Schiller was left with an uncomfortable impression of prosiness, which he accounts for in terms of his genre
theories. The novel is merely a "pseudo-epic"; it lacks the dignity
of verse which would lift it into the realm of poetry, just as *Hermann und Dorothea* is sustained merely by its tone and meter.
In the treatise on *Naive and Sentimental Poetry, Werther* is
briefly discussed as exhibiting a "sentimental" subject treated
with "naiveté." Schiller there recognizes the continuity between
Werther, Tasso, and Faust, but does not seem to be worried by
the paradox of an extremely sentimental character and subject in
the hands of a "naive" poet. He seems to rely on Goethe to keep to
the "sensuous truth of things." [34] Schiller was too much dazzled by
the Olympian Goethe, the Goethe of the Homeric *Hermann und
Dorothea* and even of the *Natürliche Tochter.*[35] He could not see
that Goethe's permanent greatness is not in his classicism, his attempts to create an idealized picture of the contemporary German
bourgeoisie in his hexameter idyll and his long novel, but in his
personal "occasional" poetry and in *Faust* (which Schiller could
have known only as a fragment). Goethe more than any other poet
would have lent himself to Schiller's analysis of "sentimental"
genres: the satire such as *Reineke Fuchs,* the idyll such as *Hermann
und Dorothea,* and the elegy such as *Tasso* or *Iphigenie.* Schiller's
solution, distinguishing "sentimental" theme and "naive" treatment, seems an awkward concession to a dualism of form and content.

In analyzing "sentimental" poetry Schiller suggests categories of
critical evaluation. Just as the naive poet runs the danger of flat

naturalism, so the "sentimental" poet is apt to fly away into the realm of fancy. He can become overwrought, extravagant, an "enthusiast" in the English 18th-century sense. His striving for the infinite and superhuman may become sheer nonsense. Schiller distinguishes between extravagance of emotion and extravagance of representation. He recognizes the truth of the emotion which St. Preux feels for Julie in Rousseau's *Nouvelle Héloïse,* or which Werther feels for Lotte; he recognizes the reality of the gallantry depicted in chivalrous romances or that of the *délicatesse* in French and English sentimental novels: but they are condemned for transgressing the limits of poetic truth, though they may describe feelings experienced in real life.[36]

Distrust of the overstrained, the purely fanciful, and the willful accounts also for Schiller's criticism of his younger contemporaries, the romanticists in the narrow sense. His relations with the Schlegels especially were clouded with personal grievances and issues of literary politics. But critically Schiller did no violence to his feelings when he condemned Friedrich Schlegel's *Lucinde* as "the very acme of modern formlessness and affectation" [37] or when he found Tieck's *Genoveva* "shapeless." [38] He was slightly amused and much more puzzled and repelled by Jean Paul, and was personally fond of his pupil Novalis without ever pronouncing on his writings.

Schiller's relation to Friedrich Hölderlin, whom today we would recognize as the greatest of his younger contemporaries, was more complex and more unfortunate. Schiller groups Hölderlin with Jean Paul as "extravagant," "one sided," and "subjective," and ascribes these failings not so much to the original nature of these authors as to a "lack of aesthetic nourishment and influx from outside and opposition of the empirical world in which they lived." [39] He saw in him only another sentimentalist who, like all the romanticists, had lost balance and wandered off into the realm of mere fancy.

Schiller tries to work out concrete criteria in a detailed discussion of the three sentimental "modes of feeling": satire, elegy, and idyll. The satiric mode is defined as that which takes as its subject the contradiction between reality and the ideal. A distinction is introduced between "punitive" satire, which must be sublime, and "laughing" satire, which must be beautiful. Juvenal, Swift, and

Rousseau are cited as examples of the first kind; Cervantes, Fielding (who occurs also among the "naive" writers), and Sterne as
examples of the second kind. Satire, Schiller insists, has its own
dangers: it would cease to be poetry if it became "avenging" satire,
mere invective, or libel, as this would make it lose its aesthetic
freedom. Nor must it become "pleasantry," as it will then have
lost the desire for the infinite. Voltaire is used as an example of
a mere "wit," deficient in feeling, though some exception is made
for *L'Ingénu* and *Candide,* works where Voltaire has not lost sight
of the ideal.

Elegy is described as the poet's putting art against nature, the
ideal against reality, with a dominance of interest in the ideal itself. Schiller here attempts to establish a criterion of value: mere
sorrow over a personal loss does not make a true elegy, for even
Ovid's *Tristia* seem to Schiller merely personal, though they mourn
the loss of Rome.[40] Rousseau is used as the example of the modern
elegiac writer, but he does not satisfy Schiller because he did not
achieve the necessary harmony of sensibility and thought. He
rarely rises to aesthetic freedom; he is too much dominated either
by his emotion or by abstract thought. He seeks physical repose and
escape from the world, not the ideal of a perfect civilization, which
for Schiller must be implicit in every elegy. A similar severe judgment is then pronounced upon the German elegiac poets, Haller,
Ewald von Kleist, and Klopstock. Klopstock, who would seem to
be Schiller's ideal "sentimental" poet yearning for the "infinite"
and "unlimited," is condemned for his lack of form, his bloodless
abstractions, and his mere "musicality." (By "musicality" Schiller
means the opposite of concrete and visualized, poetry without object, the mere evocation of a mood.[41])

In Schiller's scheme the idyll is the highest of sentimental moods.
But he does not praise the pastoral. The dream of a golden age is
only a "beautiful fiction." The world of shepherds is too narrow to
be the proper symbol of the ideal. Gessner's idylls are criticized as
being "neither wholly nature nor wholly ideal," an in-between
hybrid stage which Schiller, in a rare remark on external form,
also sees reflected in Gessner's hybrid poetic prose. The description of paradise in Milton finds favor in Schiller's eyes as the "most
beautiful idyll of the sentimental kind he knows." [42] Schiller's ideal
idyll is not Arcadia but Elysium, a utopia in which the opposition

between reality and the ideal is completely abolished. There will be calm, but the calm of perfection, not of inertia. This was not merely a theory: it seems to have assumed some concrete shape in Schiller's mind when he planned a poem on the marriage of Hercules and Hebe. The main figures in it were to be gods, though Hercules the man would introduce the human element. Schiller hoped thus to triumph "over naive poetry by means of the sentimental." [43] Such an idyll would be the counterpart of high comedy, a genre which appears only as a version of satire in Schiller's original scheme. But it is hard to see how such a bookish scheme for a mythological subject, even if carried out in Schiller's best style, could have proved anything about the theory of genres or anything fundamental about the relation between naive and sentimental poetry. It is not surprising that nothing came of it.

The coupling of the idyll with high comedy shows how Schiller became involved in the contradiction between the traditional genres and his own fourfold modes of feeling, which were certainly meant to operate quite independently of the genres and are expressly declared not to allow any other genre and to exhaust all possibilities. [44] But Schiller throughout his career thought and wrote much about the traditional genres and their function and nature, without taking too much account of his new modes of feeling even later. In the treatise on *Naive and Sentimental Poetry,* tragedy and comedy are surprisingly discussed only in the context of satire. High comedy is there exalted as the genre which allows the greatest freedom to the poet's mind. Schiller speculates that perfect comedy would make all tragedy either superfluous or impossible. "Its aim is identical with the highest aim for which man strives, to be free of passion, always to look around himself and into himself clearly and calmly, everywhere to find more of chance than of blind fate and rather to laugh about incongruity than to be angry or weep over malice." [45] In high comedy the poet thus reaches the detachment, the complete objectivity which elsewhere Schiller describes as the ideal effect of tragedy. This exaltation of comedy is isolated in Schiller's thought, though surely not unimportant if we think of later romantic theory and of the concluding position which Hegel assigned to comedy in his *Aesthetic.*

Schiller's main preoccupation as a theorist of genre was, understandably, with tragedy. His first critical writings were devoted to the theater and his own *Robbers*. "On the Contemporary German Theater" ("Über das gegenwärtige deutsche Theater," 1782) adopts Lessing's concept of drama as a kind of theodicy, as a microcosm in which we are to see the harmony of the macrocosm.[46] The better known oration "The Stage Viewed as a Moral Institution" ("Die Schaubühne als eine moralische Anstalt betrachtet," 1784) is a fulsome celebration of the civilizing effect of the theater, an all-inclusive claim for its power as a "school of practical wisdom," a "guide through civil life." [47] The stage makes men bear their sufferings and see through their own follies, teaches them toleration (see *Nathan the Wise*), welds an incoherent public into a nation, brings people together in sympathy, and hence makes them truly men. The piece is an eloquent inventory of all the clichés used in apologetics of the theater.

Schiller comes closer to grips with the theory of tragedy after he has read Kant. His paper "On the Cause of Pleasure in Tragic Subjects" ("Über den Grund des Vergnügens an tragischen Gegenständen," 1792) uses the Kantian contrast between the "purposiveness of nature" and "moral purposiveness" to account for our pleasure in tragedy. The victory of moral law over natural law (e.g., over the instinct of self-preservation in the case of the sacrifice of a martyr or patriot) or of a higher over a lower moral law (as in Shakespeare's Coriolanus, whose patriotism and filial love triumph over the desire for revenge) accounts for our pleasure in tragedy. Joy in mere purposiveness, even if it be purposive malice, accounts for the interest and pleasure we take in the machinations of villains such as Iago and Lovelace (in Richardson's *Clarissa*), provided, of course, that they are ultimately defeated. Schiller even thinks that one could draw up a kind of *a priori* table of all the possible cases of conflict between higher and lower laws.[48]

This psychological paper preceded "On Tragic Art" ("Über tragische Kunst," 1792), which returns to the account of tragic pleasure accepted by Lessing and common at that time. Tragic pleasure arises from pity, compassion for the victim. This pity must be neither too weak nor too strong. If it is too weak we remain cold; if it is too strong the pity is painful and thus ceases to be art. It is too strong when helpless or innocent people are victims of villains such as Iago or Lady Macbeth, and it is too weak when we see Lear foolishly giving away his crown and dividing his love among his

daughters. The highest pity is aroused when both the victor and
the victim arouse our sympathy: Corneille's *Le Cid,* with our sympathy divided between Rodrigue and Chimène, is thus the "master
work of tragedy," though Schiller is quick to add the qualification
"in respect to its plot." [49] At the highest point of tragedy all dissatisfaction with fate disappears and "loses itself in an intuition
or, even better, in clear awareness of a purposeful coherence of all
things, a sublime order of a benevolent will." [50] Tragedy is thus a
justification of God, a reconciliation with the order of the universe.

Schiller then reformulates Aristotle's definition: "Tragedy
would then be poetic imitation of a coherent series of events (a
complete action) which shows us men in a state of suffering and
aims at arousing our pity." [51] In elaborating the definition Schiller
draws the old distinction between historical and poetic truth,
arguing that poetic truth must always have precedence in tragedy:
he then repeats the Aristotelian view of the necessity of mixed
heroes. They must be neither "evil demons" nor "pure intelli-
gences," neither villains nor helpless martyrs. He concludes with a
strong plea that each genre pursue its peculiar end. The "most
perfect tragedy would be one in which the pity aroused would be
less the effect of the subject than of the tragic form used in the
best manner." [52] Schiller has thus embraced the theory of pathetic
tragedy which exonerates the tragic hero of all guilt and teaches
us acceptance of the inscrutably wise order of the universe: in
principle he has not gone beyond Lessing.

Within a year, however, Schiller's conception of tragedy underwent a profound change. "On the Pathetic" ("Über das Pathe-
tische," 1793) is introduced with the statement that "representation of suffering—as mere suffering—is never the aim of art. . . .
The ultimate aim of art is to represent the supersensuous, and
tragic art in particular achieves this by making sensuous the moral
independence of man from the laws of nature in a state of passion." [53] Tragedy must represent "suffering nature," but also
"moral resistance against suffering" (and moral freedom in Kantian terminology is supersensuous). Mere pity, mere compassion, is
condemned as nonartistic. The pathetic is aesthetic only insofar
as it is sublime, an act of moral freedom. Tragedy has thus ceased
to be apologetics for the world order and becomes rather the representation of human free will defying the universe. The following

article "On the Sublime" ("Über das Erhabene," 1801) argues that
we must resign ourselves to the incomprehensibility of the universe.[54] Seeing the spectacle of man's freedom in tragedy we shall
ourselves be better prepared to meet suffering in reality. Tragedy
is "inoculation against unavoidable fate." Schiller thus returns to
one of the oldest interpretations of catharsis. Tragedy is an education for stoicism, not for brotherhood and universal pity as Lessing
and a whole trend of 18th-century theory had argued.

Schiller's dramatic theory moved more and more in the direction
of a completely stylized, idealized art. Commenting on the characters of Greek tragedies, he finds them "ideal masks rather than
individuals." Ulysses in *Ajax* and *Philoctetes* is "only the ideal of a
sly, unscrupulous, narrow-minded cleverness." Creon in *Oedipus*
and *Antigone* is simply "cold royal dignity." But Schiller praises
now what he would have condemned before. "One gets along with
such characters much better, as they can be introduced much more
quickly and as their features are more permanent and firmer.
Truth does not suffer, since such characters are opposed both to
logical entities and mere individuals." [55] Similarly the handling of
the crowd in *Julius Caesar* is praised because Shakespeare looks
rather for the "poetic abstract" than for the individual and thus
comes very near the Greeks.[56] *Richard III* draws especially high
praise for the skill with which Shakespeare "represents what cannot be presented" and uses "symbols where nature cannot be depicted." [57] Schiller wants to expel vulgar imitation of nature from
the drama altogether by introducing "symbolic devices . . . which
in everything that does not belong to the true artistic world of
the poet (and thus must not be represented but only suggested)
would take the place of the object." He even expects the purification of poetry by symbolism. "Its world would contract more narrowly and significantly and within it poetry would be more effective." [58] But this desire for purer, more concentrated poetry is
somewhat belied by the hesitant hopes he immediately afterward
voices for the future of opera.

Schiller's last critical pronouncement of any weight, the preface
to the *Bride of Messina* (1803), justifies his use of the chorus and
declares open war on "naturalism" (Schiller's own term). Art must
be true, but truth is something that leaves reality behind, becoming purely ideal. "Nature," Schiller believes now, "is only an idea

of the mind." Poetry, especially dramatic poetry, demands illusion but not realistic deception. "Everything [in poetry] is only a symbol of the real." [59] Thus the chorus can be defended as a means of purging the tragic poem, raising its tone and breaking the violence of passions. But Schiller realizes the artificiality and difficulty of the modern chorus. There is a difference between the public life of the ancients, which made the chorus probable, and the privacy of the moderns. "The palace of the kings is now closed, the courts have retired from the gates of the cities to the interiors of houses, writing has supplanted the living word, and the people itself, the sensuous living mass (if it does not act with brute violence), has become the state, and thus an abstract concept, and the gods have returned to the bosoms of men." [60] The striking parenthesis, which implicitly condemns revolution and mob violence, shows how Schiller was worried by the modern lack of corporate public life and how, at least in this play, he thought of the chorus as a device of escape into a never-never world. In it he can even mix the Greek and Christian religions without a feeling of incongruity. All religions are treated as a "collective whole for the imagination," [61] a kind of universal myth.

In the years of Schiller's friendship with Goethe, the former was confronted with the question of epic theory: he reviewed *Wilhelm Meister* and discussed *Hermann und Dorothea* and several other epic plans of Goethe. He himself considered writing an epic on Frederick the Great or Gustavus Adolphus. Out of the correspondence about *Meister* arose Goethe's essay defining the differences between epic and dramatic poetry. Schiller accepted Goethe's distinctions, developing them further in accordance with his speculative bent and Kantian terminology. He argues that drama is subject to the category of causality, epic to the category of substance. Action is an end in the drama, only a means in the epic. Hence, Schiller concludes, no violent action is proper in the epic, as this would arouse too much pity and thus assimilate epic to tragedy.[62] Both *Hermann und Dorothea* and *Wilhelm Meister* are criticized for containing tragic touches. In *Meister* there is too much of the incomprehensible and marvelous, which does not agree with the clarity Schiller demands from the novel.[63] With his interest in dialectics and the reconciliation of opposites Schiller elaborates a difficult theory according to which a synthesis of the epic and tragic would be the highest poetry. He accepts Goethe's view that in the epic events are told as past, while in drama they are portrayed as present. He sees implied, however, an "opposition of genus and species," i.e., an opposition between the demands of poetry in general and the demands of the epic or drama. All poetry should make its objects sensuously concrete and present; hence in the epic there is constant piquant contrast in the endeavor to keep events in the past while making them vividly concrete. In the drama there is an analogous opposition: all poetry should make its objects distant through ideality; otherwise poetic freedom or conquest over matter will not be asserted. Thus drama, while portraying events as present, must keep them away from mere reality, must remain "semblance." These oppositions between genus and species must not, of course, in Schiller's views lead to a mixture of genres. The real aim of art is always to combine character with beauty, purity with fullness, unity with wholeness.[64] Schiller, while firmly holding to the neoclassical prescription of purity in the genres and in the different arts, still envisages some final union of the arts.

> The different arts [he speculates] are becoming more and more similar in their effect on the mind, without any change in their objective boundaries. Music in its highest perfection must become form and affect us with the quiet power of antiquity; plastic art in its highest perfection must become music and move us by its immediate sensuous presence; poetry in its most perfect development must grip us powerfully like music but at the same time surround us like sculpture with quiet clarity. The perfect style of each art is manifested when it knows how to remove its specific limitations and to assume a more general character by a wise use of its peculiarity, without, however, giving up its specific advantages.[65]

Clearly here is the germ of the theory of the Wagnerian *Gesamt-kunstwerk,* though Schiller in his insistence on preserving the limits of the arts and genres would have shied away from romantic confusions.

He had least to say on the lyric, which in a mood of self-depreciation he called "the pettiest and most ungrateful of forms." [66] The review of Bürger's poems turns rather on the general prob-

lem of idealization and popular art than on concrete problems of
the lyric. The review of Matthisson's poems (1794) is a discussion
rather of landscape poetry and art in general than of specific poems,
though in the second half an attempt is made to fit Matthisson's
poems into the theory. After general reflection that art "by a free
effect of our creative imagination must induce particular feelings"
in us, Schiller comes to the conclusion that this can be achieved
only if the artist keeps "to the objective association among appearances" and if at the same time he sheds all individual peculiarities
and becomes "man in general." Poetry demands truth of its object
and generality of its subject, the poet. Everything in a poem must
be "true nature," but nothing must be "merely real [historical]
nature." The grand style can be achieved only by throwing off
everything contingent, in order to achieve the pure expression of
necessity.[67] From this highly abstract and objective neoclassical
position Schiller concludes that there cannot be such a thing as
nature poetry. There is nothing definite and necessary about nature unless the poet by a "symbolic operation" changes inanimate
nature into human nature. This, according to Schiller, can be
achieved in two ways: either by musical effects in poetry, by an
exploitation of the analogy that exists between the movements of
our minds and appearances in nature, or by using nature as a
symbol of ideals, as "living language of spirits," a "symbol of the
internal harmony of the mind with itself." Static descriptions of
landscape are condemned by arguments substantially derived from
the *Laokoon.* Nature poetry must be musical, and "moving" in
both senses of the English word. Matthisson's poems are shown to
stand this test. But the high praise of this mediocre poet is modified
at the end of the review when Schiller expresses the hope that
Matthisson will proceed further and higher, will "invent figures
for his landscapes, and add acting humanity to his charming background." [68] Landscape poetry for Schiller always remains inferior
poetry.

One would think that didactic and philosophical poetry would
be for Schiller an extremely urgent and personal concern. It can
be argued that his own greatest poetical successes are not in the
tragedies but in his philosophical poems: "Die Künstler," "Die
Götter Griechenlands," "Das Ideal und das Leben," etc. In theory,
however, Schiller was quick in condemning philosophical poetry

as versified philosophy. In discussing Haller's and Kleist's didactic and descriptive poems on the Alps and spring, he comes to the blunt conclusion that there is no didactic poetry. Poetry may be poetry either of the senses or of ideas (in the Kantian sense) but it never can be poetry of concepts or the understanding. The concept in poetry must either be brought down to individuality or raised up to the idea. Schiller professes never to have seen a poem in which "the thought itself was poetic and would remain so." [69] The issue is obviously hidden in the term "idea," which in Schiller's and Kant's terminology means the union of the concrete and the universal which alone is poetic. Thus, when his friend Körner suggested that he write an epic on the progress of humanity, Schiller can say that a "philosophical subject is completely reprehensible for poetry." [70]

Schiller understood that language by its nature is made up of universals, and that thus the medium of poetry, language, is in constant contradiction to its aim, which must always be sensuous, concrete, and intuitive. "The object to be represented must, before it is brought to the imagination and turned into intuition, take a very long detour through the abstract realm of concepts." "Language sets everything before the understanding, but the poet must bring everything before the imagination: poetry wants intuitions, language offers only concepts." [71]

Schiller insists that the starting point of art is the unconscious; he is bent on condemning mere intellectual and contrived art.

> In experience the poet begins with the unconscious, and he must consider himself lucky if the clearest consciousness of his operations allows him to find again the first dark total idea of his work unweakened in the finished labor. Without such a dark but powerful total idea which precedes everything technical, no poetic work can arise, and poetry, it seems to me, consists just in this: to be able to express and communicate that unconsciousness, i.e., to transfer it into an object. The nonpoet can just as well as a poet be moved by a poetic idea, but he is unable to put it into an object; he cannot represent it with a claim to necessity. A nonpoet can just as well as a poet produce a work with consciousness and necessity but such a work will not begin with the unconscious and will not end

with it. It remains only a work of consciousness. But the unconscious united with the conscious makes the poetic artist.[72]

Here Schiller states with remarkable clarity an idea to which T. S.
Eliot has given formulation in his phrase about an "objective
correlative" for the poet's emotion; also he sensibly formulates the
importance of the unconscious in the poetic process without going
to the romantic extreme of ignoring the part of the conscious. It
is an entirely separate question whether Schiller in his creative
practice has lived up to the insights of his theory. It is difficult to
deny the justice of much severe criticism directed against Schiller's
dramas—by Croce, for instance, who sees in him only a second-
rate oratorical poet.[73] One could argue that his role in the history
of criticism has been obscured and overshadowed by his tremendous, though transient, national and international success as a
playwright.

Schiller offers a theory of literature which holds firmly to the
essential truth of neoclassicism without the handicap of adherence
to the "rules," the didactic fallacies and pedantries of official neoclassicism. We might object that at times his stress on the generalized, the universally human, and finally the symbolic and conventional cuts him off from a mastery of reality. Besides this reformulation of neoclassicism Schiller provides an extraordinarily fruitful
theory of modern literature and its relation to modern specialized
and mechanized society. Again, we might object that his proposed
solution in a "progressive" philosophy of history, in a future reconciliation of man and nature, is utopian. Surely also his theory of
the modes of feeling, however open to criticism in detail, moves in
the right direction toward a modern genre theory which would
abandon mere external classifications yet would not accept Croce's
rejection of all genre distinctions. Schiller also seems correctly to
have understood both the apartness of the aesthetic realm and its
relations to morality and civilization. He knew that poetry is
neither amusement nor preaching, and at the same time he avoided
the danger of romantic mysticism which, only a few years after
his great treatise, became acute for almost every German writer
on art and poetry.

Schiller's influence has not been recognized in its whole extent.
This is due in part to his unfortunate personal relations with the

Schlegels. Actually his impact on Friedrich Schlegel was enormous: the very distinction between the classic and the romantic is a modified restatement of Schiller's theory of the "naive" and "sentimental." Coleridge, either through Schelling or directly, echoes many of Schiller's leading ideas: for instance the view that art "is the mediatress between, and reconciler of, nature and man." Hegel in his *Lectures on Aesthetics* has freely acknowledged the importance of Schiller's aesthetic ideas for his own system. Even if, with the decline of German idealism, Schiller's direct influence has waned, one can observe his indirect impact even today. Surely Huizinga's *Homo Ludens* comes from Schiller. Carl Jung's types of "introvert" and "extrovert" correspond to Schiller's two types very closely. There is even a surprising affinity, possibly through the mediation of Hegel, between some of Sartre's ideas on literature and Schiller's. The final aim of art is, according to Sartre, "to recuperate this world as if it had its source in human liberty." [74] This is pure Schiller except in its skeptical reservation, "as if." Schiller's version of aesthetic illusion (*Schein*) has impressed many recent thinkers, for example, most deeply, Susanne K. Langer, who in *Feeling and Form* explicitly cites Schiller as her source.

Thus Schiller fittingly concludes these discussions of 18th-century criticism. He sums up and salvages the heritage of the 18th century and yet is the wellspring of romantic criticism which spread from Germany, mainly through the influence of the elder Schlegel, throughout Europe.

BIBLIOGRAPHIES AND NOTES

ABBREVIATIONS AND SHORT TITLES

For titles not listed here refer to the chapter bibliographies for full reference.

ELH: English Literary History
JEGP: Journal of English and Germanic Philology
JHI: Journal of the History of Ideas
MLQ: Modern Language Quarterly
MLR: Modern Language Review
MP: Modern Philology
PMLA: Publications of the Modern Language Association
PQ: Philological Quarterly
RR: Romanic Review
Saintsbury: George Saintsbury, *History of Criticism and Literary Taste in Europe*, 3 vols. Edinburgh, 1900–04
SP: Studies in Philology

BIBLIOGRAPHY: INTRODUCTION

GENERAL

THE ONLY book covering our topic is still George Saintsbury, *A History of Criticism and Literary Taste in Europe,* 3 vols. Edinburgh, 1900–04.

Histories of aesthetics overlap with much of what is discussed here. Those based on independent research are:

Rudolf Zimmermann, *Geschichte der Aesthetik als philosophischer Wissenschaft,* Vienna, 1858. Herbartian in outlook, confined virtually to classical and German authors, a lucid, solid book.

Max Schasler, *Kritische Geschichte der Aesthetik,* 2 vols. Berlin, 1872. Hegelian in outlook, compilatory.

Marcelino Menéndez y Pelayo, *Historia de las ideas estéticas en España,* 5 vols. 1883–91. Best used in revised ed. Santander, 1946. Misleadingly entitled, since Vols. *4* and *5* are devoted to French, German, and English developments in our period. The book covers much criticism and literary history, is mainly descriptive, its outlook Catholic and vaguely romantic. In spite of its wealth of information it is a disappointing, diffuse compilation.

Bernard Bosanquet, *A History of Aesthetic,* London, 1892; recent reprint 1949. Hegelian in outlook, very limited in the number of texts and problems considered, but well focused and penetrating in its analysis.

Benedetto Croce, *Estetica come scienza dell' espressione e linguistica generale,* Bari, 1902; 8th ed. 1945. Contains a history of aesthetics which, while narrowly focused on precursors of Croce's views, is still the best in existence. English translation by Douglas Ainslie as *Aesthetic,* London, 1909. The historical part is translated in full only in 2d ed. 1922.

K. Gilbert and H. Kuhn, *A History of Esthetics,* New York, 1939; new ed. Bloomington, Ind., 1953. The most recent book: well informed but unclear in its assumptions and poor in analysis of ideas.

EIGHTEENTH-CENTURY CRITICISM AND AESTHETICS

H. von Stein, *Die Entstehung der neueren Aesthetik,* Stuttgart, 1886. Still instructive, though rather elementary.

Alfred Bäumler, *Kants Kritik der Urteilskraft: Ihre Geschichte und*

Systematik, Vol. *1*, Halle, 1923. The title conceals a general history of 18th-century aesthetics, its key terms, etc., in France, England, and Germany leading up to Kant. Excellent, though doctrinaire.

Wladyslaw Folkierski, *Entre le classicisme et le romantisme. Étude sur l'esthétique et les esthéticiens du* XVIII*e siècle,* Cracow, 1925. Diffuse but instructive. Much on Diderot.

Ernst Cassirer, *Die Philosophie der Aufklärung,* Tübingen, 1932; Eng. trans. *The Philosophy of the Enlightenment,* Princeton, 1951. Contains a brilliant final chapter, "Die Grundprobleme der Aesthetik."

Benedetto Croce, "Iniziazione all' estetica del settecento," in *Ultimi saggi,* Bari, 1934; 2d ed. Bari, 1948. An important, penetrating essay.

NOTES: INTRODUCTION

1. Eliot's essay on Andrew Marvell (1921), reprinted in *Selected Essays* (London, 1932), p. 284; Richards' *Principles of Literary Criticism* (London, 1924), p. 242.

2. Ed. Shawcross (Oxford, 1909), 2, 12. The passage is quoted in full in Vol. 2, 186.

3. Stanley Edgar Hyman, *The Armed Vision* (New York, 1948), p. x.

4. The examples are drawn from Oskar Walzel, "Künstlerische Absicht," *Germanisch-romanische Monatsschrift, 8* (1920), 321–31.

5. Cf. Meyer Abrams, "Archetypal Analogies in the Languages of Criticism," *University of Toronto Quarterly, 18* (1949), 313–27.

6. Cf. Herbert Schöffler, *Protestantismus und Literatur,* Leipzig, 1922.

7. *De la Littérature allemande,* Berlin, 1780.

8. There are good suggestions on this point in Carlo Antoni, *La lotta contra la ragione,* Florence, 1942.

BIBLIOGRAPHY: NEOCLASSICISM

Besides the histories of aesthetics quoted above, J. E. Spingarn, *A History of Literary Criticism in the Renaissance* (New York, 1899) is still basic. The Italian version, *La critica letteraria nel Rinascimento* (Bari, 1905) contains additional material.

Seventeenth-century developments, mostly in England, are sketched excellently in J. E. Spingarn's introduction to *Critical Essays of the Seventeenth Century,* 3 vols. Oxford, 1908–09.

The rise of French neoclassicism is best described in René Bray, *La Formation de la doctrine classique en France,* Paris, 1927; reprint 1951. For general treatment see Henri Peyre, *Le Classicisme français* (New York, 1942), with bibliography and discussion of the history of the word "classic." E. B. O. Borgerhoff, *The Freedom of French Classicism* (Princeton, 1950) emphasizes *je ne sais quoi*.

On imitation see Richard McKeon, "Imitation and Poetry," in *Thought, Action, and Passion*, Chicago, 1954.

On the Platonic tradition of idea see Erwin Panofsky, *Idea. Ein Beitrag zur Begriffsgeschichte der älteren Kunsttheorie*, Leipzig, 1924.

On genre theory see Irene Behrens, *Die Lehre von der Einteilung der Dichtkunst, vornehmlich vom 16. bis 19. Jahrhundert* (Halle, 1940) and Mario Fubini, "Genesi e storia dei generi letterari," in *Tecnica e teoria letteraria*, a volume of A. Momigliano, *Problemi ed orientamenti critici di lingua e di letteratura italiana*, Milan, 1948.

On historicism see Friedrich Meinecke, *Die Entstehung des Historismus*, 2 vols. Munich, 1936.

On the rise of literary history see Sigmund von Lempicki, *Geschichte der deutschen Literaturwissenschaft bis zum Ende des 18. Jahrhunderts*, Göttingen, 1920; René Wellek, *The Rise of English Literary History*, Chapel Hill, N.C., 1941 (with bibliography); and Giovanni Getto, *Storia delle storie letterarie* (in Italy only), Milan, 1942.

NOTES: NEOCLASSICISM

1. Anatole France, preface to *La Vie littéraire*, 1st ser. Paris, 1888.
2. J. E. Spingarn, *Critical Essays of the Seventeenth Century*, 2, 164–5.
3. *Essays*, ed. W. P. Ker (Oxford, 1926), *1*, 228–9.
4. "The Impartial Critick" (1693), in *Critical Works*, ed. E. N. Hooker (Baltimore, 1939), p. 39 and Pope, *Essay on Criticism*, *1*, lines 88–9.
5. *Ibid.*, lines 86–7.
6. *La Pratique du théâtre*, ed. Pierre Martino (Algiers, 1927), p. 100: "Car une seule image demeurant en même état ne peut pas représenter deux choses différentes."
7. Spingarn, 2, 251.
8. *La Poétique* (Paris, 1639), p. 314: "La bassesse d'une avarice, l'infâmie d'une lâcheté, la noirceur d'une perfidie, l'horreur d'une cruauté, l'ordure d'une pauvreté."
9. *Ibid.*, p. 125: "qu'il ne fasse jamais . . . un subtil d'un Allemand, un modeste d'un Espagnol, ni un incivil d'un Français."
10. *Théâtre complet*, ed. M. Rat (Paris, 1947), pp. 476–7: "Le bon sens et la raison étaient les mêmes dans tous les siècles. Le goût de Paris s'est trouvé conforme à celui d'Athènes."
11. Told by Pliny, *Nat. hist.*, xxxv, 64; Cicero, *De inventione*, ii, i, 1;

Dionysus Halic., *De priscis script. cens.*, 1. The texts can be found assembled in J. Overbeck, *Die antiken Schriftquellen zur Geschichte der bildenden Künste bei den Griechen* (Leipzig, 1868), p. 316.

12. *Enneads,* v, viii, 1.

13. *The Grounds of Criticism in Poetry* (1704), in *The Critical Works,* ed. E. N. Hooker (Baltimore, 1939), *1*, 336.

14. Esp. "Eroici furori," in *Dialoghi morali,* ed. G. Gentile (Bari, 1908), *1*, 310–11: "Tanti son geni e specie di vere regole, quanti son geni e specie di veri poeti."

15. Cf. the chapter "Poetic Justice" in Clarence C. Green, *The Neo-Classic Theory of Tragedy in England during the Eighteenth Century* (Cambridge, Mass., 1934), pp. 139 ff. and the many remarks in Max Kommerell's *Lessing und Aristoteles* (Frankfurt, 1940), pp. 95, 206, 279, 295.

16. *Poetics,* VIII, 14. Butcher's translation, in *Aristotle's Theory of Poetry* (4th ed. New York, 1952), p. 35.

17. See Irene Behrens, *Die Lehre von der Einteilung der Dichtkunst,* Halle, 1940; James J. Donohue, *The Theory of Literary Kinds: Ancient Classifications of Literature,* Dubuque, Iowa, 1943.

18. Preface to *Albion and Albanius* (1685), *Essays,* ed. Ker, *1*, 271. Cf. pp. 272, 211.

19. Boileau, *Œuvres,* ed. Gidel (Paris, 1870), 2, 387. On France see Borgerhoff, *The Freedom of French Classicism.* On England, Paul Spencer Wood, "The Opposition to Neo-Classicism in England between 1660 and 1700," *PMLA, 43* (1928), 182–97.

20. On *je ne sais quoi* cf. Borgerhoff, and see S. H. Monk, "Grace beyond the Reach of Art," *JHI, 5* (1944), 131–50.

21. Vossius, *Poeticarum institutionum libri tres* (Amsterdam, 1647), *1*, 52: "Poetae sunt morum doctores." Molière, *Œuvres,* ed. Despois (Paris, 1873–93), *4*, 385: "Premier placet sur *Tartuffe.*" "Le devoir de la comédie est de corriger les hommes en les divertissant."

22. *Traité du poème épique* (6th ed. La Haye, 1714), *1*, 11: "pour former les mœurs par des instructions déguisés sous les allégories." Cf. p. 27.

23. The best discussion of the history of *catharsis* is in Kommerell, *Lessing und Aristoteles,* the sec. on Corneille, e.g. pp. 72–8.

24. The concluding lines of Milton's *Samson Agonistes,* 1671. In the preface Milton interprets purgation as a homeopathic cure, a theory suggested by Minturno in 1564.

25. *De arte poetica,* lines 102–3: "Si vis me flere, dolendum est primum ipsi tibi." Aristotle says substantially the same in *Poetics,* XVII.

26. Ed. Hooker, *1*, 336, 216.

27. *Essays,* ed. Ker, *1,* 210.

28. *Réflexions critiques* (Paris, 1733), *1,* 24 ff.

29. *Lettre sur les occupations de l'Académie française* (1714), ed. M. E. Despois (Paris, n.d.), p. 103: "Les héros d'Homère ne ressemblent point à d'honnêtes gens, et les Dieux de ce poète sont fort au-dessous de ces héros mêmes, si indignes de l'idée que nous avons de l'honnête homme."

30. *La Manière de bien penser* (Paris, 1687), p. 382: "Le bon goût est le premier mouvement ou, pour ainsi dire, une espèce d'instinct de la droite raison, qui l'entraîne avec rapidité, et qui la conduit plus sûrement que tous les raisonnements qu'elle pourrait faire."

31. Paris, 1747, pp. 246, 249, 255.

32. See Meyer Abrams, "Archetypal Analogies" (above, Introduction, n. 5).

33. On progress see J. B. Bury, *The Idea of Progress,* London, 1920.

34. On cyclical progress cf. Eduard Spranger, "Die Kulturzyklentheorie und das Problem des Kulturverfalls," in *Sitzungsberichte der Preussischen Akademie der Wissenschaften,* Berlin, 1926. There is much in Hubert Gillot, *La Querelle des anciens et des modernes en France,* Paris, 1914.

35. On primitivism see H. N. Fairchild, *The Noble Savage,* New York, 1928; Lois Whitney, *Primitivism and the Idea of Progress in English Popular Literature of the Eighteenth Century,* Baltimore, 1934; and several essays in A. O. Lovejoy, *Essays in the History of Ideas,* Baltimore, 1948.

36. *Discours sur Homère* (Paris, 1714), p. lviii: "Il serait ridicule de reprocher ces prétendus défauts de bienséance à un poète qui ne pouvait pas peindre ce qui n'était pas encore."

37. Hugh Blair, *Dissertation on the Poems of Ossian* (Edinburgh, 1763), p. 3.

38. *Journal littéraire, 9* (1717), 157–64. This article has been ascribed to Saint-Hyacinthe.

BIBLIOGRAPHY: VOLTAIRE

The works of Voltaire are quoted according to the standard 52-volume edition by Louis Moland, Paris, 1877–83, except that I quote the English publications according to the English texts: *The Essay upon Epic Poetry,* London, 1727; and *The Letters concerning the English Nation,* ed. Charles Whibley, London, 1926.

By far the most important treatment of Voltaire as a critic is Raymond Naves, *Le Goût de Voltaire,* Paris, n.d. [1938], 566 pp., to which this chapter is heavily indebted. In addition I have used Henri Lion,

Les Tragédies et les théories dramatiques de Voltaire, Paris, 1895; J. J. Jusserand, *Shakespeare en France sous l'ancien régime,* Paris, 1898; Thomas R. Lounsbury, *Shakespeare and Voltaire,* London, 1902; C. M. Haines, *Shakespeare in France. Criticism. Voltaire to Hugo.* London, 1925; Ernst Merian-Genast, "Voltaire und die Entwicklung der Idee der Weltliteratur," *Romanische Forschungen, 40* (1927), 1–226; Warren Ramsey, "Voltaire and Homer," *PMLA, 66* (1951), 182–96.

NOTES: VOLTAIRE

1. *Œuvres complètes,* ed. Moland, *Le Siècle de Louis XIV; 14,* 562.

2. *Ibid., Dictionnaire:* "Epopée"; *18,* 568. On Le Bossu see "Catalogue de la plupart des écrivains français"; *14,* 96. On La Motte see *8,* 317.

3. *Ibid., 2,* 53. Preface to *Œdipe,* 1730; *23,* 347: "Connaissance des beautés et des défauts de la poésie."

4. *Ibid., Le Siècle de Louis XIV; 14,* 155.

5. Joseph Warton in his 1797 ed. of Pope (*5,* 284) tells that Edmund Bladen, William Collins' uncle, gave Voltaire all information on Camoës. Warton confused William with Martin Bladen, as Churton J. Collins points out in *Voltaire, Montesquieu and Rousseau in England* (London, 1908), p. 66.

6. *Essay on Epic Poetry* (London, 1727), p. 109.

7. *Œuvres,* "Essai sur la poésie épique"; *8,* 318: "Il est impossible que toute une nation se trompe en fait de sentiment, et ait tort d'avoir du plaisir."

8. Ernst Merian-Genast, "Voltaire und die Entwicklung der Idee der Weltliteratur," *Romanische Forschungen, 40* (1927), 1–226.

9. *Letters concerning the English Nation,* ed. Whibley (1926), p. 125.

10. *Ibid.,* pp. 129–30.

11. *Ibid.,* p. 132.

12. *Ibid.,* p. 134.

13. *Ibid.,* p. 159.

14. *Ibid.,* letter to D'Argental, July 19, 1776; *50,* 58: "Ce qu'il y a d'affreux, c'est que le monstre a un parti en France; et, pour comble de calamité et d'horreur, c'est moi qui autrefois parlai le premier de ce Shakespeare; c'est moi qui le premier montrai aux Français quelques perles que j'avais trouvées dans son énorme fumier. Je ne m'attendais pas que je servirais un jour à fouler aux pieds les couronnes de Racine et de Corneille, pour en orner le front d'un histrion barbare."

15. *Œuvres, 8,* 549 ff.

16. *Ibid., 30,* 349 ff.

17. *Elements of Criticism* (9th ed. Edinburgh, 1817), *2, 311*.

18. *Œuvres,* "Lettre à l'Académie française," 1776; *30,* 363: "Oui, Monsieur, un soldat peut répondre ainsi dans un corps de garde; mais non pas sur le théâtre, devant les premières personnes d'une nation, qui s'expriment noblement, et devant qu'il faut s'exprimer de même." Similar passages in *Dictionnaire:* "Art Dramatique"; *17,* 393; and "Extrait de la Gazette littéraire," April 4, 1764; *25,* 161.

19. *Ibid.,* "Appel à toutes les nations de l'Europe," 1761; *24,* 193–203.

20. *Ibid.,* letter to Walpole, July 15, 1768; *46,* 80: "une belle nature, mais bien sauvage; nulle régularité, nulle bienséance, nul art, de la bassesse, avec de la grandeur, de la bouffonnerie avec du terrible; c'est le chaos de la tragédie, dans lequel il y a cent traits de lumière."

21. *Ibid.,* "Observations sur Jules César"; *7,* 486: "Il était inégal comme Shakespeare . . . ce qu'un seigneur est à l'égard d'un homme du peuple né avec le même esprit que lui."

22. *Ibid.,* "Lettre à l'Académie française"—preceding *Irène*—1778; *8,* 330: "On les joue depuis les rivages de la mer glaciale jusqu'à la mer qui sépare l'Europe de l'Afrique. Qu'on fasse le même honneur à une seule pièce de Shakespeare, et alors nous pourrons disputer."

23. *Ibid., Dictionnaire:* "Beau"; *17,* 556: "Demandez à un crapaud ce que c'est que la beauté . . . Il vous répondra que c'est sa crapaude."

24. *Ibid.,* "Remarques sur Pascal"; *22,* 52: "En ouvrage de goût, en musique, en poésie, en peinture, c'est le goût qui tient lieu de montre; et celui qui n'en juge que par règle en juge mal."

25. *Ibid.,* letter to Koenig, June, 1753; *38,* 37: "C'est une affaire de goût; chacun a le sien; je ne peux prouver à un homme que c'est lui qui a tort quand je l'ennuie."

26. *Ibid., Dictionnaire:* "Goût"; *19,* 278: "En général le goût fin et sûr consiste dans le sentiment prompt d'une beauté parmi des défauts et d'un défaut parmi des beautés."

27. *Ibid.,* letter to M. de la Visclède, 1776; *30,* 321: "La manie des éditeurs ressemble à celle des sacristains: tous rassemblent des guenilles qu'ils veulent faire révérer; mais de même qu'on ne juge pas les vrais saints que par leurs bonnes actions, l'on ne juge les hommes à talents que par leurs bons ouvrages."

28. *Ibid.,* "Genres de style"; *19,* 250: "La perfection consisterait à savoir assortir toujours son style à la matière qu'on traite."

29. *Ibid.,* preface to *Mariamne; 2,* 165–6: "Quand il s'agit de faire parler les passions, tous les hommes ont presque les mêmes idées; mais la façon des les exprimer distingue l'homme d'esprit d'avec celui qui n'en a point."

30. *Ibid., Dictionnaire:* "Art, anciens et modernes"; *17, 236–40:* examples of bombast from the Bible.

31. *Ibid.,* "Remarques sur Polyeucte"; *31, 373:* "Les vers doivent avoir la clarté, la pureté de la prose la plus correcte."

32. *Ibid.,* "Remarques sur deux épîtres d'Helvétius"; *23, 7:* "Aussi les idées en sont-elles liées, les mots sont propres, et cela serait beau en prose."

33. *Ibid.,* "Remarques . . ."; *23, 23:* "Les vers qui ne disent pas plus, et mieux et plus vite, que ce que dirait la prose, sont de mauvais vers."

34. *Ibid., 31, 32.* A letter to Vauvenargues (April 15, 1743) defends Corneille very warmly. See *36, 204.*

35. *Ibid.,* letter to Tressan, March 22, 1775; *49, 253:* "Tout vers, toute phrase qui a besoin d'explication, ne mérite pas qu'on l'explique."

36. *Ibid.,* preface to *Œdipe,* 1730; *2, 55.* See also *Dictionnaire:* "Epopée"; *18, 564.*

37. *Ibid.,* preface to *Œdipe,* 1730; *2, 56–7.*

38. E.g. *ibid., Dictionnaire:* "Poètes"; *20, 232:* "La poésie est la musique de l'âme."

39. *Ibid.,* 'Essai sur la poésie épique"; *8, 319:* "Qu'on ne croie point encore connaître les poètes par les traductions; se serait vouloir apercevoir le coloris d'un tableau dans une estampe."

40. See Naves, *Le Goût de Voltaire,* pp. 244, 351.

41. *Œuvres,* 2d dedicatory epistle to *Zaïre; 2, 551:* "La bonne comédie fut ignorée jusqu'à Molière, comme l'art d'exprimer sur le théâtre des sentiments vrais et délicats fut ignoré jusqu'à Racine, parce que la société ne fut, pour ainsi dire, dans sa perfection que de leur temps."

42. *Ibid.,* preface to *Œdipe,* 1730; *2, 49:* "C'est que l'esprit humain ne peut embrasser plusieurs objets à la fois. . . . une seule action ne peut se passer en plusieurs lieux à la fois."

43. Full discussion in Lion, *Les Tragédies et les théories dramatiques de Voltaire.*

44. *Œuvres, Théâtre de Pierre Corneille,* comment on *Cid; 31, 228:* "C'était l'esprit du temps."

45. *Ibid., Dictionnaire:* "Scoliaste"; *20, 403.* "Dissertation sur la tragédie ancienne et moderne," 1748; *4, 487* ff. *Dictionnaire:* "Art dramatique. Du théâtre espagnol"; *17, 395.*

46. This seems to be not sufficiently recognized by most authors praising Voltaire's cosmopolitanism: e.g. Merian-Genast, and even Naves.

47. *Œuvres, Dictionnaire:* "Goût"; *19, 278:* "La poésie sera différente chez le peuple qui renferme les femmes, et chez celui qui leur accorde une liberté sans bornes."

48. Full treatment in F. Brunot, *Histoire de la langue française, 8: Le Français hors de France au* xviiie *siècle*, Pt. 1: "Le Français dans les divers pays d'Europe," Paris, 1934.

49. This has not been shown in detail but seems obvious. Cf. Voltaire quoting Rymer in *Œuvres*, "Lettre à l'Académie française," 1776; *30*, 363.

50. *Ibid., Candide; 21*, 204 (ch. 25):

"Qui?," dit Pococurante, "ce barbare qui fait un long commentaire du premier chapitre de la Genèse en dix livres de vers durs? ce grossier imitateur des Grecs, qui défigure la création, et qui, tandis que Moïse représente l'Etre éternel produisant le monde par la parole, fait prendre un grand compas par le Messiah dans une armoire du ciel pour tracer son ouvrage? Moi, j'estimerai celui qui a gâté l'enfer et le diable du Tasse; qui déguise Lucifer tantôt en crapaud, tantôt en pygmée, qui lui fait rebattre cent fois les mêmes discours; qui le fait disputer sur la théologie; qui, en imitant sérieusement l'invention comique des armes à feu de l'Arioste, fait tirer le canon dans le ciel par les diables? Ni moi, ni personne en Italie n'a pu se plaire à toutes ces tristes extravagances. Le mariage du péché et de la mort, et les couleuvres dont le péché accouche, font vomir tout homme qui a le goût un peu délicat; et sa longue déscription d'un hôpital n'est bonne que pour un fossoyeur. Ce poème obscure, bizarre et dégoûtant, fut méprisé à sa naissance; je le traite aujourd'hui comme il fut traité dans sa patrie par les contemporains. Au reste, je dis ce que je pense, et je me soucie fort peu que les autres pensent comme moi."

John Butt's trans. in text, quoted with the permission of Penguin Books (West Drayton, Middlesex, 1947), pp. 122–3.

51. See *Paradise Lost*, vii, lines 225–7. Authority in Proverbs viii:27.

52. *Œuvres, Dictionnaire:* "Epopée"; *18*, 564. "Essai sur la poésie épique"; *8*, 358: "dégoûtante et abominable."

53. *Ibid.*, "Essai sur la poésie épique"; *8*, 360: "Un ouvrage plus singulier que naturel, plus plein d'imagination que de grâces, et de hardiesse que de choix, dont le sujet est tout idéal, et qui semble n'être pas fait pour l'homme."

54. *Ibid., Essai sur les mœurs; 12*, 106 (ch. 92). *Dictionnaire:* "Dante"; *18, 312*.

55. *Ibid.*, letter to Chamfort, Nov. 16, 1774; *49, 120*, and other passages, e.g. *Dictionnaire:* "Epopée"; *18*, 574–9.

56. *Ibid.*, "Essai sur la poésie épique"; *8*, 336 (ch. 7). On Tasso see *Essai sur les mœurs; 12*, 241 (ch. 121). Also, *Dictionnaire:* "Critique" and "Epopée"; *18*, 284, 564.

57. *Ibid.,* e.g. *Théâtre de Corneille* and preface to *Pulchérie; 32,* 291. Also, "Anciens et modernes"; *17,* 235.

58. *Ibid., Lettres sur le Nouvelle Héloïse,* 1761; *24,* 165–80.

59. *Ibid.,* letter to Helvétius, March, 1763; *42,* 447: "c'est Diogène, mais il s'exprime quelquefois en Platon."

60. Saintsbury, *2,* 515 ff.

BIBLIOGRAPHY: DIDEROT

Diderot is quoted from the standard ed.: *Œuvres complètes,* ed. J. Assézat and M. Tourneux, 20 vols. Paris, 1875–79. A convenient collection is *Œuvres,* ed. André Billy in Collection La Pléiade, Paris, 1946. See also *Writings on the Theatre* (in French), ed. F. C. Green, Cambridge, 1936. Some quotations are from *Correspondance inédite,* ed. A. Babelon, 2 vols. Paris, 1931; also, *Lettres à Sophie Volland,* ed. A. Babelon, 3 vols. Paris, 1930.

The fullest discussions of Diderot's criticism and aesthetics are Hubert Gillot, "Les Idées littéraires," in *Denis Diderot* (Paris, 1937), pp. 191–267; Wladyslaw Folkierski, *Entre le classicisme et le romantisme* (Cracow, 1925), pp. 355–516; Yvon Belaval, *L'Esthétique sans paradoxe de Diderot,* Paris, 1950 (who tries to force unity on Diderot); and Lester G. Crocker, *Two Diderot Studies: Ethics and Esthetics,* Baltimore, 1952 (containing "Subjectivism and Objectivism in Diderot's Esthetics").

A good general book is still Karl Rosenkranz, *Diderots Leben und Werke,* 2 vols. Leipzig, 1866. An important study is Leo Spitzer, "The Style of Diderot," in *Linguistics and Literary History: Essays in Stylistics* (Princeton, 1948), pp. 135–91. Eric M. Steel, *Diderot's Imagery* (New York, 1947) contains the chapter "Diderot's Theory of Imagery."

The following articles and essays discuss some of Diderot's ideas from divergent points of view:

Anne-Marie de Comaille, "Diderot et le symbole littéraire," in *Diderot Studies,* ed. Otis E. Fellows and Norman L. Torrey (Syracuse, 1950), pp. 94–120.

Herbert Dieckmann, "Diderot's Conception of Genius," *JHI, 2* (1941), 151–82.

Herbert Dieckmann, "Zur Interpretation Diderots," *Romanische Forschungen, 53* (1939), 47–82.

Margaret Gilman, "The Poet According to Diderot," *RR, 37* (1946), 37–54.

L. G. Krakeur, "Aspects of Diderot's Aesthetic Theory," *RR, 30* (1939), 244–59.

J. J. Mayoux, "Diderot and the Technique of Modern Literature,"
  MLR, 31 (1936), 518–31.
Felix Vexler, *Studies in Diderot's Esthetic Naturalism,* New York, 1922.
Eleanor M. Walker, "Towards an Understanding of Diderot's Esthetic
  Theory," *RR, 35* (1944), 277–87.

NOTES: DIDEROT

1. See Leo Spitzer's essay, "The Style of Diderot," in *Linguistics and Literary History;* also the remarks of Sainte-Beuve in *Causeries du lundi, 3,* 295, 306–7.

2. *Œuvres complètes de Diderot,* ed. Assézat-Tourneux, *4,* 279 ff.; *Hamburgische Dramaturgie,* Nos. 84, 85.

3. *Œuvres, 4,* 286, 287.

4. *Ibid., 4,* 284: "la perfection d'un spectacle consiste dans l'imitation si exacte d'une action que le spectateur, trompé sans interruption, s'imagine assister à l'action même."

5. *Ibid., 19,* 40: "Qu'à peine la première scène est-elle jouée, qu'on croit être en famille, et qu'on oublie qu'on est devant un théâtre. Ce ne sont plus des tréteaux, c'est une maison particulière."

6. *Ibid., 7,* 370:
> En général, plus un peuple est civilisé, poli, moins ses mœurs sont poétiques; tout s'affaiblit en s'adoucissant. Quand est-ce que la nature prépare des modèles à l'art? C'est au temps où les enfants s'arrachent les cheveux autour du lit d'un père moribond; où une mère découvre son sein, et conjure son fils par les mamelles qui l'ont allaité; où un ami se coupe la chevelure, et la répand sur le cadavre de son ami; où c'est lui qui le soutient par la tête et qui le porte sur un bûcher, qui recueille sa cendre et qui la renferme dans une urne qu'il va, en certains jours, arroser de ses pleurs; où les veuves échevelées se déchirent le visage de leurs ongles . . . où des bacchantes, armées de thyrses, s'égarent dans les forêts et inspirent l'effroi au profane qui se rencontre sur leur passage; où d'autres femmes se dépouillent sans pudeur, ouvrent leurs bras au premier qui se présente, et se prostituent, etc. Je ne dis que ces mœurs sont bonnes, mais qu'elles sont poétiques.

7. *Ibid., 7,* 115–6.

8. *Ibid., 7,* 314:
> Ce n'est pas ce battement de mains qui se fait entendre subitement après un vers éclatant, mais ce soupir profond qui part de l'âme après la contrainte d'un long silence, et qui la soulage. Il est une

impression plus violente encore . . . c'est de mettre un peuple comme à la gêne. Alors, les esprits seront troublés, incertains, flottants, éperdus; et vos spectateurs, tels que ceux qui, dans les tremblements d'une partie du globe, voient les murs de leurs maisons vaciller, et sentent la terre se dérober sous leurs pieds.

9. *Ibid., 5*, 223: "Et ce qui m'étonne toujours, moi, quand je suis aux derniers instants de cette innocente, c'est que les pierres, les murs, les carreaux insensibles et froids sur lesquels je marche ne s'émeuvent pas et ne joignent pas leur plainte à la mienne."

10. *Ibid., 7*, 314.

11. *Ibid., 10*, 499: "Touche-moi, étonne-moi, déchire-moi; fais-moi tressaillir, pleurer, frémir, m'indigner d'abord!"

12. *Ibid., 1*, 354–5. Cf. 2, 332.

13. *Ibid., 8*, 458.

14. *Ibid., 11*, 131–2:

Plus de verve chez les peuples barbares que chez les peuples policés; plus de verve chez les Hébreux que chez les Grecs; plus de verve chez les Grecs que chez les Romains; plus de verve chez les Romains que chez les Italiens et les Français; plus de verve chez les Anglais que chez ces derniers. Partout décadence de la verve et de la poésie, à mesure que l'esprit philosophique a fait des progrès . . . sa marche circonspecte est ennemie du mouvement et des figures. Le règne des images passe à mesure que celui des choses s'étend . . . les préjugés civils et religieux se dissipent; et il est incroyable le mal que cette monotone politesse fait à la poésie. L'esprit philosophique amène le style sentencieux et sec. Les expressions abstraites qui renferment un grand nombre de phénomènes se multiplient et prennent la place des expressions figurées . . . Quelle est, à votre avis, l'espèce de poésie qui exige le plus de verve? L'ode, sans contredit. Il y a longtemps qu'on ne fait plus d'odes . . . Quand voit-on naître les critiques et les grammairiens? Tout juste après le siècle du génie et des productions divines . . . Il n'y a qu'un moment heureux; c'est celui où il y a assez de verve et de liberté pour être chaud, assez de jugement et de goût pour être sage.

15. *Ibid., 2*, 290.

16. *Ibid., 7*, 333.

17. *Ibid., 1*, 374: "le discours n'est plus seulement un enchaînement de termes énergiques qui exposent la pensée avec force et noblesse, mais que c'est encore un tissu d'hiéroglyphes entassés les uns sur les autres qui la peignent. Je pourrais dire, en ce sens, que toute poésie est emblématique."

18. *Ibid., 11*, 19: "Une expression de génie, une physiognomie uni-

que, originale et d'état, l'image énergique et forte d'une qualité individuelle."

19. *Ibid.*, p. 147: "La clarté est bonne pour convaincre; elle ne vaut rien pour émouvoir. La clarté de quelque manière qu'on l'entende, nuit à l'enthousiasme. Poètes, parlez sans cesse de l'éternité, d'infini, d'immensité, du temps, de l'espace, de la divinité . . . Soyez ténébreux!"

20. *Ibid., 10,* 352. "Plus l'expression des arts est vague, plus l'imagination est à l'aise."

21. See the curious parallel to Jonathan Edwards' views, as discussed by Perry Miller in "Edwards, Locke, and the Rhetoric of Sensation," in *Perspectives of Criticism,* ed. Harry Levin (Cambridge, Mass., 1950), esp. p. 117.

22. *Œuvres, 2,* 177 ff.

23. See Eleanor M. Walker's unconvincing attempt, "Towards an Understanding of Diderot's Esthetic Theory," *RR, 35* (1944), 277–87.

24. *Œuvres, 11,* 268.

25. *Ibid., 1,* 376.

26. *Ibid., 5,* 242: "C'est l'âme et non l'art qui doit le produire: si vous avez pensé à l'effet, il est manqué."

27. *Ibid.*, p. 246–7:

> C'est que son corps était aux champs, et que son âme était à la ville . . . c'est qu'il n'a jamais attendu l'inspiration de la nature, et qu'il a *prophétisé,* pour me servir de l'expression de Naigeon, *avant que l'Esprit fût descendu.* S'il n'enivre pas, c'est qu'il n'était pas ivre. A l'aspect d'un beau site champêtre, il disait: O le beau site à décrire! au lieu qu'il fallait se taire, sentir, se laisser pénétrer profondément, et prendre ensuite sa lyre.

28. *Ibid.*, p. 250: "Que lui manque-t-il donc? . . . c'est une âme qui se tourmente, un esprit violent, une imagination forte et bouillante, une lyre qui ait plus de cordes."

29. *Ibid., 10,* 145: "Avant que de prendre son pinceau, il faut avoir frissoné vingt fois de son sujet, avoir perdu le sommeil, s'être levé pendant la nuit, et avoir couru en chemise et pieds nus jeter sur le papier ses esquisses à la lueur d'une lampe de nuit."

30. *Ibid., 12,* 77.

31. *Ibid., 7,* 135–6.

32. *Ibid.*, p. 137: "On n'y passe point par des nuances imperceptibles; on tombe à chaque pas dans les contrastes, et l'unité disparaît."

33. *Ibid.*, p. 151.

34. *Ibid.*

35. *Ibid., 12,* 81: "L'harmonie du plus beau tableau n'est qu'une bien faible imitation de l'harmonie de la nature."

36. *Ibid., 11,* 140: "c'est qu'en effet ces compositions prêchent plus fortement la grandeur, la puissance, la majesté de la nature, que la nature même."

37. *Ibid., 10,* 118.

38. *Ibid., 11,* 12: "le modèle le plus beau, le plus parfait d'un homme ou d'une femme, serait un homme ou une femme supérieurement propre à toutes les fonctions de la vie, et parvenu à l'âge du plus entier développement, sans en avoir exercé aucune."

39. Three versions: 1770, 1773, and 1778. Cf. Bédier's refutation of attempts to deny it to Diderot, in *Études critiques* (Paris, 1903), pp. 83–112.

40. *Œuvres, 8,* 419–20:

> Celui de la nature est moins grand encore que celui du poète, et celui-ci moins grand encore que celui du grand comédien, le plus exagéré de tous. . . . Que j'aie un récit un peu pathétique à faire, il s'élève je ne sais quel trouble dans mon cœur, dans ma tête; ma langue s'embarasse; ma voix s'altère; mes idées se décomposent; mon discours se suspend; je babultie, je m'en aperçois; les larmes coulent de mes joues, et je me tais.—Mais cela vous réussit.—En société; au théâtre, je serais hué.—Pourquoi?—Parce qu'on ne vient pas pour voir des pleurs, mais pour entendre des discours qui en arrachent, parce que cette vérité de nature dissone avec la vérité de convention . . . ni le système dramatique, ni l'action, ni les discours du poète, ne s'arrangeraient point de ma déclamation étouffée, interrompue, sanglotée.

41. *Ibid.,* p. 368: "Les grands poètes, les grands acteurs, et peut-être en général tous les grands imitateurs de la nature, quels qu'ils soient, doués d'une belle imagination, d'un grand jugement, d'un tact fin, d'un goût très sûr, sont les êtres les moins sensibles. . . . Ils sont trop occupés à regarder, à reconnaître, et à imiter, pour être vivement affectés au dedans d'eux-mêmes."

42. *Ibid.,* p. 386:

> Est-ce au moment où vous venez de perdre votre ami ou votre maîtresse que vous composerez un poème sur sa mort? Non. . . . C'est lorsque la grande douleur est passée, quand l'extrême sensibilité est amortie, lorsqu'on est loin de la catastrophe, que l'âme est calme, qu'on se rappelle son bonheur éclipsé, qu'on est capable d'apprécier la perte qu'on a faite, que la mémoire se réunit à l'imagination . . . et qu'on parle bien. On dit qu'on pleure, mais on ne pleure pas lorsqu'on poursuit une épithète énergique qui se refuse . . . lorsqu'on s'occupe à rendre son vers harmonieux:

ou si les larmes coulent, la plume tombe des mains, on se livre à son sentiment et l'on cesse de composer.

43. *Ibid.*, p. 367: "Dans ce moment elle est double: la petite Clairon et la grande Agrippine."

44. *Ibid.*, p. 372: "Ce sont les fantômes imaginaires de la poésie: je dis trop—ce sont les spectres de la façon particulière de tel ou tel poète."

45. *Ibid.:* "C'est un protocole de trois mille ans."

46. *Ibid.*, 7, 108–9.

47. *Ibid.*, p. 312: "Le parterre de la comédie est le seul endroit où les larmes de l'homme vertueux et du méchant soient confondues. Là, le méchant s'irrite contre les injustices qu'il aurait commises; compatit à des maux qu'il aurait occasionnés, et s'indigne contre un homme de son propre caractère. . . . le méchant sort de sa loge, moins disposé à faire le mal."

48. *Ibid.*, 2, 392: "là, je suis magnanime, équitable, compatissant, parce que je puis l'être sans conséquence."

49. *Correspondance inédite*, *1*, 304: "Si je préfère Homère à Virgile, Virgile au Tasse, le Tasse à Milton, Milton à Voltaire ou au Camoëns, ce n'est point une affaire de date; j'en dirais bien mes raisons."

50. *Œuvres*, *3*, 444: "faute de connaissances, ils ne chantent que des fadaises mélodieuses."

51. *Ibid.*, *18*, 109; *11*, 328.

52. *Lettres à Sophie Volland*, 3, 276.

53. *Correspondance inédite*, *1*, 304 ff. Cf. "Diderot und Horaz," in E. R. Curtius, *Europäische Literatur und Lateinisches Mittelalter* (Bern, 1948), pp. 556–64.

54. On Tacitus, *Œuvres*, *12*, 105; on Lucretius, 7, 352: "style sec et chaotique."

55. Gillot, *Denis Diderot*, p. 247: "Où il n'y a pas un mot à ajouter ni à retrancher."

56. *Œuvres*, 7, 124.

57. *Ibid.*, p. 118: "il faut, pour ce genre, des auteurs, des acteurs, un théâtre, et peut-être un peuple."

58. *Ibid.*, *5*, 233: "une muse plus tranquille et plus douce."

59. *Ibid.*, *5*, 237.

60. *Ibid.*, *3*, 482.

61. See Gillot, p. 292.

62. *Ibid.*, *19*, 15: "C'est peut-être le plus grand poète qui ait jamais existé."

63. *Ibid.*, 7, 366.

64. *Ibid.*, *19*, 396.

65. Cf. *ibid.*, *15*, 147; *2*, 85; *16*, 362.

66. *Ibid.*, *2*, 331: "le mélange extraordinaire, incompréhensible, inimitable, de choses du plus grand goût et du plus mauvais goût."

67. *Ibid.*, *7*, 374.

68. *Ibid.*, *8*, 393.

69. *Ibid.*, *15*, 37: "Le sublime et le *génie* brillent dans Shakespeare comme des éclairs dans une longue nuit, et Racine est toujours beau."

70. *Ibid.*, *8*, 384: "Ce Shakespeare, que je ne comparerai ni à l'Apollon du Belvédère, ni au Gladiateur, ni à l'Antinoüs, ni à l'Hercule de Glycon, mais bien au saint Christophe de Notre-Dame, colosse informe, grossièrement sculpté, mais entre les jambes duquel nous passerions tous, sans que notre front touchât à ses parties honteuses."

71. *Ibid.*, *5*, 213: "Combien j'étais bon! Combien j'étais juste! que j'étais satisfait de moi! J'étais, au sortir de ta lecture, ce qu'est un homme à la fin d'une journée qu'il a employée à faire le bien."

72. *Ibid.*, p. 216: "Plus on a l'âme belle, plus on a le goût exquis et pur, plus on connait la nature, plus on aime la vérité, plus on estime les ouvrages de Richardson."

73. *Ibid.*, p. 222: "Depuis qu'ils me sont connus, ils ont été ma pierre de touche; ceux à qui ils déplaisent sont jugés pour moi."

74. *Ibid.*, p. 226: "O Richardson! si tu n'as pas joui de ton vivant de toute la réputation que tu méritais, combien tu seras grand chez nos neveux, lorsqu'ils te verront à la distance d'où nous voyons Homère! Alors, qui est-ce qui osera arracher une ligne de ton sublime ouvrage?"

75. *Ibid.*, p. 224: "C'est, je vous l'avoue, une grande malédiction que de sentir et penser ainsi; mais si grande, que j'aimerais mieux tout à l'heure que ma fille mourût entre mes bras que de l'en savoir frappée. Ma fille! Oui, j'y ai pensé, et je ne m'en dédis pas."

BIBLIOGRAPHY:

THE OTHER FRENCH CRITICS

There is no general study of French criticism in this period except two chapters in Daniel Mornet, *Le Romantisme en France au* xviiie *siècle*, Paris, 1912. Alfred Michiels, *Histoire des idées littéraires en France au* xixe *siècle et de leurs origines dans les siècles antérieures* (2 vols. 4th ed. Paris, 1863), though highly partisan, is still instructive. Ferdinand Brunetière, *L'Évolution de la critique depuis la Renaissance jusqu'à nos jours* (Paris, 1890) is a good small sketch. T. M. Mustoxidi, *Histoire de l'esthétique française: 1700–1900* (Paris, 1920) is useful, though the comment is mediocre. Phillipe van Tieghem, *Petite His-*

toire des grandes doctrines littéraires en France. De la Pléiade au surréalisme (Paris, 1946), though very brief, is the best sketch available. Much also in Naves, *Le Goût de Voltaire*, Paris, 1938.

Rousseau is quoted from *Œuvres complètes,* ed. V. D. Musset-Pathay (Paris, 1824), except *Lettre à Mr. d'Alembert sur les spectacles,* which is from ed. of Max Fuchs, Geneva, 1948. I know of no general discussion of Rousseau's criticism. On stage controversy see Moses Barras, *The Stage Controversy in France from Corneille to Rousseau,* New York, 1933. Cf. E. Faguet, *Rousseau contre Molière,* Paris, 1911.

Buffon's *Discours sur le style* is available in many reprints. Good comment in Émile Krantz, *Essai sur l'esthétique de Descartes* (Paris, 1882), pp. 342–59.

Marmontel is quoted from *Poétique française,* 2 vols. Paris, 1763; and *Éléments de littérature,* 3 vols. Paris, 1879. J. Lenel, *Marmontel* (Paris, 1902) is largely biographical and descriptive. Heinrich Bauer, *Jean-François Marmontel als Literaturkritiker* (Dresden, 1937) is a useful collection of passages.

La Harpe is quoted from *Lycée ou cours de littérature ancienne et moderne,* 18 vols. Paris, 1823; and from *Œuvres,* 5 vols. Paris, 1778. Sainte-Beuve's two essays in *Causeries du lundi* (5, 1851) are largely biographical. Grace M. Sproull's *The Critical Doctrine of J. F. de la Harpe* (Chicago, 1939) is only a small fragment of what seems a valuable thesis.

Melchior Grimm's *Correspondance littéraire* is quoted from the ed. of Maurice Tourneux, 16 vols. 1877–82. Sainte-Beuve's essay is in *Causeries du lundi,* 7, 1852. Edmond Scherer, *Melchior Grimm* (Paris, 1887) is still standard. Other discussions: Karl A. F. Georges, *M. Grimm als Kritiker der zeitgenössischen Literatur,* Leipzig, 1904; Anne Cutting Jones, *F. M. Grimm as a Critic of Eighteenth Century French Drama,* Bryn Mawr, 1926. Alfred C. Hunter, "Les opinions du baron Grimm sur le roman anglais," *Revue de littérature comparée, 12* (1932), 390–400; F. Ewen, "Criticism of English Literature in Grimm's Correspondance," *SP, 33* (1936), 397–404; Joseph P. Smiley, *Diderot's Relations with Grimm,* Urbana, Ill., 1950.

Sébastien Mercier's *Du Théâtre ou nouvel essai sur l'art dramatique* is quoted from the Amsterdam ed., 1773. Also used is *Mon Bonnet de nuit,* 2 vols. Neuchâtel, 1784. Léon Béclard, *Sébastien Mercier* (Paris, 1903) is a large (810 pp.) unfinished biography (to 1789 only).

On Chassaignon, Saint-Martin, etc. see Kurt Wais, *Das antiphilosophische Weltbild des französischen Sturm und Drang, 1760–1789,* Berlin, 1934. I quote Saint-Martin, *Œuvres posthumes,* 2 vols. Tours, 1807.

Condillac's *L'Art d'écrire* is quoted from *Cours d'étude, 2,* Deux Ponts (fictitious imprint), 1782. Gustave Lanson's "Les Idées littéraires de Condillac," in *Études d'histoire littéraire* (Paris, 1929), overrates his importance. On the philosopher and psychologist see G. Le Roy, *La Psychologie de Condillac,* Paris, 1937; and Mario dal Pra, *Condillac,* Milan, 1942.

André Chénier is quoted from *Œuvres complètes,* ed. G. Walter, Paris, 1950. Cf. Paul Glachant, *André Chénier, critique et critiqué,* Paris, 1902.

Rivarol is quoted from *Œuvres complètes,* 5 vols. Paris, 1808. See Sainte-Beuve's essay in *Causeries du lundi,* 5, 1851. Quotations from Chênedollé's interviews with Rivarol are in Vol. 2 of Sainte-Beuve's *Chateaubriand et son groupe littéraire,* ed. M. Allem, Paris, 1948. André Le Breton, *Rivarol* (Paris, 1895) is mainly a biography. K. E. Gass, *Antoine de Rivarol (1753–1801) und der Ausgang der französischen Aufklärung* (Hagen, 1938) has the best analysis of his ideas.

NOTES: THE OTHER FRENCH CRITICS

1. *Lettre a Mr. d'Alembert,* ed. M. Fuchs, p. 24: "Un auteur qui voudroit heurter le goût général, composeroit bientôt pour lui seul."

2. *Ibid.,* p. 25: "On ne sauroit se mettre à la place de gens qui ne nous ressemblent point"; p. 26: "L'effet général du Spectacle est de renforcer le caractère national, d'augmenter les inclinations naturelles, et de donner une nouvelle énergie à toutes les passions."

3. *Ibid.,* p. 27: "Ne sait-on pas que toutes les passions sont sœurs, qu'une seule suffit pour en exciter mille, et que les combattre l'une par l'autre n'est qu'un moyen de rendre le cœur plus sensible à toutes?"

4. *Ibid.,* p. 32: "Une émotion passagère et vaine, qui ne dure pas plus que l'illusion qui l'a produite . . . une pitié stérile, qui se repaît de quelques larmes, et n'a jamais produit le moindre acte d'humanité."

5. Romain Rolland, *Le Théâtre du peuple,* Paris, 1904.

6. "Ces choses sont hors de l'homme, le style est l'homme même."

7. This is argued at length in Émile Krantz, *Essai sur l'esthétique de Descartes* (Paris, 1882), pp. 342–59.

8. Nikolay Ostolopov, *Slovar drevnei i novoi poezii,* 3 vols. St. Petersburg, 1821.

9. *Poétique française* (Paris, 1763), *1,* 33.

10. *Ibid., 1,* 63: "L'esprit Philosophique, l'esprit Poétique, l'esprit Oratoire ne sont qu'un"; *1,* 92: "plus un Poète, à génie égal, sera Philosophe, plus il sera Poète."

11. *Ibid., 1,* 168: "Moins les peuples sont civilisés, plus leur langage est figuré, sensible."

12. *Ibid.*, *1*, 331–2: "Un poème . . . c'est une machine dans laquelle tout doit être combiné pour produire un mouvement commun . . . les roues de la machine, ce sont les caractères; l'intrigue en est l'enchaînement."

13. *Éléments* (Paris, 1879), *3*, 421 ("Unité"): "On peu comparer l'action au polype, dont chaque partie, après qu'elle est coupée, est encore elle-même un polype vivant, complétement organisé."

14. E.g. "Génie" in *Éléments*, *2*, 196 ff.; "Imagination," *ibid.*, *2*, 279 ff.; *Poétique*, *1*, 59. One should note that much of the *Poétique* is reprinted in *Éléments*.

15. *Éléments*, *3*, 137 ff. ("Poésie"): "considérer la *poésie* comme une plante, examiner pourquoi, indigène dans certains climats, on l'y a vue naître et fleurir d'elle-même; pourquoi, étrangère partout ailleurs, elle n'a prospéré qu'à force de culture; ou pourquoi, sauvage et rebelle, elle s'est refusée aux soins qu'on a pris de la cultiver; enfin pourquoi, dans le même climat, tantôt elle a été florissante et féconde, tantôt elle a dégénéré."

16. *Éléments*, *3*, 392 ("Tragédie"): "Notre théâtre est le tableau du monde" pp. 404–5: "Chez les Grecs la *tragédie* était nationale . . . chez nous elle est universelle, comme l'empire des passions."

17. E.g. "Essai sur le goût" in *Éléments*, *1*, 14–5: "Les plus bizarres déformités . . ." See "Poésie" in *3*, 167 ff.

18. *Éléments*, *1*, 35.

19. *Ibid.*, *1*, 43, 49, 6: "qu'après avoir, comme dirait Montaigne, *artialisé* la nature, nous sommes obligés de *naturaliser* l'art."

20. The earlier criticism is collected in *Œuvres*, 5 vols. Paris, 1778; there is a *Correspondance avec le Grand Duc de Russie* [i.e. the later Tsar Paul II] *et avec M. le Comte André Schouvalow* (6 vols. Paris, 1801–07), a series of private reports from Paris, covering the years 1774–91, similar in type to Grimm's *Correspondance littéraire*.

21. *Cours*, *1*, 10: "Une histoire raisonnée de tous les arts de l'esprit et de l'imagination, depuis Homère jusqu'à nos jours."

22. "Discours sur l'état des lettres en Europe" (1797) in *Cours*, *5*.

23. All in *ibid.*, *6*, 206–51.

24. *Ibid.*, *16*, 110 ff.: "Le premier roman du monde."

25. *Ibid.*, *1*, 15–7, 20: "Les règles ne sont autre chose que ce sentiment réduit en méthode"; p. 48: "L'exact résumé des beautés et des défauts."

26. *Ibid.*, p. 89: "Notre théâtre au-dessus de tous les théâtres du monde."

27. *Ibid.*, p. 20: "Ils ont manqué de la conception d'un ensemble."

28. *Ibid.*, pp. 29–30.

29. *Ibid.*, p. 30.

30. *Œuvres, 1,* 366, misnumbered 667.

31. *Ibid., 1,* 416: "L'unintelligible galimathias."

32. *Cours,* 5, 45–6.

33. *Ibid.,* 7, 12, 324: "C'est une législation parfaite dont l'application se trouve juste dans tous les cas, un code imprescriptible dont les décisions serviront à jamais à savoir ce qui doit être condamné, ce qui doit être applaudi."

34. *Ibid., 9,* 1 ff.; *6,* 300: "Le plus tragique de tous les poètes"; *10,* 34.

35. *Ibid., 8,* 443; *14,* 324 ff.

36. *Ibid., 14,* 330: "La poésie est un art, un art de l'esprit, de l'oreille et de l'imagination"; *14,* 348: "La logique des passions"; *14,* 349: "L'esprit de système."

37. *Ibid.,* p. 366; *1,* 98; *12,* 155: "Le dernier effort de l'art, le plus beau triomphe de la tragédie." Cf. *Œuvres, 1,* 269, an essay on the three Greek tragedians, where Aristotle's *catharsis* is criticized, repeated in *Cours, 1,* 325 f.

38. *Ibid.,* 2, 303: "Image, emblême, allégorie"; *2,* 307: "Mouvemens, images, sentimens, figures, voilà, sans contredit, l'essence de toute poésie"; *2,* 332.

39. *Ibid.,* 5, 163–4: "Le langage de l'imagination conduite par la raison et le goût."

40. *Ibid.,* 5, 142, 144.

41. *Ibid., 1,* 87.

42. *Ibid., 12,* 83–4: "Il existe un rapport naturel et presque infaillible entre la manière de penser et de sentir, et celle de s'exprimer. . . . Mais généralement, l'homme qui écrit mal a mal pensé; et ce qu'on voudrait faire passer pour un simple défaut de goût dans le style est un défaut dans l'esprit, est un manque de justesse, de netteté, de vérité, de force dans les idées et dans les sentimens."

43. *Ibid.,* 2, 285.

44. *Ibid.,* 5, 63: "Une dépendance secrète et nécessaire entre les principes qui fondent l'ordre social et les arts qui l'embellissent."

45. *Ibid., 1,* 329 ff.; *1,* 97–8.

46. As Brunetière does in *L'Évolution de la critique* (Paris, 1890), pp. 162–3. Cf. Guy Michaud, *Introduction à une science de la littérature* (Istanbul, 1950), p. 16 n.: "La Harpe a du moins le mérite d'avoir créé du même coup l'histoire littéraire proprement dite et la littérature générale."

47. *Cours, 17,* 273; *18,* 5 ff.; *18,* 360: "Vil charlatan."

48. Sainte-Beuve, *Causeries du lundi*, 7, 288 (1853): "un des plus distingués de nos critiques." On La Harpe and Marmontel, p. 307. Cf. also the essay on Madame d'Epinay, in *Causeries*, 2, 203. Cf. Byron's *Diary*, January 31, 1821, in *Letters and Journals*, ed. R. E. Prothero (London, 1901), 5, 196–7: "an excellent critic and literary historian."

49. *Melchior Grimm* (Paris, 1887), p. 97: "Le véritable précurseur de la critique telle qu'elle est comprise de nos jours, de celle qui ne contente pas d'analyser et de citer, mais qui juge les ouvrages, motive les appréciations, discute les doctrines, rattache aux livres les considérations qu'ils suggèrent, et fait parfois d'un article une œuvre originale."

50. List of subscribers in *Correspondance littéraire,* ed. Tourneux, 2, 230–1. Cf. J. R. Smiley, "The Subscribers to Grimm's *Correspondance littéraire,*" *MLN, 61* (1947), 44–6.

51. *Correspondance*, 2, 397, 330; *3,* 354 ff.; *4,* 47 ff.

52. *Ibid., 10,* 27.

53. *Ibid., 3,* 229.

54. *Ibid.,* Feb. 15, 1767; *7,* 228: "cet homme ne fera jamais rien, même de médiocre."

55. *Ibid.,* Feb. 15, 1763; *5,* 236.

56. *Ibid.,* March 1, 1759; *4,* 85–6: "Il n'y a dans *Candide* ni ordonnance, ni plan, ni sagesse."

57. *Ibid.,* June 30, 1756; *3,* 255.

58. *Du Théâtre,* p. ix: "un fantôme revêtu de pourpre et d'or. . . . elles n'ont point l'âme, la vie, la simplicité."

59. *Ibid.,* pp. 76, 143–6, 105: "Tombez, tombez, murailles, qui séparez les genres!"

60. *Ibid.,* p. 1: "serve à lier entr'eux les hommes par le sentiment victorieux de la compassion et de la pitié"; p. 12: "On pourroit juger de l'âme de chaque homme par le degré d'émotion qu'il manifeste au Théâtre."

61. *Ibid.,* pp. 39, 136, 132: "Je pleure, et je sens avec volupté que je suis homme."

62. *Ibid.,* pp. 4, 23: "Il ne faudroit qu'une tragédie bien faite, bien prononcée, pour changer la mauvaise constitution d'un royaume."

63. E.g. *Mon Bonnet*, 2, 268, 199–200, 195: "Que tu es petit, ô Boileau! que tu me parois sec, froid, minutieux!"

64. *Ibid., 1,* 240 ff.; *2,* 112, 114.

65. *Neuer Versuch über die Schauspielkunst*, Leipzig, 1776. Goethe's contribution is reprinted in *Sämtliche Werke*, Jubiläumsausgabe, ed. von der Hellen (Stuttgart, 1902–07), *36,* 115–6.

66. *L'Art d'écrire,* p. 354: "Les noms d'épopée, de tragédie, de

comédie se sont conservés: mais les idées, qu'on y attache, ne sont absolument les mêmes; et chaque peuple a donné, à chaque espèce de ces poèmes, différens stiles, comme différens caractères."

67. *Ibid.*, p. 335: "Alors parce qu'on raisonne mieux sur le beau, on le sent moins"; p. 358: "Mais on le sent, et c'est assez."

68. See mainly Pt. 2 of *Essai sur l'origine des connaissances humaines,* Amsterdam, 1746.

69. *Œuvres complètes,* ed. G. Walter (Paris, 1950), p. 127.

70. E.g. *ibid.*, pp. 123, 125, 130: "En langage des Dieux fasse parler Newton."

71. *Ibid.*, pp. 621–93.

72. *Ibid.*, pp. 627, 646 ("ces convulsions barbares de Shakespeare"), 647 (Young), 681 (naiveté), 691 (Alfieri).

73. *Ibid.*, p. 676: "ces grands mouvements de l'âme qui seuls font inventer les expressions sublimes . . . ce langage ardent et métaphorique . . ." P. 406: "Il faut magnifiquement représenter la terre sous l'emblème métaphorique d'un grand animal, qui vit, se meut, est sujet à des changements, des révolutions, des fièvres, des dérangements dans la circulation de son sang."

74. Henri de Latouche published a small selection as *Œuvres complètes* in 1819. *Hermès* appeared in the 1833 edition, the fragments of the essay only in 1899.

75. *Œuvres complètes,* 2, 49: "Ce qui n'est pas clair, n'est pas français."

76. *Ibid., 3,* xxi n.: "Son vers se tient debout par la seule force du substantif et du verbe, sans le concours d'une seule épithète. Tels sont sans doute aussi les beaux vers de Virgile et d'Homère; ils offrent à la fois la pensée, l'image et le sentiment: ce sont de vrais polypes, vivants dans le tout, et vivants dans chaque partie." The last simile may have been suggested by Marmontel's, quoted above, n. 13.

77. This is brought out in Karl-Eugen Gass, *Antoine de Rivarol,* Hagen, 1938.

78. *Œuvres complètes, 1,* 115, 125: "imagination passive, vs. imagination active ou créatrice." "Le génie des idées est le comble de l'esprit; le génie des expressions est le comble du talent . . . le génie est donc ce qui engendre et enfante: c'est, en un mot, le don de l'invention."

79. *Ibid., 1,* 130–1.

80. Sainte-Beuve, *Chateaubriand et son groupe littéraire, 2,* 128: "Le poète n'est qu'un sauvage très ingénieux et très animé, chez lequel toutes les idées se présentent en images. Le sauvage et le poète font le cercle; l'un et l'autre ne parlent que par hiéroglyphes."

81. *Ibid.*, *2*, 138–9: "Rivarol aurait pu être un grand critique littéraire . . . il y a un Hazlitt français dans Rivarol.'

BIBLIOGRAPHY: DR. JOHNSON

I quote the *Lives of the Poets* from the ed. of G. Birkbeck Hill (3 vols. Oxford, 1905) and the *Preface to Shakespeare* as well as the notes to Shakespeare from Walter Raleigh's convenient *Johnson on Shakespeare,* Oxford, 1908. The other writings are quoted from *Works,* ed. Arthur Murphy, 12 vols. London, 1823. Some quotations come from the *Letters,* ed. G. B. Hill (2 vols. Oxford, 1892), from *Johnsonian Miscellanies,* ed. G. B. Hill (2 vols. Oxford, 1897), and from Boswell's *Life* (with the *Tour to the Hebrides*), ed. G. B. Hill and L. F. Powell, 6 vols. Oxford, 1934–50.

Most of the literature on Dr. Johnson is biographical and anecdotal. For a study of his criticism the compilation by Joseph E. Brown, *The Critical Opinions of Samuel Johnson* (Princeton, 1926) is most useful. The fullest analysis is J. H. Hagstrum, *Samuel Johnson's Literary Criticism,* Minneapolis, 1952. A good general account is in Joseph W. Krutch's biography, *Samuel Johnson,* New York, 1944. Discussions of different aspects of the criticism are also in Percy H. Houston, *Dr. Johnson: a Study in Eighteenth Century Humanism,* Cambridge, Mass., 1923; Walter B. C. Watkins, *Johnson and English Poetry before 1660,* Princeton, 1936; and William K. Wimsatt, *The Prose Style of Samuel Johnson,* New Haven, 1941. The following articles have some use or distinction: Irving Babbitt, "Dr. Johnson and Imagination," *Southwest Review, 13* (1927), 25–35, reprinted in *On Being Creative* (Boston, 1932), pp. 80–96; R. D. Havens, "Johnson's Distrust of the Imagination," *ELH, 10* (1943), 243–55; F. R. Leavis, "Johnson as Critic," *Scrutiny, 12* (1944), 187–204, reprinted in *The Importance of Scrutiny,* ed. E. Bentley (New York, 1948), pp. 57–75; Allen Tate, "Johnson on the Metaphysicals," *Kenyon Review, 11* (1949), 379–94; William R. Keast, "Johnson's Criticism of the Metaphysical Poets," *ELH, 17* (1950), 59–70; and "The Theoretical Foundations of Johnson's Criticism," in *Critics and Criticism: Ancient and Modern,* ed. R. S. Crane (Chicago, 1952), pp. 389–407.

NOTES: DR. JOHNSON

1. *Preface;* Raleigh, p. 14.
2. *Lives, 3* (Pope), 255.
3. *Ibid., 1* (Waller), 271.

4. *Rambler*, No. 4. *Works*, ed. Murphy, 2, 21.

5. *Works*, ed. Hawkins (1787), *1*, 217.

6. *Lives*, 2 (Addison), 129.

7. *Johnsonian Miscellanies*, 2, 15.

8. *Letters*, *1*, 162.

9. Raleigh, p. 165.

10. *Ibid.*, pp. 150–1.

11. *Lives*, *1* (Milton), 163.

12. *Ibid.* (Cowley), 6–8.

13. *Ibid.*, *3* (Pope), 235.

14. *Ibid.*, 2 (Smith), 16.

15. *Ibid.*, *3* (Gray), 439.

16. *Ibid.*, *1* (Milton), 185–6.

17. *Ibid.*, p. 163.

18. *Ibid.*, p. 164.

19. *Ibid.*

20. *Ibid.*, *3* (Lyttelton), 456.

21. Mme d'Arblay, *Diary and Letters*, ed. A. Dobson (London, 1904), *1*, 246–7.

22. Raleigh, pp. 161–2.

23. *Ibid.*, pp. 80, 187, 198.

24. *Lives*, 2 (Addison), 135.

25. *Johnsonian Miscellanies*, 2, 189–90.

26. Boswell, *Life*, ed. Hill, 2, 173–4.

27. Raleigh, pp. 20–1.

28. *Ibid.*, pp. 9–10.

29. *Lives*, *3* (Pope), 226.

30. *Rambler*, No. 125. *Works*, *3*, 346.

31. *Adventurer*, No. 99. *Works*, *11*, 485.

32. *Rambler*, No. 4. *Works*, 2, 23–4.

33. *Rasselas*, ch. 10. *Works*, *5*, 449.

34. *Rambler*, No. 36. *Works*, 2, 235.

35. Raleigh, pp. 11–12.

36. *Lives*, *1* (Cowley), 21.

37. *Ibid.*, *1* (Butler), 213–14; *1* (Cowley), 46; Raleigh, pp. 158–9.

38. *Ibid.*, *3* (Gray), 441.

39. *Le Rire* (Paris, 1950), pp. 123–4: "l'art vise toujours l'individuel. . . . Ce que le poète chante, c'est un état d'âme qui fut le sien, et le sien seulement, et qui ne sera jamais plus."

40. See below, pp. 113–14.

41. *Le Rire*, p. 124: "Rien de plus singulier que le personnage de Hamlet."

42. Johnson quotes from Dryden's *Du Fresnoy* in the *Dictionary* more frequently than from any other prose work by Dryden. Cf. W. K. Wimsatt, "Samuel Johnson and Dryden's Du Fresnoy," *SP, 48* (1951), 26–39.

43. *Lives,* 2, 76.

44. *Proposals for Printing the Dramatick Works of William Shakespeare* (1756), in Raleigh, p. 4.

45. *Preface;* Raleigh, p. 11.

46. *Ibid.,* p. 16.

47. *Rambler,* No. 92. *Works, 3,* 129.

48. *Ibid.,* No. 208. *Works, 4,* 396.

49. *Ibid.,* No. 176. *Works, 4,* 213.

50. *Ibid.,* No. 156. *Works, 4,* 96.

51. *Ibid.*

52. Raleigh, pp. 26–7.

53. *Rambler,* No. 156; *Works, 4,* 98.

54. *Ibid.*

55. Raleigh, p. 15.

56. *Ibid.,* p. 18.

57. *Ibid.,* p. 15.

58. *Adventurer,* No. 115; *Works, 11,* 520. Rambler, No. 152; *Works,* 4, 74.

59. Raleigh, p. 20.

60. *Ibid.,* p. 22.

61. *Lives, 3* (Gray), 437.

62. *Works, 9,* 313.

63. *Rambler,* No. 37. *Works, 2,* 241.

64. *Lives, 1* (Dryden), 433.

65. *Idler,* No. 70. *Works, 5,* 279.

66. *Rambler,* No. 140. *Works, 3,* 439.

67. Raleigh, p. 24.

68. *Ibid.,* p. 41.

69. *Lives, 1* (Dryden), 468.

70. *Ibid.* (Milton), p. 192.

71. *Ibid.* (Roscommon), p. 237.

72. *Ibid., 3* (Mallet), 406.

73. *Ibid., 1* (Cowley), 47.

74. *Ibid., 3* (Pope), 227.

75. *Ibid., 1* (Milton), 169, 163.

76. Boswell, *4,* 46.

77. *Lives, 1* (Milton), 177.

78. *Ibid.,* p. 180.

79. *Ibid.*, p. 183.

80. *Ibid.*, 2 (Rowe), 69–70. Cf. the story of his weeping at the death of Jane Shore, *Johnsonian Miscellanies, 1*, 283–4.

81. *Lives, 1* (Cowley), 20.

82. *Ibid.*, 2 (Congreve), 217; Raleigh, p. 9.

83. *Lives, 3* (Gray), 441.

84. *The Common Reader* (London, 1925), p. 11.

85. *Lives, 3* (Pope), 247.

86. *Ibid., 1* (Milton), 194.

87. *Works, 11*, 146–7.

88. *Lives, 1* (Cowley), 2.

89. *Tour to the Hebrides*, p. 15 (August, 1773), in Boswell, 5, 35.

90. *Idler*, No. 44. *Works, 5*, 175.

91. *Lives, 3* (Pope), 247.

92. *Rambler*, No. 125. *Works, 3*, 345.

93. *Lives, 3* (Young), 395.

94. Mme. D'Arblay, *Diary*, August 23, 1778; ed. Dobson, *1*, 77.

95. *Preface;* Raleigh, p. 11.

96. *Lives, 3* (Gray), 436.

97. *Ibid.*, p. 434.

98. *Ibid.*, 2 (Addison), 128.

99. *Ibid., 3* (Gray), 436. "Cant" means here "barbarous jargon." See No. 4 under "Cant" in *Dictionary*.

100. *Lives, 3* (Pope), 229.

101. *Ibid., 1* (Denham), 78.

102. An elaborate discussion of this passage can be found in I. A. Richards, *Philosophy of Rhetoric* (New York, 1936), pp. 120–3.

103. *Lives, 1* (Cowley), 19.

104. *Ibid.*, p. 20.

105. *Ibid.*, 2 (Addison), 130.

106. *Ibid., 1* (Cowley), 35.

107. *Ibid.*, pp. 49–50.

108. *Ibid.* (Waller), pp. 291–2.

109. *Ibid.* (Milton), p. 182.

110. *Ibid.*, p. 185.

111. *Ibid., 3* (Watts), 310.

112. *Johnsonian Miscellanies, 1*, 187.

113. *Tour of the Hebrides*, October 14, 1773; Boswell, 5, 311.

114. Boswell, 2, 11–12.

115. *Lives, 1* (Dryden), 386.

116. *Dictionary* (4th ed. 1773), *1*, signature E.

117. In Sir John Hawkins, *Life of Johnson* (London, 1787), p. 82.

118. *Lives, 1* (Dryden), 455.

119. *Ibid., 2* (Addison), 148.

120. *Ibid., 1* (Milton), 121.

121. Raleigh, p. 6.

122. Cf. Karl Young, *Samuel Johnson on Shakespeare—One Aspect*, University of Wisconsin Studies in Language and Literature (Madison, Wis.), *18*, 1923.

123. Boswell, 2, 42n., from Hannah More, *Memoirs*, ed. W. Roberts (4 vols. London, 1834), *1*, 174.

124. *Lives, 1* (Denham), 77.

125. *Ibid.* (Dryden), p. 469.

126. *Ibid.*, p. 420.

127. *Ibid., 2* (Addison), 145.

128. *Ibid., 1* (Cowley), 18.

129. *Ibid.* (Dryden), p. 411.

130. *Ibid.*, p. 438.

131. *Ibid.* (J. Philips), p. 318.

132. *Ibid.* (Waller), p. 288.

133. *Ibid., 3* (Pope), 238, 240.

134. *Ibid., 1* (Milton), 137–8.

135. *Ibid., 3* (Pope), 239.

136. *Ibid., 1* (Dryden), 421.

BIBLIOGRAPHY: THE MINOR ENGLISH AND SCOTTISH CRITICS

No part of our topic has been investigated more thoroughly and competently than this. But there is no general treatment, except in the old-fashioned surveys by Saintsbury; A. Bosker, *Literary Criticism in the Age of Johnson*, Groningen, 1930, new ed. New York, 1953; and J. W. H. Atkins, *English Literary Criticism: 17th and 18th Centuries*, London, 1951. A small but excellent sketch is Ronald S. Crane's "English Neoclassical Criticism," in *Dictionary of World Literature*, ed. Joseph T. Shipley (New York, 1941), pp. 193–203, reprinted in *Critics and Criticism: Ancient and Modern*, ed. R. S. Crane (Chicago, 1952), pp. 372–88. There is much good comment in Meyer H. Abrams, *The Mirror and the Lamp* (New York, 1953), which is, however, largely devoted to the romantic movement.

On main genres see Clarence C. Green, *The Neo-Classic Theory of Tragedy in England during the Eighteenth Century*, Cambridge, Mass., 1934; H. T. Swedenberg, Jr., *The Theory of the Epic in England, 1650–1800*, Berkeley, 1944; Norman Maclean, "From Action to Image:

Theories of the Lyric in the Eighteenth Century," in Crane's *Critics and Criticism*, pp. 408–60.

A general treatment of historicism is my *Rise of English Literary History*, which discusses many related questions. I must refer to it for a fuller development of this chapter.

The following books and articles are most relevant to the topics of the chapter, in the order in which they are taken up in the text.

Shaftesbury: see the last chapter of Ernst Cassirer, *Die platonische Renaissance in England und die Schule von Cambridge*, Leipzig, 1932, Eng. trans. Austin, Texas, 1953; R. L. Brett, *The Third Earl of Shaftesbury*, London, 1951.

Taste: see, besides Bäumler, Martin Kallich, "The Associationist Criticism of Francis Hutcheson and David Hume," *SP, 43* (1946), 644–67; Marjorie Grene, "Gerard's *Essay on Taste*," *MP, 41* (1943), 45–58.

Genius, imagination, and originality: cf. Logan Pearsall Smith, *Four Words: Romantic, Originality, Creative, Genius*, Oxford, 1924; Paul Kaufman, "Heralds of Original Genius," in *Essays in Memory of Barrett Wendell*, Cambridge, Mass., 1926; A. S. P. Woodhouse, "Collins and Creative Imagination," in *Studies in English by Members of University College, Toronto*, ed. M. W. Wallace (Toronto, 1931), pp. 59–130; Donald F. Bond, "The Neo-Classical Psychology of Imagination," *ELH, 4* (1937), 245–64; Walter J. Bate, "The Sympathetic Imagination in Eighteenth-Century English Criticism," *ELH, 12* (1945), 144–64.

Alison: see Martin Kallich, "The Meaning of Archibald Alison's *Essays on Taste*," *PQ, 27* (1948), 314–24.

Reynolds: see L. I. Bredvold, "The Tendency toward Platonism in Neo-Classic Esthetics," *ELH, 1* (1934), 91–119; Hoyt Trowbridge, "Platonism and Sir Joshua Reynolds," *English Studies, 21* (1939), 1–7; Michael Macklem, "Reynolds and the Ambiguities of Neo-Classical Criticism," *PQ, 21* (1952), 383–98.

Particularity: see Houghton W. Taylor, "Particular Character: an Early Phase of a Literary Evolution," *PMLA, 60* (1945), 161–74; Scott Elledge, "The Background and Development in English Criticism of the Theories of Generality and Particularity," *PMLA, 62* (1947), 147–82.

Burke: see Dixon Wecter, "Burke's Theory of Words, Images and Emotion," *PMLA, 55* (1940), 167–81.

Kames: see Gordon McKenzie, "Lord Kames and the Mechanist Tradition," in *Essays and Studies in English*, University of California Publications, *14*, Berkeley, 1943; Helen W. Randall, *The Critical Theory of Lord Kames*, Northampton, Mass., 1944 (good). See also comments in I. A. Richards, *The Philosophy of Rhetoric* (New York, 1936), pp. 16 ff., 98 ff.

Blair: see Robert M. Schmitz, *Hugh Blair*, New York, 1948.

Shakespearean criticism in the 18th century: e.g. Herbert S. Robinson, *English Shakesperian Criticism in the Eighteenth Century*, New York, 1932; Robert W. Babcock, *The Genesis of Shakespeare Idolatry*, Chapel Hill, 1931.

Tragic pleasure: Earl R. Wasserman, "The Pleasures of Tragedy," *ELH, 14* (1947), 283–307.

Comic theory: J. W. Draper, "The Theory of the Comic in Eighteenth-Century England," *JEGP, 37* (1938), 207–23 (a slight treatment); Edward N. Hooker, "Humour in the Age of Pope," *Huntington Library Quarterly, 11* (1947–48), 361–86.

Primitivistic theories of the epic: Lois Whitney, "English Primitivist Theories of Epic Origins," *MP, 21* (1924), 337–78.

Homer: Donald M. Foerster, *Homer in English Criticism: the Historical Approach of the Eighteenth Century*, New Haven, 1947.

Spenser: Jewel Wurtsbaugh, *Two Centuries of Spenserian Scholarship, 1609–1805*, Baltimore, 1936.

The novel: Joseph B. Heidler, *The History, from 1700 to 1800, of English Criticism of Prose Fiction*, Urbana, Ill., 1926.

Gray: William P. Jones, *Thomas Gray, Scholar*, Cambridge, Mass., 1937.

John Brown: Hermann M. Flasdieck, *John Brown (1715–1766) und seine "Dissertation on Poetry and Music,"* Halle, 1924.

Joseph Warton: Hoyt Trowbridge, "Joseph Warton on Imagination," *MP, 35* (1937), 73–87; Paul Leedy, "Genre Criticism and the Significance of Warton's *Essay on Pope*," *JEGP, 45* (1946), 140–6.

Hurd: Edwine Montague, *Bishop Hurd as Critic*, unpublished dissertation, Yale University, 1939; *idem,* "Bishop Hurd's Association with Thomas Warton," *Stanford Studies in Language and Literature*, ed. Hardin Craig (Stanford University, 1941), pp. 233–56; Audley L. Smith, "Richard Hurd's *Letters on Chivalry and Romance*," *ELH, 5* (1939), 58–81; Hoyt Trowbridge, "Bishop Hurd: A Reinterpretation," *PMLA, 58* (1943), 450–65.

Thomas Warton: Clarissa Rinaker, *Thomas Warton: a Biographical and Critical Study*, Urbana, Ill., 1916; Raymond D. Havens, "Thomas Warton and the Eighteenth Century Dilemma," *SP, 24* (1928), 36–50; David Nichol Smith, *Warton's History of English Poetry*, Oxford, 1929. For a detailed treatment see the last chapter of Wellek, *Rise*, where there are many more bibliographical references.

NOTES: THE MINOR ENGLISH
AND SCOTTISH CRITICS

1. There is a fuller discussion in my "The Concept of Romanticism in Literary History," *Comparative Literature, 1* (1949), 1–23, 147–72.

2. On title page.

3. *Essays and Treatises* (Edinburgh, 1804), *1*, 244–5.

4. *Philosophical Inquiry* (London, 1798), pp. 32, 37.

5. *Essay on Taste* (London, 1759), p. 105.

6. *Elements of Criticism* (9th ed. Edinburgh, 1814), 2, 446–7, 450.

7. *Characteristics, 1*, 207. On Germany cf. Oskar Walzel, *Das Prometheussymbol von Shaftesbury bis Goethe,* 1910; 2d ed. Munich, 1932.

8. *Conjectures on Original Composition,* ed. Edith K. Morley (Manchester, 1918), pp. 7, 11, 13, 15.

9. Blake, *Poetry and Prose,* ed. G. Keynes (London, 1927), pp. 703, 828, 844, 986, 1004, 1008, 1023, 1024, 1039–40, 1076. "Literalist of the imagination" is Yeats' phrase for Blake.

10. *Philosophical Inquiry,* pp. 330–1, 332.

11. *Essays on Poetry and Music* (3d ed. London, 1779), pp. 181–91.

12. Blair, *Lectures on Rhetoric and Belles Lettres* (London, 1820), *3,* 308 (lecture 46).

13. *Essays on the Nature and Principles of Taste* (London, 1790), p. 42.

14. *Ibid.,* pp. 117–9, 109.

15. *Essays on Poetry and Music,* pp. 189–90.

16. *Works,* ed. Edmond Malone (4th ed. London, 1809), *1,* 57, 63.

17. *Ibid., 3,* 97 (note to W. Mason's translation of Du Fresnoy); *2,* 237 (*Idler,* No. 82); *2,* 142 (thirteenth discourse).

18. *Works,* ed. Malone, *1,* 80, 86, 90.

19. *Essay on the Genius and Writings of Pope* (2 vols. 5th ed. London, 1806), *2,* 160, 168.

20. *Elements of Criticism, 1,* 215–6.

21. George Campbell, *The Philosophy of Rhetoric* (2d ed. London, 1801), *2,* 137, 140, 144.

22. William Gilpin, *Observations Relative Chiefly to Picturesque Beauty* (1772), and many other works. Sir Uvedale Price, *On the Picturesque* (1794). On the whole movement cf. Christopher Hussey, *The Picturesque,* London, 1927.

23. *Poetry and Prose,* p. 977.

24. *Philosophical Inquiry,* pp. 248, 287–8.

25. *Ibid.,* p. 333.

26. E.g. James Harris in *Three Treatises* (1744), Charles Avison in *Essay on Musical Expression* (1752), and James Beattie in *Essays on Poetry and Music* (1778). See Wellek, *Rise*, pp. 51–2.

27. In *Poems Consisting Chiefly of Translations from the Asiatick Languages* (London, 1772), p. 217.

28. Kames, *Elements*, *1*, 399.

29. *Ibid.*, pp. 81 ff.

30. *Ibid.*, *2*, 184–5, 233, 261.

31. *Ibid.*, p. 329 n.

32. Blair, *Lectures*. On fiction, *3*, 70 ff.; on Hebrew poetry, *3*, 165 ff.

33. "An Essay on the Origin of the English Stage" in *Reliques of Ancient English Poetry* (London, 1765), *1*, 118 ff.

34. *Adventurer*, Nos. 93, 97, 113, 122; 116: "General criticism is on all subjects useless and unentertaining." *Adventurer* (London, 1794), *3*, 220.

35. William Richardson, *Essays on Shakespeare's Dramatic Characters of Richard The Third, King Lear, and Timon of Athens*, 2d ed. London, 1786; *Essays on Shakespeare's Dramatic Character of Sir John Falstaff, and on his Imitation of Female Characters*, London, 1789.

36. *Essay on the Dramatic Character of John Falstaff* (London, 1777), pp. 14, 28–9, 58 n., 61, 62 n., 64, 71, 147.

37. See R. W. Babcock, *The Genesis of Shakespeare Idolatry*, Chapel Hill, 1931; and A. C. Bradley, in *Scottish Historical Review*, *1* (1904), 291.

38. Blair, *Lectures*, *3*, 275. Campbell, *Philosophy of Rhetoric*, *1*, 322.

39. Burke, *Inquiry*, pp. 75–6.

40. A letter to Mrs. Montague (June 17, 1771), quoted in Helen W. Randall, *The Critical Theory of Lord Kames* (Northampton, Mass., 1944), p. 111.

41. *Elements*, *2*, 354.

42. *Ibid.*, pp. 381, 371–3.

43. A letter to Adam Smith (July 28, 1759), in *Letters*, ed. J. Y. T. Greig (Oxford, 1932), *1*, 313.

44. *Essays and Treatises*, *1*, 236.

45. *An Analytical Inquiry into the Principles of Taste* (London, 1805), esp. pp. 324 ff.

46. "A Dissertation on the Provinces of the Drama," in Hurd, *Works* (London, 1811), 2, 81.

47. Kames, *Elements*, *1*, 329 ff.; Beattie, "Essay on Laughter and Ludicrous Composition," in *Essays on Poetry and Music* (3d ed. 1779), pp. 297 ff.

48. See p. 262 above, n. 22 to Ch. 1.

49. *A Critical Dissertation on the Poems of Ossian* (London, 1763), p. 74.

50. *Observations* (London, 1754), p. 13.

51. *Ibid.* (2d ed. 1762), *1*, 15.

52. *Works, 4*, 292; cf. pp. 296 ff.

53. *The Correspondence of Richard Hurd and William Mason*, ed. L. Whibley (Cambridge, 1932), p. 50; letter to Mason (Nov. 30, 1760).

54. *Works, 4*, 307–8, 327, 281, 290.

55. "Dissertation on the Ancient Metrical Romances," in *Reliques of Ancient English Poetry* (London, 1765), *3*, 1 ff.

56. These theories are surveyed in Wellek, *Rise*, pp. 153 ff.

57. In "Idea of Universal Poetry," *Works, 2*, 19.

58. Blair, in *Lectures;* Beattie, in *Essays.* Mrs. Clara Reeve, *The Progress of Romance* 2 vols. London, 1785. John Moore, "A View of the Commencement and Progress of Romance" (1790), in *Works,* ed. R. Anderson (Edinburgh, 1820), *5.*

59. *Essay on Pope, 2*, 405.

60. E.g. by Blackwell, Blair, Duff, and Kames. A fuller treatment in *Rise,* where the parallel with theories of origin of language is worked out.

61. *Observations on the Correspondence between Poetry and Music* (London, 1769), pp. 152 ff. *Remarks on the Beauties of Poetry* (London, 1762), pp. 70 ff.

62. Jones, *Poems,* p. 217.

63. Joseph Warton, *Essay on Pope, 1*, 5.

64. *An Enquiry into the Present State of Polite Learning* (London, 1759), p. 95. In later eds. Goldsmith dropped the whole of ch. 7. See his article in *Critical Review, 9* (1760), 10–19.

65. In his essay "Of Poetry" (1690), reprinted in J. E. Spingarn, *Critical Essays of the Seventeenth Century* (Oxford, 1908–09), *3*, 104–5.

66. Letter to John Brown (Feb. 1763), in *Correspondence,* ed. P. Toynbee and L. Whibley (Oxford, 1935), *2*, 797.

67. Essay, "Of National Characters," in *Essays and Treatises, 1*, 213 ff. Kames, *Sketches of a History of Man* (Edinburgh, 1774), *1*, 12.

68. Robert Wood, *An Essay on the Original Genius and Writings of Homer* (new ed. London, 1775), p. 15.

69. Kames, *Sketches, 1*, 109.

70. Essays, "Of Civil Liberty" and "Of the Rise and Progress of the Arts and Sciences," in *Essays and Treatises, 1*, 91 ff., 115 ff.

71. Blackwell, *An Enquiry into the Life and Writings of Homer* (London, 1735), pp. 52 ff.

72. Blair, *Dissertation*, pp. 2–3.

73. William Duff, *Essay on Original Genius* (London, 1767), pp. viii–ix.

74. More on Percy in *Rise*, pp. 68 ff. A full account of Percy's plans in Heinz Marwell, *Thomas Percy*, Göttingen, 1934. Cf. Cleanth Brooks, "The History of Percy's Edition of Surrey's Poems," *Englische Studien, 68* (1934), 424–30; V. H. Ogburn, "Thomas Percy's Unfinished Collection, *Ancient English and Scottish Poems*," *ELH, 3* (1936), 183–9. MSS of Percy's transcriptions of romances are in the Henry E. Huntington Library, San Marino, California.

75. All in *Reliques of Ancient English Poetry*, 3 vols. London, 1765.

76. Gray's scheme, in a letter to Warton (April 15, 1770), first printed in 1783. *Correspondence, 3,* 1122–5.

77. A commonplace book, quoted in W. P. Jones, *Thomas Gray, Scholar* (Cambridge, Mass., 1937), pp. 94–5.

78. Printed in Thomas Gray, *Essays and Criticisms*, ed. C. S. Northup, Boston (1911), pp. 87 ff., 118 ff.

79. Letter to W. Mason (Jan. 22, 1758). *Correspondence, 2,* 556–7.

80. Brown, *Dissertation* (London, 1763), pp. 55, 40, 101, 41, 197.

81. *Essay on Pope, 1,* 276; 2, 54.

82. *Ibid., 1,* i–ii, vi, 65, 330; 2, 403.

83. *Odes on Various Subjects* (London, 1746), advertisement.

84. *Works, 4,* 350.

85. Entry in commonplace book (1769), quoted in Edwine Montague, p. 141.

86. Preface to *History of English Poetry* (3 vols. London, 1774–81).

87. *History, 3,* 499. Many examples in Wellek, *Rise*.

88. "Verses," in *Poetical Works* (5th ed. 1802), *1,* lines 64–8.

89. *History, 2,* 462–3.

90. *Ibid., 3,* 490–1.

91. Preface to Milton's *Poems upon Several Occasions* (London, 1785), pp. iv, xii. *History, 3,* 497, 499.

BIBLIOGRAPHY: ITALIAN CRITICISM

There is no general treatment of the later eighteenth century in Italian criticism. Mario Fubini, *Dal Muratori al Baretti* (Bari, 1946) and Walter Binni, *Preromanticismo italiano* (Naples, 1947) contain distinguished essays. Benedetto Croce, "Estetici italiani della seconda metà del settecento," in *Problemi di estetica* (Bari, 1908; 4th ed. 1949), pp. 383–401, discusses minor figures.

The first half of the century has been studied much more thoroughly. Giuseppe Toffanin, *L'eredità del Rinascimento in Arcadia* (Bologna, 1923) and J. G. Robertson, *Studies in the Genesis of Romantic Theory in the Eighteenth Century* (Cambridge, 1923) discuss the critics from opposite points of view. Robertson's attempt to interpret them as forerunners of romanticism seems to me completely mistaken.

Gravina is quoted from *Prose*, ed. P. Emiliani-Guidici, Florence, 1857. Croce's essay "L'estetica del Gravina" in *Problemi di estetica* (1949), pp. 363–72, seems to reach the right conclusion. On Calepio's influence, besides Robertson, see Croce, "L'efficacia dell'estetica italiana sulle origini dell'estetica tedesca," in *Problemi di estetica* (1949), pp. 373–82; and Hugh Quigley, *Italy and the Rise of a New School of Criticism in the Eighteenth Century*, Perth, 1921.

There is a huge literature on Vico. The most convenient edition is *La scienza nuova seconda*, ed. F. Nicolini, 2 vols. Bari, 1942; Eng. trans. T. G. Bergin and M. H. Fisch, Ithaca, N. Y., 1948. See also F. Nicolini's commentary, *Commento storico alla seconda Scienza nuova*, 2 vols. Rome, 1949–50. The pioneer book is B. Croce, *La filosofia di G. Vico*, Bari, 1910; 4th ed. 1947; Eng. trans. R. G. Collingwood, London, 1913. Cf. Croce's comment on Vico's Dante criticism in *La Poesia di Dante* (6th ed. Bari, 1948), pp. 168 ff.; and "Il Vico e la critica omerica," in *Saggio sullo Hegel* (4th ed. Bari, 1948), pp. 263–76. Special works on criticism: A. Sorrentino, *La poetica e la retorica di G. B. Vico* (Torino, 1927), which is rather mediocre, and Mario Fubini, *Stile e umanità di G. Vico* (Bari, 1946), which contains an excellent essay, "Il mito della poesia primitiva e la critica dantesca di G. B. Vico." Croce's interpretation is attacked most elaborately by Franco Amerio, *Introduzione allo studio di G. B. Vico*, Torino, 1947.

Vico's fame is best studied with Croce's *Bibliografia vichiana, accresciuta e rielaborata da F. Nicolini*, 2 vols. Naples, 1947. A sketch by M. H. Fisch in T. G. Bergin's translation of Vico's *Autobiography* (Ithaca, N. Y., 1944) is somewhat vitiated by exaggerated claims for Vico's influence. See my review in *PQ, 24* (1945), 166–8.

Parini's writings are in *Prose,* ed. E. Bellorini, 2 vols. Bari, 1913–15. On Parini: Raffaele Spongano, *La poetica del sensismo e la poesia del Parini*, Messina, 1934. See Fubini, *Dal Muratori al Baretti*, pp. 125 ff.

Alfieri's *Del principe e delle lettere* is quoted from ed. Luigi Russo, Florence, 1943. There is largely ironical comment in Paul Sirvien, *V. Alfieri* (Paris, 1942), *4*, 158 ff.

Beccaria: *Ricerche intorno alla natura dello stile*, Milan, 1770.

Spalletti: *Saggio sopra la Bellezza*, ed. G. Natali, Florence, 1933. On

Spalletti: Croce, *Problemi di estetica* (1949), pp. 394 ff.; and, for a different interpretation of the text, A. Caracciolo, "Il saggio sopra la Bellezza dello Spalletti," in *Scritti di estetica,* Brescia, 1949.

Bettinelli: *Lettere virgiliane,* ed. V. E. Alfieri, Bari, 1930. On Bettinelli: Fubini, "Introduzione alla lettura delle 'virgiliane,' " in *Dal Muratori al Baretti,* pp. 133 ff.

Gasparo Gozzi: "Difesa di Dante," in *Letterati memorialisti e viaggiatori del settecento,* ed. E. Bonora, Milan, 1951.

Cesarotti: available in *Opere scelte,* ed. G. Ortolani, 2 vols. Florence, 1945. When this fails, there is *Opere,* 40 vols. Pisa and Florence, 1800–13. On Cesarotti: V. Alemanni, *Un filosofo delle lettere,* Torino, 1894; Binni, *Preromanticismo italiano;* G. Marzot, *Il gran Cesarotti,* Florence, 1949.

Baretti: *La frusta letteraria* (2 vols. Bari, 1932) and *Prefazioni e Polemiche* (Bari, 1911), both ed. Luigi Piccioni, are easily accessible in the *Scrittori d'Italia* series. Among the literature: Albertina Devalle, *La critica letteraria nel' 700: Giuseppe Baretti* (Milan, 1932) and Giuseppe I. Lopriore, *G. Baretti nella sua frusta* (Pisa, 1940) are useful. These essays present very different points of view: Croce, "G. Baretti," in *Problemi di estetica* (1949), pp. 440–5; G. A. Borgese, "Una fama ambigua," in *La vita e il libro,* 3d ser. Torino, 1913; Fubini, "G. Baretti scrittore e critico," in *Dal Muratori al Baretti,* pp. 145–76; F. Flora, in *Storia della letteratura italiana,* 2, Pt. 2 (Florence, 1947), 966–72; Binni, "La frusta letteraria e il Baretti," in *Preromanticismo italiano,* pp. 114–48.

NOTES: ITALIAN CRITICISM

1. *Prose,* pp. 8, 15: "E la poesia una maga, ma salutare, ed un delirio che sgombra le pazzie."

2. On Gravina as a precursor of romanticism see J. G. Robertson, *Studies in the Genesis of Romantic Theory. Prose,* p. 15: "I sommi poeti con la dolcezza del canto poteron piegare il rozzo genio degli uomini, e ridurli alla vita civile."

3. On Calepio see Robertson, Croce, and Quigley.

4. Some key passages in *Scienza nuova* (1744 version): pars. 185, 214, 363, 375, 384, 409, 460, 821 (paragraph numbering used by Nicolini and Bergin-Fisch).

5. *Ibid.,* pars. 873, 875, 786, 817. On Dante, also "Giudizio sopra Dante" (written 1728 or 1729) and a letter to Degli Angioli (Dec. 26, 1725).

6. Croce's fullest exposition is in *La filosofia di Vico,* Bari, 1910.

7. See the convincing arguments against Croce's interpretation in Amerio, *Introduzione allo studio di G. B. Vico,* esp. pp. 177 ff.

8. See Croce's comment in *La poesia di Dante* (6th ed. Bari, 1948), pp. 168 ff.; M. Fubini, "Il mito della poesia primitiva e la critica dantesca di G. B. Vico," in *Stile e Umanità di G. B. Vico,* Bari, 1946.

9. See documents in B. Croce's *Bibliografia vichiana,* 2 vols. Naples, 1947. An early summary is in the appendix to *La filosofia di G. B. Vico.*

10. See M. H. Fisch, "The Coleridges, Dr. Prati and Vico," *MP, 41* (1943–44), 111–22.

11. Details in Croce, quoted above. Herder's references in *Werke,* ed. Suphan, *18,* 246; *30,* 276: "ein sehr verständiger Philosoph der Humanität."

12. Fontenelle, *Œuvres* (Paris, 1790), *2,* 193: "Le règne des images fabuleuses et matérielles est passé." The piece was first published in 1751 but written, presumably, in the late 17th century, as it is introduced by an article first printed in 1678.

13. Richard Bentley, *Remarks upon a Late Discourse of Free Thinking* (London, 1713), pp. 18–9; Henry Felton, *A Dissertation on Reading the Classics* (London, 1713; 2d ed. 1715), pp. 22–3.

14. *Prose, 1,* 350: "Sentimento naturale degli uomini, che è a tutti commune e non è soggetto a verun cambiamento."

15. See the caustic comments in Paul Sirvien's *Alfieri, 4,* 152 ff.

16. Beccaria, *Ricerche intorno alla natura dello stile* (Milan, 1770), p. 27.

17. Spalletti, *Saggio,* p. 23.

18. See above p. 203, and vol. 2, 11. Bosanquet, *History of Aesthetic,* p. 272.

19. *Lettere virgiliane,* p. 12: "Poema senza azioni . . . di passagi, di salite, di andate e di ritorni."

20. Gozzi, "Difesa di Dante," *Letterati,* p. 26.

21. Especially in Binni, *Preromanticismo italiano.*

22. Letter to Macpherson (1763), in *Opere scelte, 2,* 252: "La poésie de nature et de sentiment est au dessus de la poésie de réflection et d'ésprit."

23. *Opere scelte, 2,* 125, n. to line 184 of canto 3: "Gli uomini rozzi ed appasionati singolarizzano, e parlano per sentimenti. Se questa è la qualità più essenziale del vero linguaggio poetico."

24. *Ibid.,* pp. 254, 255, 275: "Le grand poète de l'humanité." For examples from Homer comment see Binni, p. 218 n.

25. Binni, p. 209; Marzot, *Gran Cesarotti,* pp. 46 ff. Praise of Lucian, in *Opere scelte, 2,* 304. The disparagement of Aristotle and of the

"stupid adoration" of the anc ...s in "Ragionamento sopra l'origine e i progressi dell'arte poetica" (1762), in *Opere scelte, 1*, 240, 247: "La sua purgazione degli affetti è particolare e bizzarra."

26. On Metastasio, *Opere scelte, 2*, 273, 283: "Uno dei più sovrani Poeti che sieno mai stati al mondo." On *Ortis, Epistolario* (Florence, 1811), *3*, 359–60.

27. *Opere, 37*, 309; *Opere scelte, 1*, 239: "Le irregolarità e carnificine del teatro inglese."

28. E.g. *Opere scelte, 1*, 248: "Uno de' più elevati ingegni d'Italia."

29. "Ragionamento preliminare storico-critico alla Iliade," in *Opere, 6*, 28: "La lingua naturale dei popoli."

30. *Opere scelte, 1*, 273: "Uno specchio dei pericoli nostri."

31. *Ibid.,* p. 204: "orecchia armonizzata, fantasia desta, cuore presto a rispondere con fremito istantaneo alle minime vibrazioni del sentimento, prontezza a trasportarsi nella situazion dell' autore, celerità nel cogliere i cenni occulti e i lampi fuggitivi dell' espressione."

32. *Ibid.,* p. 363.

33. *La frusta letteraria, 1*, 258. The verse is by Giambattista Zappi.

34. *Ibid., 2*, 92: "Le ridenti rose de' dolci labri . . . dardi usciti della faretra di Cupido."

35. *Ibid., 1*, 369 ff.

36. *Ibid., 2*, 40–1.

37. *Ibid.,* p. 116: "manca il potere di farsi leggere rapidamente e con diletto . . . una buona dose di risolutezza e di pazienza."

38. *Ibid.,* p. 32: "Bisogna troppo studiarlo per capirlo bene."

39. *Ibid., 1*, 192, 342; *2*, 260.

40. *Ibid., 1*, 203–4: "lo scrivere vivo vivissimo e tutto pittoresco."

41. *Ibid.,* p. 347: "nel dire cose naturali, cose belle, cose grandi, cose molte, con semplicità, con forza, con entusiasmo." Cf. p. 152: "Nessuno può giudicare di poesia se non ha un' anima poetica."

42. This is convincingly demonstrated in Albertina Devalle, *La critica letteraria,* pp. 69 ff.

43. *Prefazioni,* ed. Piccioni, p. 115; on Berni, *Frusta, 1*, 212 ff.

44. *Frusta, 1*, 60, 64: "Nessuno d'essi [Dante, Petrarca, Boiardo, Ariosto] ha avuto un pensare cosí chiaro e cosí preciso come quello di Metastasio. . . . sentimenti ed affetti, che Locke e Addison potettero appena esprimere in prosa."

45. *Prefazioni,* p. 52: "Il poeta delle dame."

46. *Ibid.,* p. 265: "presque tout ce qu'il a dit de Shakespeare n'est qu'insolence, que malignité, que brutalité et que sottise." *Frusta, 1*, 211.

47. *Frusta, 1*, 333 ff.

48. *Journey from London to Genoa through England, Portugal and Spain* (3d ed. London, 1770), *3*, esp. 18, 26 (letter 57); *Tolondron* (London, 1786), pp. 165 ff.

49. *Prefazioni*, pp. 218, 225.

50. *Frusta, 1,* 89, 213, 246–8; *2,* 300. Diogene Mastigoforo quotes Johnson; *Frusta, 1,* 13–4, 93. High praise of *Rasselas* in *La scelta delle lettere familiari* (Bari, 1912), pp. 142–3.

51. *Prefazioni*, p. 254: "Depuis qu'il y a eu deux nations dans ce monde, parlant chacune sa langue, il a été impossible de trouver un goût commun aux deux."

BIBLIOGRAPHY:

LESSING AND HIS PRECURSORS

THE PRECURSORS

German literary theory and criticism in the 18th century: there is only a small sketch on criticism, Sigmund von Lempicki, "Literarische Kritik," in *Reallexikon der deutschen Literaturgeschichte,* ed. P. Merker and W. Stammler (Berlin, 1925–31), *2,* 146–68.

The period before Lessing: Emile Grucker, *Histoire des idées littéraires et esthétiques en Allemagne,* Paris, 1883; Friedrich Braitmaier, *Geschichte der poetischen Theorie und Kritik von den Diskursen der Mahler bis auf Lessing,* 2 vols. Frauenfeld, 1888–89 (diffuse but instructive); Alessandro Pellegrini, *Gottsched, Bodmer, Breitinger e la poetica dell'Aufklärung,* Catania, 1952.

Aesthetics: besides Bäumler, *Kants Kritik,* see Rudolf Sommer, *Grundzüge einer Geschichte der deutschen Psychologie und Ästhetik von Wolff–Baumgarten bis Kant–Schiller,* Würzburg, 1892.

Baumgarten: *Reflections on Poetry. Meditationes philosophicae,* trans., with the original text, by K. Aschenbrenner and William B. Holther, Berkeley, 1954 (there is a rare reprint of the *Meditationes,* ed. Croce, Naples, 1900, and a German trans. in Albert Riemann, quoted below). See also *Aesthetica* (with *Meditationes*), Bari, 1936. On Baumgarten: Ernst Bergmann, *Die Begründung der deutschen Aesthetik durch A. G. Baumgarten und G. F. Meier,* Leipzig, 1911; Benedetto Croce, "Rileggendo l' 'Aesthetica' del Baumgarten," in *Ultimi saggi* (Bari, 1948), pp. 79–105, 1st printing 1932; Albert Riemann, *Die Aesthetik A. G. Baumgartens,* Halle, 1928.

J. E. Schlegel: *Aesthetische und dramaturgische Schriften,* ed. Johann von Antoniewicz, Deutsche Litteraturdenkmale, No. 26, Heilbronn, 1887; Elizabeth M. Wilkinson, *Johann Elias Schlegel, a German*

Pioneer in Aesthetics, Oxford, 1945 (good, but greatly overrates Schlegel).

Bodmer: no modern edition. On Bodmer: Max Wehrli, *Johann Jakob Bodmer und die Geschichte der Literatur* (Frauenfeld, 1936) contains a bibliography.

Mendelssohn: many reprints. I use *Schriften zur Philosophie, Aesthetik, und Apologetik,* ed. Moritz Brach, 2 vols. Leipzig, 1880. On Mendelssohn: Ludwig Goldstein, *Moses Mendelssohn und die deutsche Ästhetik,* Königsberg, 1904.

Winckelmann: *Sämtliche Werke,* ed. J. Eiselin, 12 vols. Donaueschingen, 1825–29. Life: Carl Justi, *Winckelmann, sein Leben, seine Werke und Zeitgenossen,* 3 vols. Leipzig, 1866–72. Comment: G. Baumecker, *Winckelmann in seinen Dresdener Schriften,* Berlin, 1933 (good on sources); F. Schultz, *Klassik und Romantik der Deutschen,* Vol. *1, Stuttgart,* 1935 (has a good chapter: pp. 65–138); and in English, besides W. Pater's 1867 essay, see H. C. Hatfield, *Winckelmann and His German Critics, 1755–81,* New York, 1943.

LESSING

I quote from Lessing's *Werke,* ed. Franz Bornmüller (5 vols. Bibliographisches Institut, Leipzig, 1884) and where this fails from *Sämtliche Werke,* ed. K. Lachmann and F. Muncker, 23 vols. Leipzig, 1886–1924 (cited as Muncker).

Lessings Briefwechsel mit Mendelssohn und Nicolai über das Trauerspiel was ed. by Robert Petsch, Leipzig, 1910. See also *Laokoon,* with very full notes by Hugo Blümner (2d ed. Berlin, 1880), 756 pp. An American ed. of the German text with commentary (and a reprint of the pieces by Herder and Goethe) was ed. by William G. Howard, New York, 1910.

Of the very extensive literature on Lessing I have found these books and articles useful:

Alexander Aronson, *Lessing et les classiques français,* Montpellier, 1935.

Margaret Bieber, *Laocoon. The Influence of the Group since Its Rediscovery,* New York, 1942.

Josef Clivio, *Lessing und das Problem der Tragödie,* Wege zur Dichtung, No. 5, Zurich, 1928 (good).

Max Kommerell, *Lessing und Aristoteles. Untersuchung über die Theorie der Tragödie,* Frankfurt, 1940 (extremely learned and subtle; on Corneille and Aristotle as well).

Folke Leander, *Lessing als aesthetischer Denker,* Göteborg, 1942.

Fred O. Nolte, "Lessing's Correspondence with Mendelssohn and Nicolai," in *Harvard Studies and Notes in Philology and Literature, 13* (1931), 309–32.

Fred O. Nolte, *Lessing's Laokoon,* Lancaster, Pa., 1940.

Camille Pitollet, *Contributions à l'étude de l'hispanisme de G. E. Lessing,* Paris, 1909.

J. G. Robertson, *Lessing's Dramatic Theory. Being an Introduction to and Commentary on His Hamburgische Dramaturgie* (Cambridge, 1939), 544 pp. (important).

Erich Schmidt, *Lessing,* 3 vols. Berlin, 1884–92; 3d ed. 2 vols. Berlin, 1909.

Curtis C. D. Vail, *Lessing's Relation to the English Language and Literature,* Columbia University Germanic Studies, new ser. No. 3, New York, 1936.

———. "Lessing's Attitude toward Storm and Stress," *PMLA, 65* (1950), 805–23.

Oskar Walzel, "Lessings Begriff des Tragischen," in *Vom Geistesleben alter und neuer Zeit,* Leipzig, 1922.

Benno von Wiese, *Lessing. Dichtung, Aesthetik, Philosophie,* Leipzig, 1931.

The *Hamburgische Dramaturgie* is cited as *HD* and the *Laokoon* as *La.*

NOTES: LESSING AND HIS PRECURSORS

1. A very full description in Bruno Markwardt, *Geschichte der deutschen Poetik, 1: Barock und Frühaufklärung,* Berlin, 1937, no more published.

2. *Aesthetica,* par. 1: "Scientia cognitionis sensitivae."

3. *Meditationes,* par. 9: "Oratio sensitiva perfecta est Poema."

4. This is the interpretation of K. Aschenbrenner and William B. Holther in the intro. to their trans. of *Meditationes,* e.g. p. 6.

5. *Meditationes,* pars. 19, 39, 52, 53, 68, 70: "nexus est poeticus . . . figmenta heterocosmica . . . utopica."

6. *Aesthetica,* par. 1.

7. *Aesthetische und dramaturgische Schriften,* ed. Antoniewicz, 71 ff., 222: "Entzückung."

8. *Critische Betrachtungen über die poetischen Gemählde der Dichter* (Zurich, 1741), p. 81: "Ohne diese Dinge wäre Dantes nicht mehr Dantes."

9. *Neue critische Briefe* (Zurich, 1749), preface: "Ein nützlicher Kaufmann."

10. See above, p. 134 and n. 3 on p. 293.

11. *Critische Abhandlung von dem Wunderbaren in der Poesie* (Zurich, 1740), p. 165: "Die Kräfte der Natur in der Überbringung in den Stand der Wirklichkeit nachzuahmen."

12. *Ibid.*, pp. 31–2: ". . . dass sie die Materie ihrer Nachahmung allzeit lieber aus der möglichen als aus der gegenwärtigen Welt nimmt."

13. *Anklagung des verderbten Geschmackes* (Frankfurt, 1728), p. 112. *Neue critische Briefe* (Zurich, 1749), pp. 19, 21. Bodmer alludes to Shaftesbury's comparison of the poet with Prometheus.

14. In *Briefe die neueste Literatur betreffend* (1761), letters 166–70. Reprinted in *Schriften zur Philosophie*, ed. Brach, 2, 302–18.

15. "Über die Hauptgrundsätze der schönen Künste und Wissenschaften" (1757), in *Schriften*, ed. Brach, pp. 143–68.

16. *Morgenstunden* (Berlin, 1785), sec. 7, pp. 120–1: "Billigungsvermögen, ruhiges Wohlgefallen."

17. "Betrachtungen über die Quellen und Verbindungen," in *Bibliothek der schönen Wissenschaften*, *1* (1759), 238: "Das Genie erfordert eine Vollkommenheit aller Seelenkräfte, und eine Übereinstimmung derselben zu einem Endzwecke."

18. "Rhapsodie über die Empfindungen" (1761), in *Schriften*, ed. Brach, 2, 107: "Wir haben gesehen, dass eine gewisse Fertigkeit dazu erfordert wird, sich der Täuschung zu überlassen, und ihr zum besten dem Bewusstsein des Gegenwärtigen zu entsagen, so lange sie Vergnügen machen; sobald sie aber unangenehm zu werden anfängt, die Aufmerksamkeit zurückzurufen, und den Geist gegenwärtig sein zu lassen." *Morgenstunden*, p. 57: "Wir nehmen wirklichen Anteil an nicht wirklichen Empfindungen und Handlungen weil wir von dem Nichtwirklichsein, zu unserm Vergnügen, vorsätzlich abstrahieren."

19. "Eine edle Einfalt und eine stille Grösse," in *Gedanken über die Nachahmung der griechischen Werke* (1755), in the passage on Laocoon.

20. For proof see K. K. Eberlein, "Winckelmann und Frankreich," in *Deutsche Vierteljahrschrift für Literaturwissenschaft und Geistesgeschichte*, *11* (1933), 592–610.

21. See "Versuch einer Allegorie" (1766) in *Sämtliche Werke* (Donaueschingen, 1825–29), Vol. 9. This is a kind of iconology for painters.

22. *Geschichte der Kunst des Alterthums*, Bk. 8, in *Sämtliche Werke*, 5, 171 ff.

23. *Hamburgische Dramaturgie* [*HD*], No. 96; *Werke, 4*, 423: "Doch was halte ich mich mit diesen Schwätzern auf? Ich will meinen Gang gehen und mich unbekümmert lassen, was die Grillen am Wege

schwirren. Auch ein Schritt aus dem Wege, um sie zu zertreten, ist schon zu viel. Ihr Sommer ist so leicht abgewartet!"

24. Saintsbury, *3, 34.*

25. *HD,* No. 15; *Werke, 4,* 69: "Othello ist das vollständigste Lehrbuch über diese traurige Raserei."

26. *Ibid.,* p. 68: "Ich kenne nur eine Tragödie, an der die Liebe selbst arbeiten helfen, und das ist 'Romeo und Juliet' vom Shakespear."

27. *HD,* No. 11; *Werke, 4,* 52–3.

28. *HD,* No. 73; *Werke, 4,* 326: "Aber was man von dem Homer gesagt hat, es lasse sich dem Herkules eher seine Keule als ihm ein Vers abringen, das lässt sich vollkommen auch vom Shakespear sagen. Auf die geringste von seinen Schönheiten ist ein Stempel gedruckt, welcher gleich der ganzen Welt zuruft: Ich bin Shakespears! Und wehe der fremden Schönheit, die das Herz hat, sich neben ihr zu stellen." This is probably suggested by Diderot's use of the same simile in *Lettre sur les sourds et muets* (1751), in *Œuvres,* ed. Assézat and Tourneux, *1,* 377–8.

29. *HD,* No. 93; *Werke, 4,* 411 n.: "Es treten eine Menge der wunderlichsten Narren nacheinander auf, man weiss weder wie, noch warum."

30. *Laokoon* [*La.*], sec. 25; *Werke, 3,* 162 ff.

31. *HD,* No. 59; *Werke, 4,* 263: "er ist zugleich so gemein und so kostbar, so kriechend und so hochtrabend."

32. Intro. to Thomson; *Sämtliche Werke,* ed. Lachmann and Muncker, *7,* 68: "so wollte ich auch unendlich lieber der Urheber des *Kaufmanns von London* als des *sterbenden Cato* sein."

33. See Curtis C. D. Vail, "Originality in Lessing's *Theatralische Bibliothek*," *Germanic Review, 9* (1934), 96.

34. *La.,* appendix 2; *Werke, 3,* 221–3.

35. Muncker, *5,* 442.

36. Muncker, *5,* 408–9.

37. Robertson, *Lessing's Dramatic Theory,* p. 176.

38. *La.,* sec. 25; *Werke, 3,* 166–7.

39. *La.,* sec. 20; *Werke, 3,* 133–4.

40. *HD,* No. 37; *Werke 4,* 163.

41. See the elaborate proof in Camille Pitollet, *Contribution à l'étude de l'hispanisme de G. E. Lessing* (Paris, 1909), 342 pp.

42. *HD,* No. 97; *Werke, 4,* 425. See Robertson, p. 309.

43. Written in 1760, published posthumously, 1790. Muncker, *8,* 291–377.

44. *HD,* No. 49; *Werke, 4,* 220: "der tragischste von allen tragischen Dichtern."

45. *HD,* No. 91; *Werke, 4,* 400–1.

46. *HD*, No. 70; *Werke, 4*, 314 ff.

47. In *Theatralische Bibliothek* (1754); Muncker, *4*, 131–74, 180–93.

48. Muncker, *6*, 167–242; *5*, 272–309.

49. *HD*, No. 69; *Werke, 4*, 311; Muncker, *20*, 266.

50. E.g. Muncker, *4*, 14–5, 400–5.

51. Muncker, *18*, 170.

52. Muncker, *17*, 234: mit dem Geiste des Shakespear genährt."

53. Muncker, *17*, 244–9.

54. Letter to Wieland (February 8, 1775); Muncker, *22*, 303.

55. I.e. in *Götter, Helden und Wieland.* Lessing misinterprets Goethe as attacking Euripides.

56. Muncker, *16*, 535.

57. Letter to Eschenburg, October 26, 1774; Muncker, *18*, 115 ff.:
Glauben Sie wohl, dass je ein römischer oder griechischer Jüngling sich *so* und *darum* das Leben genommen? Gewiss nicht. Die wussten sich vor der Schwärmerei der Liebe ganz anders zu schützen . . . Solche kleingrosse, verächtlich schätzbare Originale hervorzubringen, war nur der christlichen Erziehung vorbehalten, die ein körperliches Bedürfnis so schön in eine geistige Vollkommenheit zu verwandeln weiss. Also, lieber Goethe, noch ein Kapitelchen zum Schluss; und je cynischer je besser!

58. *Literaturbriefe*, No. 33. Muncker, *8*, 75–7.

59. Muncker, *14*, 290: "Something you find by the wayside."

60. *HD*, No. 95; *Werke*, 4, 419–20: "Ich erinnere hier meine Leser, dass diese Blätter nichts weniger als ein dramatisches System enthalten sollen. Ich bin also nicht verpflichtet, alle die Schwierigkeiten aufzulösen, die ich mache. Meine Gedanken mögen immer sich weniger verbinden, ja wohl gar sich zu widersprechen scheinen: wenn es denn nur Gedanken sind, bei welchen sie Stoff finden, selbst zu denken. Hier will ich nichts als *Fermenta cognitionis* ausstreuen."

61. 1756–57. See *Lessings Briefwechsel mit Mendelssohn und Nicolai,* ed. Robert Petsch, Leipzig, 1910.

62. *Historia naturalis,* XXXVI, 37.

63. J. J. Winckelmann, *Ausgewählte Schriften und Briefe,* ed. Walther Rehm (Wiesbaden, 1948), p. 20:
Bei allen Leidenschaften eine grosse und gesetzte Seele . . . dieser Schmerz äussert sich dennoch mit keiner Wut in dem Gesichte und in der ganzen Stellung. Er erhebt kein schreckliches Geschrei, wie Virgil von seinem Laokoon singt. Die Öffnung des Mundes gestattet es nicht; es ist viel mehr ein ängstliches und beklemmtes Seufzen . . . Der Schmerz des Körpers und die Grösse der Seele sind durch den ganzen Bau der Figur mit gleicher Stärke

ausgeteilt und gleichsam abgewogen. Laokoon leidet, aber er leidet wie des Sophokles Philoktetes: sein Elend geht uns bis an die Seele; aber wir wünschten, wie dieser grosse Mann das Elend ertragen zu können.

The reference is to the *Aeneid*, II, 199.

64. Winckelmann, p. 20: "Eine edle Einfalt und eine stille Grösse." Note that Dufresnoy speaks of "majestas gravis et requies secura" in his *De arte graphica* (1668).

65. *La.*, sec. 2; *Werke, 3*, 11: "Wenn es wahr ist, dass das Schreien bei Empfindung körperlichen Schmerzes, besonders nach der alten griechischen Denkungsart gar wohl mit einer grossen Seele bestehen kann: so kann der Ausdruck einer solchen Seele die Ursache nicht sein, warum demohngeachtet der Künstler in seinem Marmor dieses Schreien nicht nachahmen wollen."

66. *La.*, sec. 2; *Werke, 3*, 18: "Er muss Schreien in Seufzen mildern; nicht weil das Schreien eine unedle Seele verrät, sondern weil es das Gesicht auf eine ekelhafte Weise verstellt."

67. *La.*, sec. 4; *Werke, 3*, 24.

68. *La.*, sec. 16; *Werke, 3*, 103:

Wenn es wahr ist, dass die Malerei zu ihren Nachahmungen ganz andere Mittel oder Zeichen gebraucht als die Poesie, jene nämlich *Figuren und Farben* in dem Raume, diese aber *artikulierte Töne* in der Zeit; wenn unstreitig die *Zeichen* ein bequemes Verhältniss zu dem *Bezeichneten* haben müssen: so können nebeneinander geordnete Zeichen auch nur Gegenstände, die nebeneinander, oder deren Teile nebeneinander existieren, aufeinander folgende Zeichen aber auch nur Gegenstände ausdrücken, die aufeinander oder deren Teile aufeinander folgen. Gegenstände, die nebeneinander oder deren Teile nebeneinander existieren, heissen Körper. Folglich sind *Körper* mit ihren sichtbaren Eigenschaften die eigentlichen *Gegenstände der Malerei*. Gegenstände, die aufeinander oder deren Teile aufeinander folgen, heissen überhaupt Handlungen. Folglich sind *Handlungen* der eigentliche *Gegenstand der Poesie*. Doch alle Körper existieren nicht allein in dem Raume, sondern auch in der Zeit. Sie dauern fort und können in jedem Augenblicke ihrer Dauer anders erscheinen und in anderer Verbindung stehen. Jede dieser augenblicklichen Erscheinungen und Verbindungen ist die Wirkung einer vorhergehenden und kann die Ursache einer folgenden und sonach gleichsam das Zentrum einer Handlung sein. Folglich kann die *Malerei* auch *Handlungen* nachahmen, aber nur *andeutungsweise durch Körper*. Auf der anderen Seite können Handlungen nicht für sich selbst bestehen, sondern müssen gewissen Wesen anhängen. Insofern nun diese Wesen Körper sind oder als Körper betrachtet werden, schildert die *Poesie* auch *Körper, aber nur andeutungsweise durch Handlungen.* Die Malerei kann in ihren koexistierenden Kompositionen nur einen einzigen Augenblick der Handlung nutzen und muss daher den *prägnantesten* wählen, aus welchem das Vorhergehende und Folgende am begreiflichsten wird. Ebenso kann auch die Poesie in ihren fortschreitenden Nachahmungen nur eine einzige Eigenschaft der Körper nutzen und muss daher diejenige wählen, welche das *sinnlichste Bild* des Körpers von der Seite erweckt, von welcher sie ihn braucht.

69. *La.,* sec. 18; *Werke, 3,* 117: "ein Eingriff des Malers in das Gebiet des Dichters, den der gute Geschmack nie billigen wird."

70. Dialogue 20, p. 311, as quoted by Lessing, *La.,* sec. 8; *Werke, 3,* 69.

71. *La.,* sec. 17; *Werke, 3,* 111 f.

72. *Orlando Furioso,* VII, 11–15.

73. *Iliad,* III, 156 ff.

74. *La.,* sec. 21; *Werke, 3,* 140–1: "Was Homer nicht nach seinen Bestandteilen beschreiben konnte, lässt er uns in seiner Wirkung erkennen. Malt uns, Dichter, das Wohlgefallen, die Zuneigung, die Liebe, das Entzücken, welches die Schönheit verursacht, und ihr habt die Schönheit selbst gemalt."

75. Act I, sc. 4: "Oder meinen Sie, Prinz, dass Raffael nicht das grösste malerische Genie gewesen wäre, wenn er unglücklicherweise ohne Hände wäre geboren worden?"

76. *La.,* appendix 2; *Werke, 3,* 238: "Ich behaupte, dass nur das die Bestimmung einer Kunst sein kann, wozu sie einzig und allein geschickt ist, und nicht das, was andere Künste ebenso gut, wo nicht besser können als sie. Ich finde bei dem Plutarch ein Gleichnis, das dieses sehr wohl erläutert, 'Wer,' sagt er (*de Audit.* p. 43. *Edit. Xyl.*) 'mit dem Schlüssel Holz spellen und mit der Axt Türen öffen will, verdirbt nicht sowohl beide Werkzeuge, als dass er sich selbst des Nutzens beider Werkzeuge beraubt.' "

77. Muncker, *17,* 290–1:

Aber das ist gewiss, dass je mehr sich die Malerei von den natürlichen Zeichen entfernt, oder die natürlichen mit willkürlichen vermischt, desto mehr entfernt sie sich von ihrer Vollkommenheit: wie hingegen die Poesie sich um so mehr ihrer Vollkommenheit nähert, je mehr sie ihre willkürlichen Zeichen den natürlichen näher bringt. Folglich ist die höhere Malerei die, welche nichts als natürlichen Zeichen im Raume braucht, und die höhere

Poesie die, welche nichts als natürliche Zeichen in der Zeit brauchte.
. . . Die Poesie muss schlechterdings ihre willkürlichen Zeichen
zu natürlichen zu erheben suchen; und nur dadurch unterscheidet
sie sich von der Prose, und wird Poesie. Die Mittel, wodurch sie
dieses tut, sind der Ton, die Worte,* die Stellung der Worte, das
Silbenmass, Figuren und Tropen, Gleichnisse, u.s.w. Alle diese
Dinge bringen die willkürlichen Zeichen den natürlichen näher;
aber sie machen sie nicht zu natürlichen Zeichen: folglich sind
alle Gattungen, die sich nur dieser Mittel bedienen, als die nie-
dern Gattungen der Poesie zu betrachten; und die höchste Gattung
der Poesie ist die, welche die willkürlichen Zeichen gänzlich zu
natürlichen macht. Das aber ist die dramatische: denn in dieser
hören die Worte auf, willkürliche Zeichen zu sein, und werden
natürliche Zeichen willkürlicher Dinge. Dass die dramatische
Poesie die höchste, ja die einzige Poesie ist, hat schon Aristoteles
gesagt, und er gibt der Epopee nur in so fern die zweite Stelle, als
sie grössenteils dramatisch ist, oder sein kann.

78. *La.*, appendix 2; *Werke, 3,* 215: "Da nämlich die Kraft der
natürlichen Zeichen in ihrer Ähnlichkeit mit den Dingen besteht, so
führt sie anstatt dieser Ähnlichkeit, welche sie nicht hat, eine andere
Ähnlichkeit ein, welche das bezeichnete Ding mit einem anderen hat,
dessen Begriff leichter und lebhafter erneuret werden kann."

79. Margaret Bieber, *Laocoon* (New York, 1942), p. 14.

80. *La.*, appendix 2; *Werke, 3,* 221: "Die höchste körperliche Schönheit existiert nur in dem Menschen, und auch nur in diesem vermöge
des Ideals."

81. *Ibid.*

82. *La.*, appendix 2; *Werke, 3,* 243: "Ja ich möchte fragen, ob es
nicht zu wünschen wäre, die Kunst, mit Ölfarben zu malen, möchte
gar nicht sein erfunden worden."

83. *A Philosophical Inquiry into the Origin of Our Ideas of the
Sublime and Beautiful* (2d ed. 1757), pp. 332, 338.

84. Muncker, *17*, 66: "Sie soll unsre Fähigkeit, Mitleid zu fühlen,
erweitern. . . . Der mitleidigste Mensch ist der beste Mensch. . . .
Wer uns also mitleidig macht, macht uns besser und tugendhafter."

85. *Ibid.*, pp. 67–8.

86. *La.*, sec. 4; *Werke, 3,* 33.

87. *HD*, Nos. 101–4; *Werke, 4,* 445: "Über den gutherzigen Einfall,

---

* The inclusion of "words" in this list is puzzling. Possibly the letter
was not transcribed accurately and should run here, "der Ton der
Worte."

den Deutschen ein Nationaltheater zu verschaffen, da wir Deutsche noch keine Nation sind! Ich rede nicht von der politischen Verfassung, bloss von dem sittlichen Charakter. Fast sollte man sagen, dieser sei, keinen eigenen haben zu wollen. Wir sind noch immer die geschworenen Nachahmer alles Ausländischen . . ."

88. *HD*, Nos. 101–4; *Werke, 4,* 448: "Man nenne mir das Stück des grossen Corneille, welches ich nicht besser machen wollte. Was gilt die Wette?"

89. *HD*, Nos. 101–4; *Werke, 4,* 446: "Indes steh' ich nicht an, zu bekennen (und sollte ich in diesen erleuchteten Zeiten auch darüber ausgelacht werden!), dass ich sie für ein ebenso unfehlbares Werk halte, als die 'Elemente' des Euklides nur immer sind . . . Besonders getraue ich mir von der Tragödie . . . unwidersprechlich zu beweisen, dass sie sich von der Richtschnur des Aristoteles keinen Schritt entfernen kann, ohne sich ebenso weit von ihrer Vollkommenheit zu entfernen."

90. *HD*, No. 74; *Werke, 4,* 328: "Zwar mit dem Ansehen des Aristoteles wollte ich bald fertig werden, wenn ich es nur auch mit seinen Gründen zu werden wüsste."

91. *HD*, Nos. 101–4; *Werke, 4,* 447–8:
Nach dieser Überzeugung nahm ich mir vor, einige der berühmtesten Muster der *französischen* Bühne ausführlich zu beurteilen. Denn diese Bühne soll ganz nach den Regeln des Aristoteles gebildet sein; und besonders hat man uns Deutsche bereden wollen, dass sie nur durch diese Regeln die Stufe der Vollkommenheit erreicht habe, auf welcher sie die Bühnen aller neueren Völker so weit unter sich erblicke. Wir haben das auch lange so fest geglaubt, dass bei unsern Dichtern den Franzosen nachahmen ebensoviel gewesen ist, als nach den Regeln der Alten arbeiten. Indes konnte das Vorurteil nicht ewig gegen unser Gefühl bestehen. Dieses war glücklicherweise durch einige *englische* Stücke aus seinem Schlummer erweckt, und wir machten endlich die Erfahrung, dass die Tragödie noch einer ganz andern Wirkung fähig sei, als ihr Corneille und Racine zu erteilen vermocht. Aber geblendet von diesem plötzlichen Strahle der Wahrheit prallten wir gegen den Rand eines andern Abgrundes zurück. . . . wir waren auf dem Punkte, uns alle Erfahrungen der vergangenen Zeit mutwillig zu verscherzen und von den Dichtern lieber zu verlangen, dass jeder die Kunst aufs neue für sich erfinden solle. . . . die Gärung des Geschmacks . . . Gerade keine Nation hat die Regeln des alten Dramas mehr verkannt als die Franzosen.

92. *HD*, No. 46; *Werke, 4,* 206: "Möchten meinetwegen Voltairens

und Maffeis 'Merope' acht Tage dauern und an sieben Orten in Grie-
chenland spielen. Möchten sie aber auch nur die Schönheiten haben,
die mich diese Pedanterien vergessen machen!"

93. *HD*, No. 7; *Werke, 4,* 34: "Das Genie lacht über alle die Grenz-
scheidungen der Kritik."

94. *HD*, No. 34; *Werke, 4,* 149: "Dem Genie ist es vergönnt, tausend
Dinge nicht zu wissen, die jeder Schulknabe weiss; nicht der erworbene
Vorrat seines Gedächtnisses, sondern das, was es aus sich selbst, aus
seinem eigenen Gefühl hervorzubringen vermag, macht seinen Reich-
tum aus."

95. *HD*, No. 96; *Werke, 4,* 422:
. . . wir haben, dem Himmel sei Dank, jetzt ein Geschlecht selbst
von Kritikern, deren beste Kritik darin besteht,—alle Kritik ver-
dächtig zu machen. "Genie! Genie!" schreien sie. "Das Genie setzt
sich über alle Regeln hinweg! Was das Genie macht, ist Regel!"
So schmeicheln sie dem Genie; ich glaube, damit wir sie auch für
Genies halten sollen. Doch sie verraten zu sehr, dass sie nicht
einen Funken davon in sich spüren, wenn sie in einem und eben
demselben Atem hinzusetzen: "die Regeln unterdrücken das
Genie!"—Als ob sich Genie durch etwas in der Welt unterdrücken
liesse! Und noch dazu durch etwas, das, wie sie selbst gestehen, aus
ihm hergeleitet ist. Nicht jeder Kunstrichter ist Genie: aber jedes
Genie ist ein geborner Kunstrichter. Es hat die Probe aller Regeln
in sich.

96. *HD, No.* 96; *Werke, 4,* 423: "Wer richtig räsonniert, erfindet auch,
und wer erfinden will, muss räsonnieren können."

97. *HD*, No. 48; *Werke, 4,* 217–8:
In den Lehrbüchern sondre man sie so genau voneinander ab als
möglich; aber wenn ein Genie höherer Absichten wegen mehrere
derselben in einem und demselben Werke zusammenfliessen lässt,
so vergesse man das Lehrbuch und untersuche bloss, ob es diese
höhere Absichten erreicht hat. Was geht mich es an, ob so ein
Stück des Euripides weder ganz Erzählung noch ganz Drama ist?
Nennt es immerhin einen Zwitter; genug, dass mich dieser Zwitter
mehr vergnügt, mehr erbaut, als die gesetzmässigsten Geburten
eurer korrekten Racinen, oder wie sie sonst heissen. Weil der
Maulesel weder Pferd noch Esel ist, ist er darum weniger eines von
den nutzbarsten lasttragenden Tieren?

98. *HD*, No. 30; *Werke, 4,* 133: "Das Genie können nur Begebenheiten beschäftigen, die ineinander gegründet sind, nur Ketten von
Ursachen und Wirkungen. Diese auf jene zurückzuführen, jene gegen
diese abzuwägen, überall das Ungefähr auszuschliessen, alles, was

geschieht, so geschehen zu lassen, dass es nicht anders geschehen können: das, das ist seine Sache."

99. *HD,* No. 24; *Werke, 4,* 108: "Die Tragödie ist keine dialogierte
Geschichte."

100. *HD,* No. 32; *Werke, 4,* 141:

> Unzufrieden, ihre Möglichkeit bloss auf die historische Glaub-
> würdigkeit zu gründen, wird er suchen, die Charaktere seiner
> Personen so anzulegen; wird er suchen, die Vorfälle, welche diese
> Charaktere in Handlung setzen, so notwendig einen aus dem an-
> dern entspringen zu lassen; wird er suchen, die Leidenschaften
> nach eines jeden Charakter so genau abzumessen; wird er suchen,
> diese Leidenschaften durch so allmähliche Stufen durchzuführen,
> dass wir überall nichts als den natürlichsten, ordentlichsten Ver-
> lauf wahrnehmen.

101. *HD,* No. 32; *Werke, 4,* 142: "die verborgne Organisation."

102. *HD,* No. 19; *Werke, 4,* 86: "die innere Wahrscheinlichkeit."

103. *HD,* No. 32; *Werke, 4,* 142: "auch uns könne ein ähnlicher
Strom dahin reissen, Dinge zu begehen, die wir bei kaltem Geblüte
noch so weit von uns entfernt zu sein glauben."

104. *HD,* No. 75; *Werke, 4,* 333: "es ist die Furcht, welche aus unserer Ähnlichkeit mit der leidenden Person für uns selbst entspringt
. . . es ist die Furcht, dass wir der bemitleidete Gegenstand selbst werden können."

105. *HD,* No. 75; *Werke, 4,* 335: "Von gleichem Schrot und Korn."
Cf. *eiusdem farinae.*

106. *HD,* No. 75; *Werke, 4,* 334: "eines von den unsrigen."

107. *Zwei Abhandlungen über die Aristotelische Theorie des Drama,*
Berlin, 1880.

108. *HD,* No. 78; *Werke, 4,* 348: "diese Reinigung beruht in nichts
anders als in der Verwandlung der Leidenschaften in tugendhafte
Fertigkeiten."

109. *HD,* No. 2; *Werke, 4,* 11: "Die Schule der moralischen Welt."

110. *HD,* No. 77; *Werke, 4,* 345: "Bessern sollen uns alle Gattungen
der Poesie: es ist kläglich, wenn man dies erst beweisen muss; noch
kläglicher ist es, wenn es Dichter gibt, die selbst daran zweifeln."

111. *Ibid.:* "Aber alle Gattungen können nicht alles bessern, wenigstens nicht jedes so vollkommen wie das andere; was aber jede am
vollkommensten bessern kann, worin es ihr keine andere Gattung
gleich zu tun vermag, das allein ist ihre eigentliche Bestimmung."

112. *HD,* No. 80; *Werke, 4,* 353: "Wozu die saure Arbeit der dramati-
schen Form; wozu ein Theater erbaut, Männer und Weiber verkleidet,
Gedächtnisse gemartert, die ganze Stadt auf einen Platz geladen, wenn

ich mit meinem Werke und mit der Aufführung desselben weiter
nichts hervorbringen will als einige von den Regungen, die eine gute
Erzählung, von jedem zu Hause in seinem Winkel gelesen, ungefähr
auch hervorbringen würde?"

113. *HD*, No. 34; *Werke, 4*, 150:

zu einer anderen Welt; zu einer Welt, deren Zufälligkeiten in
einer andern Ordnung verbunden, aber doch ebenso genau verbunden sind als in dieser; zu einer Welt, in welcher Ursachen und
Wirkungen zwar in einer andern Reihe folgen, aber doch zu eben
der allgemeinen Wirkung des Guten abzwecken; kurz, zu der Welt
eines Genies, das—(es sei mir erlaubt, den Schöpfer ohne Namen
durch sein edelstes Geschöpf zu bezeichnen!) das, sage ich, um das
höchste Genie im kleinen nachzuahmen, die Teile der gegenwärtigen Welt versetzt, vertauscht, verringert, vermehrt, um sich
ein eigenes Ganze daraus zu machen, mit dem es seine eigene
Absichten verbindet.

114. *HD*, No. 79; *Werke, 4*, 351:

Es sei; so wird es seinen guten Grund in dem ewigen unendlichen
Zusammenhange aller Dinge haben. In diesem ist Weisheit und
Güte, was uns in den wenigen Gliedern, die der Dichter heraus-
nimmt, blindes Geschick und Grausamkeit scheint. Aus diesen
wenigen Gliedern sollte er ein Ganzes machen, das völlig sich
rundet, wo eines aus dem andern sich völlig erklärt, wo keine
Schwierigkeit aufstösst, derenwegen wir die Befriedigung nicht in
seinem Plane finden, sondern sie ausser ihm in dem allgemeinen
Plane der Dinge suchen müssen; das Ganze dieses sterblichen
Schöpfers sollte ein Schattenriss von dem Ganzen des ewigen
Schöpfers sein; sollte uns an den Gedanken gewöhnen, wie sich in
ihm alles zum Besten auflöse, werde es auch in jenem geschehen;
und er vergisst diese seine edelste Bestimmung so sehr, dass er
die unbegreiflichen Wege der Vorsicht mit in seinen kleinen
Zirkel flicht und geflissentlich unsern Schauer darüber erregt?—O,
verschont uns damit, ihr, die ihr unser Herz in eurer Gewalt habt!
Wozu diese traurige Empfindung? Uns Unterwerfung zu lehren?
Diese kann uns nur die kalte Vernunft lehren; und wenn die
Lehre der Vernunft in uns bekleiben soll, wenn wir bei unserer
Unterwerfung noch Vertrauen und fröhlichen Mut behalten sollen,
so ist es höchst nötig, dass wir an die verwirrenden Beispiele
solcher unverdienten schrecklichen Verhängnisse so wenig als
möglich erinnert werden. Weg mit ihnen von der Bühne! Weg,
wenn es sein könnte, aus allen Büchern mit ihnen!

115. *HD*, No. 82; *Werke, 4*, 364: "Wir, die Religion und Vernunft

überzeugt haben sollte, dass er ebenso unrichtig als gotteslästerlich ist?"

116. *Aristotle's Theory of Poetry and Fine Art* (2d ed. London, 1898), p. 265.

BIBLIOGRAPHY: STORM AND STRESS, AND HERDER

Gerstenberg's *Briefe über Merkwürdigkeiten der Litteratur* is quoted from ed. Alexander von Weilen in Deutsche Litteraturdenkmale, *29–30*, Stuttgart, 1890. *Rezensionen in der Hamburgischen Neuen Zeitung* is from ed. Otokar Fischer in the same series, *128*, Berlin, 1904. Albert Malte Wagner, *H. W. von Gerstenberg und der Sturm und Drang* (2 vols. Heidelberg, 1920–24) contains a full discussion of the critic. Cf. the introductions to eds. and O. Fischer's "Gerstenberg als Rezensent der Hamburgischen Neuen Zeitung, 1767–1771," *Euphorion, 10* (1903), 57–76.

Hamann's writings are quoted from *Sämtliche Werke*, ed. Josef Nadler, 5 vols. Vienna, 1949–53 (cited as *Werke*). The letters are from *Schriften*, ed. Friedrich Roth, 7 vols. Berlin, 1821–25; Vol. *8* in two pts., of which the second contains a valuable index, 1842–43. An important new life and interpretation is Josef Nadler, *J. G. Hamann*, Salzburg, 1949. The best general book is Rudolf Unger, *Hamann und die Aufklärung* (2 vols. Jena, 1911), to be supplemented by his *Hamanns Sprachtheorie*, Munich, 1905. There are important comments in Carlo Antoni, *La lotta contra la ragione* (Florence, 1942), pp. 125–50. The two discussions in English, Walter Lowrie, *J. G. Hamann: an Existentialist* (Princeton, 1950) and James C. O'Flaherty, *Unity and Language: a Study in the Philosophy of J. G. Hamann* (Chapel Hill, N.C., 1952), are not relevant.

Herder's writings are quoted from the only complete ed., *Sämtliche Werke*, ed. B. Suphan, completed by C. Redlich *et al.*, 33 vols. Berlin, 1877–1913 (cited as Suphan). A selection of Herder's early critical writings is in *Sturm und Drang: kritische Schriften*, ed. Erich Loewenthal, Heidelberg, 1949. The best general book is still Rudolf Haym, *Herder*, 2 vols. Leipzig, 1877–85. A brief survey in English is Alexander Gillies, *Herder*, Oxford, 1945.

Out of the very extensive literature I have found the following most useful:

Robert T. Clark, "Herder's Conception of 'Kraft,'" *PMLA, 57* (1942), 737–52.

Robert T. Clark, "Herder, Cesarotti, and Vico," *SP, 44* (1947), 645–71.

Alexander Gillies, *Herder und Ossian*, Neue Forschung, *19*, Berlin, 1933.

Sigmund Lempicki, *Geschichte der deutschen Literaturwissenschaft* (Göttingen, 1920), pp. 372 ff.

Friedrich Meinecke, *Die Entstehung des Historismus* (2 vols. Munich, 1936), 2, 383–479.

Martin Schütze, "The Fundamental Ideas in Herder's Thought," *MP*, *18* (1920–21), 65–78, 121–302; *19* (1921–22), 113–30, 361–82; *21* (1923–24), 29–48, 113–32.

Martin Schütze, "J. G. Herder," *Monatshefte für den deutschen Unterricht*, *36* (1944), 257–87.

Rudolf Stadelmann, *Der historische Sinn bei Herder*, Halle, 1928.

Gisela Ulrich, *Herders Beitrag zur Deutschkunde*, Würzburg, 1943.

Gottfried Weber, *Herder und das Drama*, Weimar, 1922.

Hans Wolff, "Der junge Herder und die Entwicklungsidee Rousseaus," *PMLA*, *57* (1942), 753–819.

I do not think that F. G. Klopstock requires discussion in our context. K. A. Schleiden, *Klopstocks Dichtungstheorie* (Saarbrücken, 1954), makes large claims for his importance but establishes only that Klopstock embraced current ideas about poetry as moving the soul, appealing to the whole nature of man, etc.

There is a good chapter, "The Revolution in Poetics," in Roy Pascal, *The German Sturm and Drang*, Manchester, 1953.

NOTES: STORM AND STRESS, AND HERDER

1. Jakob M. R. Lenz, *Anmerkungen übers Theater*, Leipzig, 1774. Heinrich Leopold Wagner translated Mercier's *Du Théâtre*, Leipzig, 1776.

2. "Herzensausguss über Volks-Poesie," in *Deutsches Museum* (1776); reprinted e.g. in *Sturm und Drang: Kritische Schriften*, ed. Erich Loewenthal (Heidelberg, 1949), pp. 805–11.

3. "Über die Fülle des Herzens," in *Deutsches Museum* (1777); Loewenthal, *Sturm und Drang*, pp. 791 ff.; p. 798: "Was soll ich von Dir sagen, göttliche Dichtkunst? Du entströmst der Fülle des Herzens."

4. Cf. e.g. the piece on genius in Lavater, *Physiognomische Fragmente* (1775); Loewenthal, pp. 815 ff.

5. *Merkwürdigkeiten*, p. 40: "Eine Blumenlese romantischer Begebenheiten"; p. 42: "Die wunderbare Kraft einer schöpferischen Imagination."

6. *Ibid.*, p. 112: "Weg mit der Classification des Drama. . . . Nennen Sie diese *plays* . . . *history, tragedy, tragicomedy, comedy,* wie Sie wollen: ich nenne sie lebendige Bilder der sittlichen Natur."

7. *Ibid.*, p. 114.

8. *Ibid.*, p. 161: "ich sehe durchaus ein gewisses Ganze, das Anfang, Mittel und Ende, Verhältniss, Absichten, contrastirte Charakter, und contrastirte Groupen hat."

9. *Ibid.*, p. 231: "Ich sage, ein Trauerspiel sei kein Gedicht."

10. *Ibid.*, pp. 131 ff.

11. *Ibid.*, pp. 58 ff., 233 ff.; on puns, pp. 126 ff.

12. *Ibid.*, pp. 215 ff.

13. *Ibid.*, pp. 230, 232: "Unter den witzigen Köpfen giebt es Stufen; unter den dichterischen Genies gar keine. Ein Poet ohne grosses Genie ist gar kein Poet."

14. *Rezensionen in der Hamburgischen Neuen Zeitung*, ed. Fischer, pp. 57, 92, 137, 138, 233. Cf. *Merkwürdigkeiten*, p. 277, on Dryden; p. 326 on *Rambler*.

15. Kanzler von Müller, quoted in H. H. Houben, *J. P. Eckermann* (2 vols. Leipzig, 1925–28), *1*, 288 (a diary entry by Eckermann June 22, 1827): "Diesen Hamann hält Goethe für den grössten Menschen des Jahrhunderts, er setzt ihn sogar über Kant." A letter by Lavater to Zimmermann (March 15, 1775) reports that Goethe asserted Hamann is the author from whom he had learned most. See Ch. Janentzky, *Lavaters Sturm und Drang* (Halle, 1928), p. 96.

16. There are many allusions, mostly to *Hamlet* and Falstaff, "caractère unique"; *Werke*, ed. Nadler, 2, 292, but no discussion.

17. *Werke, 1*, 157: "alle unsere Erkenntnis sinnlich, figürlich." The apparent identification of these two terms gives away the whole theory.

18. *Ibid.*, 2, 197: "Sinne und Leidenschaften reden und verstehen nichts als Bilder. In Bildern besteht der ganze Schatz menschlicher Erkenntniss und Glückseligkeit."

19. *Ibid.:* "Poesie ist die Muttersprache des menschlichen Geschlechts; wie der Gartenbau, älter als der Acker: Malerei,—als Schrift: Gesang,—als Deklamation: Gleichnisse,—als Schlüsse: Tausch, als Handel."

20. Letter to Herder, April, 1765; in *Schriften*, ed. Roth, *3*, 333: "Aber *mythos*, Fabel und Erfindung, scheint mir immer dem *pathos* und Schwung der Empfindungen vorzugehen."

21. Letter to Herder, Dec. 27, 1767; *Schriften, 3*, 378: "Epos und Fabel ist der Anfang, und ausser dem nichts als Ode und Gesang."

22. *Werke, 1*, 241: "Die wahre Poesie ist eine natürliche Art der Prophezeiung."

23. *Ibid.*, *2*, 210–11: "Das Heil kommt von den Juden . . . Durch Wallfahrten nach dem glücklichen Arabien, durch Kreuzzüge nach den Morgenländern . . . Natur und Schrift also sind die Materialien des schönen, schaffenden, nachahmenden Geistes."

24. *Ibid.*, *2*, 215–6, on Latvian people singing while working.

25. Bacon, e.g. *Ibid.*, *2*, 197, 199, 202, 204, 207, 211. Lowth (with the notes of Michaelis) is constantly referred to; *ibid.*, pp. 198, 214, 215.

26. *Ibid.*, *4*, 320: "dieses wahren Lucifers unsers Jahrhunderts." Cf. *ibid.*, *2*, 417: "Le Diable des poètes modernes."

27. *Werke*, *2*, 203 n. Hamann especially attacks George Benson's "Essay Concerning the Unity of Sense [of the Scripture]," prefixed to *A Paraphrase and Notes on the Epistles of St. Paul* (London, 1734).

28. *Werke*, *2*, 217: "Lasst uns jetzt die Hauptsumme seiner neuesten Aesthetik, welche die älteste ist, hören: Fürchtet Gott, und gebt Ihm die Ehre."

29. Letter to Herder, 1760; in *Neue Hamanniana*, ed. H. Weber (Munich, 1905), p. 126: "Meine grobe Einbildungskraft ist niemals imstande gewesen, sich einen schöpferischen Geist ohne *genitalia* vorzustellen."

30. *Werke*, *2*, 294: "*Génie Auteur*, qui sonde toutes choses, mêmes les choses profondes de Dieu."

31. *Ibid.*, *2*, 75: "Was ersetzt bei Homer die Unwissenheit der Kunstregeln, die ein Aristoteles nach ihm erdacht, und was bei einem Shakespear die Unwissenheit oder Übertretung jener kritischen Gesetze? Das Genie ist die einmütige Antwort."

32. *Ibid.*, *2*, 343: "Wer Willkür und Phantasie den schönen Künsten entziehen will, stellt ihrer Ehre und ihrem Leben als ein Meuchelmörder nach."

33. In *Dichtung und Wahrheit*, Bk. 12; *Werke*, *24*, 79 ff.

34. In *Jahrbücher für wissenschaftliche Kritik* (1828), reprinted in Hegel, *Sämtliche Werke*, ed. Glockner, *17*, 38–110.

35. Cf. W. Rodemann, *Hamann und Kierkegaard*, Erlangen, 1922 (dissertation).

36. Cf. B. Croce, *Conversazioni critiche*, ser. 1 (Bari, 1942), pp. 53–58; Unger, *Hamanns Sprachtheorie*.

37. Cf. Croce, "La 'Metacritica' dello Hamann contro la critica kantiana," in *Saggio sullo Hegel* (4th ed. Bari, 1948), pp. 284–306; H. Weber, *Hamann und Kant*, Munich, 1904.

38. Letter to Herder, June 3, 1781; in *Schriften*, ed. Roth, *6*, 194: "Diese Angst in der Welt ist aber der einzige Beweis unserer Heterogeneität . . . kein Heimweh würde uns anwandeln."

39. Unger, *Hamann und die Aufklärung*, Jena, *1*, 274–5, makes much

of Hamann's supposed historicism. Antoni, *La lotta contra la ragione*, p. 130 n., protests with convincing arguments.

40. *Werke*, 2, 164: "Alle ästhetische Thaumaturgie reicht nicht zu, ein unmittelbares Gefühl zu ersetzen."

41. In Unger, *Hamann und die Aufklärung*, *1*, 377 ff., there is a complete list of literary opinions, a study of his reading, etc.

42. Cf. *Werke*, ed. Suphan, 2, 269; *4*, 364, 425; *5*, 33, 44, 117. See Hans Wolff, "Der junge Herder und die Entwicklungsidee Rousseaus," *PMLA*, 57 (1942), 753–819.

43. Cf. Robert T. Clark, "Herder, Cesarotti and Vico," *SP*, *44* (1947), 645–71.

44. Saintsbury, *3*, 355.

45. Suphan, *1*, 247: "Sein Diener, sein Freund, sein unparteiischer Richter! Suche ihn kennen zu lernen und als deinen Herrn auszustudieren; nicht aber dein eigner Herr sein zu wollen . . . Es ist schwer, aber billig, dass der Kunstrichter sich in den Gedankenkreis seines Schriftstellers versetze und aus seinem Geist lese."

46. *Ibid.*, *4*, 311: "Wir kritisieren nicht aus Hedelin, oder Racine, sondern aus unserm Gefühl."

47. *Ibid.*, *24*, 182: "im Geist eines Autors zu *wohnen*, seine *Sprachweise* sich eigen gemacht zu haben, vom Plan und Zweck seines Werks aus dessen eigner Seele gleichsam unterrichtet zu sein."

48. *Ibid.*, *17*, 338: "Niemand hat weniger Zensorgeist, als ich habe. Sonderbar ist's; aber mir gefällt das Meiste, was ich lese . . . Ich bin einmal so gebauet, dass ich allenthalben am liebsten aufsuche und bemerke, was Lobenswert ist, nicht was Tadel verdienet."

49. *Ibid.*, *5*, 330: "wenn schon Kritik über Dichter sein soll, so ist solche einem grossen Original nachtretende, nachempfindende Kritik die beste."

50. *Ibid.*, *8*, 208–9: "dies *lebendige Lesen*, diese Divination in die Seele des Urhebers . . . Solches Lesen ist Wetteifer, *Heuristik* . . . Je mehr man den Verfasser lebendig kennt und mit ihm gelebt hat, desto lebendiger wird dieser Umgang."

51. *Ibid.*, *18*, 131: "Auch die Kritik ist ohne Genius nichts. Nur ein Genie kann das Andre beurteilen und lehren."

52. *Ibid.*, *6*, 34: "Jede gesunde Kritik in der ganzen Welt sagts, dass um ein Stück der Literatur zu verstehen, und auszulegen, man sich ja in den Geist seines Verfassers, seines Publikums, seiner Nation und wenigstens in den Geist dieses seines Stücks setzen müsse."

53. *Ibid.*, *2*, 161: "es bleibt auch die unentbehrlichste Erklärung insonderheit eines Dichters, die Erklärung seiner Zeit und Nationalsitten."

54. *Ibid., 18,* 138: "Die . . . Naturmethode ist, jede Blume an ihrem Ort zu lassen, und dort ganz wie sie ist, nach Zeit und Art, von der Wurzel bis zur Krone zu betrachten. Das demütigste Genie hasset Rangordnung und Vergleichung. Es will lieber der Erste im Dorf sein, als der Zweite nach Caesar. Flechte, Moos, Farrenkraut und die reichste Gewürzblume; jedes blühet an seiner Stelle in *Gottes* Ordnung."

55. *Ibid., 5,* 527: "Aber kein Ding im ganzen Reiche Gottes . . . ist *allein* Mittel—alles *Mittel* und *Zweck* zugleich, und so gewiss auch diese Jahrhunderte."

56. *Ibid., 4,* 166, 163: "Die einzig schöne Kunst unmittelbar für die Seele."

57. *Ibid., 18,* 140: "Auf den inneren Sinn wirket sie, nicht auf das äussere Künstlerauge."

58. *Ibid., 3,* 137. Cf. Robert T. Clark, "Herder's Conception of 'Kraft,' " *PMLA, 57* (1942), 737–52.

59. Suphan, *3,* 144: "Zusammenhängende Bilderbegriffe."

60. *Ibid.,* p. 157: "Ich lerne von Homer, dass die Wirkung der Poesie nie aufs Ohr, durch Töne, nicht aufs Gedächtniss, wie lange ich einen Zug aus der Succession behalte, sondern auf meine Phantasie wirke . . . So stelle ich sie gegen die Malerei, und beklage, dass Hr. L. diesen Mittelpunkt des Wesens der Poesie 'Wirkung auf unsre Seele, Energie,' nicht zum Augenmerke genommen."

61. *Ibid., 27,* 5: "Man lese seine Gedichte nicht mit den Augen allein, sondern höre sie zugleich; oder wo es sein kann, lese man sie laut, einem andern. So wollen lyrische Gedichte gelesen sein; dazu sind sie gearbeitet. Mit dem Klange gehet ihr Geist hervor, Bewegung, Leben."

62. A letter to Merck, October 28, 1770, in Emil Gottfried Herder, *Johann Gottfried Herders Lebensbild* (Erlangen, 1846), *3,* Pt. 1, p. 230: "Sie müssen nur singen, nicht lesen."

63. Suphan, 27, 171: "die *lyrische Poesie* ist *der vollendete Ausdruck einer Empfindung, oder Anschauung im höchsten Wohlklange der Sprache.*"

64. *Ibid., 32,* 62: "Das erstgeborne Kind der Empfindung, der Ursprung der Dichtkunst, und der Keim ihres Lebens ist die *Ode.*"

65. *Ibid., 24,* 369: "Das griechische Theater war Gesang."

66. *Ibid., 9,* 543: "Ein Heldensingspiel."

67. *Ibid., 1,* 148: "Der Genius der Sprache ist also auch der Genius von der Litteratur einer Nation."

68. *Ibid., 5,* 56–7: "Ein Wörterbuch der Seele, was zugleich Mythologie und eine wunderbare Epopee von den Handlungen und Reden

aller Wesen ist! Also eine beständige Fabeldichtung mit Leidenschaft und Interesse!"

69. *Ibid.*, p. 51: "—aus Tönen lebender Natur!—zu Merkmalen seines herrschenden Verstandes!"

70. Expounded in *Vom Erkennen und Empfinden der menschlichen Seele* (1778); Suphan, *8*, 165 ff.

71. *Ibid.*, *8*, 170–1:

> Was wir wissen, wissen wir nur aus Analogie, von der Kreatur zu uns und von uns zum Schöpfer. . . . Ich schäme mich nicht . . . laufe nach Bildern, nach Aehnlichkeiten, nach Gesetzen der Übereinstimmung zu Einem, weil ich kein andres Spiel meiner denkenden Kräfte (wenn ja gedacht werden muss) kenne, und glaube übrigens, dass *Homer* und *Sophokles, Dante, Shakespear* und *Klopstock* der Psychologie und Menschenkenntniss mehr Stoff geliefert haben, als selbst die *Aristoteles* und *Leibnitze* aller Völker und Zeiten. Cf. *ibid.*, *15*, 536.

72. *Ibid.*, *15*, 526: "Unser ganzes Leben ist also gewissermassen *Poetik;* wir sehen nicht, sondern wir erschaffen uns Bilder."

73. *Ibid.*, *12*, 7: "Eine Nachahmung der schaffenden, nennenden Gottheit."

74. *Ibid.:* "der zweite Schöpfer, also auch *poietes,* Dichter."

75. *Ibid.*, *8*, 183–4: "ohne dass ers weiss, malt er die Leidenschaft bis auf die tiefsten Abgründe . . . unvermerkt malt er Hamlet bis auf seine Haare."

76. *Ibid.*, *22*, 200: "eine *Disposition sinnlicher Empfindbarkeiten* eben so wohl, als jener *heilige Trieb,* jene stille *Geisteswärme* gehöre, die *Enthusiasmus,* nicht aber Schwärmerei ist."

77. *Ibid.*, *5*, 380: "Es ist schlechthin unmöglich, dass eine philosophische Theorie des Schönen in allen Künsten und Wissenschaften sein kann, ohne Geschichte."

78. *Ibid.:* "sondern aus vielerlei *Concretis* erwachsene, in vielen Gattungen und Erscheinungen vorkommende Begriffe, in denen also *genesis* Alles ist."

79. *Ibid.*, *15*, 385: "Wollen wir je eine philosophische Poetik oder eine Geschichte der Dichtkunst erhalten: so müssen wir über einzelne Gedichtarten vorarbeiten und jede derselben bis auf ihren Ursprung verfolgen."

80. *Ibid.*, *32*, 86: "denn so wie der Baum aus der Wurzel, so muss der Fortgang und die Blüte einer Kunst aus ihrem Ursprunge sich herleiten lassen. Er enthält in sich das ganze Wesen seines Produktes, so wie in dem Samenkorn die ganze Pflanze mit allen ihren Teilen eingehüllet liegt."

81. *Ibid., 15,* 539: "auch hier zeigt die Entstehung das Wesen der Sache selbst."

82. *Ibid., 18,* 438: "Wo eine *Epigenese,* d.h. ein lebendiger Zuwachs in regelmässiger Gestalt an Kräften und Gliedern stattfinden soll, da muss, wie die ganze Natur zeigt, ein *lebendiger Keim,* ein *Natur- und Kunstgebilde* dasein, dessen Wachstum jetzt alle Elemente freudig fördern. Homer pflanzte einen solchen Keim, ein episches Kunstgebilde. Seine *Familie,* die Schule der Homeriden erzog diesen Baum."

83. E.g. *ibid., 32,* 69.

84. *Ibid., 1,* 335 ff.

85. *Ibid., 6,* 104: "Zur ältesten menschlichen Natur lasset uns zurückkehren und Alles wird sich finden und ordnen."

86. *Ibid., 25,* 11: "nur jetzt! Die Reste aller lebendigen Volksdenkart rollen mit beschleunigtem letzten Sturze in Abgrund der Vergessenheit hinab! Das Licht der sogenannten Kultur frisst, wie der Krebs um sich."

87. *Ibid.,* p. 9: "Wir sind eben am äussersten Rande des Abhanges: ein halb Jahrhundert noch und es ist zu spät!"

88. *Ibid., 1,* 266: "Scythen und Slaven, Wenden und Böhmen, Russen, Schweden und Polen."

89. But he praised *Iphigenie. Ibid., 18,* 113.

90. *Ibid., 1,* 412: "O das verwünschte Wort: Classisch! Es hat uns den Cicero zum Classischen Schulredner; Horaz und Virgil zu Classischen Schulpoeten; Cäsar zum Pedanten, und Livius zum Wortkrämer gemacht."

91. *Ibid., 9,* 522 ff.

92. *Ibid., 5,* 229.

93. *Ibid., 18,* 100–1 n.: "Wenn wir den gelehrten Fleiss betrachten, den die Engländer auf ihre alten Dichter z. B. *Warton* auf *Spenser, Tyrwhit* auf *Chaucer, Percy* auf die Balladen, und so viele, viele der belesensten Männer auf ihren *Shakespeare* und ihr altes Theater gewandt haben; und sodann Uns betrachten—was sagen wir?"

94. *Ibid., 9,* 528:

Aus ältern Zeiten haben wir also durchaus keine lebende Dichterei, auf der unsre neuere Dichtkunst, wie Sprosse auf dem Stamm der Nation gewachsen wäre; dahingegen andre Nationen mit den Jahrhunderten fortgegangen sind, und sich auf eigenem Grunde, aus Nationalprodukten, auf dem Glauben und Geschmack des Volks, aus Resten alter Zeiten gebildet haben. Dadurch ist ihre Dichtkunst und Sprache national worden, Stimme des Volks ist genutzet und geschätzt, sie haben in diesen Dingen weit mehr ein Publikum bekommen, als wir haben. Wir arme Deutsche sind von jeher bestimmt gewesen, nie unser zu bleiben.

95. *Ibid.*, pp. 529–30:

Doch bleibts immer und ewig, dass wenn wir kein Volk haben, wir kein Publikum, keine Nation, keine Sprache und Dichtkunst haben, die unser sei, die in uns lebe und wirke. Da schreiben wir denn nun ewig für Stubengelehrte und eckle Rezensenten, aus deren Munde und Magen wirs denn zurück empfangen, machen Romanzen, Oden, Heldengedichte, Kirchen- und Küchenlieder, wie sie niemand versteht, niemand will, niemand fühlet. Unsre klassische Litteratur ist Paradiesvogel, so bunt, so artig, ganz Flug, ganz Höhe und—ohne Fuss auf die deutsche Erde.

96. *Ibid.*, *25, 323*: "Volk heisst nicht, der Pöbel auf den Gassen, der singt und dichtet niemals, sondern schreit und verstümmelt."

97. *Ibid.*, p. 331.

98. *Die Gedichte Ossians*, German trans. M. Denis (Vienna, 1768), *1*, 35, note *d*. Cf. Suphan, *4*, 325; *5*, 330.

99. See Gillies, *Herder und Ossian*, for fuller discussion.

100. Suphan, *6*, 3, 108, 159.

101. *Ibid.*, *5*, 214–31: "das gleissende, klassische Ding . . . ohne Natur . . . abenteurlich . . . ekel . . . dunkle kleine Symbole zum Sonnenriss einer Theodicee Gottes . . . Nimm dieser Pflanze ihren Boden, Saft und Kraft, und pflanze sie in die Luft: nimm diesem Menschen Ort, Zeit, individuelle Bestandheit—du hast ihm Otem und Seele genommen . . . Jedes Stück ist *History* im weitesten Verstande . . . ein völliges Grösse habende Ereugniss einer Weltbegebenheit, eines menschlichen Schicksals."

102. *Ibid.*, *9, 543*: "[es] werden Zeiten kommen, die da sagen: Wir schlagen *Homer, Virgil* und *Milton* zu, und richten aus Ossian."

103. *Ibid.*, *1, 294*: "den Ursprung, das Wachstum, die Veränderungen und den Fall derselben nebst dem verschiedenen Stil der Gegenden, Zeiten und Dichter lehren."

104. *Ibid.*, *2, 25*: "Wie hat der Geist der Litteratur sich nach den verschiedenen Sprachen geändert, in die er eingetreten? Was nahm er aus allen den Örtern und Gegenden mit, die er verliess? . . . Und was entstand für ein Ding aus der Vermischung und Gährung so verschiedener Materie?"

105. *Ibid.*, p. 112: "Die gemeine Litteraturgeschichte, die mit Gelehrsamkeit beladen, im stillen Gange eines Müllertiers Völker und Zeiten durchschreitet, hat die Augen zu nahe an der Erde, um auch nur etwas überweg schwebende Erscheinungen zu sehen."

106. *Ibid.*, *1, 287*: "Zeit gegen Zeit, Land gegen Land und Genie gegen Genie."

107. *Ibid.*, p. 363: "Solch ein Werk würde den entweiheten Namen:

histoire de l'esprit humain und Geschichte des Menschlichen Verstandes wieder adeln."

108. *Ibid., 18,* 57:

Die ganze Dichterwelt vor und nach ihm verschwand vor meinen Augen; ich sahe nur ihn. Und doch wurde ich bald an die ganze Reihe der Zeiten erinnert, die vor ihm war, die nach ihm folgte. Er hatte gelernt und lehrte; er folgte andern, andre ihm nach. Das Band der Sprache, der Denkart, der Leidenschaften, des Inhalts knüpfte ihn mit mehreren, ja zuletzt mit allen Dichtern: denn—er war ein *Mensch,* er dichtete für *Menschen.* Unvermerkt werden wir also darauf geleitet, zu untersuchen, was jeder gegen jeden Ähnlichen in und ausser seiner Nation, was *seine* Nation gegen *andre* vor- und rückwärts sei; und so ziehet uns eine unsichtbare Kette ins *Pandämonium,* ins *Reich der Geister.*

109. Cf. the naive passage on pure sky, *ibid., 11,* 247.

110. *Ibid., 18,* 446 ff.

111. *Ibid., 14,* 277–80; *Ideen,* Bk. 16.

112. Suphan, *18,* 58: "denn jedes Zeitalter hat seinen Ton, seine Farbe; und es giebt ein eignes Vergnügen, diese im Gegensatz mit andern Zeiten treffend zu charakterisieren."

113. *Ibid.,* p. 107: "Die Italiänische singet; die französische *Prosa-Poesie* raisonniert und erzählet, die Englische in ihrer äusserst unmusikalischen Sprache *denket.*"

114. *Ibid.,* p. 101: "Ein darstellender Minstrel."

115. *Ibid.,* p. 103: "Eintönig, prächtig und edel."

116. *Ibid.,* p. 104: "Ein gothisches Gebäude, unzusammenhängend und unübersehbar in ihren Teilen, übertrieben in Bildern, mit Zierrat überladen."

117. *Ibid.,* p. 50: "Das poetische Meisterwerk dieser Nation."

118. *Ibid.,* p. 53: "das eigentümlichste Genie, dessen Grazie nicht veralten wird, so lange die französische Sprache dauret."

119. *Ibid., 11,* 58: "Aristoteles ist ein fester Knochenmann, wie der Tod: ganz Disposition, ganz Ordnung."

120. *Ibid., 23,* 349–62.

BIBLIOGRAPHY: GOETHE

Goethe's works are quoted from *Sämtliche Werke. Jubiläumsausgabe in 40 Bänden,* ed. Eduard von der Hellen, Stuttgart, 1902–07 (as *Werke*). *Maximen und Reflexionen* is quoted by number from Max Hecker's ed., Weimar, 1907. *Wilhelm Meisters Theatralische Sendung,* ed. Harry Maync, Stuttgart, 1911. Only when these eds. fail is the Weimar ed. (143 vols. 1887–1920) quoted (as Weimar). Eckermann's

Gespräche mit Goethe by date with reference to H. H. Houben's 23d ed. Leipzig, 1948 (cited as Houben). Other conversations are from F. von Biedermann, *Goethes Gespräche*, 5 vols. Leipzig, 1909–11.

Literature on Goethe as a critic is surprisingly meager. Ernst Robert Curtius, "Goethe als Kritiker," in *Kritische Essays zur Europäischen Literatur* (Bern, 1950) is an essay on Goethe's general method rather than on his criticism. I. Rouge, "Goethe critique littéraire," *Revue de littérature comparée, 12* (1932), 99–121, discusses only the genetic method. Oskar Walzel's important introduction to Goethe's *Schriften zur Literatur* (Vols. *36, 37,* and *38* of the *Jubiläumsausgabe*) is largely devoted to a discussion of the sources of his aesthetic concepts. Fritz Strich's *Goethe und die Weltliteratur* (Bern, 1946; Eng. trans. London, 1949) is a book of wide scope on foreign influences on Goethe and on Goethe's influence abroad, which pays some attention to Goethe's criticism. Walther Rehm, *Griechentum und Goethezeit* (1936; 3d ed. Bern, 1952) and Humphry Trevelyan, *Goethe and the Greeks* (Cambridge, 1942) discuss the whole question of the influence of the Greeks on Goethe. James Boyd, *Goethe's Knowledge of English Literature* (Oxford, 1932) and Bertram Barnes, *Goethe's Knowledge of French Literature* (Oxford, 1937) are useful compilations. Hippolyte Loiseau, *Goethe et la France* (Paris, 1930), though of wider scope, also discusses Goethe's criticism of French literature.

On symbol see I. Rouge, "Goethe et la notion du symbole," in *Goethe. Études publiées pour la centenaire de sa mort . . . sous les auspices de l'Université de Strasbourg*, Paris, 1932. Curt Richard Müller, *Die geschichtlichen Voraussetzungen des Symbolbegriffs in Goethes Kunstanschauung* (Leipzig, 1937) is important for the history of the term. Ferdinand Weinhandl, *Die Metaphysik Goethes* (Berlin, 1932), devotes a section to the symbol.

On Goethe's aesthetics there are two older books: Otto Harnack, *Die Klassische Aesthetik der Deutschen* (Leipzig, 1892), and Wilhelm Bode, *Goethes Aesthetik*, Berlin, 1901. Herbert von Einem, "Goethes Kunstphilosophie," in *Goethe und Dürer* (Hamburg, 1947) and Otto Stelzer, *Goethe und die bildende Kunst* (Braunschweig, 1949) are two good recent discussions. There is a good chapter on Goethe's aesthetics in Karl Vietor's *Goethe*, Bern, 1949; Eng. trans., *Goethe the Thinker*, Cambridge, Mass., 1950.

Friedrich Meinecke, in *Die Entstehung des Historismus* (2 vols. Munich, 1936), 2, 480–631, discusses Goethe's relation to history. Other general comments are in E. Cassirer's *Goethe und die geschichtliche Welt* (Berlin, 1932), especially the paper "Goethe und das achtzehnte Jahrhundert"; and in Cassirer's *Freiheit und Form* (Berlin, 1916), pp. 271 ff. Of general books, George Simmel, *Goethe* (Berlin, 1913) and

Ewald A. Boucke, *Goethes Weltanschauung auf historischer Grundlage* (Stuttgart, 1907) are most relevant for my purposes.

In translating I have used, wherever possible, the very convenient collection *Goethe's Critical Essays,* ed. Joel E. Spingarn, New York, 1921.

NOTES: GOETHE

1. Sainte-Beuve, "De la Tradition," *Causeries du lundi, 15,* 363; cf. *Nouveaux Lundis, 3,* 265. M. Arnold, "A French Critic on Goethe," in *Mixed Essays* (New York, 1894), p. 234.

2. *Werke,* ed. von der Hellen, *36,* 4–6:

Die erste Seite, die ich in ihm las, machte mich auf Zeitlebens ihm eigen, und wie ich mit dem ersten Stücke fertig war, stund ich wie ein Blindgeborner, dem eine Wunderhand das Gesicht in einem Augenblicke schenkt . . . Ich zweifelte keinen Augenblick, dem regelmässigen Theater zu entsagen. Es schien mir die Einheit des Orts so kerkermässig ängstlich, die Einheiten der Handlung und der Zeit lästige Fesseln unsrer Einbildungskraft . . . Schäckespears Theater ist ein schöner Raritäten Kasten, in dem die Geschichte der Welt vor unsern Augen an dem unsichtbaren Faden der Zeit vorbeiwallt. Seine Plane sind, nach dem gemeinen Stil zu reden, keine Plane, aber seine Stücke drehen sich alle um den geheimen Punkt (den noch kein Philosoph gesehen und bestimmt hat), in dem das Eigentümliche unsres Ichs, die prätendierte Freiheit unsres Willens mit dem notwendigen Gang des Ganzen zusammenstösst . . . Natur, Natur! nichts so Natur als Schäckespears Menschen . . . Er wetteifferte mit dem Prometheus, bildete ihm Zug vor Zug seine Menschen nach, nur in *kolossalischer Grösse* . . . Erst Intermezzo des Gottesdiensts, dann feierlich politisch, zeigte das Trauerspiel einzelne grosse Handlungen der Väter dem Volk mit der reinen Einfalt der Vollkommenheit, erregte ganze grosse Empfindungen in den Seelen, denn es war selbst ganz und gross. . . . Französchen, was willst du mit der griechischen Rüstung, sie ist dir zu gross und schwer. . . . Auf, meine Herren! trompeten Sie mir alle edle Seelen aus dem Elysium des sogenannten guten Geschmacks!

3. *Ibid.,* pp. 115–6: "Es ist endlich einmal Zeit, dass man aufgehöret hat, über die Form dramatischer Stücke zu reden, über ihre Länge und Kürze, ihre Einheiten, ihren Anfang, ihr Mittel und Ende. . . . Jede Form, auch die gefühlteste, hat etwas Unwahres; allein sie ist ein für allemal das Glas, wodurch wir die heiligen Strahlen der verbreiteten Natur an das Herz der Menschen zum Feuerblick sammeln."

4. *Ibid., 33, 42*: "Anbetung dem Schaffenden."

5. *Ibid.*, p. 40.

6. *Ibid.*, p. 41: "Wer allgemein sein will, wird nichts." *Ibid.*, p. 11: "Diese charakteristische Kunst ist nun die einzige wahre."

7. *Ibid.*, p. 14: "Durch alle Theorie versperrt er sich den Weg zum wahren Genuss."

8. *Ibid.*, p. 18: "Am gaffenden Publikum . . . was liegt an dem? . . . so muss sie (irgendeine spekulative Bemühung) seinem [des Künstlers] natürlichen Feuer Luft machen, dass es um sich greife und tätig erweise."

9. The exact share Goethe had in the reviews is a hotly debated question of Goethe scholarship. See *ibid., 36, 306* ff.

10. *Ibid., 36,* 28: "*Schäkespear,* der den Wert einiger Jahrhunderte in seiner Brust fühlte, dem das Leben ganzer Jahrhunderte durch die Seele webte,—und hier—Komödianten in Zendel und Glanzleinewand, gesudelte Coulissen!"

11. *Ibid.*, p. 18: "Yorick empfand, und dieser setzt sich hin, zu empfinden; Yorick wird von seiner Laune ergriffen, weinte und lachte in einer Minute, und durch die Magie der Sympathie lachen und weinen wir mit; hier aber steht einer und überlegt: wie lache und weine ich? was werden die Leute sagen, wenn ich lache und weine? was werden die Rezensenten sagen?"

12. *Ibid.*, pp. 78–9: "so misst ihr doch überall den Geist, der die Teile so verwebt, dass jeder ein wesentliches Stück vom Ganzen wird. Ebensowenig kann er Szene, Handlung und Empfindung verschmelzen."

13. The MS was discovered as late as 1910.

14. *Wilhelm Meisters Theatralische Sendung,* Bk. 2, ch. 2, pp. 76, 80, 81, 108: "edle Seele," "grosse Ader." "Lüsternheit nach dem Übel und eine dunkle Sehnsucht nach dem Genusse des Schmerzes."

15. *Ibid.*, Bk. 5, ch. 10, p. 326: "Es sind keine Gedichte, man glaubt vor den aufgeschlagnen ungeheuern Büchern des Schicksals zu stehen, in denen der Sturmwind des bewegtesten Lebens saust und sie mit Gewalt rasch hin und wieder blättert."

16. *Ibid.*, Bk. 6, ch. 8, p. 378: "eine grosse Tat auf eine Seele gelegt, die der Tat nicht gewachsen ist . . . Hier wird ein Eichbaum in ein köstliches Gefässe gepflanzt, das nur liebliche Blumen in seinem Schooss hätte aufnehmen sollen; die Wurzeln dehnen sich aus und das Gefäss wird zernichtet. Ein schönes, reines, edles, höchst moralisches Wesen, ohne die sinnliche Stärke, die den Helden macht, geht unter einer Last zu Grunde, die es weder tragen noch abwerfen kann. Jede Pflicht ist ihm heilig, diese zu schwer."

17. *Werke, 17*, 251: "wie will er das, wenn er nicht in den Sinn seines Autors, wenn er nicht in die Absichten desselben einzudringen versteht."

18. *Theatralische Sendung*, Bk. 6, ch. 11, pp. 390–1: "Jetzt, da ihr jede Gewalt über sich selbst entrissen ist, da ihr Herz auf der Zunge schwebt, wird diese Zunge ihre Verräterin, und in der Unschuld des Wahnsinns ergötzt sie sich vor König und Königin an dem Nachklange ihrer lieben losen Lieder der Einsamkeit."

19. *Werke, 18*, 24:

> Das, was diese beiden Menschen sind und tun, kann nicht durch *einen* vorgestellt werden. In solchen Kleinigkeiten zeigt sich Shakespeares Grösse. Dieses leise Auftreten, dieses Schmiegen und Biegen, dies Jasagen, Streicheln und Schmeicheln, diese Behendigkeit, dieses Schwenzeln, diese Allheit und Leerheit, diese rechtliche Schurkerei, diese Unfähigkeit, wie kann sie durch *einen* Menschen ausgedrückt werden? Es sollten ihrer wenigstens ein Dutzend sein, wenn man sie haben könnte; denn sie sind bloss in Gesellschaft etwas, sie sind die Gesellschaft, und Shakespear war sehr bescheiden und weise, dass er nur zwei solche Repräsentanten auftreten liess.

In text, Carlyle's translation, revised.

20. *Theatralische Sendung*, Bk. 6, ch. 10, p. 389: "weit entfernt zu glauben, dass der Plan dieses Stückes zu tadeln sei, halte ich vielmehr dafür, dass kein grösserer jemals ersonnen worden. Ja, er ist nicht ersonnen, er ist so . . . Hier hat der Held keinen Plan, aber das Stück hat einen."

21. *Werke, 18*, 17–8: "Es ist nicht Spreu und Weizen durch einander . . . es ist ein Stamm, Äste, Zweige, Blätter, Knospen, Blüten und Früchte. Ist nicht Eins mit dem Andern und durch das Andere?"

22. *Ibid.*, pp. 41–2: "Wie kann ich ihn am Leben erhalten . . . da ihn das ganze Stück zu Tode drückt?"

23. *Ibid.*, pp. 19–20.

24. F. W. Riemer, *Diary*, December 12, 1811. *Jahrbuch der Sammlung Kippenberg, 3* (1923), 43.

25. "Ein Wort für junge Dichter." Weimar, Pt. 2, *42*, 106: "dass der Künstler von innen heraus wirken müsse, indem er gebärde er sich, wie er will, immer nur sein Individuum zutage fördern wird."

26. *Dichtung und Wahrheit*, Bk. 7; *Werke, 23*, 83: "Bruchstücke einer grossen Confession."

27. Eckermann, *Gespräche, 1*, Sept. 18, 1823; ed. Houben, p. 38: "Gelegenheitsgedichte."

28. Eckermann, *3*, Jan. 2, 1824; Houben, pp. 430–1.

29. On *Werther:* "einem Nachtwandler ähnlich," in *Dichtung und Wahrheit*, Bk. 13; *Werke, 24,* 169. Or Eckermann, *3,* March 14, 1830; Houben, p. 577: "instinktmässig und traumartig."

30. E.g. draft of letter to Melchior Meyr, Jan. 22, 1832; Weimar, Pt. 4, *49,* 418.

31. Weimar, Pt. 1, *47,* 322: "Über den Dilettantismus." See *Maximen und Reflexionen,* ed. M. Hecker (Weimar, 1907), No. 759.

32. Eckermann, *1,* Jan. 28, 1830; Houben, p. 135: "die allgemeine Krankheit der jetzigen Zeit."

33. *Dichtung und Wahrheit,* Bk. 18; *Werke, 25,* 67: "dem Wirklichen eine poetische Gestalt zu geben."

34. "Bedeutende Fördernis durch ein einziges geistreiche Wort," i.e. "gegenständlich" (1823); *Werke, 39,* 48. Johann Christian August Heinroth was a physician who wrote a *Lehrbuch der Anthropologie.*

35. *Italienische Reise,* Sept. 6, 1787; *Werke, 27,* 108: "Diese hohen Kunstwerke sind zugleich als die höchsten Naturwerke von Menschen nach wahren und natürlichen Gesetzen hervorgebracht worden. Alles Willkürliche, Eingebildete fällt zusammen: da ist Notwendigkeit, da ist Gott."

36. "Diderots Versuch"; *Werke, 33,* 213: "Kunstgesetze, die eben so wahr in der Natur des bildenen Genies liegen, als die grosse allgemeine Natur die organischen Gesetze ewig tätig bewahrt."

37. *Werke, 33,* 56:
Gelangt die Kunst durch Nachahmung der Natur, durch Bemühung, sich eine allgemeine Sprache zu machen, durch *genaues und tiefes Studium der Gegenstände selbst* endlich dahin, dass sie die Eigenschaften der Dinge und die Art, *wie* sie bestehen, genau und immer genauer kennen lernt, dass sie die Reihe der Gestalten übersieht und die verschiedenen charakteristischen Formen nebeneinander zu stellen und nachzuahmen weiss, dann wird der *Stil* der höchste Grad . . . so ruht der *Stil* auf den tiefsten Grundfesten der Erkenntnis, auf dem Wesen der Dinge, insofern uns erlaubt ist, es in sichtbaren und greiflichen Gestalten zu erkennen.

38. "Einleitung in die Propyläen," *Werke, 33,* 108: "noch viel seltner, dass ein Künstler sowohl in die Tiefe der Gegenstände als in die Tiefe seines eignen Gemüts zu dringen vermag, um in seinen Werken nicht bloss etwas leicht und oberflächlich Wirkendes, sondern, wetteifernd mit der Natur, etwas Geistig- Organisches hervorzubringen und seinem Kunstwerk einen solchen Gehalt, eine solche Form zu geben, wodurch es natürlich zugleich und übernatürlich erscheint."

39. *Ibid.,* p. 110: "dass wir nur dann mit der Natur wetteifern können, wenn wir die Art, wie sie bei Bildung ihrer Werke verfährt,

ihr wenigstens einigermassen abgelernt haben." Cf. *Maximen,* No. 1105: "Kunst: eine andere Natur."

40. Moritz's tract was reprinted in full by S. Auerbach in *Deutsche Literaturdenkmale des 18. und 19. Jahrhunderts* (Stuttgart, 1888), Vol. *31.* Goethe's abstract is in *Italienische Reise* (1817), under March, 1788. See *Werke, 27,* 253–63. Before, there was a shorter review in *Der Teutsche Merkur,* July, 1789, reprinted in *Werke, 33,* 60 ff.: "Jedes schöne Ganze der Kunst ist im Kleinen ein Abdruck des höchsten Schönen im Ganzen der Natur."

41. Ed. Auerbach, p. 29: "Auf diese Weise entstand, ohne alle Rücksicht auf Nutzen oder Schaden, den es stiften könnte, das Schöne der bildenden Künste in jeder Art, bloss um sein selbst und seiner Schönheit willen." P. 37: "Und von sterblichen Lippen, lässt sich kein erhabneres Wort vom Schönen sagen, als: *es ist!"*

42. Review of *Des Knaben Wunderhorn,* in *Werke, 36,* 261: "die höhere innere Form."

43. Eckermann, *3,* June 20, 1831; Houben, p. 604: "Als ob es ein Stück Kuchen oder Biscuit wäre, das man aus Eiern, Mehl und Zucker zusammenrührt! Eine geistige Schöpfung ist es, das Einzelne wie das Ganze aus *einem* Geiste und Guss und von dem Hauche *eines* Lebens durchdrungen."

44. To Adam Müller, August 28, 1807, in *Goethe und die Romantik,* ed. Schüddekopf-Walzel (2 vols. Weimar, 1898–99), *2,* 68–9: "Nach meiner Einsicht scheiden sich Antikes und Modernes auf diesem Wege mehr als dass sie sich vereinigten. Wenn man die beiden entgegengesetzten Enden eines lebendigen Wesen durch Contorsion zusammenbringt, so giebt das noch keine neue Art von Organisation; es ist allenfalls nur ein wunderliches Symbol, wie die Schlange, die sich in den Schwanz beisst."

45. Eckermann, *1,* April 5, 1829; Houben, p. 269: "Die Säfte sind Teilen überflüssig zugeleitet, die sie nicht haben wollen, und andern, die sie bedurft hätten, sind sie entzogen. Das Süjet war gut, sehr gut, aber die Szenen, die ich erwartete, waren nicht da, und andere, die ich nicht erwartete, waren mit Fleiss und Liebe behandelt." Houben (p. 808) suggests Wilhelm Waiblinger's *Anna Bullen* as the target of Goethe's remarks.

46. *Werke, 38,* 21: "Schauder und Abscheu, wie ein von der Natur schön intentionierter Körper, der von einer unheilbaren Krankheit ergriffen wäre."

47. Eckermann, Jan. 29, 1826; Houben, p. 137: "ein reiner Mensch . . . es ist an ihm nichts verbogen und verbildet."

48. To Zelter, October 30, 1808; Weimar, Pt. 4, *20,* 192: "Werner,

69. "Anmerkungen zu Rameaus Neffen," *Werke, 34,* 165–6.

70. *Werke, 37,* 48: "possenhafte Intermezzisten." To Caroline von Wolzogen, Jan. 28, 1812; Weimar, Pt. 4, 22, 246: "disharmonische Allotria."

71. "Shakespeare und kein Ende" (1813–16), in *Werke, 37,* 46: "So gehört Shakespeare notwendig in die Geschichte der Poesie; in der Geschichte des Theaters tritt er nur zufällig auf."

72. Eckermann, *1,* Dec. 25, 1825; Houben, p. 133: "Er ist kein Theaterdichter, an die Bühne hat er nie gedacht, sie war seinem grossen Geiste viel zu enge."

73. Eckermann, *1,* July 26, 1826; Houben, p. 143: "Shakespeare ist ein grosser Psychologe und man lernt aus seinen Stücken wie den Menschen zu Mute ist."

74. Eckermann, *3,* April 18, 1827; Houben, p. 496: "er sah seine Stücke als ein Bewegliches, Lebendiges an, das von den Brettern herab den Augen und Ohren rasch vorüberfliessen würde, das man nicht festhalten und im Einzelnen bekritteln könnte, und wobei es bloss darauf ankam, immer nur im gegenwärtigen Moment wirksam und bedeutend zu sein."

75. To Kleist, Feb. 1, 1808; in *Goethe und die Romantik,* ed. Schüddekopf-Walzel, 2, 74–5: "Ein Jude der auf den Messias, ein Christ, der aufs neue Jerusalem, und ein Portugiese, der auf den Dom Sebastian wartet . . . Vor jedem Brettergerüste möchte ich dem wahrhaft theatralischen Genie sagen: *hic Rhodus, hic salta!* Auf jedem Jahrmarkt getraue ich mir, auf Bohlen über Fässer geschichtet, mit Calderons Stücken, *mutatis mutandis,* der gebildeten und ungebildeten Masse Vergnügen zu machen."

76. To Riemer, Dec. 26, 1813; Biedermann, 2, 221: "Eigentlich ist das, was nicht gefällt, das Rechte. Die neue Kunst verdirbt, weil sie gefallen will."

77. "Über strenge Urteile," *Werke, 33,* 100.

78. To Zelter, June 18, 1831; Weimar, Pt. 4, *48,* 241: "die Gemeinschaft der Heiligen." Cf. to Cotta, Nov. 17, 1800; Weimar, Pt. 4, *15,* 143 ff.

79. To Zelter, July 13, 1804; Weimar, Pt. 4, *17,* 151: "dass der echte Künstler oft einsam in Verzweiflung lebt."

80. To Zelter, Jan. 29, 1830; Weimar, Pt. 4, *46,* 222: "*Wir* kämpfen für die Vollkommenheit eines Kunstwerkes, in und an sich selbst, jene denken an dessen Wirkung nach aussen, um welche sich der wahre Künstler gar nicht bekümmert, so wenig als die Natur, wenn sie einen Löwen oder einen Kolibri hervorbringt."

81. To Herder, May 17, 1787, in *Italienische Reise; Werke, 27,* 4: "*sie* stellten die Existenz dar, *wir* gewöhnlich den Effekt; *sie* schilderten

das Fürchterliche, *wir* schildern fürchterlich; *sie* das Angenehme, *wir* angenehm, u.s.w."

82. "Nachlesse zu Aristoteles' Poetik," *Werke, 38,* 84–5.

Hat nun der Dichter an seiner Stelle seine Pflicht erfüllt, einen Knoten bedeutend geknüpft und würdig gelöst, so wird dann dasselbe in dem Geiste des Zuschauers vorgehen: die Verwicklung wird ihn verwirren, die Auflösung aufklären, er aber um nichts gebessert nach Hause gehen; er würde vielmehr, wenn er asketisch aufmerksam genug wäre, sich über sich selbst verwundern, dass er eben so leichtsinnig als hartnäckig, eben so heftig als schwach, eben so liebevoll als lieblos sich wieder in seiner Wohnung findet, wie er hinausgegangen.

83. To Zelter, Jan. 29, 1830; Weimar, Pt. 4, *46,* 223.

84. *Dichtung und Wahrheit,* Bk. 13; *Werke, 24,* 172: "das alte Vorurteil, dass es nämlich einen didaktischen Zweck haben müsse."

85. "Über das Lehrgedicht," *Werke, 38,* 71–2: "ein Werk aus Wissen und Einbildungskraft zusammenzuweben, zwei einander entgegengesetzte Elemente in einen lebendigen Körper zu verbinden. . . . Alle Poesie soll belehrend sein, aber unmerklich; sie soll den Menschen aufmerksam machen, wovon sich zu belehren wert wäre; er muss die Lehre selbst daraus ziehen wie aus dem Leben."

86. *Dichtung und Wahrheit,* Bk. 12; *Werke, 24,* 111–12: "Ein gutes Kunstwerk kann und wird zwar moralische Folgen haben, aber moralische Zwecke vom Künstler fordern, heisst ihm sein Handwerk verderben."

87. To Beuth, Feb. 22, 1831; Weimar, Pt. 4, *48,* 126: "Hier erscheint die Kunst vollkommen selbständig, indem sie sich sogar unabhängig erweist von dem, was dem edeln Menschen das Höchste und Verehrungswürdigste bleibt, von der Sittlichkeit. Will sie sich aber völlig frei erklären, so muss sie ihre eigenen Gesetze entschieden aussprechen."

88. *Maximen,* No. 61: "Die Kunst an und für sich selbst ist edel; desshalb fürchtet sich der Künstler nicht vor dem Gemeinen. Ja indem er es aufnimmt, ist es schon geadelt."

89. Cf. letter to Zauper, Sept. 7, 1821 (Weimar, Pt. 4, *35,* 73 f.) praising him for defending the moral of *Wahlverwandschaften.* On Sterne: "Lorenz Sterne" (1827), in *Werke, 38,* 85. *Maximen,* Nos. 773–87. Letters to Zelter, Dec. 25, 1829 (Weimar, Pt. 4, *46,* 193–4) and Oct. 5, 1830 (*ibid., 47,* 274). On Grübel: *Werke, 36,* 152 ff.

90. *Theatralische Sendung,* Bk. 2, ch. 3, p. 88: "zugleich Lehrer, Wahrsager, Freund der Götter und der Menschen."

91. "Noten und Abhandlungen zum West-östlichen Divan," Dsche-

lâl-eddîn Rumi; *Werke, 5,* 184: "endlich sein Talent am liebsten zu Preis und Verherrlichung Gottes anwendet."

92. See the elaborate discussion in F. Meinecke, *Die Entstehung des Historismus* (Munich, 1936), *2,* 544 ff.

93. To Jacobi, Jan. 2, 1800; Weimar, Pt. 4, *15,* 6: "Dabei kam mir zu statten dass ich von jeher, beim Anschauen der Gegenstände, auf dem genetischen Wege mich am besten befand."

94. To Zelter, August 4, 1803; *ibid., 16,* 265: "Natur- und Kunstwerke lernt man nicht kennen wenn sie fertig sind; man muss sie im Entstehen aufhaschen, um sie einigermassen zu begreifen."

95. To Karl August, Dec. 5, 1826; *ibid., 41,* 245.

96. To Herder, May 17, 1787. In *Italienische Reise; Werke, 27,* 5: "nun ist mir erst die *Odyssee* ein lebendiges Wort." P. 4: "Die Beschreibungen, die Gleichnisse etc. kommen uns poetisch vor und sind doch unsäglich natürlich."

97. "Noten und Abhandlungen zum West-östlichen Divan," "Urelemente orientalischer Poesie," "Lebensbezüge"; *Werke, 5,* 213.

98. "Literarischer Sansculottismus" (1795); *Werke, 36,* 141-3: "Wir wollen die Umwälzungen nicht wünschen, die in Deutschland klassische Werke vorbereiten könnten . . . eine unsichtbare Schule."

99. Biedermann, *2,* 226; May 19, 1814, to Riemer: "Goethe war mit ihrem Urteil über seine Sachen unzufrieden, da sie ihm nicht nachkommen könne und seine Sachen fragmentarisch erschienen."

100. Eckermann, *3,* May 3, 1827; Houben, p. 497: "Als einer der das Metier aus dem Grunde kennt, zeigt er die Verwandtschaft des Erzeugten mit dem Erzeuger, und beurteilt die verschiedenen poetischen Produktionen als verschiedene Früchte verschiedener Lebensepochen des Dichters."

101. "Über die neue Ausgabe der Goethischen Werke" (1816), *Werke, 37,* 83: "Den Schriftsteller in den Schriften aufsuchend, die stufenweise Entwicklung seiner geistigen Bildung zu entdecken bemüht ist."

102. To Wilhelm von Humboldt, Dec. 1, 1831; Weimar, Pt. 4, *49,* 165: "dass in meinen hohen Jahren mir alles mehr und mehr historisch wird . . . ja ich erscheine mir selbst immer mehr und mehr geschichtlich."

103. Eckermann, *2,* March 21, 1830; Houben, pp. 322-3:
Ich hatte in der Poesie die Maxim des objektiven Verfahrens, und wollte nur dieses gelten lassen. Schiller aber, der ganz subjektiv wirkte, hielt seine Art für die rechte, und, um sich gegen mich zu wehren, schrieb er den Aufsatz über naive und sentimentale Dich-

tung. . . . Die Schlegel ergriffen die Idee und trieben sie weiter, so dass sie sich denn jetzt über die ganze Welt ausgedehnt hat, und nun jedermann von Classicismus und Romanticismus redet, woran vor fünfzig Jahren niemand dachte.

104. "Shakespeare und kein Ende," *Werke, 37,* 41.

105. Eckermann, 2, April 2, 1829; Houben, pp. 263–4: "Und da sind die Nibelungen classisch wie der Homer, denn beide sind gesund und tüchtig. Das meiste Neuere, ist nicht romantisch, weil es neu, sondern weil es schwach, kränklich und krank ist, und das Alte ist nicht classisch, weil es alt, sondern weil es stark, frisch, froh, und gesund ist." Cf. *Maximen,* Nos. 1031, 1034.

106. Conversation with Riemer, August 28, 1808; Biedermann, *1,* 534.

107. "Shakespeare und kein Ende," *Werke, 37,* 41–2.

108. Cf. examples in Boucke, *Goethes Weltanschauung,* esp. pp. 406 ff.

109. *Werke, 38,* 97: "es bilde sich eine allgemeine Weltliteratur, worin uns Deutschen eine ehrenvolle Rolle vorbehalten ist."

110. *Werke, 38,* 137: "Eine jede Literatur ennuyiert sich zuletzt in sich selbst, wenn sie nicht durch fremde Teilnahme wieder aufgefrischt wird."

111. "Edinburgh Reviews"; *Werke, 38,* 170: "nur wiederholen wir, dass nicht die Rede sein könne, die Nationen sollen überein denken, sondern sie sollen nur einander gewahr werden, sich begreifen und, wenn sie sich wechselseitig nicht lieben mögen, sich einander wenigstens dulden lernen."

112. "Aus Makariens Archiv"; *Werke, 38,* 278: "Jetzt, da sich eine Weltliteratur einleitet, hat genau besehen der Deutsche am meisten zu verlieren; er wird wohltun, dieser Warnung nachzudenken."

113. Cf. e.g. the review of J. P. Hebel, *Alemannische Gedichte,* in *Werke, 36,* 236 ff.; of Grübel, *Gedichte in Nürnberger Mundart,* in *37,* 244 ff.; of *Des Knaben Wunderhorn,* in *37,* 247 ff., etc.

114. *Werke, 38,* 111 ff., 154, 199 ff.

115. *Ibid.,* p. 55: "denn eigentlich gibt es nur *eine* Dichtung, die echte, sie gehört weder dem Volke noch dem Adel, weder dem König noch dem Bauer; wer sich als wahrer Mensch fühlt, wird sie ausüben; sie tritt unter einem einfachen, ja rohen Volke unwiderstehlich hervor, ist aber gebildeten, ja hochgebildeten Nationen nicht versagt."

116. Eckermann, *1,* Jan. 31, 1827; Houben, p. 181:
Aber auch bei solcher Schätzung des Ausländischen dürfen wir nicht bei etwas Besonderen haften bleiben und dieses für musterhaft ansehen wollen. Wir müssen nicht denken, das Chinesische

wäre es, oder das Serbische, oder Calderon, oder die Nibelungen;
sondern im Bedürfniss von etwas Musterhaften müssen wir immer
zu den alten Griechen zurückgehen, in deren Werken stets der
schöne Mensch dargestellt ist. Alles übrige müssen wir nur historisch betrachten und das Gute, so weit es gehen will, uns daraus
aneignen.

117. "Antik und Modern" (1818); *Werke, 35,* 132: "Der Parnass ist
ein Montserrat, der viele Ansiedelungen in mancherlei Etagen erlaubt;
ein jeder gehe hin, versuche sich, und er wird eine Stätte finden, es sei
auf Gipfeln oder in Winkeln."

118. "Noten und Abhandlungen zum West-östlichen Divan," "Übergang von Tropen zu Gleichnissen"; *Werke, 5,* 214.

119. Review of Manzoni's *Conte di Carmagnola; Werke, 37,* 180:
"Jene ist sehr leicht; denn man darf sich nur irgend einen Massstab,
irgend ein Musterbild, so borniert sie auch seien, in Gedanken auf-
stellen, sodann aber kühnlich versichern: vorliegendes Kunstwerk passe
nicht dazu, tauge deswegen nichts, die Sache sei abgetan, und man
dürfe, ohne weiteres, seine Forderung als unbefriedigt erklären; und
so befreit man sich von aller Dankbarkeit gegen den Künstler.—Die
produktive Kritik ist um ein gutes Teil schwerer; sie fragt: Was hat
sich der Autor vorgesetzt? ist dieser Vorsatz vernünftig und verständig?
und inwiefern ist es gelungen, ihn auszuführen? Werden diese Fragen
einsichtig und liebevoll beantwortet, so helfen wir dem Verfasser
nach."

120. "Für Freunde der Tonkunst, von F. Rochlitz"; *Werke, 37,* 279–
80: "Wohlwollende Leser geben mir schon lange zu, dass ich, anstatt
über Bücher zu urteilen, den Einfluss ausspreche, den sie auf mich
haben mochten. Und im Grund ist dies doch das Urteil aller Lesenden,
wenn sie auch ihre Meinung und Gesinnung dem Publikum nicht
mitteilen."

121. Original dedication to *Sardanapalus* (1821).

122. On *Manfred; Werke, 37,* 184. On *Don Juan; 37,* 189: "Ein
grenzenlos-geniales Werk, menschenfeindlich bis zur herbsten Grausamkeit, menschenfreundlich in die Tiefen süssester Neigung sich ver-
senkend." Letter to Boisserée, March 23, 1820; Weimar, Pt. 4, *32,* 205:
"verrückter und grandioser als seine übrigen [Gedichte]."

123. *Tag- und Jahreshefte* (1816); *Werke, 30,* 293: "hypochondrische
Leidenschaft und heftiger Selbsthass." Eckermann, *1,* Dec. 25, 1825;
Houben, p. 134: "Verhaltne Parlamentsreden." Eckermann, *1,* Jan. 18,
1825; Houben, p. 111: "Aber Lord Byron ist nur gross wenn er dichtet,
sobald er reflektiert, ist er ein Kind."

124. Biedermann, *3,* 23: "Er würde mich immerfort amüsieren, aber

ich kann nichts aus ihm lernen. Ich habe nur Zeit für das Vortrefflichste."
Compared to Byron, "Walter Scott ist nichts neben ihm." *Ibid.*, p. 21.

125. Saintsbury, *3*, 375–7. Saintsbury protests against Goethe's saying
of Paul Fleming, "er kann jetzt nichts mehr helfen" (Eckermann, *1*,
Jan. 4, 1827; Houben, p. 157). But Goethe's view is sound enough,
considering that he speaks as a practicing poet.

BIBLIOGRAPHY: KANT AND SCHILLER

Kant's *Kritik der Urteilskraft* is quoted from Karl Vorländer's ed.,
6th reprint, Leipzig, 1924. From the enormous literature I found Hermann Cohen, *Kants Begründung der Aesthetik* (Berlin, 1889) and G.
Denckmann, *Kants Philosophie des Aesthetischen* (Heidelberg, 1947)
most useful for my limited purpose. There are full discussions in V.
Basch, *Essai sur l'esthétique de Kant*, 2d ed. Paris, 1927 (diffuse, exposi-
tory); H. W. Cassirer, *A Commentary on Kant's Critique of Judgment*,
London, 1938; and Luigi Pareyson, *L'estetica dell'idealismo tedesco*,
Vol. *1* with title *Kant, Schiller, Fichte*, Torino, 1950. On the sources see
O. Schlapp, *Kants Lehre vom Genie und die Entstehung der Kritik der
Urteilskraft*, Göttingen, 1901, and Bäumler.

Schiller's writings are quoted from *Sämtliche Werke*, ed. Otto
Güntter and Georg Witkowski, 20 vols. Leipzig, 1909–11 (cited as *SW*).
Schiller's letters are quoted from *Briefe*, ed. F. Jonas, 7 vols. Leipzig,
1892–96 (cited as Jonas).

Of the extensive literature the two items professedly devoted to his
criticism are of little value: Otto Pietsch, *Schiller als Kritiker*, dissertation, Königsberg, 1898; and Marta Weber, "Schiller als Kritiker," in
Dichtung und Forschung. Festschrift für Emil Ermatinger (Frauenfeld,
1933), pp. 74–87. Saintsbury's short treatment in *3*, 377–84, is thin and
prejudiced and ignores almost all the important ideas.

Most useful is Victor Basch, *La Poétique de Schiller* (2d ed. Paris,
1911), a discussion of Schiller's *Naive and Sentimental Poetry* largely
from a positivistic and psychologistic point of view. Another good exposition is Heinrich Meng, *Schillers Abhandlung über naive und
sentimentalische Dichtung*, Frauenfeld, 1936.

Georg Lukács, "Schillers Theorie der modernen Literatur" and
"Der Briefwechsel zwischen Schiller und Goethe," both in *Goethe und
seine Zeit* (Bern, 1947), pp. 48–77 and 77–109, contain brilliant criticism from a Marxist point of view.

Hermann Oertel, *Schillers Theorie der Tragödie* (Dresden, 1934)
and E. L. Stahl, "The Genesis of Schiller's Theory of Tragedy," in

German Studies Presented to Professor H. G. Fiedler (Oxford, 1938), pp. 403–23, are useful.

Melitta Gerhard, *Schiller* (Bern, 1950) is a good general book emphasizing Schiller's aesthetics. William Witte, *Schiller* (Oxford, 1949), and E. L. Stahl, *Friedrich Schiller's Drama* (Oxford, 1954), are general books in English.

NOTES: KANT AND SCHILLER

1. *Kritik der Urteilskraft* (1790), p. 181 (the page numbering of the first edition is reproduced in reprints, e.g. ed. K. Vorländer, Leipzig, 1948): "Genie ist das Talent (Naturgabe), welches der Kunst Regel gibt."

2. *Ibid.,* p. 237: "das übersinnliche Substrat der Erscheinungen."

3. Hegel, *Sämtliche Werke, 1,* 272: "Es ist der Geist der kantischen Philosophie, ein Bewusstsein über diese höchste Idee zu haben, aber sie ausdrücklich wieder auszurotten."

4. *Kritik der Urteilskraft,* pp. 215, 205; "redende Künste."

5. *Ibid.,* p. 194: "Der Dichter wagt es, Vernunftsideen von unsichtbaren Wesen, das Reich der Seligen, das Höllenreich, die Ewigkeit, die Schöpfung u. dgl. zu versinnlichen."

6. *Sämtliche Werke,* ed. Güntter, *18,* 83: "In einem wahrhaft schönen Kunstwerk soll der Inhalt nichts, die Form aber alles tun . . . Darin also besteht das eigentliche Kunstgeheimniss des Meisters, *dass er den Stoff durch die Form vertilgt.*"

7. *SW, 18,* 100: "Eine wirkliche Vereinigung und Auswechselung der Materie mit der Form."

8. *SW, 18,* 55: "Lebende Gestalt."

9. *Briefe,* ed. Jonas, *2,* 200; to Caroline von Beulwitz, January 3, 1789: "Die übertriebene Behauptung, dass ein Produkt aus dem Reiche des Schönen ein vollendetes rundes Ganze sein müsse; fehlte nur ein einziger *Radius* zu diesem Zirkel, so sinke es unter das Unnütze herunter. Nach diesem Ausspruch haben wir kein einziges vollkommenes Werk, und so bald auch keines zu gewarten."

10. Jonas, *6,* 339; to Christian G. Schütz, January 22, 1802: "Ein poetisches Werk muss, in so fern es, auch nur *in hypothesi,* ein in sich selbst organisiertes Ganze ist, aus sich selbst heraus, und nicht aus allgemeinen, und eben darum hohlen, Formeln beurteilt werden."

11. Jonas, *5,* 167; to Goethe, April 4, 1797: "Der ganze *Cardo rei* in der Kunst liegt, eine *poet*ische Fabel zu erfinden."

12. Jonas, *5,* 187; to Goethe, May 5, 1797: "ein wahrer Höllen-

richter für alle, die entweder an der äussern Form sklavisch hängen, oder die über alle Form sich hinwegsetzen."

13. Jonas, *5, 393, 394, 397;* to Humboldt, June 27, 1798: "Es ist ja überhaupt noch die Frage, ob die Kunstphilosophie dem Künstler etwas zu sagen hat . . . Ich wäre . . . zuweilen unphilosophisch genug, Alles, was ich selbst und andere von der Elementarästhetik wissen, für einen einzigen empirischen Vorteil, für einen Kunstgriff des Handwerks hinzugeben . . . dass wir die *Metaphysik* der Kunst zu unmittelbar auf die Gegenstände anwenden und sie als ein praktisches Werkzeug, wozu sie doch nicht gut geschickt ist, handhaben."

14. Jonas, *6, 332–3;* to Goethe, January 20, 1802: "Da von allgemeinen hohlen Formeln zu einem bedingten Fall kein Übergang ist. . . . man sieht aber daraus, dass, die *Philosophie* und die Kunst sich noch gar nicht ergriffen und wechselseitig durchdrungen haben, und vermisst mehr als jemals ein *Organon,* wodurch beide vermittelt werden können."

15. *SW, 17,* 517. Cf. pp. 535–6.

16. *SW, 17,* 481: *Sie* sind, was wir waren; sie sind, was wir wieder werden sollen. Wir waren Natur wie sie, und unsere Kultur soll uns, auf dem Wege der Vernunft und der Freiheit, zur Natur zurückführen."

17. *SW, 17,* 505: "Dieser Weg, den die neueren Dichter gehen, ist übrigens derselbe, den der Mensch überhaupt sowohl im Einzelnen als im Ganzen einschlagen muss. Die Natur macht ihn mit sich eins, die Kunst trennt und entzweit ihn, durch das Ideal kehrt er zur Einheit zurück."

18. *SW, 17,* 501: "Ariost, der Bürger einer späteren und von der Einfalt der Sitten abgekommenen Welt, kann bei der Erzählung dieses Vorfalls seine eigene Verwunderung, seine Rührung nicht verbergen. Das Gefühl des Abstandes jener Sitten von denjenigen, die sein Zeitalter charakterisieren, überwaltigt ihn. Er verlässt auf einmal das Gemälde des Gegenstandes und erscheint in eigener Person." Schiller quotes *Orlando Furioso, 1, 22.*

19. *SW, 17,* 499–500: "[Es] empörte mich seine Kälte, seine Unempfindlichkeit, die ihm erlaubte, im höchsten Pathos zu scherzen, die herzzerschneidenden Auftritte im *Hamlet,* im *König Lear,* im *Macbeth,* usf. durch einen Narren zu stören . . . Ich war noch nicht fähig, die Natur aus der ersten Hand zu verstehen . . . Wie die Gottheit hinter dem Weltgebäude, so steht er hinter seinem Werk; *er* ist das Werk und das Werk ist *er.*"

20. *SW, 17,* 502:

Dichter von dieser naiven Gattung sind in einem künstlichen Weltalter nicht so sehr mehr an ihrer Stelle. Auch sind sie in demselben kaum mehr möglich, wenigstens auf keine andere Weise möglich, als dass sie in ihrem Zeitalter *wild laufen,* und durch ein günstiges Geschick vor dem verstümmelndem Einfluss desselben geborgen werden. Aus der Sozietät selbst können sie nie und nimmer hervorgehen; aber ausserhalb derselben erscheinen sie noch zuweilen, doch mehr als Fremdlinge, die man anstaunt, und als ungezogene Söhne der Natur, an denen man sich ärgert.

21. *SW, 17,* 507: "Kunst der Begrenzung" vs. "Kunst des Unendlichen."

22. *SW, 17,* 310, in a note to Wilhelm von Humboldt's treatise "Über das Studium des Altertums und des griechischen insbesondere" (1793).

23. *SW, 17,* 547–8.

24. *SW, 19,* 215–7: "Durch den Fortschritt der sittlichen Kultur und den milderen Geist unsrer Zeiten unterstützt . . . die schönere Humanität unserer neueren Sitten."

25. *SW, 17,* 504: "Der Menschheit ihren möglichst vollständigen Ausdruck zu geben."

26. *SW, 17,* 545: "Eine formreiche Natur, eine dichterische Welt, eine naive Menschheit."

27. *SW, 19,* 240, 242: "ein Dichter nehme sich ja in acht, mitten im Schmerz den Schmerz zu besingen . . . Aus der sanfteren und fernenden Erinnerung mag er dichten, niemals unter der gegenwärtigen Herrschaft des Affekts . . . hatte er damit anfangen müssen, sich selbst fremd zu werden, den Gegenstand seiner Begeisterung von seiner Individualität loszuwickeln . . . Nur die heitere, die ruhige Seele gebiert das Vollkommene."

28. *SW, 17,* 558: "Der erschöpfte Geschäftsmann."

29. *SW, 17,* 560–1:

Eine Klasse von Menschen . . . welche, ohne zu arbeiten, tätig ist, und idealisieren kann, ohne zu schwärmen . . . Nur eine solche Klasse kann das schöne Ganze menschlicher Natur, welches durch jede Arbeit augenblicklich, und durch ein arbeitendes Leben anhaltend zerstört wird, aufbewahren, und, in allem, was rein menschlich ist, durch ihre Gefühle dem allgemeinen Urteil Gesetze geben. Ob eine solche Klasse wirklich existiere, oder vielmehr, ob diejenige, welche unter ähnlichen äusseren Verhältnissen wirklich existiert, diesem Begriffe auch im Inneren entspreche, ist eine andre Frage, mit der ich hier nichts zu schaffen habe.

30. Jonas, *3,* 113; to Körner, November 1, 1790: "Seine Philosophie mag ich auch nicht ganz: sie holt zu viel aus der Sinnenwelt, wo ich

aus der Seele hole. Überhaupt ist seine Vorstellungsart zu sinnlich und *betastet* mir zu viel."

31. Goethe to Schiller, August 27, 1794; Weimar, Pt. 4, *10*, 183–4: "Ihr Brief, in welchem Sie . . . die Summe meiner Existenz ziehen."

32. Jonas, *3*, 472–3; to Goethe, August 24, 1794:
> Ihr beobachtender Blick . . . Ihre richtige Intuition . . . Dadurch, dass Sie in der Natur gleichsam nacherschaffen, suchen Sie in seine verborgene *Technik* einzudringen . . . Wären Sie als ein Grieche, ja nur als ein Italiener geboren worden, und hätte schon von der Wiege an eine auserlesene Natur und eine idealisierende Kunst Sie umgeben, so wäre Ihr Weg unendlich verkürzt, vielleicht ganz überflüssig gemacht worden . . . Nun, da Sie ein Deutscher geboren sind, da Ihr griechischer Geist in diese nordische Schöpfung geworfen wurde, so blieb Ihnen keine andere Wahl, als entweder selbst zum nordischen Künstler zu werden, oder Ihrer *Imagination* das, was ihr die Wirklichkeit vorenthielt, durch Nachhülfe der Denkkraft zu ersetzen, und so gleichsam von innen heraus und auf einem *rationalen* Wege ein Griechenland zu gebären.

33. Jonas, *3*, 481; to Goethe, August 31, 1794: "Die denkenden Kräfte auf die Imagination . . . seine Anschauung zu generalisieren, seine Empfindung gesetzgebend zu machen . . . Mein Verstand wirkt eigentlich mehr symbolisierend, und so schwebe ich, als eine Zwitterart, zwischen dem Begriff und der Anschauung, zwischen der Empfindung, zwischen dem technischen Kopf und dem Genie."

34. *SW, 17*, 528: "Die sinnliche Wahrheit der Dinge."

35. Jonas, *7*, 65; to Humboldt, August 18, 1803.

36. *SW, 17*, 554.

37. Jonas, *6*, 59; to Goethe, July 19, 1799: "Der Gipfel moderner Unform und Unnatur."

38. Jonas, *6*, 270; to Körner, April 27, 1801: "Nichts Gebildetes, und voll Geschwätze."

39. Jonas, *5*, 241; to Goethe, August 17, 1797: "Ob es nur der Mangel einer aesthetischen Nahrung und Einwirkung von aussen und die *Opposition* der *empirischen* Welt in der sie leben . . ."

40. *SW, 17*, 518–9 n.

41. *SW, 17*, 524 n.

42. *SW, 17*, 540: "Die schönste, mir bekannte Idylle in der sentimentalischen Gattung."

43. Jonas, *4*, 338; to Humboldt, November 29, 1795: "Gelänge mir dieses Unternehmen, so hoffte ich dadurch mit der sentimentalischen Poesie über die naive selbst triumphiert zu haben."

44. *SW, 17,* 535–6 n.

45. *SW, 17,* 515: "Ihr Ziel ist einerlei mit dem höchsten, wornach der Mensch zu ringen hat, frei von Leidenschaft zu sein, immer klar, immer ruhig um sich und in sich zu schauen, überall mehr Zufall als Schicksal zu finden, und mehr über Ungereimtheit zu lachen, als über Bosheit zu zürnen oder zu weinen."

46. *SW, 17,* 153.

47. *SW, 17,* 173: "Eine Schule der praktischen Weisheit, ein Wegweiser durch das bürgerliche Leben."

48. *SW, 17,* 220.

49. *SW, 17,* 237: "Was die Verwicklung betrifft, das Meisterstück der tragischen Bühne."

50. *SW, 17,* 238: "sich in die Ahndung, oder lieber in ein deutliches Bewusstsein einer teleologischen Verknüpfung der Dinge, einer erhabenen Ordnung, eines gütigen Willens verliert."

51. *SW, 17,* 245: "Die Tragödie wäre demnach dichterische Nachahmung einer zusammenhängenden Reihe von Begebenheiten (einer vollständigen Handlung), welche uns Menschen in einem Zustand des Leidens zeigt und zur Absicht hat, unser Mitleid zu erregen."

52. *SW, 17,* 250: "Diejenige Tragödie würde also die vollkommenste sein, in welcher das erregte Mitleid weniger Wirkung des Stoffes, als der am besten benutzten tragischen Form ist."

53. *SW, 17,* 398: "Darstellung des Leidens—als blossen Leidens—ist niemals Zweck der Kunst, aber als Mittel zu ihrem Zweck ist sie derselben äusserst wichtig. Der letzte Zweck der Kunst ist die Darstellung des Übersinnlichen, und die tragische Kunst insbesondere bewerkstelligt dieses dadurch, dass sie uns die moralische Independenz von Naturgesetzen im Zustand des Affekts versinnlicht."

54. *SW, 17,* 630.

55. Jonas, *5,* 168; to Goethe, April 4, 1797: "Man kommt mit solchen *Charakteren* in der Tragödie offenbar viel besser aus, sie *exponieren* sich geschwinder, und ihre Züge sind *permanenter* und fester. Die Wahrheit leidet dadurch nichts, weil sie blossen logischen Wesen eben so entgegengesetzt sind als blossen Individuen."

56. Jonas, *5,* 174; to Goethe, April 7, 1797: "Ein poetisches Abstractum."

57. Jonas, *5,* 292; to Goethe, November 28, 1797: "Wie geschickt er das *repraesentiert,* was sich nicht *praesentieren* lässt, ich meine die Kunst Symbole zu gebrauchen, wo die Natur nicht kann dargestellt werden."

58. Jonas, *5,* 313; to Goethe, December 29, 1797: "Dies . . . möchte . . . am besten durch Einführung symbolischer Behelfe geschehen, die

in allem dem, was nicht zur wahren Kunstwelt des Poeten gehört, und also nicht dargestellt, sondern bloss bedeutet werden soll, die Stelle des Gegenstandes verträten . . . so müsste die natürliche Folge sein, dass die Poesie sich reinigte, ihre Welt enger und bedeutungsvoller zusammenzöge und innerhalb derselben desto wirksamer würde."

59. *SW*, *20*, 253–4: "Die Natur selbst ist nur eine Idee des Geistes, die nie in die Sinne fällt . . . Alles ist nur ein Symbol des Wirklichen."

60. *SW*, *20*, 255: "Der Palast der Könige ist jetzt geschlossen, die Gerichte haben sich von den Toren der Städte in das Innere der Häuser zurückgezogen, die Schrift hat das lebendige Wort verdrängt, das Volk selbst, die sinnlich lebende Masse, ist, wo sie nicht als rohe Gewalt wirkt, zum Staat, folglich zu einem abgezogenen Begriff geworden, die Götter sind in die Brust des Menschen zurückgekehrt."

61. *SW*, *20*, 258: "Ein kollektives Ganze für die Einbildungskraft."

62. Jonas, *5*, 181; to Goethe, April 25, 1797.

63. Jonas, *5*, 577–8; to Goethe, October 20, 1797.

64. Jonas, *5*, 310–1; to Goethe, December 26, 1797: "Es entsteht daraus eine reizender Widerstreit der Dichtung als *Genus* mit der *Species* derselben . . . Dass dieses wechselseitige Hinstreben zu einander nicht in eine Vermischung und Grenzverwirrung ausarte, das ist die eigentliche Aufgabe der Kunst, deren höchster Punkt überhaupt immer dieser ist, Charakter mit Schönheit, Reinheit mit Fülle, Einheit mit Allheit &c. zu vereinbaren."

65. *SW*, *18*, 83:

Ohne Verrückung ihrer objektiven Grenzen, [werden] die verschiedenen Künste in ihrer Wirkung auf das Gemüt immer ähnlicher. Die Musik in ihrer höchsten Veredlung muss Gestalt werden und mit der ruhigen Macht der Antike auf uns wirken; die bildende Kunst in ihrer höchsten Vollendung muss Musik werden und uns durch unmittelbare sinnliche Gegenwart rühren; die Poesie in ihrer vollkommensten Ausbildung muss uns wie die Tonkunst, mächtig fassen, zugleich aber, wie die Plastik, mit ruhiger Klarheit umgeben. Darin eben zeigt sich der vollkommene Stil in jeglicher Kunst, dass er die spezifischen Schranken derselben zu entfernen weiss, ohne doch ihre spezifischen Vorzüge mit aufzuheben, und durch eine weise Benutzung ihrer Eigentümlichkeit ihr einen mehr allgemeinen Charakter erteilt.

66. Jonas, *2*, 237; to Körner, February 25, 1789: "Das kleinlichste und undankbarste unter allen."

67. *SW*, *19*, 272–4: "Wenn man unter Poesie überhaupt die Kunst versteht 'uns durch einen freien Effekt unsrer produktiven Einbildungs-

kraft in bestimmte Empfindungen zu versetzen . . . die objektive Verknüpfung in den Erscheinungen . . . Nur in Wegwerfung des Zufälligen und in dem reinen Ausdruck des Nothwendigen liegt der *grosse Stil.*"

68. *SW, 19,* 289: "zu seinen Landschaften nun auch Figuren zu erfinden und auf diesen reizenden Grund *handelnde Menschheit* aufzutragen."

69. *SW, 17,* 522: "Noch, ich gestehe es, kenne ich kein Gedicht in dieser Gattung . . . Dasjenige didaktische Gedicht, worin der Gedanke selbst poetisch wäre und es auch bliebe, ist noch zu erwarten."

70. Jonas, *3,* 170; to Körner, November 28, 1791: "Ein philosophischer Gegenstand ist schlechterdings für die Poesie verwerflich."

71. *SW, 17,* 652–3: "Das darzustellende Objekt muss also, ehe es vor die Einbildungskraft gebracht und in Anschauung verwandelt wird, durch das abstrakte Gebiet der Begriffe *einen sehr weiten Umweg nehmen* . . . Die Sprache stellt alles vor den *Verstand,* und der Dichter soll alles vor die *Einbildungskraft* bringen (darstellen); die Dichtkunst will *Anschauungen,* die Sprache gibt nur Begriffe."

72. Jonas, *6,* 262; to Goethe, March 27, 1801:
in der Erfahrung fängt auch der Dichter nur mit dem Bewusstlosen an, ja er hat sich glücklich zu schätzen, wenn er durch das klarste Bewusstsein seiner Operationen nur soweit kommt, um die erste dunkle Totalidee seines Werks in der vollendeten Arbeit ungeschwächt wieder zu finden. Ohne eine solche dunkle, aber mächtige *Totalidee* die allem *technischen* vorhergeht, kann kein *poet*isches Werk entstehen, und die Poesie, däucht mir, besteht eben darin, jenes Bewusstlose aussprechen und mitteilen zu können, d.h. es in ein *Objekt* überzutragen. Der Nichtpoet kann so gut als der Dichter von einer poetischen Idee gerührt sein, aber er kann sie in kein Objekt legen, er kann sie nicht mit einem Anspruch auf Notwendigkeit darstellen. Eben so kann der Nichtpoet so gut als der Dichter ein Produkt mit Bewusstsein und mit Notwendigkeit hervorbringen, aber ein solches Werk fängt nicht aus dem Bewusstlosen an, und endigt nicht in demselben. Es bleibt nur ein Werk der Besonnenheit. Das Bewusstlose mit dem Besonnenen vereinigt macht den poetischen Künstler aus.

73. In *Poesia e non poesia* (4th ed. Bari, 1946), pp. 25–38.

74. "Qu'est-ce que la littérature?" in *Situations II* (Paris, 1948), p. 106: "récupérer ce monde-ci . . . comme s'il avait sa source dans la liberté humaine."

CHRONOLOGICAL TABLE
OF WORKS

FRANCE

1719	Dubos:	*Réflexions critiques sur la poésie et la peinture*
1727	Voltaire:	*Essay upon Epic Poetry* (French version 1733)
1729	Voltaire:	Preface to *Œdipe* (first performed 1718)
1730	Voltaire:	*Discours sur la tragédie* (prefixed to *Brutus*)
1731–33	Voltaire:	*Le Temple du goût*
1733	Voltaire:	*Letters concerning the English Nation* (French version: *Lettres philosophiques*, 1734)
1746	Ch. Batteux:	*Les Beaux-Arts réduits à un même principe*
1748	Voltaire:	*Dissertations sur la tragédie ancienne et moderne* (prefixed to *Sémiramis*)
1748	Diderot:	*Les Bijoux indiscrets*
1749	Rousseau:	*Essai sur l'origine des langues*
1751	Diderot:	*Lettre sur les sourds et muets*
1751	Fontenelle:	*Traité sur la poésie en général* (written about 1678)
1751–52	Voltaire:	*Le Siècle de Louis XIV*
1753	Buffon:	*Discours sur le style*
1753–63	M. Grimm:	*La Correspondance littéraire* (published 1812)
1757	Diderot:	*Le Fils naturel* (with) "Entretiens avec Dorval"
1757	Diderot:	*Salon de 1757* (published 1845)
1758	Diderot:	*Le Père de famille* (with) "Discours sur la poésie dramatique"
1758	Rousseau:	*Lettre à d'Alembert sur les spectacles*
1759	Voltaire:	*Candide*
1761	Diderot:	"Eloge de Richardson"
1761	Voltaire:	*Appel à toutes les nations de l'Europe*
1761	Voltaire:	*Lettres sur la Nouvelle Héloïse de J. J. Rousseau*

1763	Marmontel:	*Poétique française*
1764	Voltaire:	"Observations sur le Jules César de Shakespeare" (prefixed to *Jules César*)
1764	Voltaire:	*Théâtre de Pierre Corneille* (with) *Commentaires*
1764–72	Voltaire:	*Dictionnaire philosophique*
1769	Diderot:	*Le Rêve de d'Alembert* (published 1830)
1773	S. Mercier:	*Du Théâtre*
1775	Condillac:	*L'Art d'écrire*
1776	Voltaire:	*Lettre à l'Académie française*
1778	Voltaire:	"Lettre à l'Académie française" (prefixed to *Irène*)
1778	Diderot:	*Paradoxe sur le comédien* (published 1830)
1784	Rivarol:	*Discours sur l'universalité de la langue française*
1784	S. Mercier:	*Mon Bonnet de nuit*
1785	Rivarol:	Preface to Dante's *Inferno*
1787	Marmontel:	*Éléments de littérature*
1795	Mme de Staël:	*Essai sur les fictions*
1797	Rivarol:	*De L'Homme intellectuel et moral*
1799–1805	La Harpe:	*Cours de littérature* (lectures begun 1786)
1800	Mme de Staël:	*De la littérature*

ENGLAND AND SCOTLAND

1711	Alexander Pope:	*Essay on Criticism*
1711	Shaftesbury:	*Characteristicks*
1711–12	Joseph Addison:	*The Spectator*
1725	Francis Hutcheson:	*An Inquiry into the Original of Our Idea of Beauty and Virtue*
1735	Thomas Blackwell:	*An Inquiry into the Life and Writings of Homer*
1744	James Harris:	*Three Treatises*
1745	Johnson:	*Miscellaneous Observations on the Tragedy of Macbeth*
1746	Joseph Warton:	*Odes on Various Subjects*
1750–52	Johnson:	*The Rambler*
1753	Robert Lowth:	*De sacra poesi Hebraeorum* (English translation 1787)
1753–54	*The Adventurer*	(With essays by J. Warton and S. Johnson)
1754	Thomas Warton:	*Observations on the Fairie Queene of Spenser*

1755	Johnson:	*A Dictionary of the English Language*
1756	Johnson:	*Proposals for Printing . . . the Dramatic Works of W. Shakespeare*
1756	Joseph Warton:	*Essay on the Writings and Genius of Pope* (Vol. *1*)
1757	Edmund Burke:	*Philosophical Inquiry into the Origin of Our Ideas of the Sublime and Beautiful* (new edition with "Essay on Taste," 1758)
1757	David Hume:	*Four Dissertations* ("Of the Standard of Taste," "Of Tragedy," etc.)
1758–60	Johnson:	*The Idler*
1759	Alexander Gerard:	*An Essay on Taste*
1759	Johnson:	*The Prince of Abissinia* (*The History of Rasselas*)
1759	Edward Young:	*Conjectures on Original Composition*
1762	Richard Hurd:	*Letters on Chivalry and Romance*
1762	Lord Kames:	*Elements of Criticism*
1763	Hugh Blair:	*A Critical Dissertation on the Poems of Ossian*
1763	John Brown:	*A Dissertation on the Rise, Union, and Power . . . of Poetry and Music*
1765	Johnson:	Preface to the *Plays of W. Shakespeare*
1765	Thomas Percy:	*Reliques of Ancient English Poetry*
1769	Robert Wood:	*An Essay on the Original Genius and Writings of Homer* (privately printed; new edition 1775)
1769–90	Sir Joshua Reynolds:	*Discourses* (before the Royal Academy)
1772	Sir William Jones:	*Essay on the Arts Commonly Called Imitative*
1774–81	Thomas Warton:	*The History of English Poetry*
1776	George Campbell:	*The Philosophy of Rhetoric*
1777	Maurice Morgann:	*An Essay on the Character of John Falstaff*
1779	James Beattie:	*Essay on Poetry and Music*
1779–81	Johnson:	*Prefaces, Biographical and Critical, to the Works of the English Poets* (later: *The Lives of the English Poets*)
1780	Henry Mackenzie:	On *Hamlet* in the *Mirror*
1782	Hugh Blair:	*Lectures on Rhetoric and Belles Lettres*
1782	Joseph Warton:	*Essay on Pope* (Vol. 2)
1785	Thomas Warton (ed.)	*Milton's Poems*
1790	Archibald Alison:	*Essays on the Nature and Principles of Taste*
1800	Wordsworth:	Preface to *Lyrical Ballads*

ITALY

1706	Ludovico Muratori:	*Della perfetta poesia italiana*
1708	Vincenzo Gravina:	*Della ragion poetica*
1725	Giambattista Vico:	*La scienza nuova*
1732	Pietro Calepio:	*Paragone della poesia tragica d'Italia con quella di Francia*
1753	Giuseppe Baretti:	*A Dissertation upon Italian Poetry*
1757	Saverio Bettinelli:	*Lettere Virgiliane*
1758	Gasparo Gozzi:	*Difeza di Dante*
1762	Melchiorre Cesarotti:	*Ragionamento sopra il diletto della tragedia*
1763–65	Giuseppe Baretti:	*La frusta letteraria*
1765	Giuseppe Spalletti:	*Saggio sopra la bellezza*
1770	Cesare Beccaria:	*Richerche intorno alla natura dello stile*
1773–75	Giuseppe Parini:	*Sui principi di belle lettere*
1777	Giuseppe Baretti:	*Discours sur Shakespeare*
1785	Melchiorre Cesarotti:	*Saggio sulla filosofia de gusto*
1788	Vittorio Alfieri:	*Del principe e delle lettere*

GERMANY

1730	Gottsched:	*Critische Dichtkunst*
1735	Baumgarten:	*Meditationes philosophicae*
1740	Bodmer and Breitinger:	*Critische Dichtkunst*
1740	Bodmer:	*Critische Abhandlung von dem Wunderbaren*
1741	Bodmer:	*Critische Betrachtungen über die poetischen Gemählde der Dichter*
1741	J. E. Schlegel:	*Vergleichung Shakespears und Andreas Gryphs*
1742	J. E. Schlegel:	*Abhandlung von der Nachahmung*
1746	Bodmer:	*Critische Briefe*
1749	Bodmer:	*Neue critische Briefe*
1749–54	Lessing, Mylius, et al.:	*Beiträge zur Historie und Aufnahme des Theaters*
1750	Baumgarten:	*Aesthetica*
1754–59	Lessing:	*Theatralische Bibliothek*
1755	Winckelmann:	*Gedanken über die Nachahmung der griechischen Werke*
1756–57	Correspondence between Lessing, Mendelssohn and Nicolai on nature of tragedy	
1757	Mendelssohn:	*Über die Hauptgrundsätze der schönen Künste*
1759–65	Mendelssohn, Lessing, etc.:	*Briefe die neueste Literatur betreffend*

1761	Mendelssohn:	*Rhapsodie über die Empfindungen*
1762	J. G. Hamann:	*Kreuzzüge des Philologen*
1764	Winckelmann:	*Geschichte der Kunst des Alterthums*
1766	Gerstenberg:	*Briefe über Merkwürdigkeiten der Litteratur*
1766	G. E. Lessing:	*Laokoon*
1767	Herder:	*Über die neuere deutsche Litteratur: Fragmente*
1767–71	Gerstenberg:	Contributions to *Hamburgische Neue Zeitung*
1767–69	Lessing:	*Hamburgische Dramaturgie*
1769	Herder:	*Kritische Wälder*
1771	Goethe:	*Zum Shakespears Tag*
1772	Herder:	*Abhandlung über den Ursprung der Sprache*
1772–73	Goethe, Herder, etc.:	*Frankfurter Gelehrte Anzeigen*
1773	Herder, Goethe:	*Von deutscher Art und Kunst*
1775	Herder:	*Ursachen des gesunkenen Geschmacks*
1777	Herder:	"Von Ähnlichkeit der mittlern englischen und deutschen Dichtkunst"
1778	Herder:	*Vom Erkennen und Empfinden der menschlichen Seele*
		Über die Würkung der Dichtkunst auf die Sitten der Völker
		Volkslieder (Pt. 1)
1778–85	Goethe:	*Wilhelm Meisters Theatralische Sendung* (published 1910)
1782	Schiller:	"Über das gegenwärtige deutsche Theater"
1782–83	Herder:	*Vom Geist der Ebräischen Poesie*
1785	Mendelssohn:	*Morgenstunden*
1785–97	Herder:	*Zerstreute Blätter* (6 parts)
1788	Goethe:	"Einfache Nachahmung, Manier, Stil"
1788	Moritz:	*Über die bildende Nachahmung der Natur*
1790	Kant:	*Kritik der Urteilskraft*
1791	Schiller:	"Über Bürgers Gedichte"
1791	A. W. Schlegel:	"Über Dante Aligieris Göttliche Komödie"
1792	Schiller:	"Über den Grund des Vergnügens an tragischen Gegenständen"
		"Über tragische Kunst"
1793	Schiller:	"Über das Pathetische"
1793	Tieck:	"Shakespeares Behandlung des Wunderbaren" (published 1848)
1793–97	Herder:	*Briefe zu Beförderung der Humanität*

1794	Schiller:	"Über Matthissons Gedichte"
1795	Goethe:	"Literarischer Sansculottismus"
1795	Goethe:	*Wilhelm Meisters Lehrjahre*
1795	Schiller:	*Briefe über die aesthetische Erziehung*
1795	Schiller:	*Über naive und sentimentalische Dichtung*
1797	Goethe:	*Die Propyläen*
1797	Goethe:	"Über Wahrheit und Wahrscheinlichkeit der Kunstwerke"
1797	Goethe and Schiller:	"Über epische und dramatische Dichtkunst" (published 1827)
1797	A. W. Schlegel:	"Goethes Hermann und Dorothea"
1797	A. W. Schlegel:	"Shakespeares Romeo und Julia"
1797	F. Schlegel:	*Griechen und Römer*
1797	Wackenroder:	*Herzensergiessungen eines kunstliebenden Klosterbruders*
1798	F. Schlegel:	*Geschichte der Poesie der Griechen*
1798	A. W. Schlegel:	*Vorlesungen über philosophische Kunstlehre* (published 1911)
1798–99	Goethe:	"Der Sammler und die Seinigen"
1798–1800	A. W. and F. Schlegel (eds.):	*Das Athenaeum*
1799	Herder:	"Metakritik"
1799	Wackenroder and Tieck:	*Phantasien über die Kunst*
1800	Herder:	*Kalligone*
1800	F. W. Schelling:	*System der transzendentalen Idealismus*
1800	A. W. Schlegel:	"Über Bürgers Werke"
1800	Schleiermacher:	*Vertraute Briefe über Schlegels Lucinde*
1800	Tieck:	"Briefe über Shakespeare" (published 1848)

INDEX OF NAMES

Fichte, Johann Gottlieb, 228
Fielding, Henry, 67, 72, 83, 122, 198, 245
Flaxman, John, 166
Fletcher, John, 154, 162
Fontenelle, Bernard Le Bovier de, 35n.,
49, 69, 136, 189
Foscolo, Ugo, 139
Frederick the Great, 10, 42, 250
Fubini, Mario, 133n., 142n.

Galilei, Galileo, 76
Garve, Christian, 164
Gay, John, 71
Gerard, Alexander, 108
Gerstenberg, Heinrich Wilhelm, 10, 157,
158, *176–8*, 184
Gervinus, Georg Gottfried, 227
Gessner, Solomon, 72, 204, 245
Gilpin, William, 114
Goethe, Johann Wolfgang von, 2, 4, 7,
26, 30, 53, 61, 67, 73, 75, 117, 135, 137,
148, 149, 151, 157, 158, 167, 178, 179,
180, 182, 183, 190, 193, 194, 200, *201–
26*, 234, 235, 236, 237, 239, 242, 243, 244,
250, 251; the young Goethe as Herder's
disciple, 202; the speech on Shakespeare, 202; on form, 202; as reviewer,
203; on Shakespeare's *Hamlet*, 204ff.;
the change after Italian journey, 206;
on occasional poetry, 207; on art and
nature, 208; on imitation, manner, and
style, 208; on organic analogy, 209;
wholeness as criterion of judgment,
210; on symbol and allegory, 210; on
myth, 211; on types, 212; on nature of
poetry, 212; on genres as natural forms,
213; on epic and drama, 213; on mixture of genres, 214; on rules and unities, 215; on stage and theater, 215; on
artist and public, 216; on Aristotle's
view of tragedy, 217; on moral effect of
art, 217; on social setting of literature,
218; on genetic method, 219; on periods
and on romantic-classical contrast, 219;
"Shakespeare und kein Ende," 220; on
world literature, 221; on folk poetry,
222; on criticism, 223; on Byron, 224;
on Scott, 225; his stature as critic, 225
Gogol, Nikolay, 7
Goldoni, Carlo, 141, 142, 155, 178, 240
Goldsmith, Oliver, 97, 124, 143, 204, 204n.
Gottsched, Johann Christoph, 9, 72, 144,
146, 147, 151, 153, 157, 224
Gozzi, Carlo, 155
Gozzi, Gasparo, 138
Gracián y Morales, Baltasar de, 3n., 24n.

Gravina, Gian Vincenzo, *133*, 134, 136,
139
Gray, Thomas, 82, 86, 90, 97, 102, 104,
123, 125, 127
Grimm, Melchior, *70–2*
Grübel, Konrad, 218
Gryphius, Andreas, 146
Guidi, Alessandro, 133n.

Hagesandros, 159
Haller, Albrecht von, 161, 162, 245, 253
Hamann, Johann Georg, 4, 10, 135, 177,
178–81
Hamm, Victor M., 121n.
Harington, Sir John, 121n.
Harold, Baron de, 193
Harris, James, 166, 181, 186
Hawkins, Sir John, 80
Hazlitt, William, 112, 118, 137
Hebel, Johann Peter, 222
Hédelin. *See* Aubignac
Hegel, Georg Wilhelm Friedrich, 180,
212, 212n., 227, 228, 229, 231, 233, 246,
255
Heine, Heinrich, 224
Heinroth, J. C. A., 207
Heinse, Wilhelm, 151
Helvétius, Claude, 50, 70
Herder, Johann Gottfried, 2, 4, 10, 26, 29,
30, 46, 123, 124, 135, 138, 142, 143, 149,
150, 151, 167, 176, 178, 179, 180, *181–
200*, 202, 203, 205, 206, 207, 222, 224,
241; his antecedents, 181; his style, 182;
his influence, 183; his concept of criticism, 183; on empathy and relativism,
184; his historical sense, 184–5; his
aesthetics, 185; on Lessing, 186; on nature of poetry, 186; on language, 187;
on origins of poetry, 187; on poetry as
metaphor, 188; on evolution of literature, 189; on return to nature, 190; on
classical tradition, 190–1; on English
literature, 191; his concept of folk
poetry, 192; on Ossian, 192; on Shakespeare, 193; as literary historian, 195;
on social causes of literature, 197; his
sketch of literary history, 198; on German literature, 199; on French literature, 199; on Aristotle, 200
Hermann, J. G. J., 212n.
Hesiod, 192
Hickes, George, 101
Hinrichs, H. F. W., 212n.
Hirth, Alois, 137
Hobbes, Thomas, 106, 115, 120, 122
Hoffmann, E. T. A., 25

INDEX OF TOPICS AND TERMS

Acting and actors, 55, 56, 168, 173, 214, 215, 221
Aesthetics, 8; Voltaire's, 37ff.; Diderot's, 54; Dr. Johnson's, 93ff.; British, 106ff.; Vico's, 134f.; term invented by Baumgarten, 144; Lessing's, 163ff.; Herder's, 185, 203; Kant's, 227ff.; Schiller's, 233ff.; *see also* Taste, Beauty, Art and Nature, etc.
Allegory, 4, 69, 76, 80, 82, 121, 135, 148, 150, 161, 180, 188; *see also* Symbolism
Ancients vs. moderns, 31, 57, 216, 220, 234, 237
Antiquarianism, 28, 29, 101, 102, 127, 157, 191, 195
Art and history, 81, 171, 173, 202
Art and life (fiction vs. reality), 79, 115, 116, 118, 131, 140, 141, 146, 175
Art and nature, 3, 14, 16, 88, 97, 129, 208, 209, 210, 211, 212, 216, 218, 220, 225, 226, 230, 231, 233, 237, 238, 242, 245, 252, 255
Art and truth, 80, 81, 97, 131, 133, 134, 175, 220, 244, 248
Association, 52, 108, 111, 112, 115
Audience of literature (readers), 21, 95, 216, 241
Autonomy of art, 145, 207, 209, 217, 229 (Kant), 230, 233, 254

Beauty (the Beautiful), 37, 54, 93, 107, 114, 140, 149, 150, 160, 162, 166, 188, 209, 232, 233, 245
Beautiful nature (*la belle nature*), 17, 25, 55, 180, 203

Catharsis. *See* Pity and Fear
Causal explanation, 8
Character on stage or in fiction, 56, 117, 118, 163, 177, 178, 249
Characteristic, the, 137, 200, 203
Clarity (obscurity), 39, 51, 77, 112, 114, 145, 200
Classic (the classical), 16, 121, 191, 192, 207, 208, 218, 226, 227, 236, 237, 255; *see also* Neoclassicism

Climate, 124, 125, 197, 218
Comedy (comic), 21, 34, 53, 112, 119, 120, 246
Correspondences (microcosm-macrocosm parallel), 4, 148, 187, 247
Cosmopolitanism, 29, 30, 33, 42, 100, 143, 221, 228
Creating another world (heterocosmic poetry), 25, 109, 110, 145, 147, 173, 188, 194, 209
Creative imagination (creativity), 18, 26, 77, 96, 109, 121, 176, 178, 180, 203, 207, 208, 233, 252
Criticism, theory of, 2ff., 77, 88, 109, 115, 124, 127, 170, 181, 183, 184, 185, 205, 223, 224, 228; of beauties and faults, 67, 184, 223

Decorum (propriety), 15, 16, 28, 38, 45, 76, 89–90, 124, 200
Descriptive poetry (*Ut pictura poesis*, painting and poetry), 7, 52, 99, 111, 113, 114, 116, 129, 145, 154, 156, 159, 161, 162, 163, 167, 186, 252, 253
Development in literature, 27, 105, 127, 128, 135, 150, 188, 189, 190, 218, 219, 221, 236
Diction, poetic, 2, 90, 91, 100, 103; *see also* Style, Language
Domestic tragedy and drama, 40, 47, 53, 59, 72, 80, 94, 118, 167, 194
Double standard of poetry, 28, 130, 131, 132, 181, 222
Drama (*drame, Schauspiel*), 117, 164, 165, 177, 213, 214, 215, 216, 217, 250, 251

Elegy, 235, 236, 243, 244, 245
Emotionalism (feeling, pathos in poetry), 9, 22, 26, 46, 48, 49, 51, 69, 71, 74, 75, 94, 114, 115, 116, 118, 119, 120, 124, 150, 184, 186, 187
Empiricism, 8, 48, 51, 107, 108, 136
Epic, 4, 7, 17, 19, 21, 22, 32 (Voltaire), 116, 120, 121, 122, 128, 129, 165, 177, 179, 187, 189, 200, 213, 214, 215, 243, 250, 251, 253; *see also* Homer, Milton, etc.

355